THE LANGUAGE OF THE SELF

THE
LANGUAGE
OF THE SELF

The Function of Language in Psychoanalysis
By JACQUES LACAN

Translated with notes and commentary
By ANTHONY WILDEN

THE JOHNS HOPKINS PRESS: BALTIMORE AND LONDON

The Johns Hopkins Press, Baltimore, Maryland 21218
The Johns Hopkins Press Ltd., London

ISBN 0–8018–0673–9

Originally published, 1968
Second printing, 1973

"The Function of Language in Psychoanalysis" was originally published as "Fonction
et champ de la parole et du langage en psychanalyse" in *La Psychanalyse,* Vol. I (Paris,
1956), and later in Jacques Lacan's *Ecrits* (Paris: Editions du Seuil, 1966).

To P. M. P. L.

Translator's Introduction

Although the *Discours de Rome* is primarily addressed to psychoanalysts, Lacan's work has found readers in many different fields of *les sciences de l'homme,* many of whom have only a peripheral interest in psychoanalysis as such. This is often the case when a specialist employs and correlates material from different domains, as Lacan has done, especially when these correlations are daring and dramatic. Certainly in 1953, when the *Discours* was first delivered, most of the later developments of Lacan's interrogation of the Freudian texts, as well as the epistemological, linguistic, and other considerations upon which it was founded, were no more than hinted at. This, coupled with the wide range of Lacan's own interests, makes the writing of an Introduction somewhat difficult, since the writer is not at all sure to whom he is writing. The reader will find this difficulty reflected in the explanatory and amplificatory notes added to the translation, many of which will probably seem simplistic to the specialist and, in some cases, perhaps overly technical to the more general reader.

Lacan's dense and allusive style compounds the problem, for although reading Lacan is by no means as difficult as it may seem at first, the translator is continually faced with the question of knowing whether he is spelling out the obvious or contributing to the ambiguity of the ambiguous. Certainly after the struggle to put this peculiar French into less than peculiar English, the translator may still fear that his unwitting errors will lay him more than usually open to the common charge of being a traitor to his text. If the English should be difficult, awkward, or inaccurate, I can only refer the reader to the original French, recently made widely available by the publication of Lacan's *Ecrits* (Editions du Seuil, Paris, 1966).

I can think of no better way to introduce this translation than to borrow what Juliette Boutonier said of Lacan in reviewing the republication in 1950 of Lacan's "Propos sur la causalité psychique" (1947),[1] one of his less difficult texts. She said:

To attempt to sum up his thought seems as impertinent an undertaking as to try to translate certain poems. Moreover, to deprive Lacan's thought of the style with which it is born is to be completely false to it and tends to deceive the reader into thinking that he knows something about it, whereas in fact an essential aspect of the work has escaped him. Lacan's own theory justifies this importance of the *verbe*: "The use of the Word requires vastly more vigilance in the science of man than it does anywhere else, for it engages in it the very being of its object."

This caveat, which is certainly typical of any first approach to Lacan, needs only slight modification to apply to the translation offered here. Lacan obviously makes few concessions to the uninitiated, and, in 1953 at least, he displayed much of the characteristic French carelessness over references, usually relying on his audience to recognize the echoes from his own and other works. This is perhaps understandable, however, in the context of a report written in great haste within six weeks and addressed to professionals and students more or less familiar with the theses developed in his seminar since its inception in 1951. But it does not simplify matters for the reader widely separated in space and time from the climate in which Lacan addressed his audience, especially when that climate assumes a familiarity with a different intellectual tradition. For, if the full comprehension of Lacan's text depends upon a more than usual intimacy with the texts of Freud, it is further dependent upon an acquaintance with Hegel and his French commentators, upon a familiarity with the early Heidegger and the early Sartre, and upon a knowledge of the concepts of modern structural linguistics (Saussure, Jakobson) and structural anthropology (Mauss, Lévi-Strauss).

But this is not all, unfortunately. Lacan's constitutional predisposition to ambiguity, sometimes even on insignificant points, makes him difficult enough in French, where a tradition of *préciosité* gives him far greater latitude than is the case for the writer in English. And over the years since 1953, he seems progressively to have become a prisoner of his own

[1] For bibliographical information on Lacan's writings mentioned here and in the translator's notes by short title and date, or by another obvious reference, as well as other articles or books repeatedly referred to, see the bibliography.

style. Nevertheless, a number of brilliant and provoking intuitions, couched in aphoristic form, emerge through the difficulties of the text to bring together once disparate and seemingly unconnected ideas. These intuitions have such a striking relevance to contemporary thought that they provide a fertile ground for those occupied with the discourse of our own and other epochs.

I am thinking especially of literary criticism. It is only fair to say at once that this translation has been undertaken with general readers rather than with analysts in mind. Nevertheless, the unexpected revolution in the intellectual acceptance of Freud in France, the new "return to Freud" in French psychoanalysis, and the increasing realization of the subtlety of Freud's own thought, along with the new atmosphere of sophistication within the French analytical movement, would seem to indicate that the central theses of Lacan's work may well become part of the American psychoanalytical corpus.

But the reader of this text does not face an easy task, especially if its technical and philosophical vocabulary is alien to him. To a certain extent, therefore, I have tried to indicate in my notes where the English-speaking reader can find the sort of elucidation one might expect him to need, assuming that he is not necessarily familiar with many of the more recent developments in European thought, to say nothing of the minor texts of Freud. At the same time I have tried to employ Lacan to interpret himself. Thus the bulk of my notes are translations of relevant sections from his other works. These selections are confined as far as possible to the period 1949–57 (the *Discours* was first published in 1956). I have also briefly indicated definitions of certain technical terms from Freud, anthropology, and linguistics, as well as referring to the appropriate German word where it is essential to understanding the possibilities of interpretation of the German text revealed by Lacan. The word "interpretation" is especially important here, since Lacan's own "return to Freud" is manifestly an attempt to return to the spirit of the text in a modern sense, rather than an exegesis in a historical sense.

However, it is almost impossible to write any sort of substantial introduction to Lacan unless the reader has first been introduced to him. I have finally decided to relegate my own theoretical remarks to a separate study referring back to the text and notes rather than forward to them, as an extensive introduction would do. Having read the text and notes, the reader will be saved from some unnecessary repetitions, and, I hope, he will better be able to understand my preoccupation with certain aspects of the text rather than with others. A number of concepts—for example, the notion of sign, signifier, and signified—which are too complicated to be encompassed in a note are dealt with in this essay. I shall therefore confine myself here to a few generalities, which are amplified later on.

Lacan gained his Doctorat d'Etat in psychiatry in 1932 with a thesis on paranoia and its relation to the personality, which consists of a critical survey of the then-extant theories of psychosis followed by the detailed study of a female psychotic given to literary endeavor. Its concern with language—some of her work was appreciated as literature—meant an especial welcome from the surrealists. Although it is not a psychoanalysis, the thesis bears the mark of Lacan's early acquaintance with Freud, at a time when Freud was not well known in France. Lacan joined the Société psychanalytique de Paris in 1934. He became a full member just before World War II, at about the same time as his later colleague Daniel Lagache, and soon established the beginnings of his special reputation, the central concept of the *stade du miroir* having been introduced in 1936. In 1952 he and Lagache led the break with the Paris society to form the Société française de psychanalyse.

The influence of Heidegger and of the phenomenological movement of the thirties is particularly evident in his prewar writings. His acquaintance with the modern Hegel of the *Phenomenology* dates from the lectures given by Alexandre Kojève at the Ecole des Hautes Etudes between 1933 and 1939. He published nothing during the war, and it is not until 1947 that the influence of Kojève's Hegel became fully manifest in his published work, notably in the "Propos sur la causalité psychique" (1947). This was the beginning of Lacan's interpretation of the dialectic of desire and its application to Freud, especially to the concept of wish fulfillment in the dream.

Ten years before, in 1936, in his "Au-delà du 'Principe de Realité,'" Lacan had given what he called a "phenomenological description of the psychoanalytical experience." The phenomenon to be investigated, he said, is the language relationship between the analyst and patient, with the analyst seen as the *interlocutor* (a term which appears again in the *Discours*): "But the analyst, because he cannot detach the experience of Language from the situation which it implies (the situation of the interlocutor), touches on the simple fact that Language, before signifying *something,* signifies for *someone*" (pp. 76–77). By the very fact of listening without replying, said Lacan, the analyst imposes a meaning on the discourse of the subject. Even if what the subject says is "meaningless," what the subject says *to the analyst* cannot be without meaning, since it conceals what the subject *wants* to say (what he means) and the relationship he wishes to establish. The subject thus seeks to turn his auditor into an interlocutor, through the transference, and in fact imposes this role upon the silence of the analyst, revealing as he does so the *image* which he unconsciously substitutes for the person of the analyst. Lacan then goes on to develop a view of interhuman relations and interaction (dependent upon the subject's denials, the mechanism of the *Verneinung*) in opposition to the "orthodox" theory of instinctual conflict.

But in spite of the reference to the linguistic relationship—the expression of an intentionality of signification, where a word is not only a signifier *of* but also *for*—and the reference to interhuman relations, the transference is not explicitly represented as a dialectical relationship in the article of 1936. The relationship is not viewed as intersubjective, but only as a "constant interaction between the observer and the object."

In 1951, however, at the Congrès des psychanalystes de langue romane, reacting against an attempt by a colleague to view the transference in terms of Gestalt psychology, Lacan intervened in order to insist upon a dialectical view of the relationship of the analyst and patient. The psychoanalytical experience, he said, "runs its course entirely in a relationship of subject to subject, signifying in effect that it retains a dimension which is irreducible to any psychology considered as an objectification of certain properties of the individual." [2] The dialectics of analysis, he continues, are to be found in Freud's experiences of negative transference, especially in his discovery of his own countertransference in the case of Dora (1905),[3] a subject to which Lacan returns in the *Discours*. By a cumulative process of dialectic development, reversal, and further development, the analysis of Dora moves on to the stumbling block upon which it foundered: Freud's refusal to recognize Dora's attraction to Frau K, because of his own countertransference, which was the result of his having "put himself a little too much in the place of Herr K" (p. 224). The transference, said Lacan, should surely therefore be considered "as an entity entirely relative to the countertransference defined as the sum of the prejudices, the

[2] "Intervention sur le transfert" (1951); *Ecrits,* p. 216.
[3] S. Freud, *Standard Edition,* VII, 7.

passions, the embarrassments, even the analyst's insufficient information at this or that moment of the dialectical process." "In other words, the transference involves nothing real in the subject except the appearance of the permanent modes according to which it constitutes its objects, in a moment of stagnation of the dialectic of the analysis" (p. 225).

It is in the sense that the dialectical movement of the analysis is not linear, but progressively and cumulatively spiral, and in the sense that the relationship of the two subjects involved is mediated in both directions by subjects who are not present, that Lacan can speak of a "reform" —not so much a reform of psychoanalysis, since the forms upon which it depends are to be found in Freud, but a reform of our view of the subject from both sides of the couch. Hence Lacan's concern with the didactic analysis in the *Discours* (which was addressed to candidates in analysis).

For Lacan, the countertransference—whether it is viewed as something to be recognized and exploited or as something to be battled against— is therefore conjugated in the imperative mode of the "Physician, heal thyself," and it, too, must be interpreted in order to maintain the dialectical progress of the analysis, since the transference, when it is revealed, is a "dead point" blocking further movement. The technical neutrality of the analyst in his silence is not therefore a real neutrality, but a dialectical neutrality:

The analytical neutrality takes on its authentic meaning from the position of the pure dialectician who, because he knows that all that is real is rational (and inversely), therefore knows that all that exists, including the evil which he struggles against, is and will always remain equivalent to the level of his own particularity. Thus he knows that the subject progresses only by whatever integration he attains of his position in the universal: technically by the projection of his past into a discourse in the process of becoming (p. 226).

By intentionalizing his memories of the past (whether real or phantasied) and by seeking to make the analyst play a part in them, the subject projects himself towards a future dependent upon his recognition of the meaning of those memories.

Besides constant references to the journey of consciousness in the face and company of what is other in the Hegelian *Phenomenology,* Lacan's writings abound with the promotion of what he calls the *Imaginary order* (perception, hallucination, and their derivatives) and its distinction from what he calls the *Symbolic order* (the order of discursive and symbolic action) and the *Real*. This distinction is derived in part from the phase of childhood which Lacan calls the *stade du miroir*: the primary alienation of the *infans* from "himself" and his subsequent discovery of his Self. The *stade du miroir* is an interpretation of findings in both psychological and biological research concerning the perceptual relationship of the individual to others at a crucial phase in his development (from six to eighteen months in the child); for Lacan, it is the root of all later identifications. His view of the ego depends upon this primary identification seen in the light of Freud's important article on narcissism (1914)[4] and the later development of the notion of the *Idealich* and *Ichideal* in *Group Psychology and the Analysis of the Ego* (1921).[5] The Symbolic, on the other hand, is derived more or less directly from the notion of the symbolic function in human society revealed by anthropology, especially by Marcel Mauss and Lévi-Strauss.

The *stade du miroir* is what Didier Anzieu has called Lacan's heresy, in the sense that each "new way in psychoanalysis" has depended on some such central feature (the birth trauma or the inferiority complex, for instance), in somewhat the same way as the castration complex and the death instinct are privileged in Freud. But they are also privileged in Lacan, and Lacan would be the first to deny that his way is anything but a return to a long misunderstood Freud. The fact is that in the 1950's Freud was almost unavailable in French—and the available translations were uniformly bad. Indeed it is only since the 1950's that Freud has become properly available in English. Since James Strachey's monumental *Standard Edition* (superior in its scholarship to any of the German editions), since the publication of Freud's letters to Fliess and his more personal letters, since Ernest Jones's biography (however disappointing), and since the recent works of Rieff, Marcuse, and Norman O. Brown—all projects of the 1950's—Freud has surely evolved from the status of friend or enemy to more nearly the status of a truly great man.

In France, Lacan has undoubtedly been the single most important influence in that upward evaluation, and especially in sparking a return to what Freud had actually said at a time when the influence of existentialism in France and elsewhere and the work of Horney, Sullivan, Fromm, and others were diverting attention from the texts of Freud. Following the introduction of the *stade du miroir* and insights from Heidegger and Hegel into his writings, Lacan was one of the first to seek to integrate

[4] *Ibid.,* XIV, 69.
[5] *Ibid.,* XVIII, 67.

Lévi-Strauss's hypotheses about the relationship of linguistic and social structures into psychoanalysis, and the *Discours* of 1953 is his first published elaboration of what might be called the "new terminology." This is in other words the Lacanian terminology of *metaphor* and *metonymy,* of the linguistic and epistemological categories of the *signifier* and the *signified,* of the differentiation between *need, demand,* and *desire,* of the categories of the Symbolic, the Imaginary, and the Real. It is in this sense that the *Discours* was a challenge to the traditional psychoanalytic movement, as well as to "neo-Freudian revisionism," in Marcuse's unhappy phrase; and it remains a manifesto bearing the scars of the circumstances that produced it.

The result of Lacan's writings has been that his seminar, originally attended almost solely by medical men, has now become a meeting place for the most varied kinds of people,[6] including critics (the Tel Quel group, with which one associates Roland Barthes, himself a brilliant transmitter between structural anthropology, psychoanalysis, and literary criticism), philosophers (Michel Foucault, Jacques Derrida), neo-Marxists (Louis Althusser), as well as linguists, mathematicians, and students from other disciplines. To a certain extent, however, and especially since the publication of the *Ecrits,* it has simply become intellectually fashionable to hear Lacan, with the inevitable result of a period of *lacanisme* in Paris. Nevertheless, a great number of people owe their present interest in Freud to Lacan, to say nothing of their renewed readings of Freud's text. Their intellectual terrorism is not unrelated to Lacan's own, nor to the climate that Lacan helped to create. In the field of psychoanalysis itself, Laplanche and Pontalis' recent and now indispensable *Vocabulaire de la Psychanalyse* (1967), however conservatively it approaches Lacan, is the direct result of the direction of a master. No one reads Freud in quite the same way after reading Lacan—but then again, no one reads Lacan in quite the same way after reading Freud.

Remarks on the Translation

The article translated here, now known as the *Discours de Rome,* originally appeared in 1956 in the first volume of *La Psychanalyse* (pp. 81–166), the journal founded by the Société française de psychanalyse after

---

[6] Including, no doubt, the wit who, as Lacan tells it, labeled the seminar as "là où ça parle."

the secession from the Paris society in 1952. The full title of the *Discours* is: "Fonction et champ de la parole et du langage en psychanalyse." After the distribution of printed copies of the *Discours* at the new society's first congress, Lacan delivered a spoken communication, identified here as *Actes,* which, with the interventions of the other analysts present, was transcribed and published in *La Psychanalyse,* I (pp. 202-55). The full title of this volume is: *Travaux des années 1953–1955, dirigés par Jacques Lacan: De l'usage de la parole et des structures de langage dans la conduite et dans le champ de la psychanalyse.*

The *Discours* itself consisted of a Preface (apparently added for publication), an Introduction, and three sections entitled respectively: "Parole vide et parole pleine dans la réalisation psychanalytique du sujet"; "Symbole et langage comme structure et limite du champ psychanalytique"; and "Les résonances de l'interprétation et le temps du sujet dans la technique psychanalytique." Upon its republication in the *Ecrits* in 1966, the *Discours* was preceded by a further section of introductory material entitled "Du sujet enfin en question" (pp. 229-36).

The translation of Lacan must inevitably remain a more or less helpful aid to the comprehension of the original text. The translator has nevertheless tried, with what success the reader must judge for himself, to maintain a consistent and coherent approach to the French, being as careful as possible to translate key words in such a way that the reader may always remain aware of what lies behind them. The reader can with some assurance assume that when he sees "failure to recognize," for instance, it is always an equivalent—however inadequate in this case—for *méconnaissance.* It has further been necessary to establish certain conventions for this purpose (for example, "Word" for *parole*) which the reader will find elaborated in the notes and listed in the index.[7] I have also employed capitalization elsewhere to distinguish or emphasize certain words or concepts: "Language" for *langage* ("language" for *langue*); "Knowledge" for *savoir* ("knowledge" for *connaissance*); "Truth" for *vérité;* "the Symbolic," "the Imaginary," and "the Real" for *le symbolique, l'imaginaire,* and *le réel.* Because of its special meaning in Lacan, how-

---

[7] Some French terms have been retained either because of their ambiguity in a specific context (for example, *méconnaissance*) or because, like the *belle âme,* they represent accepted or sanctified expressions. In the latter case, for instance, the original German would be pointless, and the English "noble soul" lacks the French pre-Romantic connotations, Rousseau, for example.

ever, "Imaginary" is always capitalized, even as an adjective, whenever it is a question of the Imaginary order. Most of the other conventions of translation, the technical terminology, and psychoanalytical spelling—for example, "phantasy" for *fantasme*—follow those of the *Standard Edition* of Freud's works.

One or two expressions require preliminary comment, however. The word *parole* (as distinguished from *mot*) has connotations for which the convention "Word" is rather inadequate. Moreover, the use of "Word" in English tends to restrict the connotation to what in French would more commonly be the task of *verbe*. Outside its usage in French where we would employ "speech" or "speaking," "spoken word" or "faculty of speech," *parole* differs from *mot* in that it nearly always implies *somebody*'s word or words, including the sense of one's word of honor. But it still remains synonymous in certain contexts with the use of *verbe* to mean *logos* (or the Logos)—the difference being one of value and evocation rather than of meaning. In linguistics, where Saussure was the initiator of the distinction between *parole* and *langue, parole* similarly combines the sense of the individual faculty of speech and the speaker's actual words. The distinction more commonly employed in linguistics now is that between "message" and "code" (terms derived from communication theory), but obviously the similarity between *parole* and "message" is a restricted one, as is that between "code" and *langue* (and *langage* is a wider category still). The message consists of spoken or written words (*paroles*), but not of *la parole;* the term "code" is purely methodological, since it describes neither the nature nor the function of language adequately, except at the most superficial level of communication. Moreover, "code" implies an objective or fixed reference which is again true only of the less profound levels of language.

There is a similar distinction between the subjective and the objective in the expressions *sens* ("meaning," "sense") and *signification* ("signification"). Just as *mot* primarily designates an objective entity (a collection of sounds or letters), *signification* tends to emphasize objective ostensive definition (pointing) or objective verbal definition (synonyms). And just as *parole* implies the subjective intentions of the speaker, *sens,* synonymous with "direction," often implies an intentionality of meaning—which is subjective in the sense that it is what the speaker wants to say (*ce qu'il veut dire*). *Parole* and *sens,* then, like the etymological origins of the English "meaning," imply both a speaker and a listener, whereas *mot,* obviously, and *signification,* less clearly, do not. Thus Lacan defined *mot* in 1953 as characterized by the "combinatory substitution of the signifier" and *parole* as characterized by the "fundamental transsubjectivity of the signified" (*Actes,* p. 250), a distinction equivalent in English to that between "word" and "speech."

The distinction between *sens* and *signification* is obviously more intuitive than methodological, since in ordinary speech the two terms (as well as the verbs *vouloir dire* and *signifier*) are often used as synonyms. Nor is the distinction necessarily a guide to Lacan's use of the terms *sens* and *signification.* The point is that in English the distinctions hardly exist at all. The word *discours* also escapes its English equivalent, which is much more the "learned word." The French word covers "talk," "conversation," "treatise," "speech," "oration," "parlance." It is in fact much closer to the German *Rede,* which overlaps *parole,* than is the English "discourse"— by which *Rede* is also commonly translated. Thus *Gerede* (Heidegger's "idle talk") may be translated by "discours commun" in French; *Rede* has been translated by commentators on Heidegger as "discursivité." Since Lacan, unlike Heidegger, rarely defines his terms, and since he tends to use words in a deliberately evocative fashion, the reader is well-advised to keep in mind the French and German equivalents of such terms as these when they are employed in significant contexts.

The reader will also note that Lacan sometimes employs terms like *discours* or *signifiant* (but not usually *parole*) outside the domain of language itself—that is, he sometimes uses these terms figuratively in the same way as they have been employed by anthropologists or semiologists under the all-inclusive heading "interhuman communication" (for example, the "matrimonial dialogue" of kinship systems). However, where the anthropologist will speak of kinship systems and use linguistic structures as analogies, Lacan most often concentrates on the discourse itself and uses kinship nominations and their combinatory features as his analogy, under the general heading of what he calls *le symbolique.* These distinctions are taken up again from the point of view of the sign and the signifier in the essay following the translation.

The often-quoted and sometimes misused criterion of "readable English" has been only a secondary consideration in the English text. Where the English rendering of the French is particularly doubtful, or where the original is particularly idiosyncratic or poetic, I have given the French in a note. In general, etymology has been an important factor in the choice of words; thus I hope the reader will forgive the Gallicisms that have either deliberately or unconsciously been retained. In sum, accuracy has always been preferred to elegance.

The reader will perhaps more readily appreciate my concern for coherence and accuracy over style if he reflects on the fate of Freud's works.

English-speaking readers of Freud long remained unaware of the special semantic resources of the German text as a result of English translations inevitably reflecting the epistemology of the translators, translations which, before the appearance of the *Standard Edition,* not only could not reproduce these ambiguities, but succeeded in obscuring them by ignoring them. The *Standard Edition* itself can be seen becoming more and more aware of certain terms as it progresses. It is not the unavoidable distortions of Freud's early translators which must be condemned, but rather their assumption that a key word like *Vorstellung,* for instance, was to be rendered by whatever English word seemed to fit the particular context, without the reader being advised of the semantic choice that had been made. The five-volume *Collected Papers* of Freud is particularly faulty in this respect. Thus, as late as 1954 (in *The Origins of Psycho-analysis*), *Wortvorstellung* ("word presentation") and *Sachvorstellung* ("thing presentation") were still obscured by the renderings "verbal idea" and "concrete idea"—repeating the translations of the 1920's—and the English-speaking reader was left with no sure way of correlating these terms in significant contexts with *Entstellung* (translated "distortion"), with *Darstellung* ("representation," "performance"), with *Darstellbarkeit* ("representability"), or with *Vorstellung* itself ("image," "thought," "idea"). Whether or not the distinction between external reality and psychic reality is consistently maintained in the text of Freud, I do not know, but *Wirklichkeit* and *Realität*—according to Lacan, the second usually refers to psychic reality—are still not distinguished in the English translations of Freud. Since these are terms constantly used in Freud's discussions of the representation of the unconscious, it is hardly surprising that the possibilities of exploitation revealed by Lacan's commentaries on the German text should have appeared to many people as somehow "un-Freudian," whereas in fact the central question was one of translation in every sense of the term—translation not simply from German to another language, but also translation in time.

In June, 1966, on the occasion of preparing his *Ecrits,* Lacan made a number of revisions to the *Discours.* All of these revisions, the more important of which are indicated by notes added by Lacan and dated (1966), have been incorporated into the present translation. Minor stylistic changes have been incorporated without mention, but where the change was of a more substantial nature (and not indicated by Lacan), it has been indicated by a footnote or an asterisk. An asterisk following a word indicates that only that word was changed; at the end of a sentence, that the sentence was changed; at the end of a paragraph, that the paragraph was changed. The original text before the change has not been reproduced, except in one instance.

A. G. W.

Baltimore, Maryland

NOTE

I have taken the opportunity of a second printing to correct a number of minor errors in the text. Readers interested in following up my further analysis and critique of Lacan's work are referred to my *System and Structure: Essays in Communication and Exchange* (London: Tavistock, 1972) and to my *Lacan et le discours de l'Autre* (Paris: Publications Gramma, 1973).

Paris, 1973

Acknowledgments

It remains for me to express my gratitude to all those who assisted with this task in so many different ways. First, my thanks to Dr. René Girard, chairman of the Department of Romance Languages at Johns Hopkins University, whose own meditation upon literature and man has been so fruitful for his students, and whose inspiration and criticisms have been essential; to Dr. Eugenio Donato, who was the efficient cause of my introduction to Lacan via his stimulating seminar on Lévi-Strauss and who played such an indispensable role in guiding the early evolution of the translation; to Dr. Richard Macksey, who provided encouragement, a tireless sounding board, and an acute critical ear; to Mrs. Sally Donato, Miss Susanna Peters, and Mr. John Blegen, who assisted with typing the first draft; but especially to Patricia Wilden, who bore the burden of preparing an interminably revised and incomplete manuscript. I am grateful to Dr. Lacan for assistance with some difficulties in the text. Naturally, the errors and inadequacies which remain are my own.

Prefatory Note

*En particulier, il ne faudra pas oublier que la séparation en embryologie,
anatomie, physiologie, psychologie, sociologie, clinique n'existe pas
dans la nature et qu'il n'y a qu'une discipline: la* neurobiologie à
laquelle l'observation nous oblige d'ajouter l'épithète d'humaine *en ce
qui nous concerne.*[1]

(Quotation chosen as the motto of an Institute of Psychoanalysis in 1952.)

When the *Discours de Rome* was finally published in 1956, it included
a Preface outlining the circumstances under which it had been delivered,
and the above epigraph. Since this Preface was concerned primarily with
the internecine battle within the French psychoanalytical movement in
1952, it is now rather more a matter of anecdote than of history. Consequently it has seemed best simply to summarize it, rather than to reproduce it in its entirety here.

The Congrès des psychanalystes de langue française was to take place at
the Psychological Institute of the University of Rome in September, 1953.
Lacan, as a leading member of the Société psychanalytique de Paris
(founded in 1925), had been asked to deliver the usual theoretical report
at the Congress. In the meantime, however, serious disagreements, partly
technical but also personal, had arisen within the Society over the found-
ing of the Institute whose motto Lacan quotes with such disdain. The
result was a secession from the Paris society of a number of analysts and
of about half the students undergoing their didactic analysis at the time.
The secession was led by Lacan and Daniel Lagache; the eventual meeting in Rome of the fledgling Société française de psychanalyse, unrecognized by the International Association, also included Serge Leclaire, W.
Granoff, Françoise Dolto, and Didier Anzieu.

The Paris society was or had been represented by Marie Bonaparte,
Raymond de Saussure, R. Loewenstein (since allied with Ernst Kris and

[1] "In particular, it must not be forgotten that the separation into embryology,
anatomy, physiology, psychology, sociology, and clinical practice does not exist in
nature and that there is only one discipline: *neurobiology,* to which observation
obliges us to add the epithet *human* in what concerns us."

Heinz Hartmann in New York), Bénassy, Nacht, and others, most of whom are mercilessly criticized in the *Discours* or elsewhere in Lacan's writings. Unfortunately, when the matter of recognizing the new society came up for discussion at the Eighteenth Congress of the International Association, Anna Freud herself castigated the rebels, and Hartmann's committee report at the Nineteenth Congress excluded the new society for good, mainly on the grounds that its teaching was inadequate.[2]

Lacan has never been personally reconciled with the International Association, whereas the other members of the Société française de psychanalyse have since rejoined it under a new affiliation. Lacan has recently moved to the position of director of the Ecole freudienne de Paris. After many years of teaching at the Hôpital Saint-Anne, he now holds no officially recognized position, but was permitted until recently to use an auditorium at the Ecole Normale Supérieure. He was at one time associated with the Cercle d'épistémologie de l'E.N.S., which was concerned with epistemological problems related to mathematics, psychoanalysis, logic, and language. The Journal *La Psychanalyse* has been defunct since 1963; Lacan has recently published (1966) in the *Cahiers pour l'Analyse* put out by the Cercle; he is listed as the editor of *Scilicet* and the privately circulated *Lettres de l'Ecole freudienne*; his more recent seminars are now (1972) being published in about a dozen small volumes.

Epistemology for us is defined as the history and the theory of the discourse of *science* (its birth justifies the singular).

By discourse, we mean a process of language which compels and constrains truth. . . .

We call analytic any discourse insofar as it can be reduced to the putting into place of unities which produce and repeat themselves, whatever may be the principle it assigns to the transformations at work in its system. Analysis, then, properly so-called, as the theory which treats of concepts of element and combination as such.[3]

Lacan's Preface, the first half-dozen pages of the *Discours,* is thus concerned with the polemics of an old quarrel which had the fertile and auspicious result of sparking Lacan to attempt a more or less systematic

[2] See the *International Journal of Psycho-Analysis,* XXXV (1954), 267–78; XXXVII (1956), 122. See also a fuller account of the dispute by Jan Miel: "Jacques Lacan and the Structure of the Unconscious," *Yale French Studies,* No. 36–37 (1967), pp. 104ff.

[3] "Avertissement," in *Cahiers pour l'analyse,* No. i ("La Verité"), Cercle d'épistémologie de l'E.N.S. (January, 1966).

elucidation of his revolt against the "orthodoxy" of the Paris society. Like
so many psychoanalytical societies since the medical profession set out to
monopolize them, the Paris society was top-heavy with the medical superiority of therapists, largely unaware of the extent to which they themselves were mystified by the cult of the expert which bedevils society in
so many other areas as well.

Behind the dispute lay an important theoretical difference: the question
of the training or *formation* of the analyst in his dialectic with the Other
in the *unendliche* didactic analysis, and thus the question of transference
and countertransference. But above all, Lacan has always been concerned
with the question of the status of human discourse in analysis (inseparable from the discourse in general), in opposition to tendencies to reduce analysis to a study of behavior, or to a quasi-biological theory of
instincts, or to a medical therapy inclined to reduce the subject's psychical
life to a series of symptoms to be interpreted by the (all-knowing) analyst in the way that a doctor interprets the symptoms of physiological
disease. (It should be noted that the level of sophistication in analysis at
the period Lacan was writing, especially in France, was considerably less
than it is now, fifteen years later. If the French situation has changed, it
is because of Lacan.) To speak of the status of the discourse is to put
the status of the subject in question, which is surely Freud's central concern. Secondary to this central question, which has occupied philosophers
and other interpreters of the discourse—literary critics, for instance—with
increasing intensity and concern since the Cartesian discovery of the subject (but in no century more intensely than our own), was that of the
"orthodox" length of the analytic session, long set at fifty or fifty-five
minutes, and which Lacan wished to shorten or lengthen according to
the requirements of the situation of any particular patient on any particular day.[4]

Lacan's report was somewhat of a surprise to his auditors in the sense
that it departed entirely from the usual balance sheet presented at these
affairs. For the reader who has available to him a copy of the now out-

---

[4] Lacan's initiative here is of course in keeping with the effects of transference in the
discourse of analysis, since breaking off or continuing a session may well bring the
subject to recognize something which he will reject if he is simply told about it.
But the apparently typical objection recently made by an American analyst seems
to carry considerable weight: in the first place, he said, his didactic analysis consisted of fifty-minute hours, and, in the second, changing the length of the session
would make it difficult for the doctor to organize his day.

of-print Volume I of *La Psychanalyse,* a perusal of the discussion following the presentation of the *Discours* will reveal that Lacan met with both
puzzlement and objections as well as enthusiasm on the part of those
present. Some of these objections recurred in the debate following the
publication of the *Ecrits* in 1966.[5]

Lacan accused those who had sought to prevent him from speaking at
Rome of a thoroughgoing authoritarian disregard of the subjective autonomy of their students and of confusing teaching with tutelage. He
criticized the discussion of the "case" of the new group at the International Congress, pointing out that it was generally admitted among analysts that the theoretical basis of most of the principles of psychoanalysis
was far from a matter of universal agreement. The following are the concluding paragraphs of the original Preface.

In a discipline which owes its only value as a science to the theoretic
concepts which Freud forged in the process of his own experience, it
would seem premature to me to break with the traditional terminology
of these concepts—concepts which, precisely because they have as yet been
ineptly assessed and thus have retained the ambiguity of everyday speech,
continue to profit from these echoes, although not without running into
confusions.

But it does seem to me that these terms can only become that much
more clear if their equivalence to the Language of contemporary anthropology is established, or even to the latest problems of philosophy, where
psychoanalysis has often only to take back its own.

In any event what appears most urgent to me is the task of disengag-
ing the meaning of certain concepts from the deadening effect of routine
usage, a meaning which they will recover as much by a return to their
history as by a reflection on their subjective grounding.

This is unquestionably the function of the teacher, on which all the
other functions depend, and it is in this function that the value of experience is most apparent.

Let this function be neglected, and the sense of an activity that owes
its effects only to sense becomes obliterated; and technical rules, by being

[5] See in particular the illuminating comments of Didier Anzieu in *La Quinzaine,*
No. 20 (January 15–31, 1967), pp. 14–15. Anzieu had criticized Lacan's promotion
of the linguistic domain in similar terms at Rome in 1953 (*La Psychanalyse,* I
[1956], pp. 228–31).

reduced to recipes, deprive the psychoanalytic experience of the value of knowledge and even of all criterion of reality.

For nobody is less demanding than a psychoanalyst about what might give a definite status to an activity which he himself is not far from considering purely magical, since he does not know where to situate it in a theoretical conception of his field which he hardly ever dreams of conferring on his practice of analysis.

The epigraph which I used to ornament this preface is a pretty fine example of this.

In fact, this activity would seem to fall in line with a conception of the formation of the analyst that might be that of a driving school which, not content to claim the singular privilege of granting driving licenses, imagined itself to be in a position to control the automobile industry as well. . . .

Perhaps psychoanalysis, method of Truth and of the demystification of subjective camouflages, would not be manifesting an overweening ambition if it were to apply its own principles to its own body politic: whether to the conception that psychoanalysts form of their role in relation to the patient, or to their notion of their place in intellectual society, or to their idea of their relationship with their peers, or to that of their mission as teachers.

Perhaps as a result of reopening a few windows to the full daylight of Freud's thought, this exposé may alleviate for some the anguish engendered by a symbolic action when it becomes lost in its own opacity.

However all this may be, in evoking the circumstances surrounding this address, I do not intend to excuse its all too obvious insufficiencies by the haste which circumstances imposed on it, since it is from the same haste that it takes on its meaning with its form.

As a matter of fact, in an exemplary sophism concerning intersubjective time,[6] I have demonstrated the function of haste in the logical precipitation in which Truth finds its unsurpassable condition.

Nothing truly created appears except in urgency, nothing created in urgency which does not engender its own surpassing in the Word.

But there is also nothing which does not become contingent to the Word when the moment of creation comes for man, the moment when

---

[6] Lacan's note: "See: 'Le Temps logique ou l'assertion de certitude anticipée,' *Cahiers d'Art* (1945)." (See note 47 in the text.)

he is able to see the identity of the side he takes and the disorder he denounces within a single reason, in order to comprehend their coherence in the Real and to anticipate by his certitude on the action which puts them in balance.[7]

[7] "Rien de créé qui n'apparaisse dans l'urgence, rien dans l'urgence qui n'engendre son dépassement dans la parole. Mais rien aussi qui n'y devienne contingent quand le moment y vient pour l'homme, où il peut identifier en une seule raison le parti qu'il choisit et le désordre qu'il dénonce, pour en comprendre la cohérence dans le réel et anticiper par sa certitude sur l'action qui les met en balance."

Contents

THE FUNCTION OF LANGUAGE IN PSYCHOANALYSIS

Introduction

We are going to determine that while we are still at the aphelion of our matter, for, when we arrive at the perihelion, the heat will be capable of making us forget it.
  (Lichtenberg.)

"Flesh composed of suns. How can such be?" exclaim the simple ones.
  (R. Browning, *Parleying with certain people.*)

Such awe seizes man when he unveils the lineaments of his power that he turns away from it in the very action employed to lay its features bare. So it has been with psychoanalysis. Freud's truly Promethean discovery was such an action, as his works bear witness; but the same is no less present in each humble psychoanalytic experience conducted by any one of the laborers formed in his school.

As time has gone by, we can trace almost year by year this aversion of interest as far as the functions of the Word and the domain of Language are concerned. This turning aside is the reason for the "alterations in aim and technique" which are now acknowledged within the psychoanalytic movement, and whose relation to the general lessening of therapeutic effectiveness is nevertheless ambiguous. In fact the emphasis on the resistance of the object in current psychoanalytical theory and technique must itself be submitted to the dialectic of analysis, which is bound to recognize in this emphasis an alibi of the subject.

Let us attempt to outline the topography[1] of this movement. If we examine the literature—our "scientific activity," we call it—the present problems of psychoanalysis fall clearly under three headings:

a) The function of the Imaginary,[2] shall we say, or more specifically that of phantasies in the technique of the psychoanalytic experience and in the constitution of the object at the various stages of psychic development. The original impetus in this area came from the analysis of children and from the fertile and tempting field offered to the attempts of researchers by access to the formation of structures at the preverbal level. It is there also that the culmination of this impetus is now inducing a return in the same direction by posing the problem of what symbolic sanction is to be given to phantasies in their interpretation.

b) The concept of the libidinal object relations which, since it has renewed the idea of the progress of the cure, is surreptitiously altering the way in which it is conducted. Here the new perspective took its departure from the extension of the psychoanalytic method to psychoses and from the momentary opening up of the psychoanalytic technique to data based on different principles. At this point psychoanalysis merges with an existential phenomenology—one might say, with an activism animated by charity.[3] There again, a clear-cut reaction is making itself felt in favor of a return to the technical pivot of symbolization.

c) The importance of countertransference and, correlatively, of the formation of the analyst.[4] In this instance the emphasis has resulted from the difficulties besetting the termination of the cure, rejoining those which arise when the didactic analysis of the candidate culminates in his introduction into the practice of analysis. In both cases the same oscillation is evident. On the one hand, the being of the analyst is shown, not without courage, to be a by no means negligible factor in the results of the analysis—and even a factor to be brought out into the open in his conduct as the analysis draws to a close. On the other hand, it is put forward no less forcefully that no solution is possible except by an ever more thorough exploration of the mainsprings of the unconscious.

Besides the pioneer activity which they are manifesting on three different frontiers, these three problems have a trait in common with the vitality of the psychoanalytic experience which sustains them. This is the temptation for the analyst to abandon the grounding of the Word, and this precisely in areas where, because they border on the ineffable, its use would be more than ever in need of his scrutiny: that is to say, childhood training by the mother, help like that of the good Samaritan, and dialectical mastery. The danger indeed becomes great if at this point he abandons his own Language as well, in favor of others already established which offer compensations for ignorance with which he is ill-acquainted.

We would truly like to know more about the effects of symbolization in the child, and female psychoanalysts who are also mothers, even those who give our loftiest deliberations a matriarchal air, are not exempt from that confusion of tongues by which Ferenczi designated the law of the relationship between the child and the adult.[a]

Our wise men's ideas about the perfect object relation are somewhat uncertainly conceived, and, when expounded, they reveal a mediocrity which does the profession no honor.

Beyond all doubt, these effects—where the psychoanalyst corresponds to the type of modern hero famous for his vain exploits in situations entirely beyond his control—could be corrected by a proper return to that area of knowledge in which the analyst ought to be past master: the study of the functions of the Word.

But, since Freud, it seems that this central area of our domain has been left fallow. Note how he himself refrained from venturing too far into its outlying parts: he discovered the libido stages of the child through the analysis of adults and intervened in little Hans's case only through the intermediary of his parents.[5] He deciphered a whole section of the Language of the unconscious in paranoid delusion, but used for this purpose only the key text that Schreber left behind in the volcanic debris of his spiritual catastrophe.[6] On the other hand, however, as far as the dialectic of this work and the traditional view of its meaning were concerned, he assumed the position of mastery in all its eminence.

Does this amount to saying that if the master's place remains empty, it is not so much the result of his own passing as that of a growing obliteration of the meaning of his work? To convince ourselves of this, we have surely only to ascertain what is going on in the place he vacated.

A technique is being handed on in a cheerless manner, reticent in its opacity, a manner which shies at any attempt to let in the fresh air of criticism. It has in fact assumed the air of a formalism pushed to ceremonial lengths, and so much so that one might very well wonder whether it is not to be tagged with the same similarity to obsessional neurosis that Freud so convincingly defined in the observance, if not in the genesis, of religious rites.[7]

When we consider the literature that this activity produces and feeds on, the analogy becomes even more marked: the impression is often that of a curious sort of closed circuit in which a failure to recognize the origin of the basic terms is father to the problem of making them agree with

[a] Ferenczi, "Confusion of Tongues between the Adult and the Child," *International Journal of Psycho-Analysis* [henceforth abbreviated *IJP*], XXX (1949), iv, 225–30.

each other and in which the effort to solve this problem reinforces the original misconstruction.

In order to get at the roots of this deterioration of the analytical discourse, one may legitimately apply the psychoanalytical method to the collectivity which sustains it.

In point of fact, to speak of the loss of the sense of the action of analysis is as true and as pointless as to explain the symptom by its sense[8] so long as that sense is not recognized.[9] We know that if that recognition is absent, the action of the analyst will be experienced only as an aggressive action at whatever level it occurs. We know, too, that in the absence of the social "resistances" in which the psychoanalytic group used to find reassurance, the limits of its tolerance towards its own activity—now "accepted," if not approved of—no longer depend upon anything more than the numerical strength by which its presence is measured on the social scale.

These starting points are adequate to assess the Symbolic, Imaginary, and Real conditions which will determine the defense mechanisms we can recognize in the doctrine: isolation, undoing-what-has-been-done,[10] *dénégation,*[11] and, in general, *méconnaissance.*[12]

Thus, if the importance of the American group in relation to the psychoanalytic movement as a whole is measured by its mass, it will be easy enough to weigh accurately the conditions to be met with there.

In the Symbolic order first of all, one cannot neglect the importance of that factor C which I took into account at the Congress of Psychiatry in 1950 as being the constant characteristic of any given cultural milieu: here the condition of the lack of a historical dimension by which everyone recognizes the major features of "communication" in the United States, and which, according to our way of seeing it, is at the antipodes of the psychoanalytic experience. To this must be added a native mental form, known as behaviorism, which so dominates psychological concepts in America that they have clearly been entirely unfaithful ever since to the psychoanalysis inspired by Freud.[13]

As for the other two orders, we leave it in the hands of those interested to evaluate what the mechanisms which manifest themselves in the life of psychoanalytical societies owe, respectively, to the relative eminence of those within the group and to the experienced effects of their free enterprise on the whole of the social body—as well as the value to be attributed to the notion emphasized by one of their most lucid representatives, that of the convergence which makes itself felt between the foreignness of a group dominated by the immigrant, and the distancing into which it is drawn by the function which the cultural conditions indicated above call for.

In any event it appears incontestable that the conception of psychoanalysis in the United States has inclined toward the adaptation of the individual to the social environment, toward the quest for patterns of conduct, and toward all the objectification implied in the notion of "human relations." [14] And the indigenous term "human engineering" [15] strongly implies a privileged position of exclusion in relation to the human object.

It is in fact this distance—a distance from the human object without which such a position could not be held—which has contributed to the present eclipse in psychoanalysis of the most living terms of its experience: the unconscious and sexuality, which apparently will cease before long even to be mentioned.

We do not have to take sides over the faults of formalism and the corporation-man mentality, both of which are noted and denounced by the official writings of the analytical group itself. The Pharisee and the corporation man interest us only because of their common essence, the source of the difficulties which both have with the Word, and particularly when it comes to "talking shop." [16]

The fact is that the inability to communicate underlying motives, if it can sustain a magister, is not on a par with real mastery—that at least which the teaching of psychoanalysis requires. This became obvious in any case when, not long ago, in order to sustain the primacy of a magister and for the sake of appearances, it became necessary for a lesson to be given.

This is why the attachment to the traditional technique, indefectibly reaffirmed from the same tack, after a consideration of the results of the work on the frontier lines enumerated above, is not without equivocation; this equivocation is to be measured by the substitution of the term "classic" for "orthodox" in describing the traditional technique. The attachment is to decorum, for want of knowing how to make any sort of comment on the doctrine itself.[17]

As far as we are concerned, we assert that the technique cannot be comprehended, nor therefore correctly applied, if the underlying concepts are misconstrued. It is our task to demonstrate that these concepts assume their full sense only when oriented in the domain of Language, only when ordered in relation to the function of the Word.

At this point I must note that in order to handle any Freudian concept, reading Freud cannot be considered superfluous, even if it be only for those concepts which are homonyms of current notions. This has been well demonstrated, I am opportunely reminded, by the misadventure which befell a theory of the instincts in a revision of Freud's position by an author somewhat less than alert to its explicitly stated mythical content. Obviously he could hardly be aware of it, since he tackles the theory by means of the work of Marie Bonaparte, which he repeatedly cites as an equivalent of the text of Freud—without the reader being in any way advised of the fact—relying no doubt on the good taste of the reader, not without reason, not to confuse the two, but proving no less that he has not the remotest comprehension of the true level of the secondary text.*,[18] As a result, from reductions to deductions, and from inductions to hypotheses, the author comes to his conclusion by way of the strict tautology of his false premises: that is to say, that the instincts in question are reducible to the reflex arc. Like the pile of chinaware whose collapse is the main feature of the classic music hall exhibition—leaving nothing in the hands of the performer except a couple of fragments mismatched by the crash—the complex construction which moves from the discovery of the migrations of the libido in the erotogenic zones to the metapsychological passage of a generalized pleasure principle into the death instinct, becomes the binomial dualism of a passive erotic instinct, modeled on the activity of the *chercheuses de poux,* so dear to the poet,[19] and a destructive instinct, identified simply with motility. A result which merits an honorable mention for the art, voluntary or not, of drawing the ultimate logical conclusions of an original misunderstanding.

I

The Empty Word and the Full Word

Donne en ma bouche parole vraie et estable et fay de moy langue caulte.

(*L'Internele Consolacion*, XLVe Chapitre: qu'on ne doit pas chascun croire et du legier trebuchement de paroles.)[20]

Cause toujours.[21]

(Motto of "causalist" thought.)

Whether it sees itself as an instrument of healing, of formation, or of exploration in depth, psychoanalysis has only a single intermediary: the patient's Word. That this is self-evident is no excuse for our neglecting it. And every Word calls for a reply.

I shall show that there is no Word without a reply, even if it meets no more than silence, provided that it has an auditor: this is the heart of its function in psychoanalysis.

But if the psychoanalyst is not aware that this is the way it is with the function of the Word, he will only experience its appeal all the more strongly, and if the first thing to make itself heard is the void, it is within himself that he will experience it, and it is beyond the Word that he will seek a reality to fill this void.

Thus it is that he will come to analyze the subject's behavior in order to find in it what the subject is not saying. Yet in order to obtain an avowal of what he finds, he must nevertheless talk about it. Then he finds his tongue again, but his Word is now rendered suspect by having replied only to the failure of his silence, in the face of the echo perceived of his own nothingness.[22]

But what in fact was this appeal from the subject beyond the void of his speech? It was an appeal to Truth in its ultimate nature, through which other appeals resulting from humbler needs will find faltering expression. But first and foremost it was the appeal of the void, in the ambiguous *béance*[23] of an attempted seduction of the other by the means on which the subject has come compliantly to rely and to which he is going to commit the monumental construct of his narcissism.[24]

"That's it all right, introspection!" exclaims the *prud'homme* who

9

knows its dangers only too well. He is certainly not the last, he avows, to have tasted its charms, if he has exhausted its profit. Too bad that he hasn't more time to waste. For you would hear some fine profundities from him were he to arrive on your couch.

It is strange that an analyst, for whom this sort of person is one of the first encounters in his experience, should still take introspection into account in psychoanalysis. For from the moment that the wager is taken up, all those fine things that were thought to be in reserve slip away. If he does engage in it, they will appear of little account, but others present themselves sufficiently unexpected by our friend to seem ridiculous to him and to stun him into silence. The common lot.[b]

Then it is that he grasps the difference between the mirage of the monologue whose accommodating fancies used to sustain his animated outpourings, and the forced labor of this discourse without escape, on which the psychologist (not without humor) and the therapist (not without cunning) have bestowed the name of "free association."

For free association really is a labor, and so much of a travail that some have gone so far as to say that it requires an apprenticeship, even to the point of seeing in the apprenticeship its true formative value. But if viewed in this way, what does it form but a skilled craftsman?

Well, then, what of this labor? Let us consider its conditions and its fruit, in the hope of throwing more light on its aim and profit.

The aptness of the German word *durcharbeiten*—equivalent to the English "working through"—has been recognized in passing. It has confounded French translators, in spite of what the immortal words of a master of French style offered them by way of an exercise in exhausting every last drop of sense: "Cent fois sur le métier, remettez. . . ."[25] —but how does the work [*l'ouvrage*] make any progress here?

The theory reminds us of the triad: frustration, aggressivity, regression. This is an explanation so apparently comprehensible that we may well be spared the necessity of comprehending it. Intuition is prompt, but we should be all the more suspicious of the self-evident that has become an *idée reçue*. If analysis should come round to exposing its weakness, it will be advisable not to rest content with recourse to affectivity—that taboo-word of the dialectical incapacity which, with the verb *to intellectualize* (whose accepted pejorative connotation makes a

[b] Paragraph rewritten in 1966. [Minor changes were also made in the preceding paragraph.]

merit of this incapacity), will go down in the history of the language as the stigmata of our obtuseness regarding the subject.[c]

Shall we enquire instead into the source of the subject's frustration? Does it come from the silence of the analyst? A reply to the subject's empty Word, even—or especially—an approving one, often shows by its effects that it is much more frustrating than silence. Is it not rather a matter of a frustration inherent in the very discourse of the subject? [26] Does the subject not become engaged in an ever-growing dispossession of that being of his, concerning which—by dint of sincere portraits which leave its idea no less incoherent, of rectifications which do not succeed in freeing its essence, of stays and defenses which do not prevent his statue from tottering, of narcissistic embraces which become like a puff of air in animating it—he ends up by recognizing that this being has never been anything more than his construct in the Imaginary and that this construct disappoints all his certitudes? For in this labor which he undertakes to reconstruct this construct *for another,* he finds again the fundamental alienation which made him construct it *like another one,* and which has always destined it to be stripped from him *by another.*[d,27]

This ego, whose strength our theorists now define by its capacity to bear frustration, is frustration in its essence.[e] Not frustration of a desire of the subject, but frustration by an object in which his desire is alienated and which the more it is elaborated, the more profound the alienation from its *jouissance* becomes for the subject. Frustration at a second remove, therefore, and such that even if the subject were to reintroduce its form into his discourse to the point of reconstituting the preparatory image through which the subject makes himself an object by striking a

[c] Previously I had written: "in psychological matters. . . ." (1966).

[d] Paragraph rewritten in 1966.

[e] This is the crux of a deviation as much practical as theoretical. For to identify the ego with the curbing of the subject is to confuse Imaginary isolation with the mastery of the instincts. This lays one open to errors of judgment in the conduct of the treatment: such as trying to reinforce the ego in many neuroses caused by its overforceful structure—and that is a dead end. Hasn't my friend Michael Balint written that a reinforcement of the ego should be beneficial to the subject suffering from *ejaculatio praecox* because it would permit him to prolong the suspension of his desire? But this can surely not be supposed, if it is precisely to the fact that his desire is made dependent upon the Imaginary function of the ego that the subject owes the short-circuiting of the act—which psychoanalytical clinical experience shows clearly to be intimately linked to narcissistic identification with the partner.

pose before the mirror,[28] he could not possibly be satisfied with it, since even if he achieved his most perfect likeness in that image, it would still be the *jouissance*[29] of the other that he would cause to be recognized in it. This is the reason why there is no reply which is adequate to this discourse, for the subject will consider as a takedown every Word participating in his mistake.

The aggressivity which the subject will experience at this point has nothing to do with the animal aggressivity of frustrated desire. Such a reference, which most people are content with, actually masks another one which is less agreeable for each and for all of us: the aggressivity of the slave whose response to the frustration of his labor is a desire for death.

It is therefore readily conceivable how this aggressivity may respond to any intervention which, by denouncing the Imaginary intentions of the discourse, dismantles the object constructed by the subject to satisfy them. This is in effect what is called the analysis of resistances, whose perilous side appears immediately. It is already pointed to by the existence of that artless simpleton who has never seen revealed anything except the aggressive signification of his subjects' phantasies.[f]

This is the same man who, not hesitating to plead for a "causalist" analysis which would aim to transform the subject in his present by learned explanations of his past, betrays well enough by his very intonation the anxiety from which he wishes to save himself—the anxiety of having to think that his patient's liberty may be dependent upon that of his own intervention. Whether or not the expedient into which he plunges may possibly be beneficial at some moment or another to the subject, this has no more importance than a stimulating pleasantry and will not detain me any longer.

Rather let us focus on this *hic et nunc* to which some analysts feel we should confine the tactics of analysis. It may indeed be useful, provided that the Imaginary intention that the analyst uncovers in it is not detached by him from the symbolic relation in which it is expressed. Nothing must be read into it concerning the *moi* of the subject which can-

---

[f] This is the same work which I crowned at the end of my Introduction. [Added 1966:] It is clear in what follows that aggressivity is only a lateral effect of analytic frustration, even if this effect can be reinforced by a certain type of intervention; as such, this effect is not the reason for the couple frustration-regression.

not be reassumed by the subject in the form of the *"je,"* that is, in the first person.[30]

"I have been this only in order to become what I can be": if this were not the permanent fulcrum of the subject's assumption of his own mirages, where could one pick out progress here?

Hence the analyst cannot without peril track the subject down into the intimacy of his gestures, nor into that of his static state, except by reintegrating them as silent notes into his narcissistic discourse—and this has been noted very sensitively, even by young practitioners.

The danger involved here is not that of the subject's negative reaction, but much rather that of his capture in an objectification—no less Imaginary than before—of his static state or of his "statue," in a renewed status of his alienation.

Quite the contrary, the art of the analyst must be to suspend the subject's certitudes until their last mirages have been consumed. And it is in the discourse that, like verse, their resolution must be scanned.[31]

Indeed, however empty this discourse may appear, it is only so if taken at its face value: that which justifies the remark of Mallarmé's, in which he compares the common use of Language to the exchange of a coin whose obverse and reverse no longer bear any but worn effigies, and which people pass from hand to hand "in silence." This metaphor is sufficient to remind us that the Word, even when almost completely worn out, retains its value as a *tessera.*[32]

Even if it communicates nothing, the discourse represents the existence of communication; even if it denies the obvious, it affirms that the Word constitutes the Truth; even if it is destined to deceive, here the discourse speculates on faith in testimony.

Moreover, it is the analyst who knows better than anyone else that the question is to understand which "part" of this speech carries the significative term, and this is exactly how he proceeds in the ideal case: taking the recital of an everyday event for an apologue addressed to him that hath ears to hear, a long prosopopoeia for a direct interjection, or on the other hand taking a simple lapsus for a highly complex statement, or even the sigh of a momentary silence for the whole lyrical development it makes up for.

This is consequently a fortunate kind of punctuation, one which confers its meaning on the subject's discourse. This is why the adjournment of a session—which according to present-day technique is simply a chronometric break and, as such, a matter of indifference to the thread of the discourse—plays the part of a metric beat which has the full value of an actual intervention by the analyst for hastening the concluding moments. This fact should lead us to free this act of termination from its routine usage and to employ it for the purposes of the technique in every useful way possible.

It is in this way that regression is able to operate. Regression is simply the actualization in the discourse of the phantasy relations reconstituted by an ego at each stage in the decomposition of its structure. After all, this regression is not a real regression; even in language it manifests itself only by inflections, by turns of phrase, by *"trebuchements si legiers"* that in the extreme case they cannot go beyond the artifice of "baby talk" in the adult. To attribute to regression the reality of a present relation to the object amounts to projecting the subject into an alienating illusion which does no more than echo an alibi of the psychoanalyst.

It is for this reason that nothing could be more misleading for the analyst than to seek to guide himself by a so-called contact experienced with the reality of the subject. This constantly reiterated theme harped on by intuitionist and even by phenomenological psychology has become extended in contemporary usage in a way which is thoroughly symptomatic of the rarefaction of the effects of the Word in the present social context. But its obsessional power becomes flagrantly obvious by being put forward in a relationship which, by its very rules, excludes all real contact.

Young analysts who might nevertheless allow themselves to be taken in by what such a recourse implies of impenetrable gifts will find no better way of retracing their steps than to consider the successful outcome of the actual supervision they themselves undergo. From the point of view of contact with the Real, the very possibility of such supervisory control would become a problem. It is in fact exactly the contrary: here the supervisor manifests a second sight, make no mistake about it, which makes the experience at least as instructive for him as for the person supervised. And this is almost all the more so because the person under his supervision demonstrates in the process fewer of these gifts, which are held by some people to be all the less communicable in proportion as they themselves make more of a production about their technical secrets.

The reason for this enigma is that the supervised person acts as a filter, or even as a refractor, of the subject's discourse,[33] and in this way there is presented to the supervisor a ready-made stereoscopic picture, making clear from the start the three or four registers on which the musical score constituted by the subject's discourse can be read.

If the supervised person could be put by the supervisor into a subjective position different from that implied by the sinister term *contrôle* (advantageously replaced, but only in English, by "supervision"), the greatest profit he would derive from this exercise would be to learn to maintain himself in the position of second subjectivity into which the situation automatically puts the supervisor.

There he would find the authentic way to reach what the classic formula of the analyst's vague, even absent-minded, attention expresses only very approximately.[34] For it is essential to know toward what that attention is directed; and, as all our labors are there to testify, it is certainly not directed toward an object beyond the Word of the subject, in the way it is for certain analysts who make it a strict rule never to lose sight of that object.[35] If this were to be the way of analysis, then it would surely have recourse to means other than speech—or else this would be the only example of a method which forbade itself the means necessary to its own ends.

The only object within the analyst's range is the Imaginary relation which links him to the subject *qua moi*. And for lack of a way of eliminating it, he can employ it to regulate the yield of his ears, in line with the use which is normally made of them, according to both physiology and the Gospel: having ears *in order not to hear;* in other words, in order to pick up what is to be heard. For he has no other ears, no third or fourth ear to serve as what some have tried to describe as a direct transaudition of the unconscious by the unconscious.[36] I shall deal with the question of this supposed mode of communication later.

I have tackled the function of the Word in analysis from its least rewarding angle, that of the empty Word, where the subject seems to be talking in vain about someone who, even if he were his spitting image, can never become one with the assumption of his desire. I have pointed out in it the source of the growing devaluation of which the

Word has been the object in both theory and technique. I have been obliged to lift up by slow degrees, as if they were a heavy millstone which had fallen on the Word, what can serve only as a sort of "governor" for the movement of analysis: that is to say, the individual psychophysiological factors which are in reality excluded from its dialectic. To consider the goal of psychoanalysis to be to modify the individual inertia of these factors is to be condemned to a fiction of movement or evolution with which a certain trend in psychoanalytic technique seems in fact to be satisfied.

If we now turn to the other extreme of the psychoanalytic experience —if we look into its history, into its casuistry, into the process of the cure—we shall discover that to the analysis of the *hic et nunc* is to be opposed the value of anamnesis as the index and as the source of the progress of the therapy; that to obsessional intrasubjectivity is to be opposed hysterical intersubjectivity; and that to the analysis of resistance is to be opposed symbolic interpretation. Here it is that the realization of the full Word begins.

Let us examine the relation constituted by this realization.

It will be recalled that the method introduced by Freud and Breuer was very early on given the name of the "talking cure" by Anna O., one of Breuer's patients. It was the experience inaugurated with this hysterical patient that led them to the discovery of the pathogenetic event known as the traumatic experience.

If this event was recognized as being the cause of the symptom, it was because the putting into words of the event (in the patient's "stories") determined the lifting of the symptom.[37] Here the term *prise de conscience*,[38] borrowed from the psychological theory that was constructed on this fact, retains a prestige which merits the distrust we hold to be the best attitude towards explanations that do office as self-evident truths. The psychological prejudices of Freud's day were opposed to acknowledging the existence of any reality in verbalization as such, other than its own *flatus vocis*. The fact remains that in the hypnotic state verbalization is disassociated from the *prise de conscience*, and this fact alone is surely enough to require a revision of that conception of its effects.[39]

But why is it that the worthy proponents of the behaviorist *Aufhebung* do not use this as their example to show that they do not have to know whether the subject has remembered anything whatever from the past? He has simply recounted the event. But we would say that he has verbalized it—or, in order to further develop this term whose echoes in French call to mind a Pandora figure other than the one with the box (in which the term should probably be locked up for good),[40] that he has made it pass into the *verbe*[41] or more precisely into the *epos*[42] by which he brings back into present time the origins of his own person. And he does this in a Language which permits his discourse to be understood by his contemporaries, and which furthermore presupposes their present discourse. Thus it happens that the recitation of the *epos* may include some discourse of olden days in its own archaic or even foreign tongue, or may even pursue its course in present time with all the animation of the actor; but it is like an indirect discourse, isolated inside quotation marks within the thread of the narration, and, if the discourse is played out, it is on a stage implying the presence not only of the chorus, but also of spectators.

Hypnotic rememoration is doubtless a reproduction of the past, but it is above all a spoken representation[43]—and as such implies all sorts of presences. It stands in the same relation to the waking rememoration of what is curiously called in analysis "the material," as the drama in which the original myths of the City State are produced before its assembled citizens stands in relation to a history which may well be made up of materials, but in which a nation today learns to read the symbols of a destiny on the march. In Heideggerian language one could say that both types of rememoration constitute the subject as *gewesend*—that is, as being the one who thus has been. But in the internal unity of this temporalization, the existent marks the convergence of the having-beens. That is to say, other encounters being assumed to have taken place since any particular one whatever of these moments considered as having-beens, there would have issued from it another existent which would cause him to have been in quite a different way.[44]

The ambiguity of the hysterical revelation of the past does not depend so much on the vacillation of its content between the Imaginary and the Real, for it locates itself in both. Nor is it exactly error or falsehood. The point is that it presents us with the birth of Truth in the Word, and thereby brings us up against the reality of what is neither true nor false. At any rate, that is the most disquieting aspect of the problem.

For the Truth of this revelation lies in the present Word which testifies to it in contemporary reality and which grounds it in the name of that reality. Yet in that reality, it is only the Word which bears witness to that portion of the powers of the past which has been thrust aside at each crossroads where the event has made its choice.

This is the reason why the yardstick of continuity in anamnesis, by which Freud measures the completeness of the cure, has nothing to do with the Bergsonian myth of a restoration of duration in which the authenticity of each instant would be destroyed if it did not sum up the modulation of all the preceding ones. The point is that for Freud it is not a question of biological memory, nor of its intuitionist mystification, nor of the paramnesis of the symptom, but a question of rememoration, that is, of history—balancing the scales in which conjectures about the past cause a fluctuation of the promises of the future upon a single fulcrum: that of chronological certitude. I might as well be categorical: in psychoanalytical anamnesis, it is not a question of reality, but of Truth, because the effect of a full Word is to reorder the past contingent events by conferring on them the sense of necessities to come, just as they are constituted by the little liberty through which the subject makes them present.[45]

The meanders of the research pursued by Freud into the case of the Wolf Man confirm these remarks by taking their full sense from them.

Freud insists on a total objectification of proof so long as it is a question of dating the primal scene, but without further ado he takes for granted all the resubjectifications of the event which he considers necessary to explain its effects at every turning point where the subject restructures himself—that is, as many restructurings of the event as take place, as he puts it, *nachträglich,* after the event.[g] What is more, with an audacity bordering on offhandedness, he asserts that he holds it legitimate in the analysis of processes to skip over the time intervals in which the event remains latent in the subject.[h,46] In short he annuls the *times for understanding* in favor of the *moments of concluding* which precipitate the meditation of the subject towards deciding the sense to attach to the original event.

[g] *Gesammelte Werke* [henceforth abbreviated *GW*], XII, 71; *Cinq psychanalyses,* Presses Universitaires de France [henceforth abbreviated PUF], p. 356, weak translation of the term.

[h] *GW*, XII, 72, n.1, last few lines. The concept of *Nachträglichkeit* is to be found once more stressed in the note. *Cinq psychanalyses,* p. 356, n.1. [*Standard Edition,* XVII, 45, n.1.]

Let it be noted that *temps pour comprendre* and *moment de conclure* are functions which I have defined in a purely logical theorem and which are familiar to my students as having proved extremely favorable to the dialectical analysis through which we guide their steps in the process of a psychoanalysis.[47]

It is certainly this assumption of his history by the subject, insofar as it is constituted by the Word addressed to the other, which makes up the fundamental principle of the new method which Freud called psychoanalysis, and not in 1904—as was taught until recently by an authority who, when he finally threw off the cloak of a prudent silence, appeared on that day to know nothing of Freud except the titles of his works—but in 1896.[i]

In this analysis of the sense of his method, I do not deny, any more than Freud himself did, the psycho-physiological discontinuity manifested by the states in which the hysterical symptom appears, nor do I deny that this symptom may be treated by methods—hypnosis or even narcosis—which reproduce the discontinuity of these states. I simply repudiate any reliance on these states—and as deliberately as Freud forbade himself recourse to them after a certain time—whether to explain the symptom or to cure it.

For if the originality of the analytic method depends on means which it must do without, the fact is that the means which it reserves to itself are sufficient to constitute a domain whose limits define the relativity of its operations.

Its means are those of the Word, in so far as the Word confers a meaning on the functions of the individual; its domain is that of the concrete discourse, insofar as this is the field of the transindividual reality of the subject; its operations are those of history, insofar as history constitutes the emergence of Truth in the Real.

To begin with, in fact, when the subject commits himself to analysis he accepts a position more constituting in itself than all the duties by which he allows himself to be more or less enticed: that of interlocution, and I see no objection in the fact that this remark may leave the listener

[i] In an article easily available to the least exacting French reader, since it [originally] appeared [in French] in the *Revue Neurologique,* whose collected numbers usually to be found in the libraries of medical-student common rooms. ["L'hérédité et l'étiologie des névroses," *Standard Edition,* III, 143–56.]. [Added 1966:] The blunder denounced here illustrates among others how the said authority measured up to his "leadership."

nonplussed.[48] For I shall take this opportunity of stressing that the allocution of the subject entails an allocutor[j]—in other words, that the locutor[k] is constituted in it as intersubjectivity.[49]

Secondly, it is on the fundamental basis of this interlocution, insofar as it includes the response of the interlocutor, that the meaning of what Freud insists on as the restitution of continuity in the subject's motivations makes itself clear to us. An operational examination of this objective shows us in effect that it cannot be satisfied except in the intersubjective continuity of the discourse in which the subject's history is constituted.

For instance, the subject may vaticinate on his history under the influence of one or other of those drugs that anaesthetize the consciousness and which have been christened in our day "Truth serums"—an unerring *contresens* that reveals all the irony inherent in Language. But precisely because it comes to him through an alienated form, even a retransmission of his own recorded discourse, be it from the mouth of his own doctor, cannot have the same effects as psychoanalytic interlocution.

It is therefore in the position of a third term that the Freudian discovery of the unconscious becomes clearly illuminated, revealing its true grounding. This discovery can be simply formulated in the following terms:

The unconscious is that part of the concrete discourse in so far as it is transindividual, which is not at the disposition of the subject to reestablish the continuity of his conscious discourse.[50]

This disposes of the paradox presented by the concept of the unconscious if it is related to an individual reality. For to reduce this concept to unconscious drives is to resolve the paradox only by ignoring the experience which shows clearly that the unconscious participates in the functions of ideation, and even of thought—as Freud plainly insisted

---

[j] Even if he is speaking "off," or "to the wings." He addresses himself to *ce (grand) Autre* [i.e. to that Other with a big 'O'] whose theoretical basis I have consolidated since this was written and which bids a certain *epoché* in the resumption of the term to which I limited myself at that time: that of "intersubjectivity" (1966). [Cf. translator's note 49.]

[k] I borrow these terms from the late Edouard Pichon who, both in the indications he gave for the development of our discipline and in those which guided him in people's dark places, showed a divination that I can attribute only to his practice of semantics.

when, not being able to avoid a conjunction of contrary terms in the expression "unconscious thought," [51] he bestowed on it the sacramental invocation: *sit venia verbo*. In any case we obey him by throwing the blame, in effect, on the *verbe,* but on that *verbe* which is realized in the discourse which runs from mouth to mouth—like the hidden object in hunt-the-slipper—so as to confer on the act of the subject who receives its message, the sense which makes of this act an act of his history and which confers on him his Truth.

Hence the objection that is raised against the notion of unconscious thought as a contradiction in terms, by a psychology not yet properly freed from formal logic, falls to the ground with the fact of the distinction of the psychoanalytical domain insofar as this field reveals the reality of the discourse in its autonomy. And the psychoanalyst's *eppur si muove!* shares its incidence with Galileo's; an incidence which is not that of factual experience, but that of the *experimentum mentis*.

The unconscious is that chapter of my history which is marked by a blank or occupied by a falsehood: it is the censored chapter. But the Truth can be found again; it is most often already written down elsewhere. That is to say:

—in monuments: this is my body—that is to say, the hysterical nucleus of the neurosis where the hysterical symptom reveals the structure of a Language and is deciphered like an inscription which, once recovered, can without serious loss be destroyed;

—in archival documents also: these are my childhood memories, just as impenetrable as are such documents when I do not know their source;

—in semantic evolution: this corresponds to the stock of words and acceptations of my own particular vocabulary, as it does to my style of life and to my character;

—in traditions as well, and not only in them but also in the legends which, in a heroicized form, transport my history;

—and lastly, in the traces which are inevitably preserved by the distortions necessitated by the linking of the adulterated chapter to the chapters surrounding it, and whose meaning will be re-established by my exegesis.[52]

The student who has the idea that reading Freud in order to understand Freud is preferable to reading Mr. Fenichel—an idea rare enough, it is true, for our teaching to have to busy itself spreading it about—will realize, once he sets about it, that what I have just said has so little originality, even in its verve, that there appears in it not a single meta-phor that Freud's works do not repeat with the frequency of a *leitmotif* in which the very fabric of the work is revealed.

At every instant of his practice from then on, he will be more easily able to grasp the fact that these metaphors, in the manner of the nega-tion whose doubling annuls it, lose their metaphorical dimension, and he will recognize that this is so because he is operating in the charac-teristic domain of the metaphor, which is but the synonym for the sym-bolic displacement brought into play in the symptom.[53]

After that he will better be able to form an opinion of the Imaginary displacement which motivates the works of Mr. Fenichel, by measuring the difference in consistency and technical efficacy between reference to the supposedly organic stages of individual development and research into the particular events of a subject's history. The difference is pre-cisely that which separates authentic historical research from the so-called laws of history, of which it can be said that every age finds its own philosopher to diffuse them according to the prevailing scale of values.

This is not to say that there is nothing to be gathered from the differ-ent meanings uncovered in the general march of history along the path which runs from Bossuet (Jacques Bénigne) to Toynbee (Arnold), and which is punctuated by the edifices of Auguste Comte and Karl Marx. Everyone knows very well that they are worth as little for directing research into the recent past as they are for making any reasonable presumptions about the events of tomorrow. Besides, they are modest enough to postpone their certitudes until the day after tomorrow and not too prudish either to admit the retouching which permits predic-tions about what happened yesterday.

If therefore their role is somewhat too slender for the advancement of science, their interest however lies elsewhere: in their very considerable role as ideals. It is this which prompts me to make a distinction between what might be called the primary and the secondary functions of his-torization.

For to say of psychoanalysis or of history that, considered as sciences, they are both sciences of the particular, does not mean that the facts they deal with are purely accidental, or simply factitious, and that their ultimate value is reducible to the brute aspect of the trauma.

Events are engendered in a primary historization. In other words, history is already producing itself on the stage where it will be played out once it has been written down, both within the subject and outside him.[54]

At such and such a period, some riot or other in the Faubourg Saint-Antoine is lived by its actors as a victory or defeat of the Parlement or the Court; at another, as a victory or defeat of the proletariat or the bourgeoisie. And although it is "the peoples" (to borrow an expression from the Cardinal de Retz) who foot its bill, it is not at all the same historical event—I mean that the two events do not leave the same sort of memory behind in men's minds.

This is to say that, with the disappearance of the reality of the Parlement and the Court, the first event will return to its traumatic value, admitting a progressive and authentic effacement, unless its sense is deliberately revived. Whereas the memory of the second event will remain very much alive even under censorship—in the same way that the amnesia of repression is one of the most lively forms of memory—as long as there are men to place their revolt under the command of the struggle for the coming to political power of the proletariat, that is to say, men for whom we can assume that the key words of dialectical materialism have a meaning.

At this point it would be too much to say that I was about to carry these remarks over into the field of psychoanalysis, since they are there already, and since the disentanglement which they bring about in psychoanalysis between the technique of deciphering the unconscious and the theory of instincts—to say nothing of the theory of drives—goes without saying.

What we teach the subject to recognize as his unconscious is his history—that is to say, we help him to perfect the contemporary historization of the facts which have already determined a certain number of the historical "turning points" in his existence. But if they have played this role, it is already as facts of history, that is to say, insofar as they have been recognized in one particular sense or censored in a certain order.

Thus, every fixation at a so-called instinctual stage is above all a historical scar: a page of shame that is forgotten or undone, or a page of glory which compels. But what is forgotten is recalled in acts, and undoing-what-has-been-done is opposed to what is said elsewhere, just as obligation perpetuates in the symbol the very mirage in which the subject found himself trapped.

To put it briefly, the instinctual stages, when they are being lived, are already organized in subjectivity. And to put it clearly, the subjectivity of the child who registers as defeats and victories the heroic chronicle of the training of his sphincters, taking pleasure throughout it in the Imaginary sexualization of his cloacal orifices, turning his excremental expulsions into aggressions, his retentions into seductions, and his movements of release into symbols—this subjectivity *is not fundamentally different* from the subjectivity of the psychoanalyst who in order to understand them, tries his skill at reconstituting the forms of love which he calls pregenital.

In other words, the anal stage is no less purely historical when it is lived than when it is reconstituted in thought, nor is it less purely founded in intersubjectivity. On the other hand, seeing it as a momentary halt in what is claimed to be a maturing of the instincts leads even the best minds straight off the track, to the point that there is seen in it the reproduction in ontogenesis of a stage of the animal phylum which is to be looked for among threadworms, even jellyfish—a speculation which, ingenious as it may be when penned by Balint, leads in other places to the most inconsistent daydreams, or even to the folly that goes looking in the *protistum* for the imaginary blueprint of breaking and entering the body, fear of which is supposed to control feminine sexuality. Why not consequently look for the image of the *moi* in the shrimp, under the pretext that both acquire a new carapace after shedding the old?

Somewhere between 1910 and 1920, a certain Jaworski constructed a beautiful system in which the "biological plan" could be found right up to the confines of culture, and which actually sought to furnish the order of Crustacea with a historical counterpart at some period or other of the later Middle Ages, if I remember rightly, under the label of a common florescence of armor—and left no animal form without a human respondent, not excepting molluscs and bedbugs.

Analogy is not metaphor, and the use that philosophers of nature have made of it calls for the genius of a Goethe, but even his example is not encouraging. Nothing is more repugnant to the spirit of our discipline, and it was by deliberately keeping away from analogy that Freud opened up the right way to the interpretation of dreams and with it, to the concept of analytic symbolism. Analytic symbolism, I insist, is strictly opposed to analogical thinking, whose dubious tradition results in the fact that some people, even in our own ranks, still consider it to be part and parcel of our method.

This is why excessive excursions into the ridiculous must be put to use for their eye-opening value, since by opening our eyes to the absurdity of a theory, they will bring our attention to bear on dangers that have nothing theoretical about them.

This mythology of the maturing of the instincts, built out of selections from the works of Freud, actually engenders spiritual* problems whose vapor, condensing into nebulous ideals, returns to inundate the original myth with its showers. The best writers set their wits to postulating formulae which will satisfy the requirements of the mysterious "genital love" [55] (there are some notions whose strangeness adapts itself better to the parenthesis of a borrowed term), and they initial their attempt with the avowal of a *non liquet*. However, nobody appears very much disturbed by the *malaise* which results; and it can be seen rather as matter fit to encourage all the Münchhausens of psychoanalytical normalization to pull themselves up by the hair in the hope of attaining the paradise of the full realization of the genital object, indeed of the object, period.

If we, being psychoanalysts, are well placed to be acquainted with the power of words, this is no reason to turn it to account in the sense of the insoluble, nor for "binding heavy burdens and grievous to be borne, and laying them on men's shoulders," as Christ's malediction is expressed to the Pharisees in the text of Saint Matthew.

In this way the poverty of the terms in which we try to enclose a subjective* problem may leave a great deal to be desired for particularly exacting spirits, should they ever compare these terms to those which structured in their very confusion the ancient quarrels centered around Nature and Grace.[1] Thus this poverty may well leave them apprehensive concerning the quality of the psychological and sociological

---

[1] [Added 1966:] This reference to the aporia of Christianity announced a more precise one in its Jansenist culmen: a reference to Pascal in fact, whose wager, still intact, forced me to take the whole question up again in order to get at what it conceals which is inestimable for psychoanalysis—at this date (June, 1966) still in reserve. [Pascal's "pari" on the "infini-rien" is to be found in *Pensée* #233 of the Brunschvicq edition, #451 of the Pléiade edition.]

results that one may expect from their use. And it is to be hoped that a better appreciation of the functions of the *logos* will dissipate the mysteries of our phantastic charismata.

To confine ourselves to a more lucid tradition, perhaps we shall understand the celebrated maxim in which La Rochefoucauld tells us that "il y a des gens qui n'auraient jamais été amoureux, s'ils n'avaient jamais entendu parler de l'amour," [56] not in the Romantic sense of an entirely Imaginary "bringing to realization" of love which would make of this remark a bitter objection on his part, but as an authentic recognition of what love owes to the symbol and of what the Word entails of love.

In any event one has only to go back to the works of Freud to gauge to what secondary and hypothetical place he relegates the theory of instincts. The theory cannot in his eyes stand for a single instant against the least important particular fact of a history, he insists, and the *genital narcissism* [57] which he invokes when he sums up the case of the Wolf Man shows us well enough the disdain in which he holds the constituted order of the libidinal stages. Going even further, he evokes the instinctual conflict in his summing-up only to steer away from it immediately and to recognize in the symbolic isolation of the "I am not castrated" in which the subject asserts himself, the compulsive form in which his heterosexual choice remains riveted, in opposition to the effect of homosexualizing capture undergone by the *moi* traced back to the Imaginary matrix of the primal scene. This is in truth the subjective conflict, in which it is only a question of the vicissitudes of subjectivity in so far as the *"je"* wins and loses against the *"moi"* at the whim of religious catechizing or of the indoctrinating *Aufklärung,* a conflict whose effects Freud made the subject bring to realization through his help before explaining them to us in the dialectic of the Oedipus complex.

It is in the analysis of such a case that one sees clearly that the realization of perfect love is not a fruit of nature but of grace—that is to say, the fruit of an intersubjective accord imposing its harmony on the torn and riven nature which supports it.

"But what on earth is this subject then that you keep battering our understanding with?" finally protests some impatient listener. "Haven't we already learned the lesson from Monsieur de La Palice [58] that everything experienced by the individual is subjective?"

Naïve lips, whose praise will occupy my final days, open yourselves again to hear me. No need to close your eyes. The subject goes a long

way beyond what is experienced "subjectively" by the individual, exactly as far as the Truth he is able to attain, and which perhaps will
fall from those lips you have already closed again. Yes, this Truth of
his history is not all of it contained in his script, and yet the place is
marked there by the painful shocks he feels from knowing only his own
lines, and not simply there, but also in pages whose disorder gives him
little by way of comfort.

That the unconscious is the discourse of the other[59] is what appears
even more clearly than anywhere else in the studies which Freud devoted
to what he called telepathy, insofar as it manifests itself in the context
of an analytic experience. This is the coincidence of the subject's remarks with facts about which he cannot have information, but which
still bestir themselves in the liaisons of another experience in which the
same psychoanalyst is the interlocutor—a coincidence moreover constituted most often by an entirely verbal, even homonymic, convergence,
or which, if it includes an act, is concerned with an "acting out" [60] by
one of the analyst's other patients or by a child of the person being
analyzed who is also in analysis.[61] It is a case of resonance in the communicating networks of discourse, an exhaustive study of which would
throw light on the analogous facts presented by everyday life.

The omnipresence of the human discourse will perhaps one day be
embraced under the open sky of an omnicommunication of its text.
This is not to say that the discourse will be any more in harmony with
it than now. But that is the field which our experience polarizes in a
relation which is only apparently two-way, for any positing of its structure in merely dual terms is as inadequate to it in theory as it is ruinous
for its technique.[62]

II

Symbol and Language

Τὴν ἀρχὴν ὃ τι καὶ λαλῶ ὑμιν.
(Gospel according to Saint John, VIII, 25.)

"Do crossword puzzles."
(Advice to the young psychoanalyst.)

To pick up the thread of my argument again, let me repeat that it is by the reduction of the history of the particular subject that psychoanalysis touches on relational *Gestalten* which analysis extrapolates into a regular process of development. But I also repeat that neither genetic psychology nor differential psychology, on both of which analysis may throw light, is within its compass, because both require experimental and observational conditions which are related to those of analysis only by homonymy.

To go even further: what stands out as psychology in the rough in common experience (which is confused with sensuous experience only by the professional of ideas)—that is to say, the wonder which surges forth during some momentary suspension of daily care from whatever it is that matches the clashing colors of living beings in a disparity going beyond that of the grotesques of a Leonardo or of a Goya, or the surprise which the density proper to a particular person's skin opposes to the caress of an exploring hand still animated by the thrill of discovery without yet being blunted by desire—all this, it may well be said, is done away with in an experience which cannot be bothered with such caprices and which sets itself obstinately against such mysteries.[63]

A psychoanalysis normally proceeds to its termination without revealing to us very much of what our patient derives in his own right from his particular sensitivity to colors or calamities, from the quickness of his grasp of things or the urgency of his weaknesses of the flesh, from his power to retain or to invent—in short from the vivacity of his tastes.

This paradox is only an apparent one and is not due to any personal deficiency, and if it is possible to base it on the negative conditions of

29

our experience, it simply presses us a little harder to examine that experience for what there is in it that is positive.

For this paradox does not become resolved in the efforts of certain people—like the philosophers mocked by Plato for being driven by their appetite for the Real to go about embracing trees—who tend to take every episode in which that fleeting reality puts forth its shoots for the lived reaction of which they show themselves so fond. For these are the very people who, making their objective what lies beyond Language, react to our rule of "Don't touch" by a sort of obsession. Keep going in that direction, and I dare say the last word in the transference reaction will be a reciprocal sniffing between analyst and subject. I am not exaggerating: nowadays a young analyst-in-training, after two or three years of fruitless analysis, can actually hail the long-awaited arrival of the object relation in such an action between him and his subject, and can reap as a result of it the *dignus est intrare*[64] of our approval, guarantee of his abilities.

If psychoanalysis can become a science—for it is not yet one—and if it is not to degenerate in its technique—and perhaps that has already happened—we must get back to the meaning of its experience.

To this end, we can do no better than to return to the work of Freud. For an analyst to point out that he is a practitioner of the technique does not give him sufficient authority, from the fact that he does not understand a Freud III, to challenge the latter in the name of a Freud II whom he thinks he understands. And his very ignorance of Freud I is no excuse for considering the five great psychoanalyses as a series of case studies as badly chosen as they are badly expressed, however marvelous he thinks it that the grain of truth hidden within them ever managed to survive.[m]

Take up the work of Freud again at the *Traumdeutung* to remind yourself that the dream has the structure of a sentence or, rather, to stick to the letter of the work, of a rebus; that is to say, it has the structure of a form of writing, of which the child's dream represents the primordial ideography and which, in the adult, reproduces the simultaneously phonetic and symbolic use of signifying elements,[65] which can also be found both in the hieroglyphs of ancient Egypt and in the characters still used in China.[66]

[m] This remark comes from one of the psychoanalysts the most interested in this debate (1966).

But even this is no more than the deciphering of the instrument. The important part begins with the translation of the text, the important part which Freud tells us is given in the [verbal] elaboration of the dream—in other words, in its rhetoric. Ellipsis and pleonasm, hyperbaton or syllepsis, regression, repetition, apposition—these are the syntactical displacements; metaphor, catachresis, antonomasis, allegory, metonymy, and synecdoche—these are the semantic condensations[67] in which Freud teaches us to read the intentions—ostentatious or demonstrative, dissimulating or persuasive, retaliatory or seductive—out of which the subject modulates his oneiric discourse.

We know that he laid it down as a rule that the expression of a desire must always be sought in the dream. But let us be sure what he meant by this. If Freud admits, as the motive of a dream apparently contrary to his thesis, the very desire to contradict him on the part of the subject whom he had tried to convince of his theory,[n] how could he fail to admit the same motive for himself from the moment that, from his having arrived at this point, it was from another that his own law came back to him?

To put it in a nutshell, nowhere does it appear more clearly that man's desire finds its meaning in the desire of the other, not so much because the other holds the key to the object desired, as because the first object of desire is to be recognized by the other.[68]

Moreover, we all surely know from experience that from the moment that the analysis becomes engaged in the path of transference—and for us it is the index that this has taken place—each dream of the patient requires to be interpreted as a provocation, a masked avowal, or a diversion, by its relation to the analytic discourse; and that in proportion to the progress of the analysis, his dreams invariably become more and more reduced to the function of elements in the dialogue being realized in the analysis.

In the case of the psychopathology of everyday life,[69] another area consecrated by the work of Freud, it is clear that every parapraxis is a successful discourse—one might call it a nicely turned "phrase"—and that in the *lapsus* it is the muzzling effect or gag which hinges on the

[n] See *Gegenwunschtraume* in the *Traumdeutung, GW,* pp. 156–57 and pp. 163–64; *Standard Edition,* IV, 151 and 157–58; French translation, ed. Alcan, p. 140 and p. 146.

Word, and exactly from the right angle for its word to be sufficient to the wise.

But let us go straight to the part where the book goes into chance and the beliefs which it engenders, and especially to the facts where Freud applies himself to showing the subjective efficacy of number associations left to the fortune of a random choice or to the luck of the draw. Nowhere do the dominating structures of the psychoanalytical domain reveal themselves better than in this success of his. And the appeal made in passing to unknown intellectual mechanisms is no more in this instance than his distressed excuse for the total confidence he placed in the symbols, a confidence which falters as the result of being justified beyond all limits.

If for a symptom to be admitted as such in psychoanalytical psychopathology—whether a neurotic symptom or not—Freud insists on the minimum of overdetermination constituted by a double meaning (symptom of a conflict long dead apart from its function in a *no less symbolic* present conflict), and if he has taught us to follow the ascending ramification of the symbolic lineage in the text of the patient's free associations, in order to locate and mark in it the points where its verbal forms intersect with the nodal points of its structure, then it is already completely clear that the symptom resolves itself entirely in a Language analysis, because the symptom itself is structured like a Language, because the symptom is a Language from which the Word must be liberated.[70]

It is to those who have not inquired very far into the nature of Language that the experience of number association will show immediately what must be grasped here—that is, the combinatory power which is the agent of its ambiguities—and they will recognize in this the very mainspring of the unconscious.

In fact, if from the numbers obtained by cutting up the sequence of the figures in the chosen number, if from their uniting by all the operations of arithmetic, even from the repeated division of the original number by one of the numbers split off from it—if the numbers resulting°

° In order to appreciate the fruit of these procedures, the reader should acquaint himself thoroughly with the notes which I have circulated since this was written, taken from Emile Borel's book *Le Hasard,* notes on the commonplace triviality of what one obtains in this way which is "remarkable," after beginning from some number or other (1966).

from these operations, among all the numbers in the actual history of the subject, prove to be symbolizing numbers, it is because they were already latent in the choice from which they began. And if after this the idea that it was the figures themselves which determined the destiny of the subject is refuted as superstitious, we are forced to admit that it is in the order of existence of their combinations, that is to say, in the concrete Language which they represent, that everything lies which analysis reveals to the subject as his unconscious.

We shall see that philologists and ethnographers reveal enough to us about the sureness of combination which is established in the completely unconscious systems with which they deal * for them to find nothing surprising in the proposition advanced here.

But if anybody should still be in doubt about the validity of my remarks, I would appeal once more to the testimony of the man who, since he discovered the unconscious, is not entirely without credentials to designate its place; he will not fail us.

For, however neglected by our interest—and for good reason—*le Mot d'Esprit et l'Inconscient*[71] remains the most unchallengeable of his works because it is the most transparent, in which the effect of the unconscious is demonstrated to us in its most subtle confines. And the face which it reveals to us is that of the spirit in the ambiguity conferred on it by Language, where the other side of its regalian power is the *"pointe"*[72] by which the whole of its order is annihilated in an instant —the *pointe,* in fact, where its creative activity unveils its absolute gratuitousness, where its domination over the Real is expressed in the challenge of non-sense where humour, in the malicious grace of the *esprit libre,* symbolizes a Truth that has not said its last word.

We must accompany Freud through the admirably compelling detours of this book on his promenade in this chosen garden of bitterest love.

Here all is substance, all is pearl.[73] The spirit that lives as an exile in the creation whose invisible support it is, knows that it is at every instant the master capable of annihilating it. Not even the most despised of all the forms of this hidden royalty—haughty or perfidious, dandylike or debonnaire—but Freud can make their secret luster gleam. Stories of that derided Eros figure, and like him born of penury and pain: the marriage broker on his rounds of the ghettos of Moravia at the service of the riffraff whose avidity he discreetly guides—and who suddenly discomfits his client with the illuminating non-sense of his final reply. "He who lets the truth escape like that," comments Freud, "is in reality happy to throw off the mask." [74]

It is Truth in fact which throws off the mask in his words, but only in order for the spirit to take on another and more deceiving one: the sophistry which is only a stratagem, the logic which in this case is only a decoy, the comic relief itself which tends only to dazzle. The spirit is always somewhere else. "Wit in fact entails such a subjective condition-ality . . . : wit is only what I accept as such," [75] continues Freud, who knows what he is talking about. [76]

Nowhere is the intention of the individual more evidently surpassed by what the subject finds—nowhere does the distinction which I make between the individual and the subject make itself better understood—since not only is it necessary that there have been something foreign to me in what I found for me to take pleasure in it, but it is also necessary that it remain this way for this find to hit its mark. [77] This taking its place from the necessity, so clearly marked by Freud, of the third listener, always supposed, and from the fact that the *mot d'esprit* does not lose its power in its transmission into indirect speech. In short, point-ing the amboceptor—illuminated by the pyrotechnics of the "word" exploding in a supreme alacrity—towards the locus of the Other. [78]

There is only one reason for wit to fall flat: the platitude of the Truth which comes out.

Now this concerns our problem directly. The present disdain for re-search into the language of symbols—which can be seen by a glance at the summaries of our publications before and after the 1920's—corresponds in our discipline to nothing less than a change of object, whose tendency to align itself at the most commonplace level of communication, in order to come into line with the new objectives proposed for the psychoanalyti-cal technique, is perhaps responsible for the rather gloomy balance sheet which the most lucid writers have drawn up of its results.[p]

How would the Word, in fact, be able to exhaust the sense of the Word or, to put it better, with the Oxford logical positivists, the meaning of meaning—except in the act which engenders it? Thus Goethe's reversal of its presence at the origin of things, "In the beginning was the action," is itself reversed in its turn: it was certainly the *verbe* that was in the

[p] See: C. I. Oberndorf, "Unsatisfactory Results of Psychoanalytic Therapy," *Psycho-analytic Quarterly,* XIX, 393–407.

beginning, and we live in its creation, but it is the action of our spirit which continues that creation by constantly renewing it. And we can only turn back on that action by letting ourselves constantly be pushed further ahead by it.[79]

I shall try it myself only in the knowledge that *that* is its way. . . .

No one is supposed to be ignorant of the law; this formula taken direct from the heavy-handed humor of our Code of Justice nevertheless expresses the Truth in which our experience is grounded and which our experience confirms. No man is actually ignorant of it, since the law of man has been the law of Language since the first words of recognition presided over the first gifts—although it took the detestable *Danaoi* who came and fled over the sea for men to learn to fear deceiving words accompanying faithless gifts. Until that time, for the pacific Argonauts—uniting the islets of the community with the bonds of a symbolic commerce—these gifts, their act and their objects, their erection into signs, and even their fabrication, were so much part of the Word that they were designated by its name.[q]

Is it with its gifts or else with the passwords which accord to them their salutary non-sense that Language, with the law, begins? For these gifts are already symbols, in the sense that symbol means pact and that they are first and foremost signifiers of the pact which they constitute as signified, as is plainly seen in the fact that the objects of symbolic exchange—pots made to remain empty, shields too heavy to be carried, sheafs of wheat that wither, lances stuck into the ground—all are destined and intended to be useless, if not simply superfluous because of their abundance.[80]

This neutralization of the signifier is the whole of the nature of Language. On this assessment, one could see the beginning of it among sea swallows, for instance, during the mating parade, materialized in the fish which they pass between each other from beak to beak. And if the ethologists are right in seeing in this the instrument of a general setting in movement of the group which could be called the equivalent of a *fête*, they would be completely justified in recognizing it as a symbol.

It can be seen that I do not shrink from seeking the origins of symbolic behavior outside the human sphere. But this is certainly not to be done by way of an elaboration of the sign. It is on this path that Mr.

q See, among others: *Do Kamo*, by Maurice Leenhardt, chapters IX and X.

Jules H. Massermann,[r] after so many others, has set off, and I shall stop here for an instant, not only because of the knowing tone which accompanies his proceedings, but also because of the welcome which his work has found among the editors of our official journal. In conformity with a tradition borrowed from employment agencies, they never neglect anything that might provide our discipline with "good references."

Think of it—here we have a man who has reproduced neurosis ex-pe-ri-men-tal-ly in a dog tied down to a table, and by what ingenious methods: a bell, the plate of meat which it announces, and the plate of potatoes which arrives instead; you can imagine the rest. He will certainly not be one, at least so he assures us, to let himself be taken in by the "ample ruminations," as he puts it, that philosophers have devoted to the problem of Language. Not him, he's going to grab it from your throat.

We are told that a raccoon can be taught by a judicious conditioning of his reflexes to go to his feeding trough when he is presented with a card on which his menu is listed. We are not told whether it shows the various prices, but the convincing detail is added that if the service disappoints him, he comes back and rips up the card which promised too much, just as an irritated woman might do with the letters of an unfaithful lover (*sic*).

This is one of the supporting arches of the bridge over which the author carries the road which leads from the signal [81] to the symbol. It is a two-way road, and the return trip from the symbol to the signal is illustrated by no less imposing works of art.

For if you associate the projection of a bright light into the eyes of a human subject with the ringing of a bell, and then the ringing alone to the command: "Contract," [82] you will succeed in getting the subject to make his pupils contract just by giving the order himself, then by muttering it, and eventually just by thinking it—in other words you will obtain a reaction of the nervous system called autonomous because it is usually inaccessible to intentional effects. Thus, if we are to believe this writer, Mr. Hudgins "has created in a group of subjects a highly individualized configuration of related and visceral reactions from the 'idea-symbol':[83] 'Contract,' a response that could be referred back through their individual experiences to an apparently distant source, but in reality

[r] Jules H. Massermann, "Language Behaviour and Dynamic Psychiatry," *IJP* (1944), 1 and 2, pp. 1–8.

basically physiological—in this example, simply the protection of the retina against an excessively bright light." And the author concludes: "The significance of such experiments for psychosomatic and linguistic research does not even need further elaboration."

For my part, I would have been curious to learn whether subjects trained in this way also react to the enunciation of the same syllables in the expressions: "marriage contract," "bridge contract," "breach of contract," [84] or even to the word "contract" progressively reduced to the articulation of its first syllable: contract, contrac, contra, contr . . . . The control experiment required by strict scientific method would then be offered all by itself as the French reader murmured this syllable between his teeth, even though he would have been subjected to no conditioning other than that of the bright light projected on the problem by Mr. Jules H. Massermann. Then I would ask this author whether the effects observed in this way among conditioned subjects still appeared to dispose so easily of further elaboration. For either the effects would not be produced any longer, thus revealing that they do not depend even conditionally on the semanteme, or else they would continue to be produced, posing the question of the limits to be assigned to it.

In other words, they would cause the distinction of signifier and signified, so blithely confused by the author in the English term "idea-symbol," to appear in the very instrument of the word. And without needing to examine the reactions of subjects conditioned by the command "Don't contract," or even by the entire conjugation of the verb "to contract," I could draw the author's attention to the fact that what defines any element whatever of a language as belonging to Language, is that, for all the users of this language, this element is distinguished as such in any given set made up of homologous elements.[85]

The result is that the particular effects of this element of Language are intimately linked to the existence of the set or whole, anterior to any possible liaison with any particular experience of the subject. Considering this last liaison to be exterior to any reference to the first, consists simply in denying in this element the function proper to Language.

This reminder of first principles might perhaps have saved our author, in his unequaled naïveté, from discovering the textual correspondence of the grammatical categories of his childhood in the relationships of reality.

This monument of naïveté, in any case of a kind common enough in these matters, would not be worth so much attention if it were not the achievement of a psychoanalyst, or rather of someone who fits into his work as if by accident everything produced by a certain tendency in psychoanalysis—in the name of the theory of the ego or of the technique of the analysis of defenses—everything, that is, which is the most contrary to the Freudian experience. In this way the coherence of a sound conception of Language along with the maintenance of this conception is revealed *a contrario*. For Freud's discovery was that of the domain of the incidence in the nature of man of his relations to the Symbolic order and the tracing of their sense right back to the most radical instances of symbolization in being. To misconstrue this Symbolic order[86] is to condemn the discovery to oblivion, and the experience to ruin.

And I affirm—an affirmation that cannot be left out of the serious intent of my present remarks—that it would seem to me preferable to have the raccoon I mentioned sitting in the armchair where, according to our author, Freud's timidity confined the analyst by putting him behind the couch, rather than a "scientist" who discourses on the Word and Language in the way he has done.[87]

For the raccoon, at least, thanks to Jacques Prévert ("une pierre, deux maisons, trois ruines, quatre fossoyeurs, un jardin, des fleurs, un raton-laveur"),[88] has entered the poetic bestiary once and for all and participates as such and in its essence in the commanding function of the symbol. But that being resembling us who professes, as he has done, a systematic failure to recognize that function, banishes himself from everything that can be called into existence by it. From this point on, the question of the place to be assigned to our friend in the classification of nature would seem to me to be simply that of an irrelevant humanism, if his discourse, in its intersection with a technique of the Word which it is our responsibility to watch over, were not in fact too fruitful, even in engendering sterile monstrosities within it. Let it be known therefore, since he also prides himself on braving the reproach of anthropomorphism, that this is the very last term I would use to say that he makes his own being the measure of all things.

Let us return to our symbolic object, which is itself extremely consistent in its matter, even if it has lost the weight of its use, but whose imponderable sense will cause displacements of some weight. Is it there that the law and Language are to be found? Perhaps not yet.

For even if there appeared among the sea swallows some big wheel of the colony who, by gulping down the symbolic fish before the gaping beaks of the others, were to inaugurate that exploitation of swallow by swallow —a fantasy I once took pleasure in developing—this would not be in any way sufficient to reproduce among them that fabulous history, the image of our own, whose winged epic kept us captive on Anatole France's *Penguin Island*; and there would still be something else needed to create a "hirundinized" universe.

This "something else" completes the symbol and makes Language of it. In order for the symbolic object liberated from its usage to become the word liberated from the *hic et nunc,* the differentiation does not depend on its material quality as sound, but on its evanescent being in which the symbol finds the permanence of the concept.[89]

Through the word—already a presence made of absence—absence itself comes to giving itself a name in that moment of origin whose perpetual recreation Freud's genius detected in the play of the child. And from this pair [of sounds] modulated on presence and absence[90]—a coupling that the tracing in the sand of the single and the broken line of the mantic *kwa* of China would also serve to constitute—there is born a particular language's universe of sense in which the universe of things will come into line.

Through that which takes on body only by being the trace of a nothingness and whose support from that moment on cannot be impaired, the concept, saving the duration of what passes by, engenders the thing.

For it is still not enough to say that the concept is the thing itself, as any child can demonstrate against the scholar. It is the world of words which creates the world of things—the things originally confused in the *hic et nunc* of the all-in-the-process-of-becoming—by giving its concrete being to their essence, and its ubiquity to what has been from everlasting:[91] κτῆμα ἐς ἀεί.[92]

Man speaks therefore, but it is because the symbol has made him man. Even if in fact overabundant gifts welcome the stranger who has introduced himself into the group and made himself known, the life of natural groups making up the community is subjected to marriage ties which order the direction and sense of the operation of the exchange of women, and to the reciprocal exchanges of gifts and benefits determined by these marriage ties: just as the Sironga proverb says, a relative by marriage is an elephant's thigh.[93] The marriage tie is presided over by a preferential order whose law implying the kinship names, like Language, is imperative for the group in its forms, but unconscious in its structure. In this structure whose harmony or impasses regulate the restricted or generalized exchange discerned in it by the ethnologist, the startled theoretician finds the whole of the logic of combinations: thus the laws of number—that is to say, the laws of the most refined of all symbols— prove to be immanent in the original symbolism. At all events it is the richness of the forms in which are developed what have been called the elementary structures of kinship which make them legible in it. And this gives food for thought: that it is perhaps only our unconsciousness of their permanence which lets us go on believing in the freedom of choice in the so-called complex structures of marriage ties under whose law we live. If statistics have already let us glimpse that this freedom is not exercised in a random manner, it is because a subjective logic orients this freedom in its effects.

This is precisely where the Oedipus complex—insofar as we continue to recognize it as covering the whole field of our experience with its signification[94]—may be said, in this connection, to mark the limits that our discipline assigns to subjectivity: that is to say, what the subject can know of his unconscious participation in the movement of the complex structures of marriage ties, by verifying the symbolic effects in his individual existence of the tangential movement towards incest which has manifested itself ever since the coming of a universal community.

The primordial Law is therefore that which in regulating marriage ties superimposes the kingdom of culture on that of nature abandoned to the law of copulation. The interdiction of incest is only its subjective pivot, revealed by the modern tendency to reduce to the mother and the sister the objects forbidden to the subject's choice, although full licence outside of these is not yet entirely open.

This law, therefore, is revealed clearly enough as identical to an order of Language. For without kinship nominations, no power is capable of instituting the order of preferences and taboos which bind and weave the yarn of lineage down through succeeding generations. And it is indeed the confusion of generations which, in the Bible as in all traditional laws, is accused as being the abomination of the *verbe* and the desolation of the sinner.[95]

We know in fact what ravages a falsified filiation can produce, going as far as the dissociation of the subject's personality, when the constraint of the environment is used to sustain its error. They may be no less when, as a result of a man having married the mother of the woman of whom he has had a son, the son will have for a brother a child who is his mother's brother. But if he is later adopted—and the case is not invented—by the sympathetic couple formed by a daughter of his father's previous marriage and her husband, he will find himself once again the half-brother of his foster mother, and one can imagine the complex feelings with which he will await the birth of a child who will be in this recurring situation his brother and his nephew at the same time.

As a matter of fact the simple falling out of step produced in the order of generations by a late-born child of a second marriage, in which the young mother finds herself the contemporary of an older brother, can produce similar effects, as we know was the case of Freud himself.

This same function of symbolic identification through which primitive man believes he reincarnates an ancestor with the same name—and which even determines an alternating recurrence of characters in modern man —therefore introduces in subjects exposed to these discordances in the father relation a dissociation of the Oedipus relation in which the constant source of its pathogenetic effects must be seen. Even when in fact it is represented by a single person, the paternal function concentrates in itself both Imaginary and Real relations, always more or less inadequate to the Symbolic relation which constitutes it essentially.

It is in the *name of the father* that we must recognize the support of the Symbolic function which, from the dawn of history, has identified his person with the figure of the law.[96] This conception permits us to distinguish clearly, in the analysis of a case, the unconscious effects of this function from the narcissistic relations, or even from the Real relations which the subject sustains with the image and the action of the person who incarnates it; and there results from this a mode of comprehension which will tend to have repercussions on the very way in which the interventions of the analyst are conducted. Practice has confirmed its fecundity for me, as well as for the students whom I have introduced to this method. And, both in supervising analyses and in commenting on cases being demonstrated, I have often had the opportunity of emphasizing the harmful confusion engendered by failure to recognize it.

Thus it is the virtue of the *verbe* which perpetuates the movement of the Great Debt whose economics Rabelais, in a famous metaphor, extended to the stars themselves. And we shall not be surprised that the chapter in which, with the macaronic inversion of kinship names, he presents us with an anticipation of the discoveries of the ethnographers, should reveal in him the substantific divination of the human mystery which I am trying to elucidate here.[97]

Identified with the sacred *hau* or with the omnipresent mana, the inviolable Debt is the guarantee that the voyage on which wives and goods are embarked will bring back to their point of departure in a never-failing cycle other women and other goods, all carrying an identical entity: what Lévi-Strauss calls *symbole zéro,* thus reducing the power of *la Parole* to the form of an algebraic sign.[98]

Symbols in fact envelop the life of man in a network so total that they join together, before he comes into the world, those who are going to engender him "par l'os et par la chair";[99] so total that they bring to his birth, along with the gifts of the stars, if not with the gifts of the fairy spirits, the design of his destiny; so total that they give the words which will make him faithful or renegade, the law of the acts which will follow him right to the very place where he *is* not yet and beyond his death itself; and so total that through them his end finds its meaning in the last judgment where the *verbe* absolves his being or condemns it—except he attain the subjective bringing to realization of being-for-death.[100]

Servitude and grandeur in which the living would be annihilated, if desire did not preserve its part in the interferences and pulsations which the cycles of Language cause to converge on him, when the confusion of tongues takes a hand and when the orders interfere with each other in the tearing apart of the universal work.

But this desire itself, to be satisfied in man, requires that it be recognized, by the accord of the Word or by the struggle for prestige, in the symbol or in the Imaginary.

What is at stake in a psychoanalysis is the advent in the subject of that little reality which this desire sustains in him with respect to the symbolic conflicts and Imaginary fixations as the means of their accord, and our path is the intersubjective experience where this desire makes itself recognized.[101]

From this point on it will be seen that the problem is that of the relationships of the Word and Language in the subject.

Three paradoxes in these relationships present themselves in our domain.

In madness, of whatever nature, we must recognize on the one hand the negative liberty of a Word which has given up trying to make itself recognized, or what we call an obstacle to transference, and, on the other hand, we must recognize the singular formation of a delusion which—fabulous, fantastic, or cosmological; interpretative, revindicating, or idealist—objectifies the subject in a Language without dialectic.[s,102]

The absence of the Word is manifested here by the stereotypes of a discourse in which the subject, one might say, is spoken rather than speaking:[103] here we recognize the symbols of the unconscious in petrified forms which find their place in a natural history of these symbols next to the embalmed forms in which myths are presented in our storybooks. But it is an error to say that the subject takes on these symbols: the resistance to their recognition is no less strong [in psychosis] than in the neuroses when the subject is led into it by an endeavour of the analyst in the process of the cure.[104]

Let it be noted in passing that it would be worthwhile finding out what places in social space our culture has assigned to these subjects, especially as regards their assignment to social duties relating to Language, for it is not unreasonable that there is at work here one of the factors which consign such subjects to the effects of the breakdown produced by the symbolic discordances which characterize the complex structures of civilization.

The second case is represented by the privileged domain of the psychoanalytic discovery: that is, symptoms, inhibition, and anxiety in the constituent economy of the different neuroses.

Here the Word is driven out of the concrete discourse which orders the subject's consciousness, but it finds its support either in the natural functions of the subject, insofar as an organic stimulus sets off that *béance* of his individual being to his essence, which makes of the illness the introduction of the living to the existence of the subject[t,105]—or else in the images which organize at the limit of the *Umwelt* and of the *Innenwelt,* their relational structuring.[106]

The symptom is here the signifier of a signified repressed from the

---

[s] Aphorism of Lichtenberg's: "A madman who imagines himself a prince differs from the prince who is in fact a prince only because the former is a negative prince, while the latter is a negative madman. Considered without their sign, they are alike."

[t] To obtain an immediate subjective confirmation of this remark of Hegel's, it is enough to have seen in the recent [myxomatosis] epidemic a blinded rabbit in the middle of a road, lifting the emptiness of his vision changed into a *look* towards the setting sun: he was human to the point of the tragic.

consciousness of the subject. A symbol written in the sand of the flesh and on the veil of Maia, it participates in Language by the semantic ambiguity which I have already emphasized in its constitution.[107]

But it is a Word in full flight, for the Word includes the discourse of the other in the secret of its cipher.

It was by deciphering this Word that Freud rediscovered the primary language of symbols,[u] still living on in the suffering of civilized man (*Das Unbehagen in der Kultur*).

Hieroglyphics of hysteria, blazons of phobia, labyrinths of the *Zwangsneurose*—charms of impotence, enigmas of inhibition, oracles of anxiety —talking arms of character,[v] seals of self-punishment, disguises of perversion—these are the hermetic elements that our exegesis resolves, the equivocations that our invocation dissolves, the artifices that our dialectic absolves, in a deliverance of the imprisoned sense, which moves from the revelation of the palimpsest[108] to the given word of the mystery and to the pardon of the Word.[109]

The third paradox of the relation of Language to the Word is that of the subject who loses his meaning and direction in the objectifications of the discourse. However metaphysical its definition may appear, we cannot fail to recognize its presence in the foreground of our experience. For here is the most profound alienation of the subject in our scientific civilization, and it is this alienation that we encounter first of all when the subject begins to talk to us about himself: hence, in order to entirely resolve it, analysis should be conducted to the limits of wisdom.

To give an exemplary formulation of this, I could not find a more pertinent ground than the usage of common speech—pointing out that the *"ce suis-je"* of the time of Villon has become reversed in the *"c'est moi"* of modern man.[110]

The *moi* of modern man, as I have indicated elsewhere, has taken on its form in the dialectical impasse of the *belle âme* who does not recognize his very own *raison d'être* in the disorder that he denounces in the world.[111]

But a way out is offered to the subject for the resolution of that impasse when his discourse is delusion. Communication can validly be established for him in the common task of science[112] and in the posts which it

---

[u] The lines before and after this term will show what I mean by it.

[v] Reich's error, to which I shall return, caused him to take armorial bearings for an armor. [See translator's note 109.]

commands in our universal civilization; this communication will be effective within the enormous objectification constituted by that science, and it will permit him to forget his subjectivity. He will be able to make an efficacious contribution to the common task in his daily work and will be able to furnish his leisure time with all the pleasures of a profuse culture which, from detective novels to historical memoirs, from educational lectures to the orthopedics of group relations, will give him the wherewithal to forget his own existence and his death, at the same time as that to misconstrue the particular sense of his life in a false communication.

If the subject did not rediscover in a regression—often pushed right back to the *stade du miroir*—the enclosure of a stage in which his *moi* contains its Imaginary exploits, there would hardly be any assignable limits to the credulity to which he must succumb in that situation. And this is what makes our responsibility so redoubtable when, along with the mythical manipulations of our doctrine, we bring him one more opportunity to alienate himself, in the decomposed trinity of the ego, the superego, and the id, for example.[113]

Here there is a Language-barrier[114] opposed to the Word, and the precautions against verbalism which are a theme of the discourse of the "normal" man in our culture, merely serve to reinforce its thickness.

It might not be time wasted to measure its thickness by the statistically determined total of pounds of printed paper, miles of record grooves, and hours of radio broadcasting that the said culture produces per head of population in the sectors A, B, and C of its domain. This would be a fine research project for our cultural organizations, and it would be seen that the question of Language does not remain entirely within the domain of the convolutions in which its use is reflected in the individual.

> *We are the hollow men*
> *We are the stuffed men*
> *Leaning together*
> *Headpiece filled with straw. Alas!*

and so on.

The resemblance between this situation and the alienation of madness, insofar as the formula given above is authentic—that is, that here the subject is spoken rather than speaking—is obviously the result of the exigency, presupposed by psychoanalysis, that there be a true Word. If this consequence, which pushes the constituent paradoxes of what I am saying here to their limit, were to be turned against the common sense of the psychoanalytic viewpoint, I would accord to this objection all its pertinence, but only to find my own position confirmed in it—and this by a dialectical return in which I would not be lacking for authorized sponsors, beginning with Hegel's denunciation of "the philosophy of the cranium" [115] and stopping only at Pascal's warning, at the dawn of the historical era of the *"moi,"* echoing in these terms: "Les hommes sont si nécessairement fous, que ce serait être fou par un autre tour de folie, de n'être pas fou." [116]

This is not to say, however, that our culture pursues its course in shadows exterior to creative subjectivity. On the contrary, creative subjectivity has not ceased a militant struggle to renew the never-exhausted power of symbols in the human exchange which brings them to the light of day.

To take into account how few subjects support this creation would be to accede to a Romantic viewpoint by confronting what is not equivalent. The fact is that this subjectivity, in whatever domain it appears—in mathematics, in politics, in religion, or even in advertising— continues to animate the whole movement of humanity. And another look, probably no less illusory, would make us accentuate this opposing trait: that its symbolic character has never been more manifest. It is the irony of revolutions that they engender a power all the more absolute in its actions, not because it is more anonymous, as people say, but because it is more reduced to the words which signify it. And more than ever, on the other hand, the force of the churches resides in the Language which they have been able to maintain: an instance, it must be said, that Freud left in the dark in the article where he sketches for us what we would call the collective subjectivities of the Church and the Army.[117]

Psychoanalysis has played a role in the direction[118] of modern subjectivity, and it cannot continue to sustain this role without bringing it into line with the movement in modern science which elucidates it.

This is the problem of the grounding which must assure our discipline its place amongst the sciences: a problem of formalization, in truth very much off on the wrong foot.

For it seems that, caught by the very quirk in the medical mind against which psychoanalysis had to constitute itself, it is with the handicap of being half a century behind the movement of the sciences, like medicine itself, that we are seeking to join up with them again.

It is in the abstract objectification of our experience on fictitious, or even simulated, principles of the experimental method, that we find the effect of prejudices which must first be swept from our domain if we wish to cultivate it according to its authentic structure.

Since we are practitioners of the Symbolic function, it is astonishing that we should turn away from probing deeper into it, to the extent of failing to recognize that it is this function which situates us at the heart of the movement which is now setting up a new order of the sciences, with a new putting in question of anthropology.*

This new order signifies nothing other than a return to a conception of veritable science whose claims have been inscribed in a tradition beginning with Plato's *Theaetetus*. This conception has become degraded, as we know, in the positivist reversal which, by making the human sciences the crowning glory of the experimental sciences, in actual fact made them subordinate to experimental science. This conception is the result of an erroneous view of the history of science founded on the prestige of a specialized development of the experiment.

But since today the human sciences are discovering once again the age-old conception of science, they are obliging us to revise the classifications of the sciences which we inherited from the nineteenth century, in a sense indicated clearly by the most lucid spirits.

One has only to follow the concrete evolution of the various disciplines in order to become aware of this.

Linguistics can serve us as a guide here, since that is the role it plays in the vanguard of contemporary anthropology, and we cannot possibly remain indifferent to it.

The mathematicized form in which is inscribed the discovery of the *phoneme* as the function of pairs of oppositions formed by the smallest discriminate elements capable of being distinguished in the semantic structure,[119] leads us to the very grounding in which the last of Freud's doctrines designates the subjective sources of the Symbolic function in a vocalic connotation of presence and absence.

And the reduction of every language to the group of a very small number of these phonemic oppositions, since it prepares the way for an equally rigorous formalization of its most complicated morphemes, puts within our reach a precisely defined access to our own field.*

It is up to us to make use of these advances to discover their effects in the domain of psychoanalysis, just as ethnography—which is on a line parallel to our own—has already done for its own by deciphering myths according to the synchrony of mythemes.[120]

Isn't it striking that Lévi-Strauss, in suggesting the implication of the structures of Language with that part of the social laws which regulate marriage ties and kinship, is already conquering the very terrain in which Freud situates the unconscious?[w]

From now on, it is impossible not to make a general theory of the symbol the axis of a new classification of the sciences where *les sciences de l'homme* will once more take up their central position as sciences of subjectivity. Let me indicate its basic principle, which nevertheless still calls for continuing elaboration.

The Symbolic function presents itself as a double movement within the subject: man makes an object of his action, but only in order to restore to this action in due time its place as a grounding. In this equivocation, operating at every instant, lies the whole process of a function in which action and knowledge alternate.[x]

Two examples, one borrowed from the classroom, the other from the very quick of our epoch:

—the first, mathematical: phase one, man objectifies in two cardinal numbers two collections he has counted; phase two, with these numbers he realizes the act of adding them up (cf. the example cited by Kant in the introduction to the transcendental aesthetic, section IV, in the second edition of the *Critique of Pure Reason*);

—the second, historical: phase one, the man who works at the level of production in our society considers himself to rank amongst the proletariat; phase two, in the name of belonging to it, he joins in a general strike.

If these two examples come from areas which, for us, are the most contrasted in the domain of the concrete—the first involving an operation always open to a mathematical law, the second, the brazen face of capitalist exploitation—it is because, although they seem to come from a long way apart, their effects come to constitute our subsistence, and precisely by meeting each other in the concrete in a double inversion or

[w] See: Claude Lévi-Strauss, "Language and the Analysis of Social Laws," *American Anthropologist,* Vol. 53, No. 2 (April–June, 1951), pp. 155–63. [A French adaptation of the original article is published in *Anthropologie Structurale* (Paris: Plon, 1958), of which there is an English translation.]

[x] The last four paragraphs have been rewritten (1966).

reversal: the most subjective of the sciences having forged a new reality, and the shadow of social distribution arming itself with a symbol in action.[121]

Here the opposition which is traced between the exact sciences and those for which there is no reason to decline the appellation of "conjectural" seems no longer an admissible one—for lack of any grounds for that opposition.[y]

For exactitude is to be distinguished from Truth, and conjecture does not exclude rigorous precision. And even if experimental science gets its exactitude from mathematics, its relationship to nature does not remain any less problematic.

If our link to nature in fact urges us to wonder poetically whether it is not its very own movement that we rediscover in our science, in

> *. . . cette voix*
> *Qui se connaît quand elle sonne*
> *N'être plus la voix de personne*
> *Tant que des ondes et des bois,*[122]

it is clear that our physics is simply a mental fabrication whose instrument is the mathematical symbol.

For experimental science is not so much defined by the quantity to which it is in fact applied, as by the measurement which it introduces into the Real.

This can be seen in relation to the measurement of time without which experimental science would be impossible. Huyghens' clock, which alone gave experimental science its precision, is only the organ of the realization of Galileo's hypothesis on the equigravity of bodies— that is, the hypothesis on uniform acceleration which confers its law, since it is the same, on any kind of fall.

It is amusing to point out that the instrument was completed before it had been possible to verify the hypothesis by observation, and that by this fact the clock rendered the observation superfluous at the same time as it offered it the instrument of its precision.[z]

But mathematics can symbolize another kind of time, notably the

---

[y] These two paragraphs have been rewritten (1966).
[z] On the Galilean hypothesis and Huyghens' chronometer, see: Alexandre Koyré, "An Experiment in Measurement," *Proceedings of the American Philosophical Society,* Vol. 97 (April, 1953). (The last two paragraphs of my text were rewritten in 1966.)

intersubjective time which structures human action, whose formulae are beginning to be given us by the theory of games, also called strategy, but which it would be better to call *stochastics*.

The author of these lines has tried to demonstrate in the logic of a sophism the temporal sources through which human action, insofar as it orders itself according to the action of the other, finds in the scansion of its hesitations the advent of its certitude; and in the decision which concludes it, this action gives to that of the other—which it includes from that point on—along with its sanction as regards the past, its sense-to-come.

In this article it is demonstrated that it is the certitude anticipated by the subject in the *temps pour comprendre* which, by the haste which precipitates the *moment de conclure,* determines in the other the decision which makes of the subject's own movement error or Truth.

It can be seen by this example how the mathematical formalization* which inspired Boolean logic, to say nothing of the theory of sets, can bring to the science of human action that structure* of intersubjective time which is needed by psychoanalytic conjecture in order to secure itself in its own scientific rigor.

If on the other hand the history of the technique of historians shows that its progress defines itself in the ideal of an identification of the subjectivity of the historian with the constituting subjectivity of the primary historization in which the event is humanized, it is clear that psychoanalysis finds its precise bearings here: that is to say, in knowledge, as realizing this ideal, and in [curative] efficacy, as finding its justification there. The example of history will also cause to dissipate like a mirage that recourse to the lived reaction which obsesses our technique as it does our theory, for the fundamental historicity of the event which we retain suffices to conceive the possibility of a subjective reproduction of the past in the present.

Furthermore, this example makes us realise how psychoanalytic regression implies that progressive dimension of the subject's history that Freud emphasizes as lacking in the Jungian concept of neurotic regression, and we understand how the experience itself renews this progression by assuring its relief.

Finally, the reference to linguistics will introduce us to the method which, by distinguishing synchronic from diachronic structurings in Language, will allow us to comprehend better the different value or force which our Language takes on in the interpretation of resistances and transference, or even to differentiate the effects proper to repression and the structure of the individual myth in obsessional neurosis.

The list of the disciplines named by Freud as those which should make up the disciplines accessory to an ideal Faculty of Psychoanalysis is well known. Besides psychiatry and sexology, we find: "the history of civilization, mythology, the psychology of religions, literary history, and literary criticism." [123]

This whole group of subjects, determining the *cursus* of an instruction in technique, are normally inscribed within the epistemological triangle that I have described, and which would provide with its method an advanced level of instruction in analytical theory and technique.

For my part, I should be inclined to add: rhetoric, dialectic in the technical sense that this term assumes in the *Topics* of Aristotle, grammar, and, that supreme pinnacle of the esthetics of Language, poetics, which would include the neglected technique of the witticism.

And if these subject headings tended to evoke somewhat outmoded echoes for some people, I would not be unwilling to accept them, as constituting a return to our sources.

For psychoanalysis in its early development, intimately linked to the discovery and to the study of symbols, was on the way to participating in the structure of what was called in the Middle Ages, "the liberal arts." Deprived, like them, of a veritable formalization, psychoanalysis became organized, like them, in a body of privileged problems, each one promoted by some fortunate relation of man to his own measure and taking on from this particularity a charm and a humanity which in our eyes might well make up for the somewhat recreational aspect of their presentation. Let this aspect of the early development of psychoanalysis not be disdained; it expresses in fact no less than the re-creation of the sense of man during the arid years of scientism.

These aspects of the early years should be all the less disdained since psychoanalysis has not raised the level by setting off along the false paths of a theorization contrary to its dialectical structure.

Psychoanalysis will not lay down a scientific grounding for its theory or for its technique except by formalizing in an adequate fashion the essential dimensions of its experience which, along with the historical theory of the symbol, are: intersubjective logic and the temporality of the subject.

III

Interpretation and Temporality

Entre l'homme et l'amour,
  Il y a la femme.
Entre l'homme et la femme,
  Il y a un monde.
Entre l'homme et le monde,
  Il y a un mur.[124]

(Antoine Tudal in *Paris en l'an 2000*.)

Nam Sibyllam quidem Cumis ego ipse oculis meis vidi in ampulla pendere, et cum illi pueri dicerent: Σιβύλλα τί θέλεις, respondebat illa: ἀπὸ θανεῖν θέλω. [125]

(*Satyricon*, XLVIII.)

Bringing the psychoanalytic experience back to the Word and to Language as its grounding is of direct concern to its technique. Psychoanalysis may not actually be drifting off into the ineffable, but there has undoubtedly been a tendency in this direction, always along the one-way street of separating analytical interpretation more and more from the principle it depends on. Any suspicion that this deviation of psychoanalytical practice is the motive force behind the new aims to which psychoanalytical theory is being opened up is consequently well-founded.*

If we look at the situation a little more closely, we can see that the problems of symbolic interpretation began by intimidating our little group before becoming embarrassing to it. Because of the way he informed his patients about psychoanalytical theory—a heedlessness from which his successors seem in fact to proceed—the successes obtained by Freud are now a matter of astonishment, and the display of indoctrination he put on in the cases of Dora, the Rat Man, and the Wolf Man does not exactly leave us unscandalized. True, our cleverer friends do not shrink from doubting whether the technique employed in these cases was really the right one. This disaffection in the psychoanalytic movement can in truth be ascribed to a confusion of tongues, and, in a recent conversation with me, the personality the most representative of its present hierarchy made no secret about it.

It is worth noting that this confusion continues to grow. Each analyst presumes to consider himself the one chosen to discover the conditions of a completed objectification in our experience, and the enthusiasm which greets these theoretical attempts seems to grow more fervent the more dereistic they prove to be.

It is certain that the principles of the analysis of resistances, however well founded they may be, have in practice been the occasion of a growing *méconnaissance* of the subject, for want of being understood in their relation to the intersubjectivity of the Word.

If we follow the proceedings of the first seven sessions of the case of the Rat Man, and they are reported to us in full, it seems highly improbable that Freud did not recognize the resistances as they came up, and precisely in the places where our modern technicians drill into us that he overlooked them, since it is Freud's own text, after all, which permits them to pinpoint them. Once again the Freudian text manifests that exhaustion of the subject which continues to amaze us, and no interpretation has so far worked out all its resources.

I mean that Freud not only let himself be trapped into encouraging his subject to go beyond his initial reticence, but that he also understood perfectly the seductive power of this exercise in the Imaginary. To be convinced of this, it is enough to refer to the description which he gives us of his patient's expression during the painful recital of the represented torture which supplied the theme of his obsession, that of the rat forced into the victim's anus: "His face," Freud tells us, "reflected the horror of a pleasure of which he was unaware." [126] The effect of the repetition of this account at that present moment did not escape Freud, any more than did the identification of the psychoanalyst with the "cruel captain" who had forced this story to enter the subject's memory, nor therefore the import of the theoretical clarifications of which the subject required to be guaranteed before pursuing his discourse.

Far from interpreting the resistance at this point, however, Freud astonishes us by acceding to his request, and to such an extent in fact that he seems to be taking part in the subject's game.

But the extremely approximative character of the explanations with which Freud gratifies him, so approximative as to appear somewhat crude, is sufficiently instructive: at this point it is clearly not so much a question of doctrine, nor even of indoctrination, but rather of a symbolic gift of the Word, pregnant with a secret pact, in the context of the

Imaginary participation which includes it and whose import will reveal itself later in the symbolic equivalence that the subject institutes in his thought between rats and the florins with which he remunerates the analyst.

We can see therefore that Freud, far from failing to recognize the resistance, uses it as a propitious predisposition for the setting in movement of the resonances of the Word, and he conforms, as far as he can, to the first definition he gave of resistance,[127] by making use of it to implicate the subject in his message. In any case he will change tack abruptly from the moment he sees that, as a result of being carefully manipulated, the resistance is turning towards maintaining the dialogue at the level of a conversation in which the subject would from then on be able to perpetuate his seduction while maintaining his evasion.

But we learn that analysis consists in playing in all the multiple keys of the orchestral score which the Word constitutes in the registers of Language and on which depends the overdetermination [of the symptom], which has no meaning except in that order.[128]

And at the same time we discover the source of Freud's success. In order for the analyst's message to respond to the profound interrogation of the subject, it is necessary for the subject to hear and understand it as the response which is particular to him; and the privilege which Freud's patients enjoyed in receiving its good Word from the very lips of the man who was its annunciator, satisfied this exigency in them.

Let us note in passing that in the case of the Rat Man the subject had had an advance taste of it, since he had glanced over the *Psychopathology of Everyday Life,* then fresh off the presses.

This is not to say that this book is very much better known today, even by analysts, but the popularization of Freud's ideas, which have passed into the common consciousness, their collision with what we call the Language barrier, would deaden the effect of our Word, if we were to give it the style of Freud's remarks to the Rat Man.

But it is not a question of imitating him. In order to rediscover the effect of Freud's Word, it is not to its terms that we shall have recourse, but to the principles which govern it.

These principles are none other than the dialectic of the consciousness-of-self, as it is brought into realization from Socrates to Hegel, starting from the ironic presupposition that all that is rational is real, eventually to be precipitated into the scientific judgment that all that is real is rational.[129] But Freud's discovery was to demonstrate that this verifying process[130] authentically attains the subject only by decentering him from the consciousness-of-self, in the axis of which the Hegelian reconstruction of the phenomenology of the spirit maintained it: that is, that this discovery renders even more decrepit any pursuit of the *prise de conscience* which, beyond its status as a psychological phenomenon, cannot be inscribed within the conjuncture of the particular moment which alone gives body to the universal and in default of which it vanishes into generality.* [131]

These remarks define the limits within which it is impossible for our technique to fail to recognize the structuring moments of the Hegelian phenomenology: in the first place the master-slave dialectic, or the dialectic of the *belle âme* and of the law of the heart, and generally everything which permits us to understand how the constitution of the object is subordinated to the bringing to realization of the subject.

But if there still remains something prophetic in Hegel's insistence on the fundamental identity of the particular and the universal, an insistence which gives the measure of his genius, it is certainly psychoanalysis which supplies it with its paradigm by revealing the structure in which that identity comes to realization as disjoined from the subject, and without appealing to tomorrow.

Let me simply say that this is what leads me to object to any reference to totality in the individual, since it is the subject who introduces division into the individual, as well as into the collectivity which is his equivalent. Psychoanalysis is properly that which reveals both the one and the other to be simply mirages.

This would seem to be something that could no longer be forgotten, if it were not precisely the teaching of psychoanalysis that it is forgettable—concerning which we find, by a return more legitimate than it is believed to be, that confirmation comes from psychoanalysts themselves, from the fact that their "new tendencies" represent this forgetting.

For if on the other hand Hegel is precisely what we needed to confer a meaning other than that of stupor on our so-called analytic neutrality,[132] this does not mean that we have nothing to learn from the elasticity of the Socratic maieutics or "art of midwifery," or even from the fascinating technical procedure by which Plato presents it to us—be it only by our experiencing in Socrates and in his desire [to know] the still-intact enigma of the psychoanalyst, and by situating in relationship

to the Platonic skopia our own relationship to Truth—in this case, however, in a way which would respect the distance separating the reminiscence that Plato came to presuppose as necessary for any advent of the
idea, from the exhaustion of being which consumes itself in the Kierkegaardian repetition.[aa,133]

But there is also a historical difference between Socrates' interlocutor
and ours which is worth examining. When Socrates relies on an artisan
reason which he can extract equally well from the discourse of the slave,
it is in order to give authentic masters access to the necessity of an order
which makes short work of their power, and Truth of the master words
of the city.[134] But we analysts have to deal with slaves who think they
are masters, and who find in a Language whose mission is universal, the
support of their servitude along with the bonds of its ambiguity. So
much so that, as I might humorously put it, our goal is to reinstate in
them the sovereign liberty displayed by Humpty Dumpty when he reminds Alice that after all he is the master of the signifier, even if he isn't
the master of the signified in which his being took on its form.

We therefore invariably rediscover our double reference to the Word
and to Language. In order to liberate the subject's Word, we introduce
him into the Language of his desire, that is, into the *primary Language*
in which, beyond what he tells us of himself, he is already talking to
us unbeknownst to him,[135] and in the symbols of the symptom in the
first place.

In the symbolism brought to light in analysis, it is certainly a question
of a Language. This Language, corresponding to the playful wish which
can be found in one of Lichtenberg's aphorisms, has the universal character of a language which could make itself understood in all other languages, but at the same time, since it is the Language which seizes
desire at the very moment in which it becomes human desire by making
itself recognized, it is absolutely particular to the subject.

Primary Language, I say, by which I do not mean "primitive language," since Freud, whose feat in this total discovery merits comparison
with Champollion's, deciphered it in its entirety in the dreams of our
contemporaries. Moreover, the essential domain of this Language was
authoritatively defined by one of the earliest pioneers associated with
this work, and one of the few to have brought anything new to it: I

[aa] I have fully developed these indications as the opportunity presented itself
(1966). Four paragraphs rewritten.

mean Ernest Jones, the last survivor of those to whom the seven rings
of the master were given and who attested by his presence in the highest
places of an international organization that they were not reserved
simply for bearers of relics.

In a fundamental paper on symbolism,[bb] Dr. Jones points out near
page 15 that although there are thousands of symbols in the sense that
the term is understood in analysis, all of them refer to the body itself,
to kinship relations, to birth, to life, and to death.

This truth, recognized here as a fact, permits us to understand that,
although the symbol in psychoanalytical terms is repressed [136] into the
unconscious, it carries in itself no index whatsoever of regression, or
even of immaturity. For it to induce its effects in the subject, it is enough
that it make itself heard, since these effects operate without his being
aware of it—as we admit in our daily experience, explaining many
reactions of normal as well as of neurotic subjects by their response to
the symbolic sense of an act, of a relation, or of an object.

There is therefore no doubt that the analyst can play on the power
of the symbol by evoking it in a carefully calculated fashion in the
semantic resonances of his remarks.

This is surely the way for a return to the use of symbolic effects in a
renewed technique of interpretation in analysis.

In this regard, we could take note of what the Hindu tradition teaches
about *dhvani*,[cc] in the sense that this tradition brings out that it is proper
to the Word to cause to be understood what it does not say.[137] The tradition illustrates this by a tale whose ingenuousness, which appears to be
the usual thing in these examples, shows itself humorous enough to
induce us to penetrate the Truth which it conceals.

A young girl, it begins, is waiting for her lover on the bank of a
stream when she sees a Brahmin coming along towards her. She runs
to him and exclaims in the warmest and most amiable tones: "How
lucky it is that you came by today! The dog which used to frighten you

[bb] "The Theory of Symbolism," *British Journal of Psychology,* IX, 2. Reprinted
in his *Papers on Psycho-Analysis* [(London, 5th ed., 1948). See the article: "A la
mémoire d'Ernest Jones: Sur sa théorie du symbolisme," *La Psychanalyse,* V
(1960), pp. 1–20; *Ecrits,* pp. 697–717].
[cc] The reference is to the teaching of Abhinavagupta (tenth century). See: Dr.
Kanti Chandra Pandey, "Indian Esthetics," *Chowkamba Sanskrit Series,* Studies,
Vol. II, Benares, 1950.

by its barking will not be along this riverbank again, for it has just been devoured by a lion which is often seen around here. . . ."

The absence of the lion can thus have as much of an effect as his spring would have were he present, for the lion only springs once, says the proverb appreciated by Freud.[138]

The *primary* character of symbols in fact brings them close to those numbers out of which all the others are compounded, and if they therefore underlie all the semantemes of language, we shall be able to restore to the Word its full value of evocation by a discreet search for their interferences, using as our guide a metaphor whose symbolic displacement will neutralize the second senses of the terms which it associates.[139]

This technique would require for its teaching as well as for its learning a profound assimilation of the resources of one's own language, and especially of those which are concretely realized in its poetic texts. It is well known that Freud was in this position in relation to German literature, as well as to Shakespeare's dramatic works by virtue of a translation of unequaled quality. Every one of his works bears witness to it, at the same time as the continual recourse he had to it, no less in his technique than in his discovery. Not to omit his knowledge of the ancient classics, his up-to-date initiation into folklore, and his interested participation in the conquests of contemporary humanism in the domain of ethnography.

It might well be demanded of the practitioner of analysis not to denigrate any attempt to follow Freud along this road.

But the tide is against us. It can be measured by the condescending attention paid to the "wording," [140] as if to some novelty; and the English morphology of the term gives a subtle enough support to a notion still difficult to define, for people to make a point of using it.

What this notion masks, however, is not exactly encouraging when an author[dd] is amazed by the fact of having obtained an entirely different result in the interpretation of one and the same resistance by the use, "without conscious premeditation," he emphasizes, of the term "need for love" [141] instead and in the place of "demand for love," [142] which

[dd] Ernst Kris, "Ego Psychology and Interpretation," *Psychoanalytic Quarterly,* XX, No. 1 (January, 1951), pp. 15–29, in particular the passage quoted on pp. 27–28. [For further commentary on this article, see the "Réponse au commentaire de J. Hyppolite" (1956), pp. 52–58.]

he had first put forward, without seeing anything deeper in it (as he emphasizes himself). If the anecdote is to confirm this reference of the interpretation to the "ego psychology" in the title of the article, it is rather, it seems, a reference to the "ego psychology" of the analyst, insofar as this interpretation makes shift with such a weak use of English that this writer can push his practice of analysis to the limits of a nonsensical stuttering.[ee]

The fact is that "need" and "demand" have a diametrically opposed sense for the subject, and to hold that their use can be confused even for an instant amounts to a radical failure to recognize the "intimation" of the Word.[143]

For in its symbolizing function the Word is moving towards nothing less than a transformation of the subject to whom it is addressed by means of the link which it establishes with the one who emits it—in other words, by introducing an effect of the signifier.[*]

This is why it is necessary for us to return once more to the structure of communication in Language[*] and to dissipate once and for all the mistaken notion of Language as a system of signs,[144] a source in this domain of confusions of the discourse as well as of malpractice of the Word.

If the communication of Language is conceived as a signal by which the sender informs the receiver of something by means of a certain code, there is no reason why we should not give as much credence and even more to any other sign when the "something" in question is of the individual: there is even every reason for us to give preference to any mode of expression which comes close to the natural sign.

It is in this way that the technique of the Word has fallen into discredit among us. We can be seen in search of a gesture, a grimace, an attitude, a moment of mimicry, a movement, a shudder, nay, an arrestation of habitual movement; shrewd as we are, nothing can now stop us from letting our bloodhounds off the leash to follow these tracks.

I shall show the insufficiency of the conception of Language-as-a-sign by the very manifestation which best illustrates it in the animal kingdom, a manifestation which, if it had not recently been the object of an authentic discovery, it seems it would have been necessary to invent for this purpose.

[ee] Paragraph rewritten (1966).

It is now admitted generally that when the honeybee returns to the hive from his foraging expedition, he transmits to his companions by two sorts of dance instructions about the existence of nectar-bearing flowers and their relative distance, near or far, from the hive. The second type of dance is the most remarkable, for the plane in which the bee traces the figure-of-eight curve which has caused it to be called the "wagging dance," [145] and the frequency of the figures executed within a given time, designate exactly the direction to be followed, determined in relation to the inclination of the sun (on which bees are able to take a fix in all weathers, thanks to their sensitivity to polarized light) on the one hand, and on the other, the distance, up to several miles, at which the source of nectar may be found. And the other bees respond to this message by setting off immediately for the designated spot.

It took some ten years of patient observation for Karl von Frisch to decode this mode of message, for it is certainly a question of a code, or of a system of signaling, whose generic character alone forbids us to qualify it as conventional. [146]

But is it necessarily a Language? We can say that it is distinguished from a Language precisely by the fixed correlation of its signs to the reality which they signify. For in a Language, signs take on their value from their relationships to each other in the lexical sharing-out of semantemes as much as in the positional, or even flectional, use of morphemes, in sharp contrast to the fixity of the coding used by bees. And the diversity of human languages takes on its full value from this enlightening discovery.

What is more, while the message in the mode described here determines the action of each *socius*, it is never retransmitted by him. This means that the message remains fixed in its function as a relay of the action from which no subject detaches it as a symbol of communication itself.[ff]

The form alone in which Language is expressed defines subjectivity. Language says: "You will go such and such a way, and when you see

---

[ff] This for the use of whoever can still understand it, after going to Littré to look for the justification of a theory which makes of the *parole* an "action beside," by the translation which Littré does in fact give of the Greek *parabole* (but why not "action towards"?) without having noticed at the same time that if this word always designates what it means, it is because of ecclesiastical usage which since the tenth century, has reserved the word *verbe* for the Logos incarnate.

such and such, you will turn off in such and such a direction." In other words, it refers itself to the discourse of the other. As such it is enveloped in the highest function of the Word, inasmuch as the Word commits its author by investing the person to whom it is addressed with a new reality, as for example, when by a "You are my wife," a subject marks himself with the seal of wedlock.*

This is in fact the essential form from which every human Word derives rather than the form at which it arrives.

Hence the paradox by which one of my most penetrating listeners, when I began to make my views known on analysis as dialectic, thought he could oppose my position by a remark which he formulated in the following terms: "Human Language (according to you) constitutes a communication in which the sender receives his own message back from the receiver in an inverted form." This was an objection that I had only to reflect on for a moment before recognizing that it carried the stamp of my own thinking—in other words, that the Word always subjectively includes its own reply,[147] that Pascal's "Tu ne me chercherais pas si tu ne m'avais trouvé" [148] simply confirms the same Truth in different words, and that this is the reason why, in the paranoiac refusal of recognition, it is in the form of a negative verbalization that the inavowable feeling comes to the point of surging forth in the persecutory "interpretation."

Furthermore, when you congratulate yourself on having met someone who speaks the same Language as you do, you do not mean that you meet with him in the discourse of everybody, but that you are united to him by a special form of Word.

Thus the antinomy immanent to the relations of the Word and Language becomes clear. As Language becomes more functional, it becomes improper for the Word, and as it becomes too particular to us, it loses its function as Language.

One is aware of the use made in primitive traditions of secret names in which the subject identifies his own person or his gods, to the point that to reveal these names is to lose himself or to betray these gods; and the confidences of our subjects, as well as our own memories, teach us that it is not at all rare for children spontaneously to rediscover the virtue of such a usage.

Finally, it is by the intersubjectivity of the "we" which it takes on that the value of a Language as Word is measured.

By an inverse antinomy, it can be observed that the more the duty of

Language becomes neutralized by its moving closer to information, the more Language is imputed to be laden with *redundancies*. This notion of redundancy in Language came from research which was all the more precise because a vested interest was involved, having been prompted by the economic problem of long-distance communication, and in particular that of the possibility of carrying several conversations at once on a single telephone line. It can be asserted that a substantial portion of the phonetic material * is superfluous to the realization of the communication actually sought.[149]

This is highly instructive for us,[gg] since what is redundant as far as information is concerned is precisely that which does duty as resonance in the Word.

For the function of Language is not to inform but to evoke.

What I seek in the Word is the response of the other. What constitutes me as subject is my question. In order to be recognized by the other, I utter what was only in view of what will be. In order to find him, I call him by a name which he must assume or refuse in order to reply to me.

I identify myself in Language, but only by losing myself in it like an object.* What is realized in my history is not the past definite of what was, since it is no more, or even the present perfect of what has been in what I am, but the future anterior of what I shall have been for what I am in the process of becoming.

If I now place myself in front of the other to question him, there is no cybernetic computer imaginable that can make a reaction out of what the response will be. The definition of response as the second term in the circuit "stimulus-response" is simply a metaphor sustained by the subjectivity imputed to the animal, a subjectivity which is then glossed over in the physical schema to which the metaphor reduces it. This is

---

[gg] Every Language to its own taste in transmission, and since the legitimacy of such research is founded on its success, nothing forbids us to draw a moral from it. Consider, for example, the maxim pinned to the prefatory note as an epigraph. Since it is so laden with redundancies, its style may possibly appear a little flat to you. But lighten it of them, and its audacity will get the enthusiasm it deserves: "Parfaupe ouclaspa nannanbryle anaphi ologi psysocline ixispad anlana —égnia kune n'rbiol' ô blijouter têtumaine ennouconç . . . ." There we have the purity of its message finally laid bare. There meaning raises its head, there the avowal of being outlines itself, and our victorious *esprit* bequeaths to the future its immortal imprint.

what I have called putting the rabbit into the hat so as to be able to pull it out again later. But a reaction is not a reply.

If I press an electric button and a light goes on, there is no response except for *my* desire. If in order to obtain the same result I must try a whole system of relays whose correct position is unknown to me, there is no question except as concerns my anticipation, and there will not be one any longer, once I have learned enough about the system to operate it without mistakes.

But if I call the person to whom I am speaking by whatever name I choose to give him, I intimate to him the subjective function that he will take on again in order to reply to me, even if it is to repudiate this function.

Henceforth the decisive function of my own reply appears, and this function is not, as has been said, simply to be received by the subject as acceptance or rejection of his discourse, but really to recognize him or to abolish him as subject. Such is the nature of the analyst's *responsibility* whenever he intervenes by means of the Word.

Moreover, the problem of the therapeutic effect of inexact interpretation posed by Mr. Edward Glover[hh] in a remarkable paper has led him to conclusions where the question of exactitude moves into the background. In other words, not only is every spoken intervention received by the subject in terms of his (and its) structure, but the intervention takes on a structuring function in him in proportion to its form. It is precisely the scope of nonanalytic psychotherapy, and even of the most ordinary medical "prescriptions," to be interventions that could be described as obsessional systems of suggestion, as hysterical suggestions of a phobic character, or even as persecutory supports, each one taking its particular character from the sanction which it gives to the subject's failure to recognize his own reality.

The Word is in fact a gift of Language, and Language is not immaterial. It is a subtle body, but body it is. Words are trapped in all the corporeal images which captivate the subject; they can make the hysteric pregnant, be identified with the object of *penis-neid,* represent the flood of urine of urethral ambition, or the retained faeces of avaricious *jouissance.*

[hh] "The Therapeutic Effect of Inexact Interpretation; a Contribution to the Theory of Suggestion," *IJP*, XII, p. 4.

What is more, words themselves can undergo symbolic lesions and accomplish Imaginary acts of which the patient is the subject. You will remember the *Wespe* (wasp), castrated of its initial W to become the S. P. of the Wolf Man's initials at the moment when he brings to realization the symbolic punishment whose object he was on the part of Grusha, the wasp.[150]

You will remember also the S which constitutes the residue of the hermetic formula into which the conjuratory invocations of the Rat Man became condensed after Freud had extracted the anagram of the name of his beloved from its cipher, and which, tacked on to the final "amen" of his jaculatory prayer, eternally floods the lady's name with the symbolic ejection of his impotent desire.[151]

Similarly, an article by Robert Fliess,[ii] inspired by Abraham's inaugural remarks, shows us that the discourse as a whole may become the object of an erotization, following the displacements of erogeneity in the corporeal image as they are momentarily determined by the analytic relation.

The discourse then takes on a phallic-urethral, anal-erotic, or even an oral-sadistic function. It is in any case remarkable that the author catches the effect of this function above all in the silences which mark the inhibition of the satisfaction experienced through it by the subject.

In this way the Word may become an Imaginary, or even Real object in the subject and, as such, swallow up in more than one respect the function of Language. We shall then place the Word inside the parentheses of the resistance which it manifests.

But this will not be in order to put the Word on the index of the analytic relation, for that relation would then lose everything, including its *raison d'être*.

Analysis can have for its goal only the advent of a true Word and the bringing to realization of his history by the subject in his relation to a future.

Maintaining this dialectic is in direct opposition to any objectifying orientation of analysis, and emphasizing this necessity is of first importance in order to see through the aberrations of the new tendencies being manifested in psychoanalysis.

[ii] "Silence and Verbalization. A Supplement to the Theory of the 'Analytic Rule,'" *IJP*, XXX, 1.

I shall illustrate my remarks on this point again by a return to Freud, and in fact, since I started by using this case, by the observation of the Rat Man.

Freud even goes so far as to take liberties with factual accuracy when it is a question of attaining to the Truth of the subject. At one moment he perceives the determining role played by the proposal of marriage brought to the subject by his mother at the origin of the present phase of his neurosis. In any case, as I have shown in my seminar, Freud had had a lightning intuition of it as a result of personal experience. Nevertheless he does not hesitate to interpret its effect to the subject as that of his dead father's prohibition against his liaison with the lady of his thoughts.

This interpretation is not only materially inaccurate. It is also psychologically inaccurate, for the castrating action of the father, which Freud affirms here with an insistence that might be considered systematic, played only a secondary role in this case. But the apperception of the dialectical relationship is so apt that Freud's act of interpretation at that moment sets off the decisive lifting of the death-bearing symbols which bind the subject narcissistically both to his dead father and to the idealized lady, their two images being sustained, in an equivalence characteristic of the obsessional neurotic, one by the phantasmatic aggressivity which perpetuates it, other by the mortifying cult which transforms it into an idol.

In the very same way, it is by recognizing the forced subjectification of the obsessional debt[jj] in the scenario of the vain attempts at restitution —a scenario which too perfectly expresses the Imaginary terms of this debt for the subject even to try to bring it to realization—by recognizing the forced subjectification of an obsessional debt whose pressure is exploited by the subject to the point of delusion, that Freud achieves his goal. This is the goal of bringing the subject to rediscover—in the history of his father's lack of delicacy, his marriage with the subject's mother, the "poor but pretty" girl, his marred love-life, the distasteful memory of the beneficent friend [to whom the father had never made restitution of

---

[jj] Here equivalent for me to the term *Zwangsbefurchtung* [literally: "obsessional or compulsive (transitive) fearing," "apprehension"], which needs to be rendered into its component elements without losing any of the semantic resources of the German language.

his own debt]—to rediscover in this history, along with the fateful constellation[152] which had presided over the subject's very birth, the *béance,* impossible to fill, of the symbolic debt of which his neurosis is the notice of nonpayment.

There is no trace here at all of a recourse to the ignoble specter of some sort of original "fear," nor even to a masochism which it would be easy enough to wave about, less yet to that obsessional counterforcing propagated by some analysts in the name of the analysis of defenses. The resistances themselves, as I have shown elsewhere, are used as long as possible in the sense or direction of the progress of the discourse. And when it is time to put an end to them, it is in acceding to them that the end is reached.

For it is in this way that the Rat Man succeeds in introducing into his subjectivity his true mediation in the transferential form of the Imaginary daughter which he ascribes to Freud in order to receive through her a marriage tie with him, and who unveils her true face to him in a key dream: that of death gazing at him with her yellow-brown eyes.[153]

Moreover, if it is with this symbolic pact that the ruses of the subject's servitude came to an end, reality did not fail him, it seems, in consummating these nuptials. And the footnote of 1923 [on p. 249] which Freud dedicated by way of epitaph to this young man who had found in the risks of war "the end that awaited so many young men of value on whom so many hopes could be founded," thus concluding the case with all the rigor of destiny, elevates it to the beauty of tragedy.

In order to know how to reply to the subject in analysis, the procedure is to recognize first of all the place where his ego is, that ego which Freud himself defined as an ego formed of a verbal nucleus; in other words, to know through whom and for whom the subject poses *his question.* So long as this is not known, there will be the risk of a *contresens* concerning the desire which is there to be recognized and concerning the object to whom this desire is addressed.

The hysterical subject captures this object in an elaborate intrigue, and his ego is in the third party by whose intermediary the subject enjoys that object in which his question is incarnated. The obsessional subject drags into the cage of his narcissism the objects in which his question reverberates back and forth in the multiplied alibi of mortal figures and, subduing their heady acrobatics, addresses its ambiguous homage towards the box in which he himself has his seat, that of the master who cannot be seen or see himself.[154]

Trahit sua quemque voluptas; one identifies himself with the spectacle, and the other puts one on.

For the hysterical subject, for whom the technical term "acting out" takes on its literal meaning since he is acting outside himself, you have to get him to recognize where his action is situated. For the obsessional neurotic, you have to get him to recognize you in the spectator, invisible from the stage, to whom he is united by the mediation of death.[155]

It is therefore always in the relationship of the subject's *moi* to the *je* of his discourse that you must understand the sense of the discourse in order to achieve the dealienation of the subject.

But you cannot possibly achieve this if you cling to the idea that the *moi* of the subject is identical to the presence which is speaking to you.

This error is fostered by the terminology of the analytic topography, which is all too tempting to objectifying thought and which lets the objectifying thinker make an almost imperceptible transposition from the concept of the *moi* defined as the system perception-consciousness— that is, as the system of the objectifications of the subject—to the concept of the *moi* as correlative to an absolute reality and thus, in a singular return of the repressed in psychologistic thought, to rediscover in the *moi* the "function of the Real" in relation to which Pierre Janet, for instance, orders his psychological conceptions.

Such a transposition can occur only when it has not been recognized that in the works of Freud the topography of the ego, the id, and the superego is subordinated to the metapsychology whose terms he was propounding at the same period and without which the new topography loses its sense. Thus analysts became involved in a sort of psychological orthopedics which has not yet finished bearing its fruit.

Michael Balint has analyzed in a thoroughly penetrating way the intricate interaction of theory and technique in the genesis of a new conception of analysis, and he finds no better term to indicate the problem than the catchword borrowed from Rickman of the advent of a "Two-body psychology."

It couldn't be better put. Analysis is becoming the relation of two bodies between which is established a phantasmatic communication in which the analyst teaches the subject to apprehend himself as an object;

subjectivity is admitted into it only inside the parentheses of the illusion, and the Word is put on the index of a search for the lived experience which becomes its supreme aim, but the dialectically necessary result appears in the fact that, since the subjectivity of the analyst is free of all restraint, his subjectivity leaves the subject in a state of complete surrender to every summons[156] of his Word.

Once the intrasubjective topography has become entified, it does in fact come to realization in the division of labor between the subjects in the presence of each other. And this deformed usage of Freud's formula that all that is of the id must become of the ego appears under a demystified form; the subject, transformed into a *cela*,[157] has to conform to an ego in which the analyst has little trouble in recognizing his ally, since in actual fact it is to the analyst's ego that the subject is expected to conform.[158]

This is precisely that process expressed in many a theoretical formulation of the "splitting of the ego" in analysis. Half of the subject's ego passes over to the other side of the wall which separates the person being analyzed from the analyst, then half of that half, and so on, in an asymptotic procession which will never succeed, however far it is pushed in the opinion which the subject has reached on his own, in canceling out any margin from which he can go back on the aberration of the analysis.

But how could the subject of a type of analysis whose axis is the principle that all his formulations are systems of defense, be defended against the total disorientation in which this principle leaves the dialectic of the analyst?

Freud's interpretation, whose dialectical progression appears so clearly in the case of Dora,[159] does not present these dangers, for, when the analyst's prejudices and presumptions (that is, his countertransference, a term whose use in my opinion cannot be extended beyond the dialectical reasons for the error) have misled him in his intervention, he pays the price for it on the spot by a negative transference. For this negative transference manifests itself with a force which is all the greater the further such an analysis has already set the subject going in an authentic recognition, and what usually results is the breaking off of the analysis.

This is exactly what happened in Dora's case, because of Freud's relentless persistence in wanting to make her recognize the hidden object of her desire in the person of Herr K, in whom the constituting presumptions of his countertransference lured him into seeing the promise of her happiness.

Dora herself was undoubtedly deceived in this relation, but she did not resent any the less the fact that Freud was fooled along with her. But when she came back to see him, after a delay of fifteen months in which the fateful cipher of her *"temps pour comprendre"* is inscribed, we can sense her entering into the path of a pretense that she had been pretending, and the convergence of this second-degree pretense with the aggressive intention imputed to her by Freud—and not inaccurately, but without his recognizing what it actually sprang from—presents us with the rough outline of the intersubjective complicity which any "analysis of resistances" sure of its rights would have been able to perpetuate between them. No doubt that with the means now offered us by the progress of our technique, this human error could have been extended beyond the limits of the diabolical.

None of this is of my own invention, for Freud himself afterwards recognized the prejudicial source of his defeat in his own failure to recognize at the time the homosexual position of the object at which the hysterical subject's desire was aimed.[160]

No doubt the whole process which has culminated in this present tendency of psychoanalysis goes back, and from the very first, to the analyst's guilty conscience about the miracle produced by his Word. He interprets the symbol, and lo and behold, the symptom, which inscribes the symbol in letters of suffering in the subject's flesh, disappears. This unseemly thaumaturgy is unbecoming to us, for after all we are scientists, and the practice of magic is hardly something we can defend.[161] So we escape the difficulty by attributing magical thinking to the patient. Before long we'll find ourselves preaching the Gospel according to Lévy-Bruhl to him. But in the meantime, lo and behold, we have become thinkers again and have re-established the proper distance between ourselves and our patients—a traditional distance which was perhaps a little too recklessly abandoned, a distance expressed so nobly in the words of Pierre Janet when he spoke of the feeble abilities of the hysterical subject compared to our own lofty position. The poor little thing, he confides to us, "she understands nothing about science, and doesn't even imagine how anybody could be interested in it . . . . If we consider the absence of control which characterizes their thinking, instead of allowing ourselves to be scandalized by their falsehoods, which are in any case naïve enough, we should rather be astonished that there are so many truthful ones," and so on.

These words, since they represent the sentiments of many present-day analysts who have come back to condescending to talk to the patient "in his own Language," can be used to understand what has happened in between times. For if Freud had been capable of putting his name to them, how would he have been able to hear and understand as he did the Truth enclosed within the little stories of his first patients, or yet decipher a gloomy delusion like Schreber's to the point of extending it to the measure of man eternally enchained by his symbols?

Is our reason so weak that it cannot recognize itself on equal terms in the mediation of scientific discourse and in the primary exchange of the Symbolic object, and that it cannot rediscover there the identical measure of its original guile?

Is it going to be necessary to recall what the yardstick of "thought" is worth to practitioners of an experience which is occupied rather more closely with an intestinal erotism than with an equivalent of action?

Is it necessary for me, as I speak to you, to point out that I do not have to fall back on thought in order to understand that if I am talking to you in this moment of the Word, it is insofar as we have in common a technique of the Word which enables you to understand me when I speak to you, and which disposes me to address myself through you to those who understand nothing of that technique?

No doubt that we have to lend an ear to the "not-said" which lies in the holes of the discourse, but this does not mean that we are to do our listening as if it were to someone knocking from the other side of a wall.

For if from this point on we are no longer to concern ourselves except with these noises, as some analysts pride themselves on doing, it must be admitted that we will not have put ourselves in the most propitious set of conditions to decipher their sense. Without first racking our brains to comprehend [such a sign from the subject, something quite unnecessary for a signifier], how is one supposed to *translate* what is not of itself Language? Led in this way to appeal to the subject,[162] since it is after all to *his* account that we have to disburse this understanding, we shall implicate him in a wager along with us, a wager that we have properly understood [his sign] and then wait until a return makes winners out of both of us. As a result, in continuing to perform this shuttling back and forth, he will learn very simply to beat time himself, a form of suggestion worth as much as any other—in other words, a form of suggestion in which, as in every other form of suggestion, one does not know who is keeping the score. The procedure is recognized as being sound enough when it is a question of being six feet under.[kk,163]

Halfway to this extreme the question arises: Does psychoanalysis remain a dialectical relation in which the nonaction of the analyst guides the subject's discourse towards the bringing to realization of his Truth, or is it to be reduced to a phantasmatic relation where "two abysses brush against each other" without touching, while the whole gamut of Imaginary regressions is exhausted—like a sort of "bundling"[ll] pushed to its extreme limits as a psychological experience?

In actual fact, this illusion which impels us to seek the reality of the subject beyond the Language barrier is the same as that by which the subject believes that his Truth is already given in us and that we know it in advance; and it is moreover as a result of this that he is wide open to our objectifying intervention.

But for his part, no doubt, he does not have to answer for this subjective error which, whether it is avowed or not in his discourse, is immanent in the fact that he has entered analysis and that he has already concluded the original pact involved in it. And the fact that we find in the subjectivity of this moment the reason for what can be called the constituting effects of transference—insofar as they are distinguished by an index of reality from the constituted effects which succeed them —is all the more ground for not neglecting this subjectivity.[mm]

[kk] Two paragraphs rewritten (1966).

[ll] This term refers to the custom, of Celtic origin and still employed among certain American Biblical sects, of allowing a couple engaged to be married, or even a passing guest and the daughter of the house, to pass the night together in the same bed, provided that they keep their outdoor clothes on. The word takes its meaning from the fact that the girl is usually wrapped up tightly in several sheets.

(Quincey speaks of it. See also the book by Aurand le Jeune on this practice amongst the Amish people.)

In this way the myth of Tristan and Iseult, and even the complex which it represents, would henceforth act as a sponsor for the analyst in his quest for the soul betrothed to mystifying nuptials via the extenuation of its instinctual phantasies.

[mm] Thus what I have designated in what follows as the support of transference: namely, le sujet-supposé-savoir, is to be found defined here (1966). [Lacan: It is insofar as he is "supposed to know"—however incorrect this is, of course—that the analyst becomes the support ($\dot{v}\pi o\kappa\epsilon i\mu\epsilon\nu o\nu$) of the transference.]

Freud, let it be recalled, in touching on the feelings involved in transference, insisted on the necessity of distinguishing in it a factor of reality.
He concluded that it would be an abuse of the subject's docility to want
to persuade him in every case that these sentiments are a simple transferential repetition of the neurosis.[164] Consequently, since these real
feelings manifest themselves as primary and since the charm of our own
person remains a contingent factor, there would seem to be some mystery
here.

But this mystery becomes clarified if it is viewed within the phenomenology of the subject, insofar as the subject constitutes himself in
the quest for Truth. One has only to go back to the traditional data—
which the Buddhists could furnish us with, although they are not the
only ones who could—to recognize in this form of the transference the
normal error of existence, and under three headings which they figure as
follows: love, hate, and ignorance. It is therefore as a countereffect of
the movement of analysis that we shall understand their equivalence in
what is called an originally positive transference—each one being illuminated by the other two under this existential aspect, if one does not except
the third, which is usually omitted because of its proximity to the subject.

Here I evoke the invective through which I was called on as a witness
to the lack of discretion shown by a certain work (which I have already
cited too often) in its senseless objectification of the play of the instincts
in analysis, by someone whose debt to me can be recognized by his use
of the term "real" in conformity with mine. It was in these words that,
as people say, he "liberated his heart": "It is high time to put an end
to the fraud which tends to make it believed that anything real whatsoever takes place during the treatment." Let it not be said what has befallen
it, for alas, if analysis has not cured the dog's oral vice of which the
Gospel speaks, its condition is worse than before: it is other people's
vomit which it laps up.

For this sally was not ill directed, since it sought in fact to distinguish
between those elementary registers whose grounding I later put forward
in these terms: the Symbolic, the Imaginary, and the Real—a distinction
never previously made in psychoanalysis.*

Reality in the analytic experience does in fact often remain veiled by
negative forms, but it is not too difficult to situate it.

Reality is encountered, for instance, in what we usually condemn as active interventions; but it would be an error to define the limit of reality in this way.

For it is clear on the other hand that the analyst's abstention, his refusal to reply, is an element of reality in analysis. More exactly, it is in this negativity insofar as it is a pure negativity—that is, detached from any particular motive—that lies the junction between the Symbolic and the Real. This naturally follows from the fact that this nonaction of the analyst is founded on our firm and stated Knowledge of the principle that all that is real is rational, and on the resulting precept that it is up to the subject to show what he is made of.

The fact remains that this abstention is not indefinitely maintained; when the subject's question has taken on the form of a true Word, we give it the sanction of our reply, but thereby we have shown that a true Word already contains its own reply and that we are simply adding our own lay to its antiphon. What does this mean except that we do no more than to confer on the subject's Word its dialectical punctuation?

The other moment in which the Symbolic and the Real come together is consequently revealed, and I have already marked it theoretically: that is to say, in the function of time, and this makes it worth stopping for a moment to consider the technical effects of time.

Time plays its role in analytical technique from several angles.

Time presents itself first of all in the total duration of the analysis, and implies the sense to be given to the termination of the analysis, which is the question which must precede that of the signs of its end. I shall touch on the problem of fixing its termination. But it is clear right now that this duration can only be anticipated for the subject as indefinite.

This is for two reasons which can only be distinguished in a dialectical perspective:

The first, which is linked to the limits of our domain and which confirms our remarks on the definition of its confines: we cannot predict for the subject what his *temps pour comprendre* will be, insofar as it includes a psychological factor which escapes us as such.

The second, which is properly of the subject and through which the fixing of a termination is equivalent to a spatializing projection in which he finds himself already alienated from himself at the very beginning: from the moment that the coming-to-term of his Truth can be predicted —whatever may come about in the ensuing interval in the intersubjective relation of the subject and analyst—the fact is that the Truth is already there. That is to say that in this way we re-establish in the subject his original mirage insofar as he places his Truth in us, and that if we then give him the sanction of our authority, we are setting the analysis off on an aberrant path whose results will be impossible to correct.

This is precisely what happened in the celebrated case of the Wolf Man, and Freud so well understood its exemplary importance that he took support from it again in his article on finite or indefinite analysis.[nn]

The advance fixing of a termination to an analysis, first form of active intervention, inaugurated (*proh pudor!*) by Freud himself,[165] whatever may be the divinatory sureness (in the proper sense of the term)[oo] of which the analyst may give proof in following his example, will invariably leave the subject in the alienation of his Truth.

Moreover, we find the confirmation of this point in two facts from Freud's case:

In the first place, in spite of the whole cluster of proofs demonstrating the historicity of the primal scene, in spite of the conviction which he shows concerning it—remaining imperturbable to the doubts which Freud methodically cast on it by way of testing him—the Wolf Man never managed in spite of it all to integrate his rememoration of the primal scene into his history.

Secondly, the same patient later demonstrated his alienation in the most categorical way, in a paranoid form.

[nn] For this is the correct translation of the two terms which have been rendered, with that unfailing *contresens* already noted, by "terminated and interminable analysis." [The usual French translation of the title "Die endliche und die unendliche Analyse" (1937), *Standard Edition*, XXIII, is "Analyse terminée et analyse interminable"; the English: "Analysis Terminable and Interminable." Lacan renders the title by "analyse finie ou indéfinie."]

[oo] Cf. Aulus-Gellius, *Attic Nights*, II, 4: "In a trial, when it is a question of knowing who shall be given the task of presenting the accusation, and when two or more people volunteer for this office, the judgment by which the tribunal names the accuser is called divination .... This word comes from the fact that since accuser and accused are two correlative terms which cannot continue to exist without each other, and since the type of judgment in question here presents an accused without accuser, it is necessary to have recourse to divination in order to find what the trial does not provide, what it leaves still unknown—that is to say, the accuser."

It is true that here there is at work another factor through which reality intervenes in the analysis—namely, the gift of money whose symbolic value I shall save to treat of elsewhere, but whose import is indicated in what I have already brought out concerning the link between the Word and the constituting gift of primitive exchange. In this case the gift of money is reversed by an initiative of Freud's in which, as much as in his insistence on coming back to the case, we can recognize the unresolved subjectification within him of the problems which this case leaves in suspense. And nobody doubts that this was a factor in the subsequent onset of the psychosis, however without really being able to say why.

Surely it is understood nevertheless that admitting a subject to be nurtured in the prytaneum[166] of psychoanalysis in return for services he renders to science as a case available for study (for it was in fact through a group collection that the Wolf Man was supported), is also to initiate and establish him in the alienation of his Truth? *

The material of the supplementary analysis of the Wolf Man undertaken by Dr. Ruth Mack Brunswick[167] illustrates the responsibility of the previous treatment with Freud by demonstrating my remarks on the respective places of the Word and Language in psychoanalytic mediation.

What is more, it is in the perspective of the Word and Language that one can grasp the fact that Dr. Mack Brunswick has not at all taken her bearings incorrectly in her delicate position in relation to the transference. (The reader will be reminded of the very wall of my metaphor of the Language barrier, in that the wall figures in one of the Wolf Man's dreams, the wolves of the key dream showing themselves eager to get around it . . . .) Those who follow my seminar know all this, and the others can try their hand at it if they like.[pp]

What I want to do is to touch on another aspect of analysis which is particularly ticklish at the moment, that of the function of time in the technique of analysis; more precisely, the question of the length of the session.

Once again it is a question of an element which manifestly belongs to reality, since it represents our working time, and from that angle it falls under the heading of the prevalent professional rule.

[pp] Two paragraphs rewritten (1966).

But its subjective incidences are no less important—and in the first place for the analyst. The taboo nature which has recently characterized discussion of this time limit proves well enough that the subjectivity of the psychoanalytical group is not at all entirely free in this respect, and the scrupulous, not to say obsessional, character which the observation of a standard time limit takes on for some if not most analysts—a standard whose historical and geographical variation seems nevertheless to bother no one—is certainly the sign of the existence of a problem which they are all the more reluctant to deal with because they realize to what extent it would entail a putting into question of the function of the analyst.

On the other hand, nobody can possibly fail to recognize its importance for the subject in analysis. The unconscious, it is said, in a tone which is all the more businesslike in proportion as the speaker is less capable of justifying what he means—the unconscious needs time to reveal itself. I quite agree. But I ask: how is this time to be measured? Is its measure to be that of what Alexandre Koyré calls "the universe of precision"? Obviously we live in this universe, but its advent for man is relatively recent, since it goes back precisely to Huyghens' clock—in other words, to 1659—and the *malaise* of modern man does not exactly indicate that this precision is in itself a liberating factor for him. Are we to say that this time, the time of the fall of heavy bodies, is in some way sacred in the sense that it corresponds to the time of the stars as they were fixed in the Eternal by God who, as Lichtenberg put it, winds up our sundials? Perhaps we might get a somewhat better idea of time by comparing the time [required for] the creation of a symbolic object with the moment of inattention when we let it fall.

However this may be, if the labor of our function during this time remains problematic, I believe I have brought out clearly enough the function of labor in what the patient brings to realization during that time.

But the reality of this time, whatever that reality may be, consequently takes on a localized value from it: that of receiving the product of this labor.*

We play a recording role by assuming the function, fundamental in any symbolic exchange, of gathering what *do kamo,* man in his authenticity, calls *la parole qui dure.*[168]

As a witness called to account for the sincerity of the subject, depositary of the minutes of his discourse, reference as to his exactitude, guarantor of his straightforwardness, custodian of his testament, scrivener of his codicils, the analyst participates in the nature of the scribe.

But above all he remains the master of the Truth of which this discourse is the progress. As I have said, it is he above all who punctuates its dialectic. And here he is apprehended as the judge of the value of this discourse. This entails two consequences.

The suspension of a session cannot *not* be experienced by the subject as a punctuation in his progress. We know very well how he calculates its coming-to-term in order to articulate it upon his own delays, or even upon his escapist refuges, how he anticipates its end by weighing it like a weapon, by watching out for it as he would a place of shelter.

It is a fact, which can be plainly seen in the study of the manuscripts of symbolic writings, whether it is a question of the Bible or of the Chinese canonicals, that the absence of punctuation in them is a source of ambiguity. The punctuation, once inserted, fixes the sense; changing the punctuation renews or upsets it; and a faulty punctuation amounts to a change for the worse.

The indifference with which the cutting up of the "timing" [169] interrupts the moments of haste within the subject can be fatal to the conclusion towards which his discourse was being precipitated, or can even fix a misunderstanding or misreading in it, if not furnish a pretext for a retaliatory act of guile.

Beginning analysts seem more struck by the effects of this fact than others—which makes one think that for the others it is simply a matter of submitting to routine.

Certainly the neutrality which we manifest in strictly applying the rule concerning the length of the session maintains us in the path of our nonaction.

But this nonaction has its limits, otherwise there would be no interventions at all—and why make an intervention impossible at this point, which is consequently privileged in this way?

The danger that this point may take on an obsessional value for the analyst rests simply in the fact that it lends itself to the connivance of the subject, a connivance which is not only overt for the obsessional subject, but which takes on a special force for him, precisely in relation to the vigorousness of his feeling about his labor. The keynote of forced labor which envelops everything for this subject, even the activities of his leisure time, is only too well known.[170]

This sense is sustained by his subjective relation to the master insofar as it is the master's death for which he waits.

In fact the obsessional subject manifests one of the attitudes that Hegel did not develop in his dialectic of the master and the slave. The slave has given way in face of the risk of death in which mastery was being offered to him in a struggle of pure prestige. But since he knows that he is mortal, he also knows that the master can die. From this moment on he is able to accept his laboring for the master and his renunciation of *jouissance* in the meantime; and, in the uncertainty of the moment when the master will die, he waits.

Such is the intersubjective reason, as much for the doubt as for the procrastination which are character traits of the obsessional subject.

In the meantime, all his labor falls under the heading of this intention, and becomes doubly alienating by this fact. For not only is the subject's handiwork stripped from him by another—which is the constituting relation of all labor—but the subject's recognition of his own essence in his handiwork where this labor finds its justification, does not any the less escape from him, for he himself "*is* not in it." He *is* in the anticipated moment of the master's death, from which moment he will begin to live, but in the meantime he identifies himself with the master as dead, and as a result of this he is himself already dead.[171]

Nevertheless he makes an effort to deceive the master by the demonstration of the good intentions manifested in his labor. This is what the dutiful children of the analytical catechism express in their rough and ready way by saying that the subject's ego is trying to seduce his superego.

This intrasubjective formulation becomes immediately demystified once it is understood in the analytical relation, where the subject's "working through" is in fact employed for the seduction of the analyst.

Nor is it by chance that, from the moment that the dialectical progress begins to approach the questioning of the intentions of the ego in our subjects, the phantasy of the analyst's death—often felt in the form of fear or even of anguish[172]—never fails to be produced.

And the subject then sets off again in an even more demonstrative elaboration of his "good will."

How can we consequently have doubts about the effect of any disdain shown by the master towards the product of such a labor? The subject's resistance may even become completely out of tune because of it.

From this moment, his alibi—hitherto unconscious—begins to unveil itself for him, and he can be seen passionately in quest of the justification of so many efforts.

I would not have so much to say about it if I had not been convinced that, in experimenting with what have been called our short sessions, in a moment of my experience which has now come to its conclusion, I was able to bring to light in a certain male subject phantasies of anal pregnancy as well as the dream of its resolution by Caesarean section, in a delaying of the end of the session where I would otherwise have had to go on listening to his speculations on the art of Dostoïevsky.[173]

However, I am not here in order to defend this procedure, but to show that it has a precise dialectical sense in its technical application.[qq]

And I am not the only one to have made the remark that it ultimately becomes one with the technique known as *Zen,* which is applied as the means of the subject's revelation in the traditional ascetic practice of certain Far Eastern teachings.

Without going to the extremes to which this technique is carried, since they would be contrary to certain of the limitations imposed by ours, a discreet application of its basic principle in analysis seems much more admissible to me than certain modes of analysis known as the analysis of resistances, insofar as this technique does not in itself entail any danger of the subject's alienation.

For this technique only breaks the discourse in order to bring about the delivery of the Word.

Here we are then, at the foot of the wall, at the foot of the Language barrier. We are in our place there, that is to say, on the same side as the patient, and it is on this wall—the same for him as for us—that we shall try to respond to the echo of his Word.[174]

Beyond this wall, there is nothing for us but outer darkness. Does this mean that we are entirely masters of the situation? Certainly not, and on this point Freud has bequeathed us his testament on the negative therapeutic reaction.

The key to this mystery, it is said, is in the instance of a primordial

[qq] Stone which the builders rejected or headstone of the corner, my strong point is that I have never yielded over this (1966).

masochism—in other words, in a manifestation in the pure state of that death instinct[175] whose enigma Freud propounded for us at the apogee of his experience.

We cannot turn up our noses at this problem, any more than I shall be able to postpone examination of it here.

For I note that this same refusal to accept this culminating point of Freud's doctrine is shared by those who conduct their analysis on the basis of a conception of the ego whose error I have denounced, and by those who, like Reich, go so far with the principle of seeking the ineffable organic expression beyond the Word that, like him, in order to deliver it from its armor, they might symbolize, as he does, the orgasmic induction that, like him, they expect from analysis, in the superimposition of the two vermicular forms whose stupefying schema may be seen in his book on character analysis.

Such a combination will no doubt allow me an optimistic view of the rigor of the formations of the spirit, when I have demonstrated the profound relationship uniting the notion of the death instinct to the problems of the Word.

As a moment's reflection shows, the notion of the death instinct involves a basic irony, since its sense has to be sought in the conjunction of two contrary terms: instinct in its most comprehensive acceptation being the law which regulates in its succession a cycle of behavior whose goal is the accomplishment of a vital function; and death appearing first of all as the destruction of life.

Nevertheless, both the definition of life, given by Bichat at the dawn of biology, as being the whole set of forces which resist death; as well as the most modern conception of life—to be found in Cannon's notion of homeostasis—as the function of a system maintaining its own equilibrium, are there to remind us that life and death are compounded in a polar relation at the very heart of phenomena related to life.

Consequently the congruence between the contrasted terms of the death instinct and the phenomena of repetition to which Freud's explanation in fact related them under the heading of automatism[176] ought not to cause difficulty, if it were simply a question of a biological notion.

But we all know very well that it is not a question of biology, and this is what makes this problem a stumbling block for so many of us. The fact that so many people come to a halt on the apparent incompatibility of these terms might well be worth our attention in that it manifests a dialectical innocence that would probably be somewhat disconcerted by the classical problem posed to semantics in the determinative declaration: a hamlet on the Ganges,[177] by which Hindu aesthetics illustrates the second form of the resonances of Language.[rr]

This notion must be approached through its resonances in what I shall call the poetics of the Freudian corpus, the first way of access towards the penetration of its sense, and the essential dimension, from the origins of the work to the apogee marked in it by this notion, for an understanding of its dialectical repercussions. It must be remembered, for example, that Freud tells us he found his vocation for medicine in the call heard during a public reading of the Goethe's famous "Hymn to Nature"—in that text brought to light by a friend in which the poet, in the declining years of his life, agreed to recognize a reputed child of the most youthful effusions of his pen.

At the other end of Freud's life, we find in the article on analysis considered as finite or indefinite, the express reference of his new conception to the conflict of the two principles to which the alternation of universal life was subjected by Empedocles of Agrigentum in the fifth century B.C.—that is, in the pre-Socratic period where nature and mind were not distinguished.[178]

These two facts are a sufficient indication that here it is a question of a myth of the dyad, whose exposition by Plato is in any case evoked in *Beyond the Pleasure Principle,* a myth which can only be understood in the subjectivity of modern man by its elevation to the negativity of the judgment in which it is inscribed.[179]

This is to say that, in the same way as the compulsion to repeat—all the more misconstrued by those who wish to divide the two terms from each other—has in view nothing less than the historizing temporality of the experience of transference,[180] so does the death instinct essentially express the limit of the historical function of the subject. This limit is death—not as an eventual coming-to-term of the life of the individual, or as the empirical certitude of the subject, but, as Heidegger's formula puts it, as the "possibilité absolument propre, inconditionnelle, indépassable, certaine et comme telle indéterminée du sujet," [181] "subject" understood as meaning the subject defined by his historicity.

[rr] This is the form called *Laksanalaksana.*

Moreover this limit is at every instant present in what this history possesses as achieved. This limit represents the past in its absolutely real form—that is to say, not the physical past whose existence is abolished, or the epic past as it has become perfected in the handiwork of memory, or the historic past in which man finds the guarantor of his future, but the past which reveals itself reversed in repetition.[ss]

This is the dead partner taken by subjectivity in the triad which its mediation institutes in the universal conflict of *Philia,* "love," and *Neikos,* "discord."

There is consequently no further need to have recourse to the outworn notion of primordial masochism in order to understand the reason for the repetitive utterances in which subjectivity brings together mastery over its abandonment and the birth of the symbol.[182]

These are the acts of occultation[183] which Freud, in a flash of genius, revealed to us so that we might recognize in them that the moment in which desire becomes human is also that in which the child is born into Language.

We can now grasp in this the fact that in this moment the subject is not simply mastering his privation by assuming it, but that here he is raising his desire to a second power. For his action destroys the object which it causes to appear and disappear in the anticipating *provocation* of its absence and its presence. His action thus negatives the field of forces of desire in order to become its own object to itself. And this object, immediately taking body in the symbolic couple of two elementary jaculations, announces in the subject the diachronic integration of the dichotomy of the phonemes, whose synchronic structure existing Language offers to his assimilation; moreover, the child begins to become engaged in the system of the concrete discourse of the environment, by reproducing more or less approximatively in his *Fort!* and in his *Da!* the vocables which he receives from it.[184]

Fort! Da! It is precisely in his solitude that the desire of the little child has already become the desire of another, of an *alter ego* who dominates him and whose object of desire is henceforth his own affliction.[185]

Let the child now address himself to an Imaginary or Real partner,

[ss] The four words ["renversé dans la répétition"] in which is inscribed my latest formulation of repetition (1966) are substituted for an improper recourse to the "eternal return" ["toujours présent dans l'éternel retour"], which was all that I could put across at that time.

and he will see this partner in equal obedience to the negativity of his discourse, and since his appeal has the effect of making the partner disappear, he will seek in a banishing summons the provocation of the return which brings the partner back to his desire.

Thus the symbol manifests itself first of all as the murder of the thing,[186] and this death constitutes in the subject the eternalization of his desire.

The first symbol in which we recognize humanity in its vestigial traces is the sepulture, and the intermediary of death can be recognized in every relation where man comes to the life of his history.

This is the only life which goes on enduring and is true, since life is transmitted without being lost, in the perpetuated tradition of subject to subject. How is it possible not to see how loftily this life transcends that inherited by the animal in which the individual disappears into the species, since no memorial distinguishes his ephemeral apparition from that which will reproduce it again in the invariability of the type. In fact, apart from those hypothetical mutations of the phylum that must be integrated by a subjectivity which man is still only approaching from outside—nothing, except the experiments to which man associates it, distinguishes a rat from the rat, a horse from the horse, nothing except this inconsistent passage from life to death—whereas Empedocles, by throwing himself into Mount Etna, leaves forever present in the memory of men this symbolic act of his being-for-death.

Man's liberty is entirely inscribed within the constituting triangle of the renunciation which he imposes on the desire of the other by the menace of death for the *jouissance* of the fruits of his serfdom—of the consented-to sacrifice of his life for the reasons which give to human life its measure—and of the suicidal renouncement of the vanquished partner, balking of his victory the master whom he abandons to his inhuman solitude.

Of these figures of death, the third is the supreme detour through which the immediate particularity of desire, reconquering its ineffable form, rediscovers in *dénégation* a final triumph. And we must recognize its meaning, for we have to deal with it. This third figure is not in fact a perversion of the instinct, but rather that desperate affirmation of life which is the purest form in which we recognize the death instinct.

The subject says "No!" to this intersubjective *jeu de furet* in which desire makes itself recognized for a moment, only to become lost in a will which is will of the other.[187] Patiently, the subject withdraws his precarious life from the sheeplike conglomerations of the Eros of the symbol in order to affirm it at the last in a Wordless malediction.

Therefore, when we wish to attain in the subject what was before the serial articulations of the Word, and what is primordial to the birth of symbols, we find it in death, from which his existence takes on all the meaning it has. It is in effect as a desire for death that he affirms himself for others; if he identifies himself with the other, it is by fixing him solidly in the metamorphosis of his essential image, and no being is ever evoked by him except among the shadows of death.

To say that this mortal meaning reveals in the Word a center exterior to Language is more than a metaphor and manifests a structure. This structure is different from the spatialization of the circumference or of the sphere in which some people like to schematize the limits of the living being and his environment:[188] it corresponds rather to the relational group which symbolic logic designates topologically as an annulus.

If I wished to give an intuitive representation of it, it seems that, rather than have recourse to the surface aspect of a zone, I should call on the three-dimensional form of a torus, insofar as its peripheral exteriority and its central exteriority constitute only one single region.[tt]

This schema satisfactorily expresses the endless circularity of the dialectical process which is produced when the subject brings his solitude to realization, be it in the vital ambiguity of immediate desire or in the full assumption of his being-for-death.

But by the same fact it can be grasped that the dialectic is not individual, and that the question of the termination of the analysis is that of the moment when the satisfaction of the subject finds a way to come to realization in the satisfaction of everyone—that is, of all those whom this satisfaction associates with itself in a human undertaking. Of all the undertakings which have been put forward in this century, that of the psychoanalyst is perhaps the loftiest, because the undertaking of the psychoanalyst acts in our time as a mediator between the man of care and the subject of absolute Knowledge.[189] This is therefore why it requires a long subjective ascesis, and one which can never be interrupted, since the end of the didactic analysis itself is not separable from the engagement of the subject in its practice.

[tt] Premises of topology which I have been putting into practice over the past five years (1966).

Let it be renounced, then, by whoever cannot rejoin at its horizon the subjectivity of his epoch. For how could he possibly make his being the axis of so many lives if he knew nothing of the dialectic which engages him with these lives in a symbolic movement? Let him be well acquainted with the whorl into which his epoch draws him in the continued enterprise of Babel, and let him be aware of his function as interpreter in the discord of Languages. As for the darkness of the *mundus* around which the immense tower is coiled, let him leave to the mystic vision the task of seeing in it the putrescent serpent of life raised on an everlasting rod.[190]

I may be permitted a laugh if these remarks are accused of turning the sense of Freud's work away from the biological basis he would have wished for it towards the cultural references with which it overflows. I do not want to preach to you the doctrine of factor *b*, designating the first, nor of factor *c,* designating the second. All I have tried to do is to remind you of the misconstrued *a*, *b*, *c*, of the structure of Language, and to teach you to spell once again the forgotten *b-a, ba*, of the Word.[191]

For what recipe would guide you in a technique which is composed of the first and draws its effects from the second, if you did not recognize the domain and the function of both of them?

The psychoanalytical experience has rediscovered in man the imperative of the *verbe* as the law which has formed him in its image. It manipulates the poetic function of Language to give to his desire its symbolic mediation. May that experience bring you to understand at last that it is in the gift of the Word [uu] that all the reality of its effects resides; for it is by way of this gift that all reality has come to man and it is by his continued act that he maintains it.

If the domain which defines this gift of the Word is to be sufficient for your action as also for your Knowledge, it will also be sufficient for your devotion. For it offers it a privileged field.

When the Devas, the men, and the Asuras were ending their novitiate with Prajapâti, so we read in the second Brâhmana of the fifth lesson of the Bhrad-âranyaka Upanishad, they addressed to him this prayer: "Speak to us."

[uu] Let it be understood that it is not a question of those "gifts" which are always supposed to be in default in novices, but of a gift which is in fact lacking to them more often than they lack it.

"Da," said Prajapâti, god of thunder. "Have you understood me?" And the Devas answered and said: "Thou hast said to us: *Damyata,* master yourselves"—the sacred text meaning that the powers above submit to the law of the Word.

"Da," said Prajapâti, god of thunder. "Have you understood me?" And the men answered and said: "Thou hast said to us: *Datta,* give"— the sacred text meaning that men recognize each other by the gift of the Word.

"Da," said Prajapâti, god of thunder. "Have you understood me?" And the Asuras answered and said: "Thou hast said to us: *Dayadhvam,* be merciful"—the sacred text meaning that the powers below resound to the invocation of the Word.[vv]

That, continues the text, is what the divine voice caused to be heard in the thunder: Submission, gift, grace. *Da da da.*[192]

For Prajapâti replies to all: "You have understood me."

[vv] Ponge writes it: *réson* (1966). [In his *Pour un Malherbe.* "Resound" is "résonner" in French; *réson* is a homonym of *raison.*]

TRANSLATOR'S NOTES

Translator's Notes

¹ "La topique," the French rendering of the Freudian "die Topik" (literally: "arrangement of material"). The accepted English term, which there seems no reason to change, is "topography," and it does in fact match the Freudian metaphor of the "double inscription." But another candidate would be "topology," especially since Lacan seems to use it from time to time as a synonym for *Topik*.

For the nontechnical reader, it may be of assistance to state briefly some of the varying "points of view" used by Freud to represent the psychic system:

(1) the functional: Freud's earliest attempt to systematize his discovery, concerned with the difference between memory and perception and with the unsolved problem of consciousness, is usually described as functional (*Standard Edition*, V, 571);

(2) the descriptive: conscious/unconscious—that is, *Cs./Pcs.Ucs.;*

(3) the topographical (or structural): *Cs.Pcs./Ucs.* This includes the concept of the double inscription (*Niederschrift*);

(4) the dynamic: where the unconscious is equated with the repressed;

(5) the systematic: equivalent to the topographical plus the dynamic, where the division is: secondary system/primary system;

(6) the economic (essentially functional): concerned with the "principle of constancy" expressed in the opposition of pleasure and unpleasure with the attempt of the system to re-establish an original inertia, and with the notion of cathexis.

(7) the "new topography" (1920): the ego, the id, and the superego.

In reference to the "new topography," the last diagrammatic representation of it by Freud in the *New Introductory Lectures* (1933), *Standard*

Edition, XXII, 78, is of value in clearing up some popular misconceptions about the status of these "divisions." But perhaps the most important point of view in the present context is that to be found in the quotation from Freud in note 66. It is essentially systematic, but if one were to give it a label, it would be the "linguistic view."

Note that the "new topography" is intimately connected with Freud's later attempts to deal with "disavowal" (*Verleugnung*—note 11), outside the perversions, in the terms of a "splitting" of the ego (*Ichspaltung*). See, for example, p. 58 of the *New Introductory Lectures* and the unfinished article: "The Splitting of the Ego in the Process of Defense" (1940), *Standard Edition* XXIII, 273, where a number of other references will be found.

[2] *Le symbolique, l'imaginaire,* and *le réel* are the three "orders"— basically, the discursive, the perceptive, and the real orders—introduced into psychoanalytical terminology by Lacan in 1953.

For some remarks on the Imaginary and its relation to the Symbolic and the Real, see the 1958 article by Leclaire on psychosis. Leclaire says in part: "The experience of the Real presupposes the simultaneous use of two correlative functions, the Imaginary function and the Symbolic function. That is Imaginary which, like shadows, has no existence of its own, and yet whose absence, in the light of life, cannot be conceived; that which, without power of distinction inundates singularity and thus escapes any truly rational grasp. That is Imaginary which is irremediably opposed or which is indistinctly confused, without any dialectical movement; the dream is Imaginary . . . just as long as it is not interpreted." And later: "no symbol can do without Imaginary support" (pp. 383–84).

The topographical regression of the "dream thoughts" to images in the dream might be described as a process of the Symbolic becoming Imaginary.

[3] Lacan's views on phenomenology and existentialism are not explicitly developed in the *Discours,* but are significant for its comprehension. Their most extended development will be found in the 1961 article on Merleau-Ponty. In 1953, after referring to the condemnation of the autonomy of the consciousness-of-self in Hegel, to Freud's discovery of "the contrary power," to the logico-mathematical theory of sets, and to the linguistic theory of the phoneme, he goes on:

In this light the whole phenomenological—or even existentialist—movement appears like an exasperated compensation of a philosophy which is no longer sure of being master of its motives; and one that must not be confused, although this movement plagiarizes them, with Wittgenstein's and Heidegger's interrogations of the relationships of being and Language, an interrogation so pensive because it knows itself to be enclosed within what it questions, so slow to seek out its time (*Actes*, p. 251).

An analyst would obviously be less than sympathetic to philosophies taking their departure, or their certitude, directly from the *cogito,* or centered on it. The following extract from the article on the *stade du miroir* (1949) is of particular significance in this respect:

The term 'primary narcissism' by which analytical doctrine designates the libidinal cathexis proper to this moment [that of the completion of the *stade du miroir* by the identification with the *imago* of the counterpart], reveals in its discoverers [Näcke, Havelock Ellis, Freud. See: "Narcissism" (1914), *Standard Edition,* XIV, 67], as I see it, a truly profound feeling for the latencies of semantics. But semantics also clarifies the dynamic opposition of this libido to the sexual libido, which they sought to define when they invoked instincts of destruction, even the death instinct, in order to explain the evident relation of narcissistic libido to the alienating function of the *je,* to the aggressivity which arises out of it in every relation with the other, be it that of the most Samaritan kind of help.

The fact is that they touched on that existential negativity whose reality is so vividly promoted by the contemporary philosophy of being and nothingness.

But this philosophy unhappily grasps this negativity only within the limits of a self-sufficiency of consciousness, which, by the fact of being inscribed in its premises, binds to the constitutive misconstructions of the *moi,* the illusion of autonomy in which it puts its trust. Word play in the mind which, nourishing itself in singular fashion on borrowings from analytic experience, culminates in the pretension of setting up an existential psychoanalysis.

At the end of the historical enterprise of a society which now no longer recognizes in itself any but a utilitarian function, and in the anguish of the individual in the face of the concentrationary form of the social tie, the anguish whose surging forth seems to be a compensation for that effort, existentialism is judged by the justifications which it gives for the subjective impasses which in fact result from it: a liberty which never affirms itself so authentic as when within the walls of a prison, an exigency of *engagement* in which the impotence of pure consciousness to surmount any situation is expressed, a voyeur-sadistic idealization of the sexual relationship, a personality which can only realize itself in suicide, a consciousness of the other which can only be satisfied by the Hegelian murder [that is, by a refusal of the master-slave dialectic in the mutual annihilation of both one and the other].

Everything in our experience is opposed to these views, insofar as it dissuades us from conceiving the *moi* as centered on the *system perception-consciousness,* as organized by the "reality principle" in which is formulated the prejudice of scientism the most contrary to the dialectic of *connaissance* —so as to indicate to us to make our departure from the function of *méconnaissance* which characterizes the *moi* in all the structures so forcefully articulated by Miss Anna Freud: for if the *Verneinung* represents the patent form of this misconstruction, its effects will remain latent for the most part so long as they are not clarified by a gleam of light reflected on the level of fatality, where it is the *id* that manifests itself (pp. 454–55).

[4] For Lacan, the didactic analysis is far from being a simple business of learning the "rules" of a therapeutic technique; it puts the student himself in question. He uses the word "formation" in a sense very similar to the German *Bildung,* as in Hegel, or in the concept of the *Bildungsroman.* See: *La Phénoménologie de l'Esprit,* I, 165ff.; II, 50ff., particularly Hyppolite's note 14, p. 55. (*Phänomenologie,* p. 148ff; p. 350ff.) Cf. Hyppolite on *Bildung, Entaüsserung,* and *Entfremdung* in his *Genèse et Structure de la Phénoménologie de l'Esprit,* II (1946), 371ff.

[5] "Analysis of a Phobia in a Five-Year-Old Boy" (1909). *Standard Edition,* X, 5.

[6] "Psychoanalytic Notes on an Autobiographical Account of a Case of Paranoia (Dementia Paranoides)" (1911), *Standard Edition,* XII, 9.

[7] Cf. Freud, *An Autobiographical Study* (1925), *Standard Edition,* XX, 66:

I myself set a higher value on my contributions to the psychology of religion, which began with the establishment of a remarkable similarity between obsessive actions and religious practices or ritual ["Obsessive Actions and Religious Practices" (1907), *Standard Edition,* IX, 117]. Without as yet understanding the deeper connections, I described the obsessional neurosis as a distorted private religion and religion as a kind of universal obsessional neurosis.

[8] "Sens" presents difficulties. In the present context, it is not simply a question of choosing between "sense," "meaning," "direction," "feel," and so forth, but also that of maintaining the difference between *sens* and *signification.* For example:

But it is not because the enterprises of grammar and lexicology exhaust themselves at a certain limit that we must think that signification [*significa-tion*] reigns over it all alone. This would be an error.

For the signifier of its very nature invariably anticipates on the meaning [*sens*] by a sort of unfolding ahead of itself of the dimension of sense. This can be seen at the level of the sentence when it is interrupted before the significative term: 'I never . . . ,' 'It is always . . . ,' 'Again, perhaps . . . .' The sentence doesn't make any less sense, and all the more oppressively because the meaning expresses itself adequately by making one wait for it. [. . .]

As a result, one can say that it is in the chain of the signifier that the sense *insists,* but that none of its elements *consists* in the signification of which the sense is capable at that particular moment ("L'Instance de la lettre" [1957], p. 56).

Although I doubt whether Lacan always maintains an observable differ-ence between the two words, the convention has been adopted of translat-ing *signification* by "signification" and *sens* by "sense" or by "meaning," except where the best rendering seems to be something like the hendiadys of "sense and direction." *Nonsens* will be rendered "non-sense," *contre-sens* left as in the French.

[9] That is, if the subject refuses to recognize the meaning of a symptom it is quite pointless to *tell* him about it (as Freud repeatedly explains). For Lacan, cognition depends on recognition, and is necessitated by an original mis-cognition. See note 12 on *méconnaissance*.

[10] For "isolation" and "undoing what has been done" (*annulation*), both technical terms used by Freud, see "Inhibitions, Symptoms and Anxiety" (1926), *Standard Edition,* XX, especially pp. 119–20.

Both are mechanisms of defense characteristic of obsessional neurosis. In the first, after some significant but unacceptable occurrence in his life, the subject seeks to break its continuity with the rest of his existence by interpolating an isolating interval in which nothing further must hap-pen. In the second, he seeks to "blow away"—in a fashion even closer to the magical and the ceremonial—what he does not wish to accept. Both are consequently forms of *Verneinung,* or denegation.

Both were originally referred to in the case of the Rat Man: "Notes upon a Case of Obsessional Neurosis" (1909), *Standard Edition,* X, 235–36, 243, 246.

[11] I have retained the French word because it is Lacan's emendation of the usual translation of Freud's *Verneinung* as *"négation"* (for the

English, see the article "Die Verneinung" ["Negation" (1925)] in *Standard Edition,* XIX, 223). The *Verneinung* is not simply "negation," nor is it simply "denial," which in any case entails confusion with the Freudian *Verleugnung,* usually translated "denial," but which the *Standard Edition* now translates "disavowal." (See the note on p. 143 of Vol. XIX.) Freud uses *Verneinung* in the 1925 article to refer both to the concrete attitude of "no-saying" met with in experience ("You ask who this person in the dream can be. It's *not* my mother.") and to the creation of the symbol of negation, constitutive of judgment itself. See J. Hyppolite, "Commentaire parlé sur la *Verneinung* de Freud" (1956), and the introduction and commentary by Lacan. Needless to say, it is the first sense that is in question here.

[12] There is no simple equivalent for *méconnaissance* in English. It is an important term in the Lacanian vocabulary of the *moi.* The problem is to render it by terms that will bring out the sense of a "failure to appreciate," a "refusal to recognize," a "mis-cognition," and at the same time to remind the reader of its etymological affinity with *connaissance* ("knowledge," "understanding," "acquaintance with") and *reconnaissance* ("recognition," "appreciation"). Depending upon the English context, therefore, *méconnaissance* will be rendered "misconstruction" (that is, "something misconstrued") or "failure to recognize," and *méconnaître* by similar expressions.

The following passage, related to Lacan's theory of *la connaissance paranoïaque,* will illustrate Lacan's use of these terms:

Quel est donc le phénomène de la croyance délirante?—Il est, disons-nous, méconnaissance, avec ce que ce terme contient d'antinomie essentielle. Car méconnaître suppose une reconnaissance, comme le manifeste la méconnaissance systématique, où il faut bien admettre que ce qui est nié soit en quelque façon reconnu.

. . . Il me paraît clair en effet que dans les sentiments d'influence et d'automatisme, le sujet ne reconnaît pas ses propres productions comme étant siennes. C'est en quoi nous sommes tous d'accord qu'un fou est un fou. Mais le remarquable n'est-il pas plutôt qu'il ait à en connaître? et la question, de savoir ce qu'il connaît là de lui sans s'y reconnaître?

[What in fact is the phenomenon of delusional belief? It is, I insist, failure to recognize, with all that this term contains of an essential antinomy. For to fail to recognize presupposes a recognition, as is manifested in systematic failure to recognize, where it must obviously be admitted that what is denied is in some fashion recognized.

. . . It seems clear to me that in his feelings of influence and automatism, the subject does not recognize his productions as his own. It is in this respect that we all agree that a madman is a madman. But isn't the remarkable part rather that he should have to take cognizance of it? And isn't the question rather to discover what he knows about himself in these productions without recognizing himself in them?] ("Propos sur la causalité psychique" [1950], pp. 33–34.)

[13] Cf. Freud's succinct rejection of behaviorism in the posthumous *Outline of Psychoanalysis* (1940), *Standard Edition*, XXIII, 157.

[14] English in the original.

[15] English in the original.

[16] English in the original.

[17] This and the preceding paragraph were slightly modified in 1966.

[18] As noted in the Translator's Introduction, the asterisks refer to revisions made by Lacan in 1966.

[19] The reference is to "The Lice Seekers" by Rimbaud. The author in question is the French analyst Bénassy.

[20] "Give [me] a true and stable Word in my mouth and make of me a cautious tongue" (The Internal Consolation, Forty-fifth Chapter: that one must not believe everyone and of the lapses of spoken words). The French title of this chapter is "Parole vide et parole pleine dans la réalisation psychanalytique du sujet." On this notion, compare Heidegger's *Gerede* and *Rede* and Kojève's view of the *discours adéquat, Introduction à la lecture de Hegel* (1947), pp. 550f. "Idle talk" in Heidegger (*Being and Time* [1962], pp. 211–14 *et passim*) is not, however, disparaging, as the *parole vide* (the *discours imaginaire*) is for Lacan. Compare also the empty discourse of the *belle âme: Phénoménologie*, II, 189 (*Phänomenologie*, p. 462).

[21] "Always a cause" or "keep talking."

[22] The French text reads as follows:

Mais si le psychanalyste ignore qu'il en va ainsi de la fonction de la parole, il n'en subira que plus fortement l'appel, et si c'est le vide qui d'abord s'y fait entendre, c'est en lui-même qu'il l'éprouvera et c'est au delà de la parole qu'il cherchera une réalité qui comble ce vide.

Ainsi en vient-il à analyser le comportement du sujet pour y trouver ce qu'il ne dit pas. Mais pour en obtenir l'aveu, il faut bien qu'il lui en parle. Il retrouve alors la parole, mais rendue suspecte de n'avoir répondu qu'à la défaite de son silence, devant l'écho perçue de son propre néant.

[23] *Béance,* another key word, lacks any usable equivalent in English ("openness," "yawningness," "gapingness"). The following quotation from Leclaire will bring out the weaker sense in which *béance* is used in general, and also the stronger sense in which it is used by Lacan in reference to psychosis:

> If we imagine experience to be a sort of tissue, that is, taking the word literally, like a piece of cloth made of intersecting threads, we can say that repression would be represented in it by a snag or rip of some sort, perhaps even a large rent, but always something that can be darned or rewoven, whereas foreclusion [*Verwerfung*] would be represented by a *béance* of some sort, resulting from the way in which the original tissue itself was woven; foreclusion would be a sort of *'original hole,'* never capable of finding its own substance again since it had never been anything other than *'hole-substance'*; this hole can be filled, but never more than imperfectly, only by a 'patch,' to take up the Freudian term [already cited].

This reference is to "Neurosis and Psychosis" (1924), *Standard Edition,* XIX, 151: "In regard to the genesis of delusions, a fair number of analyses have taught us that the delusion is found applied like a patch over the place where originally a rent had appeared in the ego's relation to the external world."

Lacan has brought out Freud's distinction between the concept of *Verwerfung* ("rejection," "repudiation," "censure"), which he now translates *"forclusion,"* and that of "normal" neurotic repression or *Verdrängung.* In 1954 he translated it *"retranchement"* ("cutting off," "cutting out," "withdrawal") and spoke of the repression of a specific signifier (Freud's Signorelli) as "une parole retranchée" ("Introduction au commentaire de J. Hyppolite" [1956], p. 27). In relation to the concept of *béance,* it is worth noting the various meanings of the verb *verwerfen* (basically: "throw away," "throw in the wrong direction," "reject"), especially the reflexive forms meaning "to become warped," "to show a (geological) fault," *Verwerfung* itself also meaning "fault" in this sense. For *faille,* see note 116. The concept of *Verwerfung* is further referred to as "a primordial deficiency [*carence*] in the signifier" (Seminar of January, 1958, p. 293).

In 1949, Lacan expressed the concept of *béance* in a more strictly biological context, and one without particular reference to psychosis. Speaking of the "spatial capture" of the *stade du miroir* as manifested in man, he characterizes it as the effect of "an organic insufficiency of his natural reality" (man always being prematurely born in relation to other animals) and then relates it to the function of the *imago* (see passage quoted in note 106). He continues: "But this relation to nature is impaired in man by a certain dehiscence of the organism within itself, by a primordial Discord which is revealed by the signs of *malaise* and the lack of motor co-ordination of the neonatal months" ("Le Stade du miroir" [1949], p. 452).

[24] The French text reads as follows:

Mais qu'était donc cet appel du sujet au dela du vide de son dire? Appel à la vérité dans son principe, à travers quoi vacilleront les appels de besoins plus humbles. Mais d'abord et d'emblée appel propre du vide, dans la béance ambigue d'une séduction tentée sur l'autre par les moyens où le sujet met sa complaisance et où il va engager le monument de son narcissisme.

[25] Boileau, *L'Art Poétique*, I:

> *Hâtez-vous lentement; et, sans perdre courage,*
> *Vingt fois sur le métier remettez votre ouvrage:*

In Pope's translation:

> *Gently make haste, of labor not afraid*
> *A hundred times consider what you've said:*

[26] Freud does not normally use the usual German expressions for frustration (*Vereitelung, Verhinderung*). The Freudian term translated "frustration," which is obviously that in question here, is *Versagung,* which might be defined as a particular kind of denial of satisfaction or of an object *to* the subject *by* his own ego. Cf. Freud on *Versagung,* "Types of Onset of Neurosis" (1912), *Standard Edition*, XII, 231–42, especially p. 234 and the Editor's Notes.

Lacan later characterized *Versagung* as being essentially "promesse et rupture de promesse" in the seminar of January–February 1957, p. 743, and again as being a process in which the subject "goes back on his word," "gainsays himself" (*se dédire: ver-sagen*).

[27] The French text reads as follows:

Le sujet ne s'y engage-t-il pas dans une dépossession toujours plus grande de cet être de lui-même, dont, à force de peintures sincères qui n'en laissent pas moins incohérente l'idée, de rectifications qui n'atteignent pas à dégager son essence, d'étais et de défenses qui n'empêchent pas de vaciller sa statue, d'étreintes narcissiques qui se font souffle à l'animer, il finit par reconnâître que cet être n'a jamais été que son oeuvre dans l'imaginaire et que cette oeuvre déçoit en lui toute certitude. Car dans ce travail qu'il fait de la reconstruire *pour un autre,* il retrouve l'aliénation fondamentale qui la lui a fait construire *comme une autre,* et qui l'a toujours destinée à lui être dérobée *par un autre.*

Referring to the work of Charlotte Bühler on the behavior of very young children, Lacan speaks of the (paranoid) phenomenon of "transitivism" as "a veritable capture by the other" in a "primordial ambivalence which appears to us . . . 'as in a mirror,' in the sense that the subject identifies his sentiment of Self in the image of the other." "Thus, and this is essential, the first effect of the *Imago* which appears in human beings is an effect of alienation in the subject. It is in the other that the subject identifies and even senses himself at first" ("Propos sur la causalité psychique" [1950], p. 45).

Compare the following:

In order for us to come back to a more dialectical view of the analytic experience, I would say that analysis consists precisely in distinguishing the person lying on the analyst's couch from the person who is speaking. With the person listening, that makes three persons present in the analytical situation, among whom it is the rule that the question at the base in all cases of hysteria be put: Where is the *moi* of the subject? Once this is admitted, it must be said that the situation is not three-way, but four-way, since the role of dummy [*le mort*], as in bridge, is always part of the game, and so much so that if it is not taken into account, it is impossible to articulate anything of any sense whatsoever in regard to obsessional neurosis (*Actes,* p. 210).

See also Leclaire in the 1958 article on psychosis: "'*The* moi *is the locus of the Imaginary identifications of the subject.*' My intention is above all to indicate by this definition the Imaginary function of the '*moi*' (formation, deformation, information) in opposition to the symbolic character of the 'subject'" (p. 399).

For the "first person," see note 110.

28 ". . . jusqu'à l'image passivante par où le sujet se fait objet dans la parade du miroir . . . ." See the description of the child's behavior before a mirror at the beginning of the article on the *stade du miroir* (1949). "Passivation" describes the chemical process of "pickling" metal to make it ready to receive a coating, such as paint or plating.

[29] *Jouissance* has no simple English equivalent. In a less significant context, it might be translated "enjoyment," "possession," "appropriation," "right," "pleasure." Since in Lacan's view the enjoyment of possession of an object is dependent for its pleasure on others, the ambiguity of the French *jouissance* nicely serves his purpose.

[30] The words *ego, moi,* and *je* are left as in the French. The ambiguity of Freud's use of the term *das Ich* is well known, but Lacan's concept of the *moi* is essentially that of the *Idealich* or the *Ichideal*. There is a nice distinction between the ego-ideal and the ideal-ego, a distinction never methodologically clarified by Freud, and Lacan's assimilation of narcissism to identification is in the tradition of that same ambiguity. At the same time, Lacan's use of *moi* shares the *Ich*'s sense of "self," as Freud sometimes employs it, especially in the earlier works.

The concept of the *moi* which Freud demonstrated particularly in the theory of narcissism viewed as the source of all enamoration or 'falling in love' (*Verliebtheit*)—and in the technique of resistance viewed as supported by the latent and patent forms of *dénégation* (*Verneinung*)—brings out in the most precise way its function of irreality: mirage and misconstruction. He completed the concept by a genetic view which situates the *moi* clearly in the order of the Imaginary relations and which shows in its radical alienation the matrix which specifies interhuman aggressivity as essentially intrasubjective (*Actes,* p. 209).

[31] Compare the following:

. . . The subject may take pleasure in the desire of the Other. He may respond to it, or believe he is responding to it, by minting his own signs, the gifts by virtue of which he may believe himself to be loved. But the analytic attitude is designed to suspend his certitudes on this subject, and the analyst's interpretation, when the opportunity offers, is designed to show him what Lacan calls the 'vanity' of his gifts, or in other words, their regressive character. To this extent, the analytic way is that which leads towards anxiety (M. Safouan, "Le Rêve et son interprétation," *La Psychanalyse,* VIII [1964], p. 119).

[32] The allusion is to the function of the *tessera* as a token of recognition, or "password." The *tessera* was employed in the early mystery religions where fitting together again the two halves of a broken piece of pottery was used as a means of recognition by the initiates—and in Greece the *tessera* was called the *sumbolon.* Note that the central concept involved in the symbol is that of a *link,* but that Lacan views this

link as one between systems, not between terms or between terms and things. See note 80.

The allusion to Mallarmé is to a passage in his preface to René Ghil's *Traité du Verbe* (1886); it can be found in the *Oeuvres complètes* (Paris: Pléiade, 1945), pp. 368, 857.

[33] That is, the discourse of the subject being treated by the analyst under the supervision of another analyst:

... If the intermediary of the Word were not essential to the analytic structure, the supervision of an analysis by another analyst who has only a verbal relationship to that analysis would be absolutely inconceivable, whereas it is in fact one of the clearest and most fruitful modes of the analytic relation (cf. my report) (*Actes*, p. 210).

[34] That is, the analyst's "evenly suspended attention." This, or a similar expression, appears in *Standard Edition,* X, 23 ("Little Hans"); XII, 111; and XVIII, 239; and elsewhere.

[35] Compare the following:

I beg you simply to note the link which I affirm to exist between the second position [that psychoanalysis is the resolution of the symbolic exigency that Freud revealed in the unconscious and which his last topography linked so strikingly with the death instinct], the only correct one for us, and the recognition of the validity of Freud's often debated position on the death instinct. You will agree with me on this when I say that any abrogation of that part of his work is accompanied among those who pride themselves on it by a repudiation which extends all the way to Freud's basic principles, in the sense that these are the same people—and not by chance—who no longer seek anything in the subject of the analytical experience that they do not situate beyond the Word (*Actes*, pp. 207–8).

[36] The reference is to Reik's *Listening with the Third Ear.*

Cf. Freud's papers on technique, particularly *Standard Edition,* XII, 115–16:

[The different rules I have brought forward] are all intended to create for the doctor a counterpart to the 'fundamental rule of psycho-analysis' which is laid down for the patient. Just as the patient must relate everything that his self-observation can detect, and keep back all the logical and affective objections that seek to induce him to make a selection from among them, so the doctor must put himself in a position to make use of everything he is told for the purposes of interpretation and of recognizing the concealed unconscious material without substituting a censorship of his own for the selection that the patient has foregone. To put it in a formula: he must turn his own unconscious like a receptive organ towards the transmitting unconscious of the patient . . . . Just as the [telephone] receiver converts back into sound-waves the electric oscillations in the telephone line which were set up by sound waves, so the doctor's unconscious is able, from the derivatives of the unconscious which are communicated to him, to reconstruct that unconscious, which has determined the patient's free associations.

See also XII, 112.

[37] See: Breuer and Freud, "Preliminary Communication" (1893):

For we found, to our great surprise at first, that each individual hysterical symptom immediately and permanently disappeared when we had succeeded in bringing clearly to light the memory of the [traumatic] event by which it was provoked and in arousing its accompanying affect, and when the patient had described that event in the greatest possible detail and had put the affect into words. Recollection without affect almost invariably produces no result. The psychical process which originally took place must be repeated as vividly as possible; it must be brought back to its *status nascendi* and then given verbal utterance [most of this passage is italicized in the original] (*Standard Edition*, II, 6).

And further on, p. 17: "[The psychotherapeutic method] brings to an end the operative force of the idea [*Vorstellung*] which was not abreacted in the first instance, by allowing its strangulated affect to find a way out through speech [*Rede = discours*] . . . ." See also pp. 225, 288–89.

[38] "Act of becoming aware." Compare the following:

It will . . . be understood why it is as false to attribute the analytical dénouement to the *prise de conscience* as it is to be surprised at its not happening to have the power to do it. It is not a question of passing from the unconscious, plunged in obscurity, to consciousness, site of clarity, by some sort of mysterious elevator. This really *is* objectification—by which the subject ordinarily tries to avoid his responsibility—and it is here that the bully-boys of intellectualization show their intelligence by involving him in it yet again.

It is not a question of a passage into consciousness, but of a passage into the Word . . . (*Actes*, p. 206).

See also note 66.

[39] Freud's rejection of his early "intellectualist" views and the *prise de conscience* is elaborated in his papers on technique, in particular: "On Beginning the Treatment" (1913), *Standard Edition*, XII, 141–42. See also the paper on "Negation" (XIX, 233).

[40] *Verbaliser,* in its legal sense, would be the equivalent of "to write a traffic ticket." *Pandore* is a slang term for gendarme. But *verbaliser* also retains its older, pejorative sense of "to discourse at needless length" and, in a rather special technical sense, "to certify in writing."

[41] The term *verbe* will be left untranslated since it is more or less synonymous with *mot, parole, logos,* and the Logos (*le Verbe*), depending on the context—and "more or less" means precisely that it has a particular flavor of its own. The following translation of a citation from Littré may assist the reader unfamiliar with French to appreciate the usage of the term: "Your wise men, says Tertullian, agree that the *logos,* that is to say, *le verbe, la parole,* seems to be the craftsman of the universe; we believe, moreover, that the proper substance of this *verbe,* of this reason, by which God has made all things, is *l'esprit"* (Condillac). This reference to the father of the ideologists is not without particular relevance to the tradition in which Lacan is writing.

Verbe was in fact very early on reserved for religious and ecclesiastical contexts (as Lacan later points out), and as such it has remained the (poetical) "word" par excellence.

[42] It will assist the reader to take into account the several meanings of this Greek term: "word," "speech," "tale," "song," "promise," "saying," "word" (opposed to deed), "message," and in the plural: "epic poetry," "lines of verse." On this whole passage, see Hegel on the Homeric epos, *Phénoménologie,* II, 242ff., especially p. 243 (*Phänomenologie,* 570ff.).

[43] "Représentation" also means "performance" (of a play) (*Darstellung*). It also translates both the Hegelian and the Freudian *Vorstellung.* The word translated "stage" is the French *scène.*

Cf. Freud on transference: "So what he is showing us is the kernel of his intimate life history: *he is reproducing it tangibly, as though it were actually happening, instead of remembering it."* "The Question of Lay Analysis" (1926), *Standard Edition,* XX, 226. This is referred to in the next paragraph as the patient's obligation "to stage a revival of an old piece." See also: "Remembering, Repeating and Working-Through" (1914), *Standard Edition,* XII, 147.

[44] The French text reads as follows:

On peut dire dans le langage heideggerien que l'une et l'autre constituent le sujet comme *gewesend,* c'est-à-dire comme étant celui qui a ainsi été. Mais dans l'unité interne de cette temporalisation, l'étant marque la convergence des ayant été. C'est-à-dire que d'autres rencontres étant supposées depuis l'un quelconque de ces moments ayant été, il en serait issu un autre étant qui le ferait avoir été tout autrement.

Compare with Heidegger:

As authentically futural, Dasein *is* authentically as *"having been"* [*gewesen*]. Anticipation of one's uttermost and ownmost possibility [death] is coming back understandingly to one's ownmost "been." Only insofar as it is futural can Dasein *be* authentically as having been. The character of "having been" [*Gewesenheit*] arises, in a certain way, from the future (*Being and Time,* trans. Macquarrie and Robinson [1962], p. 373).

[45] Compare the following:

To tell the truth, the subject who is invited to speak in analysis doesn't demonstrate a great deal of liberty. Not that he is enchained by the rigor of his associations: no doubt they oppress him, but it is rather that they open up onto a free Word, onto a full Word which is painful to him ("La Direction de la cure" [1961], p. 179).

[46] On the "theory of deferred action," see also the "Project" of 1895 in *The Origins of Psychoanalysis* (1954), Part II, particularly Section 4 (pp. 410–13). This theory crops up constantly in Freud's early writings on psychoanalysis—for example, in the French article of 1896 referred to in Lacan's note i,—as well as throughout the case of the Wolf Man. See the editor's remarks at the end of the note cited by Lacan (*Standard Edition,* XVII, p. 45, n.1), and also the further references given at the end of the lengthy note on p. 167 in *Standard Edition,* III.

[47] See: "Le temps logique et l'assertion de certitude anticipée" (1945).

Lacan's analysis of this sophism is concerned with the psychological and temporal process involved between three hypothetical prisoners of which the first to discover whether he is wearing a black or a white patch on his back has been offered his freedom by the prison governor. The prisoners are not allowed to communicate directly. The governor has shown them three white and two black patches and has then fixed a white patch on each man's back.

Lacan analyzes the intersubjective process in which each man has to put himself in the place of the others and to gauge the correctness of his deductions through their actions in time, from the *instant du regard* to the *moment de conclure.* The first moment of the *temps pour com-*

prendre is a wait (which tells each man that no one can see two black patches), followed by a decision by each that he is white ("If I were black, one of the others would have *already* concluded that he is white, because nobody has as yet started for the door"). Then they all set off towards the door and all hesitate in a retrospective moment of doubt. The fact that they *all* stop sets them going again. This hesitation will only be repeated twice (in this hypothetically ideal case), before all three leave the prison cell together.

[48] The word-play is between "interlocution" and "interloqué."

[49] The following passages from his later writings will be of assistance in clarifying Lacan's further elaboration of this concept. In opposition to what he calls a certain "phenomenological" trend in psychoanalysis, Lacan refers to the divergence between himself and his colleague Daniel Lagache in the following terms:

[Our divergence] lies in the actual function which he confers on inter-subjectivity. For intersubjectivity is defined for him in a relation to the other[ness] of the counterpart [*l'autre du semblable*], a symmetrical relation in principle, as can be seen from the fact that Daniel Lagache sets up the formula that the subject learns to treat himself as an object through the other. My position is that the subject has to emerge from the given of the signifiers which cover him in an Other which is their transcendental locus: through this he constitutes himself in an existence where the manifestly constituting vector of the Freudian area of experience is possible: that is to say, what is called desire ("Remarque sur le rapport de Daniel Lagache" [1961], p. 119).

In the article on Merleau-Ponty in *Les Temps Modernes* (1961), Lacan points out the problematic involved in philosophizing from the primacy of the *cogito,* or from that of the *percipio:*

To put it in a nutshell, it seems to me that the 'I think,' to which it is intended that presence be reduced, continues to imply, no matter how in-determinate one may make it, all the powers of the reflection [*réflexion*] by which subject and consciousness are confounded—namely, the mirage which psychoanalytic experience places at the basis [*principe*] of the *méconnaissance* of the subject and which I myself have tried to focus on in the *stade du miroir* by concentrating it there (pp. 248–49).

The structure of intersubjectivity is further elaborated as follows:

Thus it is that if man comes to thinking the Symbolic order, it is because he is caught in it from the first in his being. The illusion that he has formed it by his consciousness results from the fact that it was by the way of a *béance* specific to his Imaginary relation to his counterpart, that he was able to enter into this order as a subject. But he was only able to make this entrance by the radical defile of the Word, the same, in fact, of which we have recognized a genetic moment in the play of the child [the *Fort! Da!* of *Beyond the Pleasure Principle*] but which, in its complete form, is reproduced each time that the subject addresses himself to the Other as absolute, that is to say, as the Other who can nullify the subject himself, in the same way as he can do for him, that is, by making himself an object in order to deceive him. This dialectic of intersubjectivity, whose use I have shown to be necessary —from the theory of transference to the structure of paranoia itself—during the past three years of my seminar at Sainte-Anne, is readily backed up by the following schema which has long been familiar to my students:

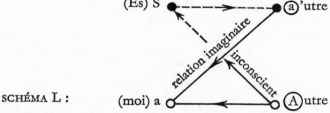

SCHÉMA L :

The two middle terms represent the coupled reciprocal Imaginary objectification which I have emphasized in the *stade du miroir"* ("Le Séminaire sur *La lettre volée* [1956], p. 9).

There is a simplified and slightly different version of the schema in the "Traitement possible de la psychose" (1958), p. 18, with the following comments:

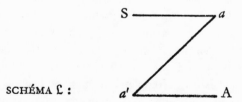

SCHÉMA £ :

This schema signifies that the condition of the subject S (neurotic or psychotic) depends on what is being unfolded in the Other A. What is being unfolded there is articulated like a discourse (the unconscious is the discourse of the Other)—a discourse whose syntax Freud first sought to define for those fragments of it which come to us in certain privileged moments, dreams, slips of the tongue or pen, flashes of wit.

How would the subject be an interested party in this discourse, if he were not taking part? He is one, in fact, in that he is drawn to the four corners of the schema, which are: *S*, his ineffable and stupid existence; *a*, his objects; *a'*, his *moi*—that is, what is reflected of his form in his objects; and *A*, the locus from which the question of his existence may be put to him.

The rest of this article is given over to an analysis of the Schreber case, accompanied by a topological transformation of the schema seeking to represent the distortion of the psychotic's relation to others and to reality.

See also Leclaire in the 1958 article on psychosis, pp. 399f., where *a* and *a'* are explicitly the *moi*'s of *S* and *A*, and the axes *S—A* and *a—a'* are, explicitly, the Symbolic axis and the Imaginary axis, respectively.

For Freud's " 'defile' of consciousness" see: "The Psychotherapy of Hysteria" (1895), *Standard Edition*, II, 291.

[50] On the theoretical background of the preceding remarks, see the posthumous *Outline of Psychoanalysis* (1940), *Standard Edition*, XXIII, 144, especially pp. 157ff., where it is a question of the representation of the *lacunae* in the "broken sequences" of consciousness, as well as of the *prise de conscience*. Cf. also p. 177: "For a patient never forgets again what he has experienced in the form of transference; it carries a greater force of conviction than anything he can acquire in other ways."

[51] "La pensée inconsciente." The *sit venia verbo* ("let the word be pardoned") occurs in the analysis of the Wolf Man (XVII, 84), where the expression in question is rendered "an unconscious concept."

[52] One immediately recognizes in this passage a whole series of allusions to the Freudian metaphors about the unconscious, as Lacan mentions in the next paragraph. One recognizes the metaphor of the ancient city undergoing excavation through various layers: that of the somatic compliance of the hysterical symptom, which may exhibit the condensation and displacement to be found in language and which "joins in the conversation" (*mitsprechen*), as Freud put it; that of Freud's view that resonances of unconscious meanings and linguistic relationships from a mythical earlier time are exhibited in the language of dreams; that of the double inscription. Moreover, we are reminded of Freud's constant recourse to the myth and to the fairy tale as exhibiting universal structures or as serving as representatives in the subject's discourse—the whole analysis of the Wolf Man revolves around the attempted integration of a fable by the subject into his own history—as well as to the personal or individual myth of the subject, normal, neurotic, or psy-

chotic. And lastly, there is the instance of "secondary revision" and of the *Entstellungen* ("distortions") in the dream and in the symptom, where the subject, unbeknownst to himself, seeks to "make it all make better sense"—notably after the topographical regression to perception in the dream, the fundamental meaning being finally restored only by the putting into words of the "images" (the thing presentations) and their assumption by the subject's discourse in the dream text, where the dialectical working through of associations enables the subject to provide himself (unconsciously at first) with the exegesis of his own dream (or symptom).

[53] The relationship made by Lacan between metaphor (condensation) and the symptom, and that between metonymy (displacement) and desire, is elaborated in the notes to Chaper II (for example, note 67) and dealt with in further detail in the essay following these notes. In 1953 Lacan did not make the later distinction between metaphor and metonymy.

Freud first came to recognize the mechanism of condensation (*Verdichtung*) in the simple fact that the dream itself is much shorter and much more compressed than its verbal representation (the dream text). Dreams are "laconic," as is the dream text itself in relation to its later interpretation. Condensation represents the "nodal point" (*Knotenpunkt*) of the dream and will be like a railroad switch in the dream work, always allowing multiple interpretations (overdetermination).

After noting that it is impossible ever to know whether a dream has been fully interpreted, Freud goes on to the use of words in dreams: "The work of condensation in dreams is seen at its clearest when it handles words and names. It is true in general that words are frequently treated in dreams as though they were things, and for that reason they are apt to be combined in just the same way as thing presentations" (*Interpretation of Dreams, Standard Edition*, IV, 295–96).

Freud often employs the related concepts of "password" and "switchword" in his analyses of symptoms and dreams. In the *Psychopathology of Everyday Life* and the work on jokes, condensation is revealed to be essential to the joke, the forgetting of words, slips of the tongue or pen, and so forth.

Displacement (*Verschiebung*) is less clearly defined. It is a form of distortion (*Entstellung*) and "indirect representation" in dreams, in respect of both words and images. The censorship will displace the center of the dream onto objects or words of minor importance, and thus reveal its latent content. Displacement in dreams, for Freud, not only covers any kind of "diversion from a train of thought but every sort of indirect representation as well," including "substitution by a piece of symbolism, or an analogy, or something small" (*Jokes and the Unconscious, Standard Edition,* VIII, 171). In this context (the context of presentations), he also employs the term *Verschiebungersatz:* "displacement-substitute." Connected with the concept of displacement in his early writings are a number of other terms, including "dislodge" (*dislozieren*), "transpose" (*transponieren*), and *Uebertragung* itself ("transference," "translation") in the usual nontechnical German sense, as well as concepts involving "false connections" and "conversion."

In mental illness itself, displacement as a mode of symptom formation is one of Freud's earliest methodological terms, referring to the transfer of a "quantity of affect" from one presentation to another, or from a presentation to the body itself (hysteria). This mechanism is especially evident in obsessional neurosis.

[54] ". . . au for interne comme au for extérieur."

In the paragraphs which follow, the reader should consider what Lacan has just said about the domain of the metaphor, as well as keeping in mind the Freudian metaphors translated as the "primal scene" and the "other scene" (the dream).

[55] English in the original.

[56] "There are people who would never have been in love, if they had never heard talk of love" (Maxim CXXXVI, Garnier ed.).

[57] "From the History of an Infantile Neurosis" (1918), *Standard Edition,* XVII, 46, 102, 110–11, 118.

[58] "Une vérité de La Palice" is a self-evident truth, a truism.

[59] "Le discours de l'autre." After 1955, this "autre" is more precisely "l'Autre." See note 49 and Lacan's note j added in 1966.

In the "Subversion du sujet et dialectique du désir" (1966), Lacan clarified the "de" as to be read in the sense of the Latin *de* (objective determination): *"de Alio in oratione* (to complete the phrase: *tua res agitur*)" (*Ecrits,* p. 814).

[60] English in the original.

[61] This incident is described at the end of Lecture XXX of the *New Introductory Lectures* (1933), *Standard Edition,* XXII, following the analysis of the "Forsyte" incident alluded to in the first part of this sentence. This last is the "third case" omitted (as a result of Freud's unconscious resistance to the occult) from the article "Psychoanalysis and Telepathy" (1941 [1921]), XVIII, 177–93.

[62] The orientation of psychoanalysis after World War II, both in England and in the United States, had especially concentrated on the countertransference (of the analyst onto the patient), that is to say, on the two-way or dual nature of transference (first mentioned by Freud in 1910). See, for instance: Michael Balint, "Changing Therapeutical Aims and Techniques in Psycho-analysis," *International Journal of Psycho-Analysis* (1950), XXXI, 117.

[63] The French text reads as follows:

. . . ce qui se détache comme psychologie à l'état brut de l'expérience commune (qui ne se confond avec l'expérience sensible que pour le professionel des idées)—à savoir dans quelque suspension du quotidien souci, l'étonnement surgi de ce qui apparie les êtres dans un disparate passant celui des grotesques d'un Léonard ou d'un Goya—ou la surprise qu'oppose l'épaisseur propre d'une peau à la caresse d'une paume qu'anime la découverte sans que l'émousse encore le désir—ceci, peut-on dire, est aboli dans une expérience, revêche à ces caprices, rétive à ces mystères.

[64] This is the phrase employed by the chorus in the macaronic Latin of the burlesqued ceremony which closes Molière's *Le Malade Imaginaire.* The example is a real one. The allusion to Plato is to the *Sophist,* 249b.

[65] "Des elements signifiants." "The dream-work follows the laws of the signifier." "The unconscious is not the primordial, nor the instinctual, and elementarily it is acquainted only with the elements of the signifier" ("L'Instance de la lettre" [1957], pp. 65, 74). As Lacan points out elsewhere, the dream is not the unconscious, but rather what Freud called the "royal road" to the unconscious, the latter being revealed not by the manifest text of the dream as such, but by the *lacunae* latent within it.

Cf. Freud: "The Unconscious" (1915), *Standard Edition,* XIV, 167:

All these conscious acts [parapraxes, dreams, symptoms, obsessions, ideas that "come into our head we do not know from where"] remain *disconnected* and unintelligible if we insist upon claiming that every mental act that occurs in us must also necessarily be experienced by us through consciousness; on the other hand they fall into a demonstrable connection if we *interpolate between them* the unconscious acts which we have inferred.

[66] Cf. Freud: "The Claims of Psycho-Analysis to Scientific Interest" (1913), *Standard Edition*, XIII, 177:

If we reflect that the means of representation in dreams are principally visual images [*Bilden*] and not words, we shall see that it is even more appropriate to compare dreams with a system of writing than with a language. In fact the interpretation of dreams is completely analogous to the decipherment of an ancient pictographic script such as Egyptian hieroglyphs. In both cases there are certain elements which are not intended to be interpreted (or read, as the case may be) but are only designed to serve as 'determinatives,' that is to establish the meaning of some other element.

For the specific reference of this passage of Lacan's (and for Freud's use of the metaphor of the rebus), see *Standard Edition*, IV, 277–78.

The reader will note the relationship, in Freud's own system of metaphors, between the "double inscription" (*Niederschrift*), as a means of accounting for the coexistence of conscious and repressed ideas, and the reference to hieroglyphs (*Bilderschriften*).

These passages should be read with the later analysis of the topographical regression in the dream from the dream-thoughts to visual images (the *Rücksicht auf Darstellbarkeit*, or "concern for representability") where Freud makes the distinction between "word presentations" (*Wortvorstellungen*) and "thing presentations" (*Sachvorstellungen* or *Dingvorstellungen*) and where these two types of *Vorstellungen* are used in relating the dream-language to the language of schizophrenia. This "backward course, through the *Ucs.* to perception" is discussed in the "Metapsychological Supplement to the Theory of Dreams" (1917), *Standard Edition*, XIV, 222–35. This paper was written at the same time as the article "The Unconscious" (1915), *Standard Edition*, XIV, 166–204, where the following passage occurs, part of which is quoted by Leclaire and Laplanche in their structural analysis of the two modes of representation in their article on the unconscious:

What we have permissibly called the conscious presentation [*Vorstellung*] of the object can now be split up into the presentation of the *word* and the presentation of the *thing* . . . . We now seem to know all at once what the difference is between a conscious and an unconscious presentation. The two are not, as we supposed, different registrations of the same content in different psychical localities, nor yet different functional states of cathexis [*Beset-*

zung] in the same locality; but the conscious presentation comprises the presentation of the thing plus the presentation of the word belonging to it, while the unconscious presentation is the presentation of the thing alone . . . . Now, too, we are in a position to state precisely what it is that repression denies to the rejected presentation in the transference neuroses: what it denies to the presentation is translation into words which shall remain attached to the object. A presentation which is not put into words, or a psychical act which is not hypercathected, remains thereafter in the *Ucs.* in a state of repression (pp. 201–2).

Lacan takes up the whole question of representation in greater detail in "L'Instance de la lettre" (1957), where he also deals with the hieroglyphic "determinatives."

[67] Lacan elaborates on his use of the concepts of metaphor and metonymy and explains the algorithmic representation he uses, in "L'Instance de la lettre" (1957) and "La Direction de la cure" (1961).

Metonymy represents the connection of "word to word" (*mot à mot*) in the signifying chain, or the combination of signifier to signifier (S . . . S'), and represents the subject's desire; metaphor—the substitution of "one word for another one" in which the first signifier is occulted and falls to the level of the signified while retaining its metonymic connection with the rest of the chain—represents the symptomatic passage across the bar of the Lacanian algorithm $\left(\dfrac{S'}{S}\right)$. The articles in question should be consulted, but in the first, basing his elaboration on the *Traumdeutung,* Lacan proceeds as follows:

Entstellung, translated *transposition* ["distortion" in English], where Freud demonstrates the general precondition of the dream, is what I designated earlier in this article, following Saussure, as the *glissement* [sliding] of the signified under the signifier, always in action (unconscious action, let it be noted) in the discourse.

But the two aspects of the incidence of the signifier over the signified are to be found again in it.

Verdichtung, condensation, is the structure of the superimposition of the signifiers in which the field of the metaphor is found, and whose name, condensing within itself the word *Dichtung* [poetry], indicates the natural affinity of the mechanism to poetry, to the point that this mechanism envelops the traditional function proper to poetry.

Verschiebung, or displacement: this transfer [*virement*] of signification demonstrated by metonymy is closer to the German term. From its first appearance in Freud, displacement is represented as the most appropriate means used by the unconscious to foil the censorship.

What is it that distinguishes these two mechanisms, which play such a privileged role in the dream-work (*Traumarbeit*), from their homologous function in the discourse? Nothing, except a condition imposed upon the signifying material, called *Rücksicht auf Darstellbarkeit* ["considerations of representability"], which is to be translated: concern for the means of the *mise en scène* . . . (p. 64).

[And later:] . . . It is the connection of signifier to signifier which permits the elision through which the signifier installs the lack of being in the object relation, by using the power of 'reference back' of signification in order to invest it with the desire aimed at this lack which it supports (p. 68).

See the *Interpretation of Dreams, Standard Edition,* IV, 279–338, notably p. 308; and V, 339–49; 506–7.

Freud brings out the sense of *Entstellung* as meaning "to put something in another place," "to displace," in *Moses and Monotheism* (1939), *Standard Edition,* XXIII, 43.

⁶⁸ In 1946 Lacan paraphrased Hegel as follows:

The very desire of man, [Hegel] tells us, is constituted under the sign of mediation; it is desire to make its desire recognized. It has for its object a desire, that of the other, in the sense that there is no object for man's desire which is constituted without some sort of mediation—which appears in his most primitive needs: for example, even his food has to be prepared—and which is found again throughout the development of satisfaction from the moment of the master-slave conflict throughout the dialectic of labor ("Propos sur la causalité psychique" [1950], p. 45).

See also the first chapter of Kojève's *Introduction à la lecture de Hegel* (1947).

In the "Direction de la cure" (1961), Lacan summarizes his remarks on the nature of desire:

One of the principles which follow from these premises is that:
—if desire is an effect in the subject of that condition which is imposed on him by the existence of the discourse, to make his need pass through the defiles of the signifier;
—if on the other hand . . . , by opening up the dialectic of transference, we must ground the notion of the Other with a big O as being the locus of the deployment of the Word (the other scene, *eine andere Schauplatz,* of which Freud speaks in the *Traumdeutung*);
—it must be posited that, as a facet of an animal at the mercy of Language, man's desire is desire of the Other.

This formulation is aimed at quite another function than that of the primary identification [with objects—see note 183] mentioned earlier in this article, for it is not a question of the assumption by the subject of the *insignia* of the other, but rather the condition that the subject has to find the constituting structure of his desire in the same *béance* opened up by the effect of the signifiers in those who come [through transference] to represent the Other for him, insofar as his demand is subjected to them (p. 190).

For some further remarks on the dialectic of desire, and concerning its relation to need and to demand, see notes 143 and 183; for the *andere Schauplatz* (a remark of Fechner's) see: *Standard Edition,* IV, 48; V, 536; and Letter 83 (1898) in *The Origins of Psychoanalysis* (1954).

For further clarification, see the "Subversion du sujet" (1966), especially p. 814. The "de" is a subjective genitive—that is, man desires insofar as he is Other. Man's ignorance (*nescience*) of his desire is "less ignorance of what he demands, which can after all be defined or limited, than ignorance of *whence* he desires."

[69] *Standard Edition,* VI (1901). See in particular Lacan's commentary on the repression of the signifier "Signorelli," the first parapraxis in the text, in the introduction to the *Verneinung* articles (1956), pp. 27–28, and Freud's structural representation of the mechanism in the article "The Psychical Mechanism of Forgetfulness" (1898), *Standard Edition,* III, 287, which is reproduced again in the *Psychopathology of Everyday Life* (p. 5). Freud reported the incident to Fliess in Letter 96 of the *Origins of Psychoanalysis* (1954).

See also the seminar of November, 1957, pp. 295–96, and "La Psychanalyse et son enseignement" (1957), p. 75, for further comments on the forgetting of "Signorelli."

[70] Compare the following:

Symptoms of conversion, inhibition, anguish, these are not there to offer you the opportunity to confirm their nodal points, however seductive their topology may be; it is a question of untying these knots, and this means to return them to the Word function that they hold in a discourse whose signification determines their use and sense (*Actes,* p. 206).

The letter of the message is the important thing here. In order to grasp it, one must stop an instant at the fundamentally equivocal character of the Word, insofar as its function is as much to hide as to uncover . . . . It is this [division into the different parts of an] orchestral score inherent in the ambiguity of Language which alone explains the multiplicity of the ways of access to the secret of the Word. The fact remains that there is only one text where it is possible to read what the Word says and what it does not say, and that it is to this text that the symptoms are connected just as intimately as is a rebus to the sentence it represents.

For some time now there has been utter confusion between the multiple ways of access to the deciphering of this sentence, and what Freud calls the overdetermination of the symptoms which represent it (*Actes,* p. 207).

Freud is as a matter of fact too coherent in his thinking to consider that [this] overdetermination . . . actually enters into a present conflict insofar as this conflict reproduces an old conflict of a sexual nature; and the support—which is not adventitious—of an organic *béance* (some lesional stimulus or somatic compliance) or of an Imaginary one (fixation) would have appeared to him as something other than a verbal loophole to be scorned, if in these circumstances it were not a question of the structure which unites the signifier to the signified in Language (*Actes,* p. 207).

What the linguistic conception which must form the worker from the beginning will teach him, is to look for the symptom to provide proof of its function as a signifier—that is, proof of what distinguishes it from the 'natural indicator' that the same term currently designates in medicine ("La Chose freudienne" [1956], p. 238).

The psychoanalyzable symptom, whether normal or pathological, is distinct not only from the diagnostic 'indicator,' but also from every distinguishable form of pure expressivity, in the sense that it is sustained by a structure which is identical to the structure of Language. And by this, I do not mean a structure to be situated in some sort of so-called generalized semiology drawn from the limbo of its periphery, but the structure of Language as it manifests itself in the languages which I might call positive, those which are actually spoken by the mass of human beings ("La Psychanalyse et son enseignement" [1957], p. 72).

Speaking of the two registers of the signifier and the signified— "register" designating "two chained-sequences taken in their globality" which are related as system to system (in the mathematical sense of group theory) and not as term to term—Lacan continues:

Thus it is that if the symptom can be read, it is because it is already itself inscribed in a process of writing. Insofar as a particular formation of the unconscious, it is not a signification, but its relation to a signifying structure which determines it. If I may be permitted a play on words, I would say that it is always a question of the agreement of the subject with the *verbe*. (*Ibid.,* p. 73).

[71] *Jokes and Their Relation to the Unconscious* (*Der Witz und seine Beziehung zum Unbewussten*) (1905), *Standard Edition,* VIII.

[72] "Witty phrase," or "conceit."

[73] "Perle" is used colloquially for "goof," "howler." The metaphor of the promenade, the defile, and the garden is one applied by Freud to the plan of the *Traumdeutung,* an "imaginary walk" through the wood of the authorities, "who cannot see the trees," out into the open through the defiles of his analysis of the dream. See Letter 114 in *The Origins of Psycho-Analysis* (1954), or *Standard Edition,* IV, p. 122, editor's note.

[74] *Standard Edition,* VIII, 106: "Anyone who has allowed the truth to slip out in an unguarded moment is in fact glad to be free of pretence."

[75] *Standard Edition,* VIII, 105: "Thus jokes can also have a subjective determinant of this kind. . . . It declares that only what I allow to be a joke *is* a joke."

[76] The difficulty of translating the word *esprit,* which covers most of both *Witz* and *Geist,* is well known, but in this passage it becomes an insoluble problem. I have chosen to translate it by the least objectionable term, "spirit," except in the quotation from Freud in which the word *Witz* is used in the German, and in the expression *esprit libre* ("mind free from care").

The substance of the passage on *l'esprit* is as follows:

. . . et le visage qu'il nous révèle est celui même de l'esprit dans l'ambiguïté que lui confère le langage, où l'autre face de son pouvoir régalien est la 'pointe' par qui son ordre entier s'anéantit en un instant,—pointe en effet où son activité créatrice dévoile sa gratuité absolue, où sa domination sur le réel s'exprime dans le défi du non-sens, où l'humour, dans la grâce méchante de l'esprit libre, symbolise une vérité qui ne dit pas son dernier mot. [. . .]

Ici tout est substance, tout est perle. L'esprit qui vit en exilé dans la création dont il est l'invisible soutien, sait qu'il est maître à tout instant de l'anéantir. [. . .]

C'est la vérité en effet, qui dans sa bouche jette là le masque, mais c'est pour que l'esprit en prenne un plus trompeur, la sophistique qui n'est que stratagème, la logique qui n'est là qu'un leurre, le comique même qui ne va là qu'à éblouir. L'esprit est toujours ailleurs. 'L'esprit comporte en effet une telle conditionnalité subjective . . . : n'est esprit que ce que j'accepte comme tel,' poursuit Freud qui sait de quoi il parle.

[77] The French text reads as follows:

Nulle part l'intention de l'individu n'est en effet plus manifestement dépassée par la trouvaille du sujet,—nulle part la distinction que nous faisons de l'un à l'autre ne se fait mieux comprendre,—puisque non seulement il faut que quelque chose m'ait été étranger dans ma trouvaille pour que j'y aie mon plaisir, mais qu'il faut qu'il en reste ainsi pour qu'elle porte.

78 The French text reads as follows:

Ceci prenant sa place de la necessité, si bien marquée par Freud, du tiers auditeur toujours supposé, et du fait que le mot d'esprit ne perd pas son pouvoir dans sa transmission au style indirect. Bref pointant au lieu de l'Autre l'ambocepteur qu'éclaire l'artifice du mot fusant dans sa suprême alacrité.

The first sentence was modified in 1966, and the last sentence replaces that in the original text. An amboceptor, a medical entity, has a double affinity for opposites.

For the "third person" see *Jokes and the Unconscious, Standard Edition,* VIII, 140–58 ("Jokes as a Social Process"); 173; 179–80.

79 Compare the following:

Setting off from the action of the Word in that it is what grounds man in his authenticity, or seizing it in the original and absolute position of the 'In the beginning was the Word [*le Verbe*] . . . of the Fourth Gospel, with which Faust's 'In the beginning was the action' cannot be in contradiction, since this action of the *Verbe* is coextensive with it and renews its creation every day—this is to go straight along both routes, beyond the phenomenology of the *alter ego* in Imaginary alienation, to the problem of the mediation of an Other [who is] not second when the One *is* not yet (*Actes,* p. 203).

The *alter ego* is the *autre du semblable* referred to in note 49, the "counterpart whose image captures and supports us" (Seminar of April–June 1958, p. 252).

Compare also:

Who is this other to whom I am more attached than to my[self], since at the most profound level of approbation of my identity to myself, it is he who agitates me?

His presence can only be understood at a second degree of otherness, which therefore situates him in a position of mediation in relation to my own doubling, in relation to my division from myself as from a counterpart ("L'Instance de la lettre" [1957], p. 77).

80 This passage abounds in allusions to the Greek terms from which *parole* and *symbole* are derived. Although etymologies are notoriously false friends and although they are often abused, a few references may clarify Lacan's apparent intent.

Parole and *symbole,* as is well known, are derived from the same root verb, "to throw," the two compounds meaning literally "to throw towards," "to throw besides," and "to throw with." The verb *sumballo* means "to meet," "to unite," "to join," "to make a contract," "to lend," "to contribute," "to join (battle)," and, with *logous* understood, "to converse" (or so say Liddell and Scott). Lacan has already referred to the function of the Word as a *tessera* or "token of recognition," even "password" (see note 32), and he refers it explicitly—and in a wider context—to the etymology of *symbole* in the "Introduction au commentaire de J. Hyppolite" (1956), p. 28. (Cf. also Freud's use of the expression "verbal bridge" and *Passwort* in the case of the Rat Man, *Standard Edition,* X, 213, 318.)

The noun *sumbolon,* with its associated forms, has a wide variety of meanings. In a legal sense, it is used in the plural to refer to covenants or pacts entered into by states for the protection of commerce. In a religious context, it came to refer to the distinctive Credo or confession of faith of the early Christians. In its widest sense ("the sign or token by which one infers a thing"), Euripides uses it to refer to marks on the body (recognition of Orestes); Galen employs it for "symptom." It has also the sense of "seal," "signet" (*sceau*), "impression in wax," "insignia."

Sophocles uses *sumbolaion* in the plural for "symptom"; the general sense of the term is that of a debtor's note or contract. The feminine form, *sumbolē,* "meeting," is also used in contexts where it would be translated "knotting," "twisting together," "bond" (*noeud*), "intercourse," and in a rather specific sense "contribution to a common meal or feast," which might be referred to the *potlatch.*

Compare C. S. Peirce on the symbol in his writings on semiosis—for example, "Logic as Semiotic: The Theory of Signs" in: *The Philosophy of Peirce,* pp. 112–15. For the specific psychoanalytical reference of these terms, see: Rosolato, "Le Symbolique" (1959).

The verb *paraballo,* with its derivatives, has a similar network of meanings: "to hold out as bait," "throw towards," "set beside," "entrust to," "approach," "meet," "cross over," "go by sea," and, in the middle voice, "to deceive." Various derivatives have the sense of "thrown to or besides," "venturesome," "deceitful."

It is worth remarking that "Danaoi" echoes the network of words derived from the root "da" ("give," "share," even "lend"). The "Argonautes pacifiques" suggests the title of Malinowski's book: *Argonauts of the Western Pacific*.

If Language is a process of the degradation of the symbol into the sign, and if the symbol "manifests itself first of all as the murder of the thing," this death constituting in the subject "the eternalization of his desire"—which takes us back to the conjecture of Freud in 1914: "things that are symbolically connected today were probably united in prehistoric times by conceptual and linguistic identity" (*The Interpretation of Dreams* [1900], *Standard Edition*, V, 352)—then the poetic intuition of Schiller, quoted by Freud in a different but more heavily symbolic context (*Moses and Monotheism* [1939], *Standard Edition*, XXIII, 101) is perhaps of relevance here:

> Was unsterblich im Gesang soll Leben,
> Muss im Leben untergehn.

> ["What is to live immortal in song must perish in life,"]

The anthropological echoes in these two paragraphs, as Lacan notes, are derived in part from Maurice Leenhardt's *Do Kamo: La personne et le mythe dans le monde mélanésien* (1947), which is referred to by Lacan as "sometimes confused" but "highly suggestive" (*Actes,* p. 246).

In the two chapters referred to ("La parole" and "La parole constructive," pp. 164–97), Leenhardt deals with the Melanesian concepts *no* and *ewekë,* in the Houailou and Lifou languages, respectively, translated by the natives themselves as *parole* and later, after missionaries introduced them to the New Testament, by *verbe*. The native words cover a vast range of concepts including "thought," "act," "action," and "discourse," all of which are fundamentally related to the myth, to the structure of society, and to the being of the native himself. (He and all living beings considered to be human, or to have an element of humanity, are *kamo*.)

. . . The gift carries in itself its signification, and the declaration that accompanies it in many a ritual is a non-essential act. One often sees pieces of *balassor* [a type of bark] folded like remnant pieces at the fabric counter of a store. These are offered on the occasion of births and deaths. They are the body of the message: the object and the sense of this message are made more precise by means of a symbolic palm-branch laid across the *balassor* at the time of the presentation. And this branch is called: the 'indicating stem' of the *balassor*. It explicates the message, but the message is entirely in the bark-cloth itself whose fibres are the symbol of the fibres of all beings.

The discourse which supports these gifts is an extraneous addition. It may be poetic; it is itself another gift, not an offering but a homage. However, the *parole, no,* is not this discourse, but the *balassor* itself and its stem (p. 167).

In reference to *ewekë,* whose use complements and overlaps that of *no,* Leenhardt states:

All that belongs to man is *ewekë,* his eloquence, the object he fashions, what he creates, what he possesses in his own right, his work, his speech, his goods, his garden, his wife, his psychic health, his sex. All this is *parole* . . . .
. . . The two terms clearly translate what the Melanesian understands by *parole:* the manifestation of a being, or of an existent, if the word 'being' appears too precise; the manifestation of the human, in all its aspects, from pyschic life to work done by the hands and to the expression of thought. This is an indication of the little differentiation established between being and thing. But the thing can be substance or object, it can be no more than a detached, but essential, part of him to whom it belongs. From this point of view, the *parole* is an object. This object comes forth from man, and man finds his support in it. And without this object, man goes astray and the group falls apart (pp. 172–73).

Before the coming of the white man, the Caledonians employed the word *êvië* for gift, meaning "friendship-gift"—to give was to give of oneself in order to establish a reciprocal correspondence with the other. The term was replaced after some years of white administration by *apo,* a corruption of *impôt,* "tax" (p. 147).

The title *do kamo,* which refers to the native who has "evolved" from the predominantly "mythical" to the predominantly "rational" mentality under the pressure of economic and religious influences—*kamo* no longer being sufficient to express what he feels himself to be—is translated by the author: "man in his authenticity" (p. 10), "truly human" (p. 38). The native who is able to detach himself from the "personage" whose "self" has no existence for him apart from the circle of relationships in which he is constituted as a locus—invariably as part of a duality—in other words, the native who no longer confuses the first and third person, who can say "I" and who can distinguish the figure "one," who knows the difference "between me and thee," who has become a person without becoming an "individual," says: "*Go do kamo:* I am real person" (p. 219).

Referring to the work of Cassirer and to Leenhardt's "Ethnologie de la parole," Lévi-Strauss summarizes: ". . . It is evident from this that the conception of the Word as *verbe,* as power and as action, certainly represents a universal trait of human thought" (*Les Structures élémentaires de la parenté* [1949], p. 613).

Leenhardt had translated the New Testament into Houailou in 1922.

[81] Compare the following:

The *signal* does not go beyond the level of *communication:* its function is to be perceived, without entailing a search for signification, the anticipation of its message offering only a restricted amount of free play, of a binary type: the presence or absence, affirmation or negation, positive or negative (for example, the password, a red light, the tilt light on a pinball machine, a white flag) (Rosolato, "Le Symbolique" [1959], p. 226).

[82] English in the original.

[83] English in the original.

[84] English in the original.

[85] Compare the following:

The first network, that of the signifier, is the synchronic structure of the material of Language insofar as each element takes on in it its exact usage as being different from the others; this is the principle of distribution which alone regulates the function of the elements of the language at its different levels, from the phonemic pair of oppositions to compound expressions of which the task of the most modern research is to disengage its stable forms.

The second network, that of the signified, is the diachronic set of concretely pronounced discourses, which set reacts historically on the first, in the same way in which the structure of the latter governs the paths of the second. Here what dominates is the unity of signification which establishes itself as never becoming resolved into a pure indication of the Real, but always as referring to another signification. This is to say that if the significations 'grasp' the things, it is only by constituting their set by enveloping it in the signifier; and that if their web always covers this set enough to overflow it, it is because the set of the signifier is not a signification of anything. This point confirms that Language is never signal, but always dialectical movement ("La Chose freudienne" [1956], p. 235).

'What link do you make,' I heard myself asked, 'between that instrument of Language, whose given data man must accept every bit as much as those of the Real, and that grounding function which you say is the function of the Word insofar as it constitutes the subject in an intersubjective relation?'

I reply: in making Language the intermediary in which to set the analytic experience to rights, it is not the sense of means implied by this term that I emphasize, but that of locus . . . .

I add that it is from the point of view of the notion of communication that I deliberately orient my conception of Language; its function as expression, as far as I know, was mentioned only once in my report.

Let me therefore say precisely what Language signifies in what it communicates: it is neither signal, nor sign, nor even sign of the thing insofar as the thing is an exterior reality. The relation between signifier and signified is entirely enclosed in the order of Language itself, which completely conditions its two terms.

Let us examine the term signifier first of all. It is constituted by a set of material elements linked by a structure of which I shall indicate presently the extent to which it is simple in its elements, or even where one can situate its point of origin. But, even if I have to pass for a materialist, it is on the fact that it is a question of material that I shall insist first of all, and in order to emphasize, in this question of locus which we are discussing, the place occupied by this material. This is with the sole purpose of destroying the mirage which by a process of elimination seems to assign to the human brain the locus of the phenomenon of language. Well, where could it be then? Replying for the signifier: 'everywhere else.' [Lacan then mentions modern communication theory which has given to the reduction of the signifier into nonsignifying units (Hartley units) the "scientific" status of use in industry, and then to the "frozen words" of Rabelais, which anticipate the "two pounds or so of signifier" rolled up in the recorder in front of him.]

Let us move on to the signified. If it is not the thing, as I told you, what is it then? Precisely the sense. The discourse which I am delivering to you here . . . is concerned with an experience common to all of us, but you will estimate its value insofar as it communicates to you the sense of that experience, and not the experience itself . . . .

And this sense, where is it? The correct reply here, 'nowhere,' if opposed —when it is a question of the signified—to the correct reply that suited the signifier, will not disappoint my questioner any the less, if he expected in it something approaching the 'denomination of things.' For, besides the fact that no 'part of speech' has the privilege of such a function, contrary to the grammatical appearances which attribute this function to the substantive, meaning is never capable of being sensed except in the uniqueness of the signification developed by the discourse.

Thus it is that interhuman communication is always information on information, put to the test of a community of Language, a numbering and a perfecting of the target which will surround the objects, themselves born of the concurrence of a primordial rivalry.

No doubt that the discourse is concerned with things. It is in fact in this encounter that from realities they become things. It is so true that the word is not the sign of the thing, that the word tends to become the thing itself. But it is only insofar as it abandons the sense . . . .

If someone should oppose me with the traditional view that it is the definition that gives a word its meaning, I would not say no: after all it was not I who said that every word presupposes by its use the entire discourse of the dictionary . . . —or even that of all the texts of a given language (*Actes,* pp. 242–44).

[86] "L'ordre symbolique" or "le symbolique" is to be distinguished from "la symbolique" (*die Symbolik*):

La symbolique, descriptive 'science,' enumerates signs and compares them in order to constitute the keys to dreams, to make inventories of myths, to arrange the repertories of esthetic qualities, to set up heraldries. Paradoxically, it neglects the Symbol, in its characters (Rosolato, "Le Symbolique" [1959], p. 226).

The symbol is that transmuted sign ["giving access to *le Symbolique,*" Rosolato's note] which comprises a *network* of relations between signifiers and signifieds, themselves, by this fact, plurivalent. This entails the consequence that the Symbolic does not take into account "some-thing," nor does it represent (*Ibid.,* p. 225).

Cf. *The Interpretation of Dreams* (1900), *Standard Edition,* V, 350–404, where the material added from 1909 to 1925, mainly as a result of the influence of Stekel, sets forth Freud's theory of a fixed symbolic code.
Compare the following:

The concepts of psychoanalysis are to be grasped in a field of Language, and its domain extends to the point that a function used as an apparatus of display [*une fonction d'appareil*], a mirage of consciousness, a segment of the body or of its image, a social phenomenon, a metamorphosis of the symbols themselves can serve as signifying material for what the unconscious subject has to signify.
This is the essential order in which psychoanalysis is situated, and I shall call it henceforth the Symbolic order (*Actes,* p. 206).

It remains to say that, apart from the case of living species, from which Aristotle's logic takes its support [in the] Real, and whose link to nomination is already sufficiently indicated in the Book of Genesis, all reification [*chosification*] entails a confusion between the Symbolic and the Real, an error we must know how to correct.
The so-called physical sciences have guarded against this error in radical fashion by reducing the Symbolic to the function of a tool with which to carve up the Real—no doubt with a success which, on this principle, takes on more obviously every day the renunciation which it entails of any knowledge of being or even of the existent, however much *l'étant* might answer to the etymology—in any case entirely forgotten—of the term 'physical' [φύω: "grow," "beget," *être-là, dasein.*] (*Actes,* p. 245).

[87] Compare the following:

. . . Man will soon no longer appear [in the human sciences] in any serious way except in the techniques where he is 'taken into account' like so many head of cattle; in other words, he would soon be more effectively effaced in the human sciences than nature has been in the physical sciences, if we psychoanalysts did not know how to bring to the fore what in his being is dependent only upon the Symbolic.
The fact remains that the Symbolic is something that cannot possibly be reified in any way at all—any more than we think of doing so for the series of whole numbers or the notion of a mathematical expectation (*Actes,* p. 245).

[88] "A stone, two houses, three ruins, four ditchdiggers, a garden, some flowers, a raccoon."

[89] Cf. Hegel on language in the *Phenomenology, passim;* for example, (in the French translation): I, 83–86, 91–92; II, 69ff., 184ff., 242ff. etc.; and also Kojève's *Introduction à la lecture de Hegel* (1947), especially pp. 364ff.

[90] That is, the *Fort! Da!* where a child's (phonemic) opposition O/A was related by Freud to the presence and absence of persons and things, *Beyond the Pleasure Principle* (1920), *Standard Edition,* XVIII, 14–17. (See also note 183.)
The allusion to the Chinese *kwa* which follows is presumably based on the fact that what the child actually uttered was an "o-o-o-o" (disappearance) followed by a *"da"* (return).

[91] The French text reads as follows:

Par ce qui ne prend corps que d'être la trace d'un néant et dont le support dès lors ne peut s'altérer, le concept, sauvant la durée de ce qui passe, engendre la chose.
. . . C'est le monde des mots qui crée le monde des choses d'abord confondues dans *l'hic et nunc* du tout en devenir, en donnant son être concret à leur essence, et sa place partout à ce qui est de toujours . . . .

Compare: "No doubt that the discourse is concerned with things. It is in fact in this encounter that from realities they become things" (*Actes,* p. 244).

[92] "An eternal possession." Thucydides, I, xxii: "My history has been composed to be an everlasting possession, not the showpiece of an hour."

[93] This proverb is the epigraph to Claude Lévi-Strauss, *Les Structures élémentaires de la parenté* (1949), which is alluded to more directly in the two sentences that follow.

[94] In 1947, Lacan expressed himself on the Oedipus complex as follows:

I have often taken a stand against the risky way in which Freud interpreted sociologically the capital discovery for the human mind that we owe to him [in the discovery of the Oedipus complex]. I do not think that the Oedipus complex appeared with the origin of man (if indeed it is not completely senseless to try to write the history of that moment), but rather at the dawn of history, of 'historical' history, at the limit of 'ethnographic' cultures. Obviously the Oedipus complex can appear only in the patriarchal form of the institution of the family—but it has a no less incontestable value as a threshold, and I am convinced that in those cultures which exclude it, its function must be or have been fulfilled by initiation experiences, as ethnology in any case still permits us to see this fact today, and the value of the Oedipus complex as a closing-off of a psychic cycle results from the fact that it represents the family situation, insofar as by its institution this situation marks the intersection, in the cultural sphere, of the biological and the social ("Propos sur la causalité psychique" [1950], p. 47).

[95] Compare the following:

For where on earth would one situate the determinations of the unconscious if it is not in those nominal cadres in which marriage ties and kinship are always grounded for the speaking being that we are, in those laws of the Word where lineages found their right, in this universe of discourse with which these laws mingle their traditions? And how would one apprehend the analytical conflicts and their Oedipean prototype outside the engagements which have fixed, long before the subject came into the world, not only his destiny but his identity itself? (*Actes*, p. 205.)

[96] What is meant by *le nom du père* is elaborated in the later theoretical article on psychosis (1958), especially pp. 22–24. "The name of the father" is the signifier of "the function of the father," and the question of the sense in which these terms are to be taken is briefly dealt with in "La Psychanalyse et son enseignement" (1957). The signifier is not only "to be taken *au pied de la lettre,* it *is* the letter."

. . . The incidence of the signifier over the signified is something completely sensible at the level of the B, A, Ba of the analyst's experience. Consider for instance the function of the father; this function is absolutely unthinkable in this experience if the signifier which is its term is not brought out in it: this signifier is the name of the father, as one says in religious invocations; absolutely unthinkable if the 'name of the father' does not have that signifying value which condenses, orients, and polarizes in its direction a whole series of significations which are on a number of extremely diverse planes (p. 94).

Certain primitive societies, against all the evidence, do not attribute procreation to the father. But, says Lacan, whether they do or not is of no significant importance,

. . . since, if the symbolic context requires it, paternity will nonetheless be attributed to the fact that the woman met a spirit at some fountain or some rock in which he is supposed to live.

This is certainly what demonstrates that the attribution of procreation to the father can only be the effect of a pure signifier, of a recognition, not of the real father, but of what religion has taught us to invoke as the Name-of-the-Father.

There's no need of a signifier, of course, to be a father, no more than there is to be dead, but without the signifier no one would ever know anything at all about either of these two states of being ("Traitement possible de la psychose" [1958], p. 24).

It is this article, by way of a detailed commentary on Schreber's book, which elaborates the concept of *Verwerfung,* of "the hole hollowed out in the field of the signifier by the foreclusion of the Name-of-the-Father" (p. 31), and its relationship to the symbolic father of *Totem and Taboo* (1912–13).

[97] *Tiers Livre,* iii, iv; *Quart Livre,* ix.

Debts, says Panurge, are "the connecting link between Earth and Heaven, the unique mainstay of the human race; one, I believe, without which all mankind would speedily perish;" they are "the great soul of the universe."

[98] Notably in his "Introduction à l'oeuvre de Marcel Mauss" (1950), where he compares the notion of mana to the concept of the zero-phoneme introduced into phonology by Roman Jakobson.

Concepts like that of mana devolve from what Lévi-Strauss conceives of as an "overabundance of signifier" in relation to the actual signifieds (that is, the universe, the cosmos) which are available to human "symbolic thought." Thus a concept like mana seeks to fulfil the function of representing all this "floating signifier," and consequently all the antinomies and contradictions involved—since mana may in fact mean almost anything. Mauss's celebrated *Essai sur le don* depends upon the notion of *hau* or mana as the *raison d'être* of the symbolic exchange (whose prime importance lies in the act or transmission of mana or *hau* rather than in any profit or advantage), and Lévi-Strauss seeks to interpret this mysterious anthropological entity in scientific terms as something like an algebraic symbol, representing an "indeterminate value of signification," in the same way as the zero-phoneme is one whose function is simply to be opposed to all other phonemes, without entailing any constant phonetic or differential value in itself. Just as the function of the zero-phoneme is also to exist in opposition to the absence of phonemes, mana is viewed by Lévi-Strauss as a significative symbol empty of meaning in itself, but therefore capable of taking on any meaning required. The function of mana is therefore to fill a gap between signifier and signified at whatever level a lack of adequation between them is revealed. For the native, mana is simply "the subjective reflexion of the exigencies of a totality which he cannot perceive." Mana is a category of thought rather than a category of the Real; it fulfils for the native the role of explanation that modern science fulfils for us. On this view, like the zero-phoneme, mana is pure form without specific content, pure symbol, a symbol with the value of zero (pp. xliv–l).

[99] "By flesh and blood," an allusion to an anthropological binary opposition brought out by Lévi-Strauss in *Les Structures élémentaires de la parenté* (1949).

[100] The French text reads as follows:

Les symboles enveloppent en effet la vie de l'homme d'un réseau si total qu'ils conjoignent avant qu'il vienne au monde ceux qui vont l'engendrer 'par l'os et par la chair,' qu'ils apportent à sa naissance avec les dons des astres, sinon avec des dons des fées, le dessin de sa destinée, qu'ils donnent les mots qui le feront fidèle ou rénégat, la loi des actes qui le suivront jusque-là même où il n'est pas encore et au delà de sa mort même, et que par eux sa fin trouve son sens dans le jugement dernier où le verbe absout son être ou le condamne—sauf à atteindre à la réalisation subjective de l'être-pour-la-mort.

The Heideggerian *Sein-zum-Tode* is normally rendered in English as "Being-towards-death."

[101] The French text reads as follows:

Servitude et grandeur où s'anéantirait le vivant, si le désir ne préservait sa part dans les interférences et les battements que font converger sur lui les cycles du langage, quand la confusion des langues s'en mêle et que les ordres se contrarient dans les déchirements de l'oeuvre universelle.

Mais ce désir lui-même, pour être satisfait dans l'homme, exige d'être reconnu, par l'accord de la parole ou par la lutte de prestige, dans le symbole ou dans l'imaginaire.

L'enjeu d'une psychanalyse est l'avènement dans le sujet du peu de réalité que ce désir y soutient au regard des conflits symboliques et des fixations imaginaires comme moyen de leur accord, et notre voie est l'expérience intersubjective où ce désir se fait reconnaître.

[102] Further to Lichtenberg's aphorism cited by Lacan in note s, see the "Propos sur la causalité psychique" (1950), which examines what Lacan calls "paranoiac knowledge." Summing up the substance of his doctoral thesis of 1932, Lacan refers to that analysis of a "Romantic" paranoiac patient as follows:

In this way I sought to focus on psychosis in its relationship with the totality of the biographical antecedents of the patient, with the totality of her intentions, avowed or not, and, finally, with the totality of the motives, perceived or not, which came out of the contemporary situation of her delusion—that is, as the title of my thesis indicates, psychosis in its relationships with the personality.

Out of this, it seems to me, and from the very first, there emerges the general structure of *méconnaissance*. But we must be careful how we understand this.

Certainly it can be said that the madman thinks he is other than he is, a view expressed in the remark about 'those who think themselves arrayed in gold and purple' by which Descartes revealed himself conforming with the most anecdotal of stories about madmen, and a view with which an authority on the subject contents himself—that is to say, the author for whom the concept of 'Bovarysme,' adapted to the measure of his sympathy for the mentally ill, was the key to paranoia.

But besides the fact that Gaultier's theory [of *Bovarysme*] concerns one of the most normal relationships of the human personality—his ideals—it is worth adding that if a man who believes he's a king is mad, a king who believes he's a king is no less so (pp. 37–38).

For Lacan, the Language "without dialectic" is to be found in schizophrenic or psychotic language, where a "regression" to treating words like things leaves the speaker in the grip of an uncontrollable shifting between opposites in which binary differential elements (for example, inside, outside; good, bad; O, A) are not "anchored" to the *"points de capiton"* supposed by Lacan's theory of the "paternal metaphor." His discourse is incomprehensible; for him all the Symbolic is

Real, in Lacan's terms, or in other words, there has been a *Verwerfung* (foreclusion) of the Symbolic. The thing presentations of the language of the unconscious (see note 66) have become conscious for him; there is no dialectic, no "dia-logos," because his discourse, in Lacan's view, is composed of nothing but words, rather than of the Word. This is the "obstacle to transference" in certain types of psychosis.

Speaking of the Schreber case and of his theory of psychosis as founded on "a primordial deficiency of the signifier" (the concept of *Verwerfung*), Lacan goes on to say:

The *Other* as the seat of the Word and guarantor of Truth is compensated for in psychosis by the *other;* it is the suppression of the duality between the symbolic Other and the other who is an Imaginary partner that causes the psychotic such difficulty in maintaining himself in the human Real, that is to say in a Real which is symbolic (Seminar of November, 1957, p. 293).

[103] Lévi-Strauss has brought out the notion that the myth, like the discourse of the "they" (*Gerede*) in Heidegger, speaks itself through the subject—that is, the subject is being spoken by the myth. Sartre has taken up the idea again in his analysis of Flaubert's almost paranoid horror of the *bêtise* of the *idée reçue*, where "one is spoken rather than speaking," in "La conscience de classe chez Flaubert" (Part II), *Temps Modernes,* No. 241 (June, 1966), pp. 2113–153.

[104] Cf. Lacan's analysis of the Wolf Man's rejection (*Verwerfung*) of castration "in the sense of repression" in the reply to Hyppolite's commentary on the *Verneinung* (1956).

[105] The following note was kindly supplied by Jean Hyppolite:

'Man is the sick animal, or sickness is the becoming of the subject': all these texts (taken up again by Nietzsche) are to be found in Hegel's work at Jena (*Realphilosophie,* ed. Hoffmeister, vol. II, pp. 167–75) and eventually in the *Encyclopedia,* towards the end of the section on the philosophy of nature (ed. Lanson, #371 to #376). If the *Phenomenology* does not explicitly contain this view of illness, the same process is very much in the spirit of Hegel's remarks on death (the master-slave dialectic, and so forth).

See also Kojève's *Introduction à la lecture de Hegel* (1947), pp. 553ff.

[106] Compare: "The function of the *stade du miroir* establishes itself for me . . . as a special case of the function of the *imago,* which is to establish a relation of the organism to its reality—or, as it is said, of the *Innenwelt* to the *Umwelt*" ("Le Stade du miroir" [1949], p. 452).

[107] Maia, associated by the Romans with an old Italian earth goddess, is derived from the Greek for "O mother earth," whence it came to mean "mother," "nurse," "grandmother," "midwife," eventually emerging as *mamma. Voile* is presumably to be read in the sense of the Latin *velum,* sometimes used in distinctions between female clothing and the toga.

"Different from the perverse subject who clasps the rag that the Word has permitted him to tear from the veil of Maia, to make of it the object of his satisfaction, the neurotic is the question articulated on what is beyond the veil" ("La Psychanalyse et son enseignement" [1957], p. 89). (Cf. Freud: "Fetishism" [1927], *Standard Edition,* XXI, 152–57.)

See also the discussion of fetishism and the veil in the seminar of January–February 1957. In the Hindu writers, of course, the veil of Maya conceals "the illusion to which this whole world is due," an illusion "begotten of entrenched selfhood," as Whorf once put it.

On the symptom and the signifier, see "L'instance de la lettre" (1957):

. . . If the symptom is a metaphor, it is not a metaphor to say so, no more than it is to say that man's desire is a metonymy. For the symptom *is* a metaphor, whether it be admitted or not, just as desire *is* a metonymy, even if man mocks the notion that it is so.

. . . Nothing of value has so far been articulated concerning what links the metaphor to the question of being and metonymy to lack of being . . . (pp. 80–91).

In the Sartrean terminology, "lack of being" (*manque d'être*) is the ontological absence which provides the possibility of the *pour-soi*'s desire: "For the *pour-soi* is described ontologically as *manque d'être,* and the possible belongs to the *pour-soi* as *what is lacking to it.*" "Liberty is the concrete mode of being of the lack of being . . . . Man is fundamentally desire of being . . . [since] desire is a lack . . . ." "And the being lacking to the *pour-soi* is the *en-soi*" (*L'Etre et le Néant* [Paris: Gallimard, 1943], p. 652).

[108] The palimpsest is a piece of parchment or other writing material from which the writing has been partially or completely erased (literally: "scraped again") to make way for a new text. This is perhaps to be viewed in the light of Freud's discussion of rememoration and memory in "A Note on the Mystic Writing Pad" (1925), *Standard Edition,* XIX, 227–32.

But see also the metaphor of the palimpsest (common in the nineteenth century) applied to the dream by James Sully (1893), quoted by Freud in an approving note added to the *Traumdeutung* in 1914, *Standard Edition,* IV, p. 135, note 2.

[109] This passage seems to echo Vico's *Scienza Nuova* (1725), where Vico examines what he calls Poetic Wisdom: "[This] second kind of speech, corresponding to the age of heroes, was said by the Egyptians to have been spoken by symbols. To these may be reduced the heroic emblems, which must have been the mute comparisons which Homer calls *semata* (the signs in which the heroes wrote). In consequence they must have been metaphors, images, similitudes, or comparisons, which, having passed into articulate speech, supplied all the resources of poetic expression" (II, iv). The first language, corresponding to the age of the gods when men believed themselves governed by divinities, auspices, and oracles, was "a mute language of signs and physical objects having natural relations to the ideas they wished to express" ('Idea of the Work'), it was a "hieroglyphic" language, "with natural significations" (II, iv). The third language, corresponding to the age of men, the age of equality, is a language "using words agreed on by the people, a language of which they are the absolute lords" (unlike the secret languages of the priests and nobles of the earlier stages); he calls it the "epistolary or vulgar language"; its purpose is the communication necessary in ordinary life; it consists of words which are arbitrary signs.

Part of Vico's demonstration, which is too diffuse, repetitive, and complicated to be reproduced here, is to derive the origins of all insignia, emblems, blazons, markers, and coats of arms, through a repeated series of etymologies, from his theory of the three languages and his theory of signs, based upon the idea of the necessity of marking ownership of property by recognizable signs. These views are developed under the heading: "Corollaries concerning the Origins of Languages and Letters; and, Therein, the Origins of Hieroglyphics, Laws, Names, Family Arms, Medals, and Money; and Hence of the First Language and Literature of the Natural Law of the Gentes." In Book IV, Section v, he summarizes: "The first [the hieroglyphic language] was a divine mental language by mute religious acts or divine ceremonies . . . . The second [the symbolic language] was by heroic blazonings, with which arms are made to speak . . . . The third [the epistolary language] is by articulate speech, which is used by all nations today." (The above quotations are taken

from the translation of the *Scienza Nuova* by Thomas Bergin and Max
Fisch [Anchor Books, New York: 1961].)

These passages from Vico illustrate Lacan's cryptic note v about
Reich's theory of the protective "character armor" of the neurotic, from
which there arises "character resistances" (as opposed to symptom resistances): ". . . Reich made only one mistake in his character analysis:
What he called 'armor' (character armor) and treated as such is only an
armorial bearing. After the treatment, the subject keeps the weight of the
arms nature gave him; all he has done is to erase the blazon or bearings"
("Variantes de la cure-type" [1955], *Ecrits,* p. 342).

[110] This linguistic phenomenon is mentioned again by Lacan in dealing
with the *Ich* of Freud's "Wo es war soll Ich werden," deformed by the
French translators into "Le moi doit déloger le ça" and originally rendered
in English by "Where the id was there the ego shall be" (the definite
articles have since been dropped—the id is *das Es* and the ego *das Ich*—
see the *New Introductory Lectures* [1933], *Standard Edition,* XXII, 80).
The reader should refer to "La Chose freudienne" (1956), pp. 237–38,
for the development of Lacan's "translation" and its justification as: "Là
où c'était, peut-on dire, là où s'était, voudrions-nous faire qu'on entendit,
c'est mon devoir que je vienne à être." The created verb *s'être* being used
to express "absolute subjectivity insofar as Freud properly discovered it
in its radical ex-centricity," the English would be approximately " 'There
where *it* was,' one might say, 'where *es* was an absolute subject,' I
would like it understood, 'it is my duty that *I* come to be.' " For Lacan it
would seem that since "soll," "vienne," and "come" can each be read as
either first or third person verb forms, they are not necessarily in agreement with the *moi qui parle.*

See also the seminar of November, 1958–January, 1959, p. 266, and
"L'Instance de la lettre" (1957), p. 76, where Lacan adds: "This aim is
one of reintegration and of accord, I would say, one of reconciliation
(*Versöhnung*)." The problem of this reconciliation is perhaps as central
for Freud as it is for Hegel, but in the context of analysis, it is an essentially asymptotic return to "unity" (see note 113). Cf. Hegel on reconciliation:

The promise of reconciliation [*das Wort der Versöhnung*] is the objectively-
existing spirit which contemplates [*anschaut*] the pure Knowledge of itself
as universal essence in its counterpart [*Gegenteil*], in the pure Knowledge of

self as *individuality* [*Einzelheit*] which is absolutely within itself—a reciprocal recognition which is the *Absolute Spirit* (*Phänomenologie,* p. 471; *Phénoménologie,* II, 198).

Lacan's constant insistence upon a number of radical translations of this aphorism of Freud's results in part from the fact that in the passage in question Freud is discussing the strengthening of the ego.

[111] For the *moi* of modern man:

One cannot insist too heavily in fact on the correlation which links psychological objectification to the growing dominance that the function of the *moi* has taken on in the lived experience of modern man, beginning from a set of sociotechnological and dialectical conjunctures, whose cultural *Gestalt* is visibly constituted by the beginning of the seventeenth century (*Actes,* p. 208).

For the *belle âme:*

One might . . . remark that every verbal denunciation of a disorder participates in the disorder against which it protests, in the sense that the disorder has been set up by its discourse. Hegel, in the dialectic of the *belle âme,* had already shown that this remark is tautologous only if the tauto-ontic effect in which it is rooted is not recognized—that is to say that being is primary in the disorder on which the *belle âme* lives in all the senses (including the economic sense) which can be found in the expression, "enough to live on," and that in denouncing the disorder, the *belle âme* proceeds only to the still misconstrued mediation of himself by the conduct through which he subsists on it ("La Chose freudienne" [1956], p. 235).

See: *Phénoménologie,* II, 168ff. (*Phänomenologie,* pp. 460ff.), and J. Hyppolite, *Genèse et structure de la "Phénoménologie de l'Esprit"* (1946), II, 495ff.

At the time of the delivery of the *Discours* the "elsewhere" mentioned in the text was the "Propos sur la causalité psychique" (1947), where the example of the *belle âme* is the Alceste of Molière's *Le Misanthrope.*

[112] Used without a modifier, *science* has of course a much wider connotation than the English "science"—for example, "knowledge," "learning."

[113] In the article on the *stade du miroir,* writing of the child's experience of himself when placed in front of a mirror (Köhler's *Aha-Erlebnis*), which is quite different from that of the chimpanzee (which does

not recognize what it sees), Lacan speaks of this fundamental "onto-logical structure of the human world" as follows:

It suffices to comprehend the *stade du miroir as an identification* in the full sense of the term in analysis—that is, the transformation produced in the subject when he assumes an image . . . .

The joyful assumption of his specular image by a being still unable to control his motor functions and still dependent on his mother to nurse him, as is the *infans* at this stage, therefore seems to me to reveal in an exemplary situation the symbolic matrix in which the *je* precipitates itself in a pri-mordial form, before it becomes objectified in the dialectic of the identification with the other, and before Language restores to it in the universal its function as subject.

This primordial form would probably be best designated as *je-idéal*, if I wished to fit it into the usual terminology of psychoanalysis, in the sense that it would also be the root stock of secondary identifications, whose functions of libidinal normalization we recognize in this term. But the important point is that this form situates the instance of the *moi*, from be-fore its social determination, in a fictional line, eternally irreducible for the single individual—or rather, an instance which will only asymptotically re-join the becoming of the subject, whatever may be the success of the dialectical syntheses by which the subject is to resolve as *je* his discordance with his own reality ("Le Stade du miroir" [1949], p. 450).

Lacan's translation of "Ich" by "je" had been dropped by 1953.

[114] "Un mur de langage." See note 174.

Compare the early Freud on the technique of following the patient's associations past his resistances: "It is at first as though we were standing before a wall which shuts out every prospect and prevents us from having any idea whether there is anything behind it, and if so, what" ("Psychotherapy of Hysteria" [1895], *Standard Edition*, II, 293).

[115] For example, *Phénoménologie*, I, 268ff (*Phänomenologie*, pp. 237ff.).

[116] "Men are so necessarily mad that it would be being mad by another kind of madness *not* to be mad" (*Pensées*, Brunschvicq ed. #414 [Pléiade ed. #184]).

Compare the following:

For a characteristic which is much more decisive for the reality which the subject confers on these phenomena [of madness], than the sensorality which he experiences by them or the belief which he attaches to them, is that all of them, whatever they are—hallucinations, interpretations, intuitions, and with whatever extraneousness and strangeness they are lived by him—these phenomena are aimed at him personally: they split him into two, respond to him, echo him, read in him as he identifies them, interrogates them, provokes them, and deciphers them. And when the point comes where he lacks any further way of expressing them, his perplexity reveals to us a questioning *béance* within him: in other words, madness is lived wholly in the register of meaning.

The moving interest which madness arouses gives a first reply to the question I proposed concerning the human value of the phenomenon of madness. And its metaphysical import is revealed in the fact that the phenomenon of madness is not separable from the problem of signification for being in general—that is, from the problem of Language for man ("Propos sur la causalité psychique" [1950], p. 34).

For the risk of madness can be measured by the very attractiveness of identifications, in which man commits at one and the same time his Truth and his being.

Madness is therefore far from being the contingent fact of the fragilities of his organism; it is the permanent virtuality of an open fault [*faille*] in his essence.

Madness is far from being an 'insult' to liberty: it is her most faithful companion, it follows her movement like a shadow.

And the being of man not only cannot be understood without madness, but it would not be the being of man if it did not carry madness within it as the limit of its liberty (*Ibid.*, p. 41).

[117] Chapter V, in particular, of *Group Psychology and the Analysis of the Ego* (1921), *Standard Edition*, XVIII.

[118] That is, "guidance," as in the religious sense of "direction de consciences."

[119] See: Jakobson and Halle, "Phonology and Phonetics" (1955). Morphemes, the ultimate constituents of language endowed with meaning, are composed of syllables which are in turn composed of sequences of phonemes. Phonemes are bundles of concurrent distinctive features (for example, tone, force, quantity, and the twelve inherent binary oppositions of qualities like grave/acute, voiced/voiceless, and so forth), these last being the ultimate components of language (equivalent to Saussure's "éléments différentiels"). A phoneme has "no singleness of reference" (Sapir). All phonemes "denote nothing but mere otherness" (p. 11). "This lack of individual denotation sets apart the distinctive features, and their combinations into phonemes, from all other linguistic units" (*Ibid.*).

[120] Notably in Lévi-Strauss, "The Structural Study of Myth," in: MYTH: A Symposium, *Journal of American Folklore*, Vol. 78, No. 270, (Oct.–Dec., 1955), pp. 428–44 (republished with modifications in his *Anthropologie Structurale* [1958]). The mytheme is described and employed by Lévi-Strauss as a "gross constitutive element" of the myth—that is, an element "higher" than the morpheme or the semanteme in language, and one to be analyzed in its occurrence within "bundles of relations" at the sentence level. (The mytheme is more or less equivalent to the use of "concept" in the general sense.)

Lévi-Strauss's point is that the view of myth as having some sort of "natural," "symbolic," or "archetypal" meaning (in the Jungian sense) is a view still on the level of the investigations of the ancient philosophers into the "natural" relationship between sound and sense in language (Plato's *Cratylus,* for instance, which ends with a *non liquet*)—a relationship which many poets, theorists of synaesthesia, and linguists (Roman Jakobson, for example) agree exists at the level of the affective power of phonemes. (Mallarmé complains that *jour* is "dark" and *nuit* is "light" in French.)

Obviously for all *words* the relationship is clearly arbitrary, however. Thus Lévi-Strauss claims as a working hypothesis that (1) the meaning of the myth does not reside in the isolated elements which make it up, but "only in the way these elements are combined," (2) that myth, although it is language, has specific properties, which (3) are "above the ordinary linguistic level" because they are "more complex than those to be found in any kind of linguistic expression."

See also the intervention of Lacan in the discussion following Lévi-Strauss's lecture: "Sur les rapports entre la mythologie et le rituel" (1956), pp. 113–18.

The application of this type of structural analysis (but at a much less formal and less methodological level) can be seen in Lacan's use of the elements of the Oedipus complex in analysis of a myth. See: "Le Mythe individuel du névrosé" (1953) and the seminars on "La Relation d'objet et les structures freudiennes."

[121] The French text reads as follows:

Si ces deux exemples se lèvent, pour nous des champs les plus contrastés dans le concret: jeu toujours plus loisible de la loi mathématique, front d'airain de l'exploitation capitaliste, c'est que, pour nous paraître partir de loin, leurs effets viennent à constituer notre subsistance, et justement de s'y croiser en un double renversement: la science la plus subjective ayant forgé une réalité nouvelle, la ténèbre du partage social s'armant d'un symbole agissant.

There is an allusion, apparently, to Lassalle's *loi d'airain,* the iron law of wages.

122

> ". . . *that* [*august*] *voice*
> *Who knows herself when she sings*
> *To be no longer the voice of anyone*
> *As much as the voice of the waves and the woods."*
> *Valéry:* La Pythie.

The whole stanza is as follows:

Honneur des Hommes, Saint LANGAGE, *Voici parler une Sagesse*
Discours prophétique et paré. *Et sonner cette auguste Voix*
Belles chaines en qui s'engage *Qui se connaît quand elle sonne*
Le dieu dans la chaire égaré, *N'être plus la voix de personne*
Illumination, largesse! *Tant que des ondes et des bois!*

[123] In "The Question of Lay Analysis" (1926), *Standard Edition,* XX, 246.

[124] "Between man and love, there is woman. Between man and woman, there is a world. Between man and the world, there is a wall."

[125] "For I have seen with my own eyes the Cumean Sibyll hanging inside a jar, and whenever boys asked her: 'What do you wish, O Sibyll,' she would reply: 'I wish to die.'" This is the epigraph to *The Waste Land* (1922); Lacan has already quoted from *The Hollow Men* (1925). There seems to be a connection between Lacan's choice of this epigraph on death and Heidegger's commentary on Heraclitus in "Logos," translated by Lacan in *La Psychanalyse,* I (1956). On p. 75 Heidegger comments on the sense of ἐθέλω (θέλω)—not simply "to wish" but "to be ready to . . ." in the sense of "admitting something in retroactive reference to oneself." Lacan adds the note: "Soit le français: con-sentir à," which is echoed in the later remarks in the *Discours* on the master, the slave, and the *absolut Herr:* death.

Compare Kojève, *Introduction à la lecture de Hegel* (1947), p. 379:

> The Concept is Time . . . . Man is the empirical existence of the Concept in the World. He is therefore the empirical existence in the World of a future which will never become present. This Future—is for Man his *death* . . . . Man is *essentially* mortal; and he is only the Concept, i.e. abso-

lute Knowledge, incarnate Wisdom, if he *knows* it. The Logos only becomes flesh, only becomes Man, on condition of wanting to and being able to *die."*

[126] *Standard Edition,* X, 167–68. The word translated "pleasure" is *jouissance* in the French. The "clarifications" mentioned later in this sentence occur on pp. 175–78. This paragraph was slightly modified in 1966.

[127] In "The Psychotherapy of Hysteria" (1895), *Standard Edition,* II, 288–92.

[128] That is, in the order of Language. The metaphor of the *partition* and the *registre* is to be found very frequently in Lacan's writings. This topic is taken up again in the introduction to the commentary on the *Verneinung* (1956).

The metaphor of the orchestra score derives its value for Lacan (and for Lévi-Strauss; see the reference in note 120) from the fact that it is read both vertically and horizontally at the same time.

[129] Referring to the statement that, when all is said and done, "neurotics are really incomprehensible," in his analysis of desire in "La Direction de la cure" (1961), Lacan continues:

But this is precisely what was said long ago, and has always been said—and yet there are analysts who have only just come round to it, analysts who are stuck on this fact. The simpleton calls it the irrational, since he hasn't even realized that Freud's discovery is confirmed [*s'homologue*] by Freud's considering it certain, from the very first—a fact which draws the teeth of our exegesis from the start—that the Real is rational, and then by his affirming that the rational is real. As a result Freud can articulate the fact that what presents itself as unreasonable in desire is an effect of the passage of the rational insofar as it is real—that is to say, the passage of Language, into the Real, in so far as the rational has already traced its circumvallation there (p. 199).

And in the *Actes,* he described analysis as embodying "the most developed of dialectical methods" in the

essential procedure through which the psychoanalyst, in his experience, conjugates the particular to the universal; through which, in his theory, he subordinates the Real to the rational; through which, in his technique, he recalls the subject to his constituting role for the object; through which, in short, in his strategy, he often intersects with the Hegelian phenomenology —as in the turning back [*rétorsion*] on the discourse of the *belle âme* of the support which he brings to the disorder of the world where his revolt takes on its theme (p. 209).

Since the adjective Hegel uses in the aphorism on the rational and the real from the *Philosophy of Right* is *wirklich,* it should probably be translated: "What is rational is actual (or effectively real), and what is actual (or effectively real) is rational." In the *Phenomenology* a similar notion is expressed by the phrase "the spiritual [*das Geistige*] alone is the effectively real [*das Wirkliche*]" (*Phänomenologie,* p. 24; *Phénoménologie,* I, 23). When linked with Hegel's statements about the relationship between the spirit, language, and consciousness at various stages of the *Phenomenology*—for example: that the "non-mediate *Dasein* of the spirit is consciousness" (p. 32; I, 31), that "language is the *Dasein* of the pure Self as Self" (p. 362; II, 69), that "once more we see language as the *Dasein* of the spirit" (p. 458; II, 184), and that "language is the [non-mediate] consciousness-of-self which is for others" (*ibid.*)—it seems clear that both his statement and Lacan's application of it to Freud are open to wide interpretation in relation to Heidegger's view of the *logos* and in relation to theories of intersubjective communication.

[130] Or process of attaining *vérité.*

Cf. Kojève, *Introduction à la lecture de Hegel* (1947), p. 375, n. 1: "For Man the adequation of Being and Concept is a process (*Bewegung*), and truth (*Wahrheit*) is a *result*. It is only this 'result of the process' which merits the name of (discursive) 'truth,' for only this process is Logos or Discourse."

[131] Compare the following:

The discovery of Freud is that the movement of this dialectic does not simply determine the subject unbeknownst to him even by the paths of his *méconnaissance*—which Hegel had already formulated in the 'cunning of reason' which is the first principle of the phenomenology of the spirit—but that this movement constitutes him in an order which can only be ex-centric in relation to any bringing to realization of the consciousness-of-self. . . . (Actes, p. 206).

[132] Hegel, says Lacan, is always sure that Truth will be found again in his final accounting, because it is already there. If the analyst could be equally sure of it—which he cannot, because the Truth is only there in the form of the symptom, that is to say, pretty well twisted—he would be able to be neutral in a much more fundamental way.

"It is to this Other beyond the other that the analyst cedes place by the neutrality through which he becomes *ne-uter,* neither one nor the other of the two who are there, and if he keeps silent, it is in order to let the Other speak" ("La Psychanalyse et son enseignement" [1957], p. 67).

[133] The Kierkegaardian repetition is taken up again in the "Séminaire sur *La lettre volée*" (1956). Here Lacan links the "compulsion to repeat" (*Wiederholungswang*) and the death instinct of *Beyond the Pleasure Principle* to the necessity of refinding the object originally lost which Freud declared to be the characteristic of the system ψ in the "Project for a Scientific Psychology" (1895):

Thus it is that Freud takes a position from the very beginning in the opposition, which Kierkegaard has taught us about, concerning the two notions of existence founded respectively on reminiscence and on repetition. If Kierkegaard discerns in this opposition, and admirably so, the difference between the classical and modern conceptions of man, it nevertheless appears that Freud, by taking away from the human agent—identified with consciousness—the necessity included in this repetition, causes the second conception to take a decisive step forward. Since this repetition is a symbolic repetition, the fact becomes established as a result that the order of the symbol can no longer be conceived as constituted by man, but rather as constituting him (p. 2).

[134] ". . . qui fasse justice de leur puissance et vérité des maîtres-mots de la cité." A master word would be, for example, δημοκρατία.

[135] The sense of this passage takes its support from the *je-moi* distinction and from the difference between the full Word and the empty Word.

"The subject . . . begins the analysis by talking about him[self] without talking to *you,* or by talking to you without talking about him[self]. When he can talk to you about him[self], the analysis will be over" ("Introduction au commentaire de Jean Hyppolite" [1956], p. 21, n. 1).

In the resistance displayed by the subject's *Verneinung,* Freud

uncovers for us a phenomenon which structures all revelation of Truth in the dialogue. There is the fundamental difficulty encountered by the subject in what he has to say; the most common difficulty being that which Freud demonstrated in repression—in other words, that sort of discordance between the signified and the signifier determined by every censorship of social origin. The Truth can always be communicated between the lines in this case. That is to say, that whoever wants to make it heard can always have recourse to the technique which is indicated by the identity between the Truth and the symbols which reveal it; in other words, he can attain his ends by deliberately introducing into a text discordances which will correspond cryptographically to those imposed by the censorship.

The true subject, that is, the subject of the unconscious, does not proceed differently in the Language of his symptoms which, although it is in a sense deciphered by the analyst, is more a process of the subject's coming around to address himself to him in a more and more consistent way, for the ever-renewed satisfaction of our experience. This is in fact what our experience has recognized in the phenomenon of transference.

What the subject who is speaking says, however empty his discourse may be at first, takes on its effect from the process of approaching to the Word which is realized in his discourse, a coming closer to the Word into which he will fully convert the Truth which his symptoms express" [that is, the *parole vide* will become a *parole pleine*] (*Ibid.,* pp. 20–21).

[136] "Refoulé." It is perhaps worth remarking at this point on certain lexical distinctions. Psychoanalytic "repression" (*Verdrängung*) is rendered by the French *refoulement; répression* in French, best translated "suppression," or "conscious repression," corresponds to the Freudian *Unterdrückung*. There is the further distinction between what Freud called the "primal repression" (*refoulement originaire: Urverdrängung*) and what he first called *Nachdrängen* ("after pressure") and referred to as "repression proper" (*Standard Edition,* XIV, 148), later *Nachverdrängung* (*refoulement après coup:* "after repression") (*Standard Edition,* XXIII, 227). But for there to be a primal repression, a "mythical" earlier stage must be supposed; for Freud, the primal repression is inaccessible to consciousness; moreover, it never was "conscious." Leclaire and Laplanche develop their own theory around these distinctions in "L'Inconscient" (1961). The reader will note the relationship between these concepts and the theory of deferred action (*Nachträglichkeit*).

[137] The early schools of poetic theory in the Hindu writers were (1) the school of *rasa* (sentiment), (2) the school of *riti* (style), (3) the school of *dhvani,* (4) the school of *vakrokti* (beautiful expression), as well as the school of *citra* (picture), of which only the third is still of any importance.

Dhvani means "sound, murmur, roar," even "thunder"; but most important here are the meanings: "tone," "allusion." *Dhvani* represents "that power of a word or sentence," says Apte's dictionary, "by virtue of which it conveys a sense different from its primary or secondary meaning, suggestive power." The doctrine of *dhvani,* tone, long dominant in Hindu poetics and one of which Abhinavagupta was a leading exponent, is usually called the doctrine of "suggestion," but no doubt it would be better described in this context as a theory of metaphor or metonymy. See below on *lakshanalakshana* (note 177).

[138] In his "Analysis Terminable and Interminable" (1937), *Standard Edition,* XXIII, 219.

[139] Compare the following:

The creative spark of the metaphor does not fly forth from the making-present of two images, that is, of two signifiers equally actualized. It surges forth between two signifiers of which one is substituted for the other by taking its place in the chain of signifiers, the occulted signifier remaining present because of its (metonymic) connection to the rest of the chain ("L'Instance de la lettre" [1956], p. 60).

The supplantation of one signifier by another means that "the one which is supplanted falls to the level of the signified and as a latent signifier perpetuates at that level the interval in which another chain of signifiers can be grafted on to it" ("Théorie du symbolisme" [1959], p. 12).

[140] English in the original.

[141] English in the original.

[142] English in the original.

[143] *"L'intimation* de la parole."

The relation of *need, demand,* and *desire* and the relation of desire to the signifier are elaborated throughout the later writings of Lacan, and in detail in the unpublished seminars (see the summaries of J.-B. Pontalis): "It must be granted that it is the concrete incidence of the signifier in the submission of need to demand which, by repressing desire into the position of being faultily recognized, confers on the unconscious its order" ("Théorie du symbolisme" [1959], p. 13).

The question is further delineated by Leclaire in "L'Obsessionel et son désir" (1959). After stating that "need aims at the object and is satisfied by it"; that demand "puts the other as such into question"; that it is "that sort of appeal to the Other" whose nature is "to open up on to a *béance* and to remain unsatisfied"; and that desire participates of both, he summarizes:

[Desire] is the necessary mediation between the implacable mechanism of need and the dizzy solitude of demand . . . .
. . . Desire is proper to the Imaginary; it is to be conceived as *significative mediation of a fundamental antinomy.* Thus it participates in need insofar

as it is relatively satisfied by an object, but only sustains itself insofar as it participates in demand by its perennially unsatisfied quest of the being of the Other, *locus of the signifier* (pp. 386–90).

[144] "Le malentendu du langage-signe."

The varied technical use of terms like "sign (*signum*)," *"signans,"* *"signatum,"* "signifier (*significans*)," "signified (*significatum*)," "signal," "index," "referent," "object," and so forth readily leads to confusion among different authors and in different domains.

Lacan has clarified his point verbally as follows:

The *langage-signe* is any language which aims at basing itself only on its 'reference' to the object, any language which thus confuses the signified with the object, and which consequently misses the point that it is constituted of signifiers and not of signs—with this further condition that it is never a question of a *code* but rather of *une batterie de signifiants.*

For Lacan the *signifier* seems to take over the role of the *sign* for Saussure or for Lévi-Strauss. The further Lacan pursues his epistemology of the signifier, the less one hears about the signified (Saussure's "concept") as such.

[145] English in the original.

[146] That is, as a code arrived at by convention, such as the alphabet, or a traffic system, or a spectrograph, and so forth.

Further to what follows, see the discussion of von Frisch's discoveries (the precise significance of the "wagging dance" was only made public in 1948, whereas the original observations date from 1923) in E. Benveniste, "Communication animale et langage humain," *Problèmes de linguistique générale* (1966), pp. 56–62.

[147] Compare the following:

For this revelation of meaning [in the practice of analysis] requires that the subject be already ready to hear it—that is to say, that he would not be waiting for it if he had not already found it. But if his comprehension requires the echo of your word, is it not that it is in a Word, which from the fact of being addressed to you was already yours, that the message which he is to receive from it is constituted? Thus the act of the Word appears less as communication than as the grounding of the subjects in an essential annunciation (*Actes,* p. 204).

Later, in the formal discussion in 1953, Lacan gave what he called "the general equation of transsubjective communication": "This formula is as follows: the action of the Word, as far as the subject means to ground himself in it, is such that the sender, in order to communicate his message, must receive it from the receiver, and all the same he only manages to do it by emitting his message in an inverted form" (*Actes,* p. 248).

"The unconscious is that discourse of the Other where the subject receives, in the inverted form suited to the promise, his own forgotten message" ("La Psychanalyse et son enseignement" [1957], p. 67).

[148] "You would not be looking for me if you had not already found me," the words of Christ in *Le mystère de Jésus, Pensées* (Brunschvicq ed. #553 [Pléiade ed. #736]).

[149] Jakobson also combats the notion of "redundancy" as meaning "something superfluous." See: "On Linguistic Aspects of Translation" in R. A. Brower, ed., *On Translation* (Cambridge: Harvard University Press, 1959), pp. 232–39.

There is a distinction to be made between the formal necessity of redundancy uncovered by the theory of information—undifferentiated information being intransmissible as such—and the existential redundancy of speech. Since the theory of communication is concerned with the transmission of messages between all sorts of senders and receivers (for example, man and Nature, man and machine, machine and machine), it poses the possibility of reducing human language to a (theoretically) one-to-one relationship of signifier and signified, or of signifier and signifier, on the assumption that the unconscious code of language is in fact a convention.

[150] See: *Standard Edition,* XVII, 89–97, 107–8, 112–13 (and note). The *Wespe* incident is reported on p. 94.

[151] *Standard Edition,* X, 225, 260, 280–81, 294–95. The original formula is decondensed on pp. 280–81, where the condensation of "Gisela" into "S" is also demonstrated.

[152] This is the "constellation familiale" of the subject, the history and the internal relationships of the subject's family—and "history" in the precise sense of both a lived experience as well as of what the subject is told by his parents about their lives (as the incidents mentioned indicate). See: "Le Mythe individuel du névrosé" (1953), pp. 8ff., where Lacan deals with these aspects of the case of the Rat Man in detail, and

particularly with the theme of the double therein, which he relates to an obsessional episode in the life of the young Goethe, taken from *Dichtung und Wahrheit*.

The reference in the preceding paragraph to Freud's "inexact interpretation" of the father's role will clarify what Lacan means by the role of "dummy" in analysis (as in bridge: *le mort* in French), as well as the role of the "Symbolic father" (the dead father—see note 96) in the subject's history, if it is compared to the following passage:

[This interpretation of Freud's] is contradicted by the reality it assumes, but [it] is nevertheless a true interpretation in that Freud's intuition anticipates on what I have brought out about the function of the Other in obsessional neurosis. I have demonstrated that this function is particularly suited to being held by a dead man (or "dummy") and that in this case it could not be better held than by the father, insofar as by his death the Rat Man's father had rejoined the position which Freud recognized as that of the absolute Father ("La Direction de la cure" [1961], p. 161).

[153] "Ses yeux de bitume." See *Standard Edition*, X, 200, 293, and Genesis, XI, 3 ("and slime they had for mortar").

[154] The French text reads as follows:

L'hystérique captive cet objet dans une intrigue raffinée et son *ego* est dans le tiers par le médium de qui le sujet jouit de cet objet où sa question s'incarne. L'obsessionel entraîne dans la cage de son narcissisme les objets où sa question se répercute dans l'alibi multiplié de figures mortelles et, domptant leur haute voltige, en adresse l'hommage ambigu vers la loge où lui-même a sa place, celle du maître qui ne peut se voir.

[155] For Lacan, the mediation of the Word "is conceivable only if a third term is supposed to be present in the Imaginary relationship itself: mortal reality, the death instinct, which has been shown to condition the marvels of narcissism," notably in analyses conducted to their termination as relationships of *moi* to *moi*.

In order for the transference relation to escape these effects henceforth, it would be necessary for the analyst to strip the narcissistic image of his *moi* of all the forms of the desire in which this image has been constituted, so as to reduce it to the sole figure which can sustain it under their masks: the face of the absolute master, death ("Variantes de la cure-type" [1955], *Ecrits,* p. 348).

And death, for Lacan, is the fourth term to be integrated into the triangle of the three persons making up the oedipal relationship (*ibid.,* p.

362). (For the phallus as the fourth term, see the last part of the essay following the translator's notes.)

[156] "Toutes les intimations."

Now the Real confronted by analysis is a man who must be allowed to go on speaking. It is in proportion to the sense that the subject effectively brings to pronouncing the *"je"* which decides whether he is or is not *the one who is speaking*. But the fatality of the Word, in fact the condition of its plenitude, requires that the subject by whose decision is actually measured at every instant the being in question in his humanity, be the one who is listening as much as the one who is speaking. For at the moment of the full Word, they both take an equal part in it (*Actes,* p. 204).

[157] Literally "that (thing)." The French for the *id* is *le ça,* but this *cela* —the "phenomenological" object—is precisely not the *ça.* For Freud's "Wo es war soll Ich werden," see note 110.

[158] Compare the following:

The *moi* of which we speak is absolutely impossible to distinguish from the insidious Imaginary captures [*captations*] which constitute it from head to foot, in its genesis as in its status, in its function as in its actuality, by another and for another. In other words, the dialectic which sustains our experience, situated as it is at the most enveloping level of the efficacy of the subject, obliges us to comprehend the *moi* through and through in the movement of progressive alienation in which the consciousness-of-self is constituted in the Hegelian phenomenology.

This means that if you are dealing with the ego of the subject, in the moment which we are studying, the fact is that you are at this moment the support of his *alter ego* ("Introduction au commentaire de J. Hyppolite" [1956], p. 22).

[159] "Fragment of an Analysis of a Case of Hysteria" (1905), *Standard Edition,* VII, 7. It is here (pp. 117–18) that Freud for the first time indicates the importance of transference in the progress of analytical therapy. (The term *Uebertragung* first appears in the *Studies on Hysteria* [1895].)

See Lacan's dialectical interpretation of the progress of this analysis in a lengthy intervention at the Congrès des psychanalystes de langue romane (1951), published in the *Revue Française de Psychanalyse,* XVI, No. 1–2 (January–June, 1952), pp. 154–63, and republished in the *Ecrits* (pp. 215–26).

Freud first raised the question of countertransference in 1910 ("Future Prospects of Psycho-Analysis," *Standard Edition,* XI, 144–45). He returned to it in the paper on transference love cited below. The editor of the *Standard Edition* notes that these are probably the only two explicit discussions of countertransference in Freud's published works.

[160] *Standard Edition,* VII, 120. The account itself was published four years after the breaking off of the analysis in 1901.

[161] Compare the following passage from "The Question of Lay Analysis" (1926), where Freud engages in an imaginary dialogue with an "impartial critic."

Nothing takes place between [the analyst and patient] except that they talk to each other . . . .
The Impartial Person's features now show signs of unmistakable relief and relaxation, but they also clearly betray some contempt. It is as though he were thinking: 'Nothing more than that? Words, words, words, as Prince Hamlet says.'
'. . . So it is a kind of magic,' he comments: 'you talk, and blow away his ailments.'
Quite true. It *would* be magic if it worked rather quicker . . . . And incidentally do not let us despise the *word*. After all it is a powerful instrument; it is the means by which we convey our feelings to one another, our method of influencing other people. Words can do unspeakable good and cause terrible wounds. No doubt 'in the beginning was the deed' ["Im Anfang war die Tat," Goethe, *Faust* I, sc. 3] and the word came later; in some circumstances it meant an advance in civilization when deeds were softened into words. But originally the word was magic—a magical act; and it has retained much of its ancient power (*Standard Edition,* XX, 187-88).

[162] See the passage quoted from the French in note 22.

[163] The French text reads as follows:

Car pour ne plus nous occuper dès lors, comme l'on s'en targue, que de ces bruits, il faut convenir que nous ne nous sommes pas mis dans les conditions les plus propices à en déchiffrer le sens: comment, sans mettre bille-en-tête de le comprendre, traduire ce qui n'est pas de soi langage? Ainsi menés à en faire appel au sujet, puisque après tout c'est à son actif que nous avons à faire virer ce comprendre, nous le mettrons avec nous dans le pari, lequel est bien que nous le comprenons, et attendons qu'un retour nous fasse gagnants tous les deux. Moyennant quoi, à poursuivre ce train de navette, il apprendra fort simplement à battre lui-même la mesure, forme de suggestion qui en vaut bien une autre, c'est-à-dire que comme en toute autre on ne sait qui donne la marque. Le procédé est reconnu pour assez sûr quand il s'agit d'aller au trou.

The *pari* does not occur in the original paragraphs, which were translated as follows:

For if we grasp in the Word only a reflection [*reflet*] of thought hidden behind the Language barrier, before long we shall come to the point of not wanting to hear anything more than the rapping from behind this wall, to the point of seeking it not in the punctuation, but in the holes of the discourse.

This would mean our being occupied henceforth solely in decoding this mode of communication and, since it must be admitted that we have not put ourselves in the most favorable set of conditions for receiving its message, we would have to get it repeated sometimes so as to be sure of understanding it, or even so as to get the subject to understand that we are understanding it. And it might well be that after a sufficient number of these comings and goings the subject will have simply learned from us how to make his rappings keep time, a form of 'falling into step' which is worth as much as any other.

[164] See: "Observations on Transference-Love" (1915), *Standard Edition,* XII, 159, especially 168ff.

[165] In the case of the Wolf Man, *loc. cit.,* pp. 10–11. This is where the lion only springs once. See: "Analysis Terminable and Interminable" (1937), XXIII, 217–19, and the lengthy discussion following, which brings out Freud's concept of the castration complex as the "bedrock" beyond which analysis cannot go.

[166] In France, a type of boarding school.

[167] "A Supplement to Freud's 'History of an Infantile Neurosis' " (1928), reprinted in: *The Psycho-Analytic Reader* (1950). See the further details and references in E. Jones, *Sigmund Freud,* II, 306–12. Dr. Mack Brunswick notes that she was simply the mediator between the Wolf Man and the absent Freud.

[168] "The lasting Word." See: Leenhardt, "La parole qui dure (Tradition, mythe, statut)," *Do Kamo* (1947), pp. 173ff.:

After my elucidation of what these terms *no* and *ewekë* signify, it will be readily understood that the Caledonian considers *la parole* as a solid reality. He likes to say '*la parole qui dure.*' It is *la parole* in fact which links together the rhythms of life and marks their continuity through the time lived by the succeeding generations (p. 173). [. . .]

The name of the ancestor to be 'reimbursed' [for a debt, an injury, a woman 'lent' by his generation, and so forth] may be forgotten, but the thought, the act previously pledged, are not. They are *la parole qui dure.* And this dominates time (p. 173).

Thus *la parole* maintains the integrity of social life. It constructs the social behavior of the members of the group. It is an object which consolidates what goes on within man, and it plays the role of a stabilizer for him (p. 176).

See also note 80.

[169] English in the original. The following "moments of haste" refer to the 1945 article in *Cahiers d'Art.*

[170] The preceding six paragraphs were rearranged and slightly modified in 1966.

[171] The French text reads as follows:

Cependant tout son travail s'opère sous le chef de cette intention, et devient de ce chef doublement aliénant. Car non seulement l'oeuvre du sujet lui est dérobée par un autre, ce qui est la relation constituante de tout travail, mais la reconnaissance par le sujet de sa propre essence dans son oeuvre où ce travail trouve sa raison, ne lui échappe pas moins, car lui-même 'n'y est pas,' il est dans le moment anticipé de la mort du maître, à partir de quoi il vivra, mais en attendant quoi il s'identifie à lui comme mort, et ce moyennant quoi il est lui-même déjà mort.

For the echo of this passage in a different context, see note 27.

[172] "Angoisse." Both the Freudian and the Heideggerian *Angst* have been generally translated "anxiety" in English, "angoisse" in French. But Freud, unlike Heidegger, by no means uses this term, sanctified since "existentialism," in an entirely coherent way, although he does stress the anticipatory element and the absence of an object in *Angst,* as Heidegger does. The *Standard Edition* uses "anxiety" as the technical term (for example, *Angstneurose*), but where *Angst* is used by Freud as an "everyday term," it is translated accordingly. In his French papers, Freud uses both "angoisse" and "anxiété." See the editor's note on *Angst, Standard Edition,* III, 116; also the Macquarrie and Robinson translation of *Sein und Zeit* (1927), Division I, 6, Secs. 39–40, especially the translators' note on page 277 where it is pointed out that *Angst* appears as "dread" in translations of Kierkegaard and in a number of discussions of Heidegger. In the seminar of May–July, 1957, on "La Relation d'objet et les structures freudiennes," speaking in relation to little Hans, Lacan defined "angoisse" as follows: "*Angoisse* is not the fear of an object, but the con-

frontation of the subject with an absence of object, with a lack of being in which he is stuck or caught, in which he loses himself and to which anything is preferable, even the forging of that most strange and alien of objects: a phobia" (p. 32).

[173] In the "Traitement possible de la psychose" (1958), pp. 14–15, Lacan describes this incident as "une voie qui a fait date dans ma carrière."

[174] In the discussion at Rome Lacan elaborated: "If you will permit me the metaphor, we should act with Language as one does with sound: move at its speed to break its barrier." After referring to the "bang-bang de l'interprétation," he continued:

You can make use [of this *mur du langage*] in order to reach your interlocutor, but on condition that you understand, from the moment that it is a question of using this wall, that both you and he are on this side, and that you must aim to reach him along it, like a cue-shot along the cushion, and not objectify him beyond it.

This is what I wanted to point out by saying that the normal subject shares this position along with all the paranoiacs in the world insofar as the psychological beliefs to which this subject is attached in modern civilization constitute a variety of delusion that must not be considered less harmful just because it is more general . . . .

In no possible way does this justify your putting on the leaden shoes of pedagogy, decked out as it may be in the name of the analysis of resistances, to play at being a bear explaining to the showman how to dance (*Actes*, p. 252).

[175] "Instinct de mort." Lacan more usually employs the expression "pulsion de mort" for the Freudian *Todestrieb,* and especially since one of his repeated contentions has been that *"Trieb"* ("drive") is to be distinguished from *"Instinkt"* in the text of Freud. (Whether the two words may or may not be synonymous in modern German is irrelevant.) But the *Standard Edition* has settled on "instinct"—and indeed one does not often hear the expression "death drive." Cf. the editor's introduction to "Instincts and their Vicissitudes" (1915), *Standard Edition,* XIV, 109.

[176] Notably in *Beyond the Pleasure Principle.*

[177] See Lacan's note[rr]. The Sanskrit noun *lakshana* means "mark," "token," "sign," "symptom," "definition," "designation," "name," "secondary signification," "mark on the body," *"sign or organ of virility."* The compound *lakshanalakshana* is defined as follows in Macdonell's dictionary: "indicative indication (e.g. a herd station on the Ganges = on the

bank of the Ganges)." This is to be explained by reference to the doctrine of *dhvani* mentioned in note 137. The following quotation is from Keith's *History of Sanskrit Literature* (Oxford: 1928), p. 387:

> The theory [of *dhvani*] finds its origin in the analysis of language and meaning. The phrase, a herdsmen's station on the Ganges is obviously as it stands absurd; the denotation (*abhidha*) gives no sense, and we are obliged to find a transferred sense (*lakshana*) which gives us the sense of a station on the bank of the Ganges . . . . There is brought to us by such a phrase deliberately used in poetry a sense of the holy calm of such a station on the sacred stream with all its associations of piety.

On the views of those who held the doctrine of *dhvani*, Keith comments (p. 388):

> Suggestion, however, can be expressed in two ways, for it may rest on the metaphorical sense of words . . . a species of Dhvanikavya [suggested sense] where the literal meaning is not intended at all . . . . Or, again, the literal sense may be intended; but a deeper suggestion implied . . . .

[178] See: "Analysis Terminable and Interminable" (1937), *Standard Edition*, XXIII, 245ff.; and: *An Outline of Psychoanalysis* (1940), *ibid.*, 148f.

[179] See: *Beyond the Pleasure Principle* (1920), *Standard Edition*, XVIII, 57ff.; and the *Three Essays* (1905), VII, 136. For the elaboration of these remarks, see Freud on *dénégation* (*Standard Edition*, XIX, 235) and the previously cited commentaries on this article by Lacan and Hyppolite.

[180] See: "Remembering, Repeating and Working-Through" (1914), *Standard Edition*, XII, 145.

[181] See: *Being and Time* (1962), p. 294: "Thus death reveals itself as that *possibility which is one's ownmost, which is non-relational, and which is not to be outstripped* (*unüberholbare*)."

[182] ". . . la raison des jeux répétitifs où la subjectivité fomente tout ensemble la maîtrise de sa déréliction et la naissance du symbole." *Déréliction* echoing the Heideggerian sense of "Man's particular and tragic destiny." ("Some Reflections on the Ego" [1953], p. 16.) See following note.

[183] "Jeux d'occultation." The child in question would associate the appearance and disappearance of a toy which he alternately threw away and drew back again with the vowel sounds "ŏ" and "ā," which Freud interpreted as those of the German words for "gone!" (*Fort!*) and "here!" (*Da!*). The repetition of this game was apparently evidence of the child's beginning to master his environment actively through speech, for the

active repetition seemed clearly to replace the passivity of the situation where the child's mother was alternately present and absent. Freud notes the eventual detachment of the game from the figure of the mother, and he notes the importance of the antithesis of disappearance and return rather than the content of the opposition: by means of his image in a mirror, the child soon discovered how to make himself disappear. See: *Beyond the Pleasure Principle* (1920), *Standard Edition,* XVIII, 14ff.

Although it is not referred specifically to the *Fort! Da!* and although it is expressed in the universal terms which Lacan regularly applies to particular cases, the following passage seems to be a more informative later statement of what Lacan is saying in the *Discours* at this point:

> It is worth recalling that it is in the oldest demand that the primary identification is produced, that which is brought about by the all-powerful [status] of the mother, that is to say, the identification which not only suspends the satisfaction of needs from the signifying apparatus, but also that which carves them up, filters them, and models them in relation to the defiles of the structure of the signifier.
>
> Needs become subordinate to the same conventional conditions as those of the signifier in its double register: the synchronic register of opposition between irreducible elements and the diachronic register of substitution and combination, through which Language, even if it obviously does not fulfil all functions, structures the whole of the relationship between humans ("La Direction de la cure" [1961], p. 181).

Lacan goes on to point out that it is from this fact that result Freud's ambiguities about the relationship of the superego to reality—Freud says somewhere that the superego is the source of reality, which it obviously cannot be. It was eventually in the unconscious, says Lacan, that Freud rediscovered "the first ideal marks where the tendencies [*Triebe*] are constituted as repressed in the substitution of the signifier for needs" (*ibid.*)—presumably at the level of the "primal repression."

Earlier in this article (p. 177), Lacan had said that the Kleinian dialectic of phantasied objects is usually considered to refer to identification,

> for these objects, partial or not, but certainly significant [*signifiants*]—the breast, excrement, the phallus—are doubtless won or lost by the subject. He is destroyed by them or he preserves them, but above all he *is* these objects, according to the place where they function in his fundamental phantasy. This mode of identification simply demonstrates the pathology of the slope down which the subject is pushed in a world where his needs are reduced to exchange values . . . .

Thus Lacan concludes that the identification with the analyst, which is sometimes how transference is described, notably by English analysts, amounts ultimately to "an identification with signifiers."

These remarks are taken up from another point of view in the essay following the translator's notes.

In "La Direction de la cure" (1961), p. 158, Lacan describes this moment as: "The point of the insemination of a Symbolic order which pre-exists in relation to the child and according to which it will be necessary for him to structure himself."

[184] For the notion of the couple or pair as anterior to the isolated element, see Henri Wallon, *Les Origines de la pensée chez l'enfant* (1945), Chapter III, "The Elementary Structures":

Even at the very beginning, the thought of the child is far from being totally unorganized. It is not simply a question of a content resulting from formations of an empirical or subjective origin which contact with objects and experience of events have succeeded in juxtaposing between these formations. By themselves, they would never be more than an amorphous succession of psychic moments, one replacing another or simply conglomerating, with no real principle of unity. In reality, thought only exists insofar as it introduces structures into things—very elementary structures at first. What can be ascertained at the very beginning is the existence of coupled elements. The element of thought is this binary structure, not the elements which constitute it. Duality has preceded unity. The couple or pair are anterior to the isolated element. Every term identifiable by thought, every thinkable term, requires a complementary term in relation to which it will be differentiated and to which it can be opposed . . . . Without this initial relationship of the couple, the whole later edifice of relationships would be impossible (p. 41).

On the intellectual plane also the couple is oriented in neither time nor space. It is the act which unifies at the same time as it distinguishes, without at first being able to specify the nature of the relationship (pp. 130–31).

This work is one cited by Jakobson and Halle in discussing Chao's question as to whether the dichotomous scale is actually inherent in the structure of language, or whether it is an imposition on the linguistic code by the analyzer:

. . . The phonemic code is acquired in the earliest years of childhood and, as psychology reveals, in a child's mind the pair is anterior to isolated objects. The binary opposition is a child's first logical operation. Both opposites arise simultaneously and force the infant to choose one and to suppress the other of the two alternative terms" ("Phonology and Phonetics" [1956], p. 47).

See also pp. 37–38 on "pa."

[185] ". . . dont l'objet de désir est désormais sa propre peine"; that is, the object of the desire of the other is what makes it possible for the child to desire the desire of the Other—and this is "sa propre peine."

For the "Imaginary partner," see the remark on the mirror in note 183. The "Real partner" is presumably related to the fact that when the child could talk, he replaced the "o-o-o" with "Go to the fwont!" as he threw the toy down. His father was fighting "at the front" in World War I, and the child was not displeased by his absence, which left him in sole possession of his mother. On the other hand, when the child's mother died in 1920, shortly before he was six, Freud reports that the child (his eldest grandson) "showed no signs of grief."

[186] For "le meurtre de la chose," see Kojève, *Introduction à la lecture de Hegel* (1947), pp. 372ff. Lacan takes up another Kojevian formula when he says in "La Direction de la cure" (1961), p. 189, that "the being of Language is the non-being of objects." ("The mind [*Manas*]," said the author of the *Voice of the Silence,* "is the great slayer of the real.") Kojève expresses the idea as follows:

What distinguishes Being from the concept 'Being' is purely and simply the *Being* of Being itself . . . . Thus one obtains the concept 'Being' by *subtracting* being from Being: Being minus being equals the concept 'Being' (and not Nothing or 'zero'; for the negation of A is not Nothing, but 'non-A,' that is, 'something'). This subtraction . . . takes place literally 'at every instant'; it is called 'Time.' (*Introduction à la lecture de Hegel* [1947], p. 375, n. 1.)

[187] ". . . dans un vouloir qui est vouloir de l'autre." The double sense of "vouloir de l'autre" ("to want of the other") cannot be brought out in the English. On this whole passage, see the *Verneinung* articles.

[188] Leenhardt, for example, employs this spatial representation in his *Do kamo* to represent the native's existence as a locus of relationships with others.

[189] ". . . comme médiatrice entre l'homme du souci et le sujet du savoir absolu." *Souci* is the usual French rendering of the Heideggerian *Sorge,* and *savoir,* of the Hegelian *Wissen.*

[190] The French text reads as follows:

Qu'il connaisse bien la spire où son époque l'entraîne dans l'oeuvre continuée de Babel, et qu'il sache sa fonction d'interprète dans la discorde des langages. Pour les ténèbres du *mundus* autour de quoi s'enroule la tour immense, qu'il laisse à la vision mystique le soin d'y voir s'élever sur un bois éternel le serpent pourrissant de la vie.

The serpent is Moses' brazen serpent, god of healing (*Numbers,* xxi, 9).

[191] Cf. Freud's analysis of Dora, *Standard Edition,* VII, 39: "It is a rule of psycho-analytic technique that an internal connection which is still undisclosed will announce its presence by means of a contiguity—a temporal proximity—of associations; just as in writing, if 'a' and 'b' are put side by side, it means that the syllable 'ab' is to be formed out of them." Lacan's allusion plays on the fashion in which French children learn to read. Freud's first use of this metaphor occurs in the *Traumdeutung, Standard Edition,* IV, 247, 314.

[192] "Soumission, don, grâce." The three Sanskrit nouns (*damah, dânam, dayâ*) are also rendered: "maîtrise de soi," "aumône," "pitié" (Senart); "self-control," "giving," "compassion" (Rhadhakrishnan); the three verbs: "control," "give," "sympathize" (T. S. Eliot: *The Waste Land,* Part V: "What the Thunder Said").

LACAN AND THE DISCOURSE OF THE OTHER

Lacan and the Discourse of the Other

by Anthony Wilden

Nous ne sommes hommes et ne nous tenons les uns aux autres que par la parole.
　　(Montaigne.)

I

It is especially difficult to know where to begin with Lacan, partly because of the range of the echoes one finds in his work and partly because Lacan is not prone to define or employ his terms unambiguously. It appears that most of this explication has been attended to in his seminar, now in its sixteenth year, of which very little has ever been published. This is a situation which accentuates Lacan's tendency to write forever in suspense; only time will tell whether he has fulfilled the promises of his manifesto, the *Discours de Rome.* Nevertheless a great deal of the ground he once staked out for future occupation is a fairly solid acquisition now, and, provided he is read in the light of his sources, his interpretation of Freud has consequences both for us and for our reading of Freud of which we can hardly fail to take cognizance.

The Stade du Miroir *and the Imaginary Order*

Let me begin with the *stade du miroir,* which has been fairly extensively covered in the notes (translator's notes 3, 27, 49, 106, 113). As Laplanche and Pontalis point out in their *Vocabulaire de la Psychanalyse* (1967), the original concept is derived from Henri Wallon.[1] Lacan develops the idea further in the light of the observations of children by Charlotte Bühler, Elsa Köhler, and the Chicago school in the thirties. To evidence concerning the role of the other in childhood—the situation known as "transitivism," for instance, where the child will impute his own actions to another—Lacan adds evidence from animal biology,

---

[1] In his article: "Comment se développe chez l'enfant la notion du corps propre," *Journal de Psychologie* (1931), pp. 705–48.

where it has been experimentally shown that a perceptual relationship to another of the same species is necessary in the normal maturing process. Without the visual presence of others, the maturing process is delayed, although it can be restored to a more nearly normal tempo by placing a mirror in the animal's cage.

The "mirror phase" derives its name from the importance of mirror relationships in childhood. The significance of children's attempts to appropriate or control their own image in a mirror (cf. t.n. 183) is that their actions are symptomatic of these deeper relationships. Through his perception of the image of another human being, the child discovers a form (*Gestalt*), a corporeal unity, which is lacking to him at this particular stage of his development. Noting the physiological evidence for the maturing of the cortex after birth—which Freud sought to relate to the genesis of the ego—Lacan interprets the child's fascination with the other's image as an anticipation of his maturing to a future point of corporeal unity by identifying himself with this image. Although there are certain difficulties in Lacan's expression of his views on this extremely significant phase of childhood, the central concept is clear: this primordial experience is symptomatic of what makes the *moi* an Imaginary construct. The ego is an *Idealich*, another self, and the *stade du miroir* is the source of all later identifications (cf. t.n. 113).

It is worth noting that this theory—which is what lies at the basis of the later distinction between the Symbolic, the Imaginary, and the Real —was first put forward in 1936, during the heyday of Husserlian phenomenology, and that it was repeated and expanded in 1946, 1949, and 1951, during the heyday of Sartrean existentialism. One recalls the importance of the *regard de l'Autre* in the early Sartre, as well as the lack of emphasis on language in *L'Etre et le Néant* (1943), for the *stade du miroir* has obvious philosophical and ideological consequences, especially for those accustomed to the Cartesian tradition of the *cogito* or that of its correlative, the *moi profond,* supposedly available to conscious exploration in depth. Lacan's view of the *moi* as an alienated self makes an interesting commentary on the early Sartre's concept of the ego as transcendent and not interior to consciousness, that is, as something we are conscious *of.* Lacan's *moi* corresponds to the internalization of the other through identification; we are conscious of this self, but unconscious of its origins.

In the "Schema L" (t.n. 49), Lacan shows the dual relationship between *moi* and other as a dual relationship of objectification (and, inevitably, of aggressivity) along the lines of Sartre's analysis of our sadomasochistic relationship to the other who is an object for us, or for whom we make ourselves an object. Aggressivity is intimately linked to identification, notably in paranoia, where the subject's persecutors may turn out to be those with whom he had once identified himself: the other we fear is often the other we love. The *moi* is thus another, an *alter ego*. In Lacan's interpretation, perception is certainly primary in human existence, but it is the notion of self, rather than that of subjectivity, which perception generates. The child's release from this alienating image, if indeed he is released from it, will occur through his discovery of subjectivity by his appropriation of language from the Other, which is his means of entry into the Symbolic order in the capacity of subject. (As will be clear presently, he is already constituted in it as an object, from before his birth.) He begins that crucial moment of entry through the phonemic organization of reality evident in the *Fort! Da!,* which Lacan has never ceased to stress. Later the child will appropriate personal pronouns for himself and others, along with the whole category of what linguists call "shifters." It is well known that personal pronouns present important difficulties for the child, who usually tends to prefer the apparent solidity of a proper name (a case of valid ostensive definition) to an "alienable" word like "I," which seems to be the property of others and not something designating the child himself. (These difficulties may be repeated in reverse in some kinds of aphasia and schizophrenia.)

Since the Symbolic, the Imaginary, and the Real co-exist and intersect in the subject—the Real is not synonymous with external reality, but rather with what is real for the subject—at the same time as they are functions linking the subject to others and to the world, any change in one order will have repercussions on the others. The Symbolic is the primary order, since it represents and structures both of the others; moreover, since it is ultimately only in language (or in judgment) that synonyms, ambiguities, and interpretations operate, Lacan avers that it is not possible to view the Freudian concept of overdetermination (of the symptom) as originating outside the Symbolic order. A specific instance of the way in which these repercussions may take place will be given in the discussion of Lacan's remarks on psychosis at the end of Section IV. But the relationship between these "systems" is invariably problematic. A symbol in the traditional sense is not necessarily part of the Symbolic order, for instance, nor an image necessarily part of the Imaginary, since these terms define functions rather than the elements entering into these functions. However, not all the difficulties involved in reading Lacan stem immediately from these concepts or from their objects; some stem directly from the structural approach itself.

The Schema L, for example, is obviously ambiguous in that it seeks to represent both an initial and a later relationship, as well as a dynamic process. The ambiguity is of course ultimately inherent in what the schema seeks to represent. But at the same time the whole notion behind the structural approach is that any structural metaphor must be multivalent if it is to have any value at all. In other words, since the emphasis of the structural view is upon relationships rather than upon objects, the various *loci* of an algorithm like the Schema L must perform the algebraic function of allowing all sorts of substitutions, whereas the *functions* represented by the relationships between these *loci* remain more or less constant.

It is not the purpose of this introduction to Lacan's thought to go into detail about the more recent developments of Lacan's views; nor do I wish or intend to become very deeply involved in the specific psychoanalytical problems of the object relation as originally developed by English analysts. Nevertheless, the difficulties of interpreting Lacan's algebraic metaphors can be put into correct perspective only if one recalls that the general concept of the object relation in psychoanalysis involves several levels: the genetic and the structural, the psychological and the metapsychological, the logical and the existential. Lacan's works up to about 1953 concentrate upon the genetic view; here he is concerned about the *stade du miroir* as a specific phase in development. At the same time he employs the psychological data to construct a metapsychology of the *moi,* and he speaks in existential terms, as the reader has seen from the translator's notes. In his later works, however, Lacan's emphasis becomes almost exclusively structural, and he concentrates upon the logical level of the *chaîne signifiante* in an attempt to construct a "logic of the signifier" on the basis of the child's earliest relation to objects.

What is especially important in the development of his views is the notion of the "partial object," derived from English psychoanalysis. Whereas Lacan says little about the object relation in the earlier works which is not a restatement in psychoanalytical terms of the Hegelian theory of desire (t.n. 68), the growing emphasis in the later works is upon a reinterpretation of the Kleinian theories about the object relation. Thus there is a significant difference in the nature of the object involved: in the early works it is *"l'autre (petit a)"*; in the later ones it is *"l'objet a,"* which is a much more primordial relationship, a relationship to objects which is anterior to the child's relationship to a person as an object.

In the Hegelian view, the object of one's desire is what mediates any relationship to others, since we desire that object because it is desired by the other. But the child's relationship to the "partial object" is anterior to the constitution of the other in his world, and his desire for unity with this object (the mother's breast, for example) is at a different level from his desire for unity with the other—or in other words his desire to identify with the other—at a later stage in his life. Nevertheless, the *function* of the object relation remains the same when one moves from the genetic to the structural view, and at the same time the Freudian concept of *Nachträglichkeit* (t.n. 46) enables one to see how an earlier relationship may be interpreted by the subject at a level quite different from the original level, as specific objects come to play their part in the relationship of the subject to objects.

Lacan's concern for a psychoanalytical epistemology has led him to develop this essentially psychological notion of the object relation into what he calls *une logique du signifiant.* This theory is heavily dependent upon a radical interpretation of the *Fort! Da!* in *Beyond the Pleasure Principle.* Lacan sees this phonemic opposition as directly related not to any specific German words but rather to the binary opposition of presence and absence in the child's world. At this level the child is repeating at the level of the *Vorstellung* a relationship which he discovered at a much more primordial level. Lacan would view the newborn child as an "absolute subject" (t.n. 110) in a totally intransitive relationship to the world he cannot yet distinguish from himself. For the object to be discovered by the child it must be *absent.* At the psychological level the partial object conveys the lack which creates the desire for unity from which the movement toward identification springs—since identification is itself dependent upon the discovery of *difference,* itself a kind of absence. At the logical or epistemological level, says Lacan, the "lack of object" is the gap in the signifying chain which the subject seeks to fill at the level of the signifier. This is the condition which makes it possible to discover the subject's truth in the linear movement of his discourse, since all other relationships, phantasies, and so forth will eventually be represented at this level of representation. Here Lacan is seeking to answer the question of the *movement* of the discourse. Whereas linguists tend to view speech as essentially static—that is to say, as subject to the mechanics of articulation and to time in a nonessential way—Lacan views speech as a movement toward something, an attempt to fill the gaps without which speech could not be articulated. In other words, speech is as dependent upon the notion of *lack* as is the theory of desire. Since Lacan does not distinguish thought from speech, there is no question for him of speech articulating in time and space something already "given" in thought. It is the relationship to absence which accounts for the rather peculiar fact that Freud's grandson found it necessary to substitute for a phantasy relationship to the lack of object (at one level, the breast; at another, the mother's comings and goings) the signifier relationship of speech, at the same time as he employed a substitute (the toy) for the more primordial object. It is this relationship between phantasy, signifier, and absence which allows Lacan to speak of the *parole vide* as an Imaginary discourse and to describe the "transposition" of word to word in metonymy as desire.

But for the nonspecialist reader, the concept of the *stade du miroir* is primarily of psychological importance, and it is this aspect which I shall emphasize here. The reader interested in examining Lacan's logic of the signifier and the way in which he relates it to Frege's theory of integers will want to turn to the articles of 1966 and later as well as to the studies now appearing in *Les Cahiers pour l'Analyse* (c.f. the Prefatory Note), since these aspects of Lacan's views will not be dealt with in detail here.

The fascination of the subject with an image, and the alienation revealed by the *stade du miroir,* are clearly demonstrable both in the study of the child and in psychopathology, as well as in literature. Oedipus' debate with Tiresias (the situation of what René Girard calls the *frères ennemis*), the subject who says "I" in Montaigne's *Essays,* Balzac's Sarrasine in the short story of that name, and the hero of Rousseau's *Confessions* (or, more vividly, the hero of his *Pygmalion*) are instances which come immediately to mind, in addition to the more obvious literature of the double from Chrétien de Troyes' Yvain to Molière's *sosie,* the Romantic *Doppelgänger,* Dostoievsky's schizoid heroes, and Proust's snobs. Insofar as the *moi* of the subject is still embroiled in the dialectics of narcissism and identification at later stages in his life, one can say that the subject is involved in the objectification of the Imaginary axis at the same time as in the Symbolic and unconscious relationship between *Es* (later related to $, the subject barred from consciousness) and the Other, which is his means to the radical intersubjectivity of the full Word, through recognition of his unconscious desire. As I read it, the relationship of Imaginary objectification and identification is directly reciprocal in that it is a dual dialectic of activity and passivity. The subject may constitute the other as an object, he may be constituted as an object by the other, or he may constitute himself as an object in the eyes of the other (as in masochism, for instance). The process of objectification and identification is an infinite dialectic of images (*a* and *a'* are the images of ego and other); it is symmetrical.

Its very symmetry makes it a closed system from which the subject could never escape without the mediation of the third term, the unconscious. The pathological quest for the self in the other—Don Juan, for instance—is no more than an advanced degree of the normal dialectic of love and hate revealed by Freud's observations on narcissism and known to psychologists of literature at one time as the Renaissance theory of love. "My soul is totally alienated in you," says Rousseau's Saint-Preux to his Julie, and she replies: "Come back [to me] and reunite yourself with yourself." This is precisely the fate Saint-Preux must avoid: Julie marries Wolmar; Saint-Preux is safe again—in the Oedipal triangle he has never wanted to escape. Wolmar is the defense which enables Saint-Preux to live out a "normal" life in the rest of *La Nouvelle Héloïse,* for he has unconsciously recognized the same incestual danger which menaces the Frédéric of Flaubert's *L'Education sentimentale,* an education in the atrophy of desire. For the boy, the specular identification with an ideal, notably with the father, constitutes the subject in the *position* of the real father and thus in an untenable rivalry with him; what the subject must seek is what Lacan calls the symbolic identification with the father—that is to say, he must take over the *function* of the father through the normalization of the Oedipus complex. This is an identification with a father who is neither Imaginary nor real: what Lacan calls the Symbolic father, the figure of the Law.

At another level, the specular relationship, however "normal," generates an image of unity where there is in fact discord. If the child does not escape the attraction of this alienated self, he is potentially embroiled in the pathological search for the lost object of which Freud spoke in his earliest works. Since the discovery of the lack of object is for Lacan the condition and the cause of desire, the adult quest for transcendence, lost time, lost paradises, lost plenitude, or any of the myriad forms the lack of object may take—including the most grotesque and the most absurd—can be reduced, if one wishes, to the question at the root of neurosis and psychosis, the question asked by Oedipus: "Who (or what) am I?" The subject, like Oedipus, always knows the answer, but the distinction between Knowledge (*savoir*) and truth repeatedly emphasized by Lacan points up the function of *méconnaissance* and *reconnaissance* in human life. Truth for the subject is not knowledge but recognition. Mental illness on the other hand is precisely the refusal to recognize that truth; the mechanisms of negation, disavowal, rejection, isolation, and so forth flow from it. But a certain *méconnaissance*—which we might call sublimation—is essential to health; Dostoievskian hyperconsciousness is no solution. The point is of course that hyperconsciousness or hyperrecognition simply corresponds to the intensity of the loss. To pose the question at all is the subject's way of recognizing that he is neither who he thinks he is nor what he wants to be, since at the level of the *parole vide* he will always find that he is another. For the Freudian analyst (and for Lacan), the question will eventually be answered at the level of the phallus (the object of symbolic exchange between parents and generations); for the Dasein-analyst, it will be answered with equal conviction in the terms of "ontological insecurity," simply because to be an object for the other is to have lost one's being as a person. In the same way as the quest for being—the quest for the lost "authentic" self (however interminable)—depends upon an original loss and the discovery of difference, self-knowledge depends upon an original misconstruction. For Lacan this is the Imaginary misconstruction of the ego. But since the only valid definition of mental illness is that it can always be found somewhere in psychiatrists' offices, this *méconnaissance* has no a priori value in determining the subject's future: like history, the subject can only be read backwards. All that can be said about the Imaginary relationship a priori is that because it denies the unconscious elements within it, it is correlative to the notion that "consciousness" and "subject" are synonyms.

At whatever level one views the Imaginary relationship as it is expressed in Lacan's earlier works—whether from the static or the dynamic point of view—it is a relationship of love and aggressivity between two egos. The Imaginary battle of mutual objectification is quite different from the symbolic objectification in which the child becomes an object for the parents in a system of symbolic exchange, from long before his birth. In this instance the child functions primarily not as a subject to be reduced to an object (a slave) in a Hegelian struggle for recognition, but more nearly as what Lacan would call a *signifier* in a system of communication between other people. Thus, at the later level of the interpersonal relationships in which the subject is involved as a subject (who may become an object), Lacan's formulation of the Imaginary relationship—whose paradigm is the *stade du miroir*—is significant because it is a development of the notion of the *imago* (Jung) and of the dialectics of narcissism throughout the works of Freud. At the same time it involves a reversal of the usual sense of the word ego (*moi*) both in Freud and in most contemporary psychoanalysis. It is on this return from contemporary "ego psychology" to the problem of the subject that Lacan articulates his "return to Freud."

An example from the *Standard Edition* will serve to illustrate the traditional usage of the notion of "object-choice" in Freudian analysis. Freud is discussing "the establishment of a connection" between a pre-conscious and an unconscious presentation in the dream, and he employs the word "transference" in doing so, a concept "which provides an explanation of so many striking phenomena in the mental life of neurotics." The editor comments: "In his later writings, Freud regularly used this same word . . . (*Uebertragung*) to describe a somewhat different, but not unrelated, psychological process . . . —namely the process of 'transferring' on to a contemporary object feelings which originally applied, and still unconsciously apply, to an infantile object." [2]

The reader will have noted to what extent the notion of transference within the dialectic of analysis is inseparable from any comprehension of interhuman relationships outside it—whether in a contemporary or genetic sense. At the most elementary level, the silent "neutrality" of the analyst (his role as "dummy") enables the subject to project onto him the image of the significant other to whom the subject is addressing his *parole vide*. This *alter ego* of the subject is the ego of the subject himself insofar as his ego is the product of a capture by the other (ultimately reducible

[2] *Interpretation of Dreams* (1900), V, 562, note 2.

to the ideal of the ego). The relationship is a purely dual one for the subject; he is in fact maintaining a sort of short circuit between his narcissistic image of himself and the image of the other, in order to resist any attempts to change that image. But the analyst himself is neither an object nor an *alter ego*; he is the third man. Although he begins by acting as a mirror for the subject, it is through his refusal to respond at the level consciously or unconsciously demanded by the subject (ultimately the demand for love), that he will eventually (or ideally) pass from the role of "dummy," whose hand the subject seeks to play, to that of the Other with whom the barred subject of his patient is unconsciously communicating. The mirror relationship of ego and *alter ego* which was the obstacle to recognition of his unconscious desires which the subject has set up and maintained will be neutralized, the subject's mirages will be "consumed," and it will be possible for the barred subject to accede to the authenticity of what Lacan calls "the language of his desire" through his recognition of his relationship to the Other. This relationship is represented by the broken line in the Schema L between S and A, the latter representing the unconscious or what Lacan calls "the locus of the Other." The triangular relationship between ego, *alter ego,* and the analyst is mediated by the reciprocal interaction of the analyst's unconscious and that of the patient; thus the relationship requires the four terms of the Schema L: two triangles that can be folded one upon the other. In spite of the difficulties of bringing Lacan's algebraic metaphors into the analysis of concrete relationships, it will be seen at once how important the concept of *locus* is for his views. Identification and narcissism, or the relationship between ego and *alter ego,* are not relationships of identity; it is always a question of each trying to take the other's *place*—as in what Lacan defined and demonstrated as an "inmixing of subjects" in his commentary on Poe's *Purloined Letter* (1956). But no one can take another's place, whereas he can be constituted there as in a locus of relationships and functions.

Before dealing further with the *stade du miroir* and the Imaginary, I should indicate something of the status of narcissism and identification in Freud, since the reader will recall that Lacan claims the *stade du miroir* to be an extension of Freud's views.

Näcke's description of narcissism (1899), with which Freud begins his article on the subject,[3] is concerned with autoeroticism in clinical

[3] "On Narcissism" (1914), *Standard Editon*, XIV, 67.

cases. Freud begins his assimilation of narcissism into the mental life of all of us by dealing with it in the terms of the libido which was to become the all-encompassing Eros in his later works. He then distinguishes for the first time between "ego libido" (narcissism) and "object-libido" (sexual choice), which leads him to the significant conclusion that "a unity comparable to the ego cannot exist in the individual from the start; the ego has to be developed" (p. 77). After a lengthy digression on the dangers of hypothesis, a cautionary approach so typical of Freud, he develops the following thesis:

A person may love:

(1) According to the narcissistic type:
    (a) what he himself is [i.e. himself]
    (b) what he himself was
    (c) what he himself would like to be
    (d) someone who was once part of himself [i.e. his children].
(2) According to the anaclitic (attachment) type:
    (a) the woman who feeds him
    (b) the man who protects him and the succession of substitutes who take their place (p. 90).

He goes on to develop the notion of the "ego ideal" or "ideal ego" which becomes the target (by displacement) of the originally narcissistic love. This conception of the model, which becomes internalized as conscience in certain respects, was later to reappear in the concept of the superego. He explains the ideal of the ego (Type 1c) as follows:

In addition to its individual side, this ideal [ego] has a social side; it is also the common ideal of a family, a class or a nation. It binds not only a person's narcissistic libido, but also a considerable amount of his homosexual libido, which is in this way turned back into the ego. The want of satisfaction which arises from the non-fulfilment of this ideal liberates homosexual libido, and this is transformed into a sense of guilt (social anxiety) (pp. 101–2).

In 1916, in *Mourning and Melancholia,*[4] Freud developed a view of narcissism as identification with the lost loved object, which tends to confirm Lacan's assimilation of narcissism to identification. But, as Laplanche and Pontalis point out, neither of these terms is very clear. There are at least three types of identification (*Identifizierung*, not *Einfühlung*) involved: (1) primary identification, which Freud describes as the original, pre-Oedipean affective link to an object, related

---

[4] *Standard Edition,* XIV, 249–51.

to incorporation, the oral stage, and the mother; (2) identification as the regressive substitute for an abandoned object choice; and (3) non-sexual identification with another insofar as one person has something in common with another (the desire of schoolgirls to be involved in love, for instance).[5]

But in *Group Psychology and the Analysis of the Ego,* Freud also mentions two other kinds of relationship: (1) the nonobjectal primary narcissism (replacing the primary narcissism of "On Narcissism," which then becomes "secondary narcissism"), a view which seems to send us back to the theory of the monad; and (2) a presexual identification with the father: "It is easy to state in a formula the distinction between an identification with the father and the choice of the father as [a love] object. In the first case one's father is what one would like to *be,* and in the second he is what one would like to *have.* The distinction, that is, depends upon whether the tie attaches to the subject or to the object of the ego" (p. 106). This presexual identification with an ideal is viewed as "the earliest and original form of emotional tie" (p. 107). It is through this last conception and through the further mechanism of identification as "active" (identification of oneself with the other), or "passive" (identification of the other with oneself), or "reciprocal" that Freud comes to view the psychology of the group (the masses) as an identification with the leader who replaces the ego ideal of the group and the consequent identification of each member with each other on the basis of that ideal.

The reader might well wonder at the inconclusiveness of these remarks, but the term "identification" is commonly used so loosely that it is essential to have some notion of the complexity of what we are actually talking about. As far as Freud's own views are concerned, the contradictions forced upon him by empirical facts can be resolved only by further reference to the facts, and further interpretation. What is immediately noticeable is the paradoxical way in which Freud regards the hydraulics of that somewhat unfortunate metaphor, the libido. In the article on narcissism all forms of identification, including the identification with an ideal, are assimilated to sexual choice in the end, and primacy is given to the mother ("the attachment type"). In the later article on

---

[5] See: *Group Psychology and the Analysis of the Ego* (1921), *Standard Edition,* XVIII, 105ff. Note that the German term is *Masse,* with its somewhat derogatory connotations.

group psychology, however, the notion of identification with the father as an ideal is supposedly "presexual." Later in this work, nevertheless, identification with the ideal of a group is again subsumed under the libido, which seems always to be a masculine notion, although the identification with another on the basis of a common element is described as nonsexual. Nothing is said at this level to relate the dialectic of identification with persons to the more primordial question of introjection and expulsion of primary objects as it was developed by Freud in the 1925 article "Die Verneinung," to which I shall return later. Moreover Freud's use of the expression *das Ich* is much looser—closer to "self"—in the earlier article. As far as the relationship of the group and the relationship of the subject to an ideal is concerned, however, the implication is clearly that all types of identification, at all sorts of levels, operate in these instances, without any one type being assigned a primacy: "Each individual is a component part of numerous groups, he is bound by ties of identification in many directions, and he has built up his ego ideal upon the most various models. Each individual therefore has a share in numerous group minds . . ." (*Group Psychology,* p. 129). Whatever the difficulties of interpretation involved, however, Lacan's view of the *moi* ("I," "me," "self") as an alienation can be clarified to a certain extent by another passage from the same chapter: "In many individuals the separation between ego and the ego ideal is not very far advanced; the two still coincide readily; the ego has often preserved its earlier narcissistic self-complacency" (p. 129).

Norman O. Brown offers an interpretation of Freud's contradictions on this subject by reference to the concept of Eros, which he feels underlies the distinctions Freud tries unsuccessfully to maintain. Fundamentally, he suggests, love is for Freud the concept of a desire for union with the love object, rather than a desire to possess it, an interpretation which is similar in some respects to Sartre's negative view of desire as the desire to appropriate the other's liberty (which cannot be appropriated at the level of having). Although Brown's view of the assimilation of identification and narcissism seems totally opposed in intent to Lacan's, it is certainly instructive here: ". . . In some of his writings [Freud] uses the terms 'narcissistic object-choice' and 'anaclitic object-choice,' corresponding to his later terminology of 'identification' and 'true object-choice' (or 'object-cathexis'). Summarizing the distinction, Freud says that the human being has originally two sexual objects: himself and the woman who tends him" ["On Narcissism," p. 88]. But Freud's distinction between identification and object choice, or between narcissistic and anaclitic object choices, does not, in Freud's own terms, seem to be tenable. As I have indicated, Freud does not maintain the correlation of identification with love of the father and object choice with love of the mother. Thus Brown concludes: "Close examination of Freud's own premises and arguments suggests that there is only one loving relationship to objects in the world, a relation of being-one-with-the-world which, though closer to Freud's narcissistic relation (identification), is also at the root of his other category of possessive love (object-choice)." [6] Consequently, for Brown, being the other is at the basis of our desire to have the other.

Some further clarification of Lacan's early view of the metapsychology of identification and narcissism can be found in his "Aggressivité en psychanalyse" (1948). In speaking of the relationship of aggressivity and narcissism, the one being correlative to the other, Lacan views the *stade du miroir* as the primary identification allowing the possibility of the secondary identification described by Freud as part of the function of the Oedipus relationship. The function of the Oedipus complex

is one of sublimation, which designates very precisely an identificatory reorganization of the subject, and, as Freud put it when he felt the necessity of making a "topographical" coordination of psychic dynamisms, a *secondary identification* by the introjection of the *imago* of the parent of the same sex.
. . . But it is clear that the structural effect of identification with the rival is not self-evident, except at the level of the fable, and can only be conceived of if it is previously prepared by a primary identification which structures the subject as a rival of himself (p. 382).

Thus aggressivity, for Lacan, is primarily intrasubjective. But is the *infans* of the *stade du miroir* a subject? Lacan employs the term with a fine distinction: the child is a subject, he says, because, unlike the chimpanzee before a mirror, he recognizes what he sees and celebrates his discovery. But he is an alienated subject (a *moi*) by this very fact. His "true" subjectivity, as I interpret it, is only "restored" to him "in the universal" (that is, in the world of language) by his learning to speak.

The *stade du miroir* is further the "crossroads" through which the child is introduced to human desire:

[6] *Life against Death* (New York: Vintage Books, 1959), p. 42.

It is this capture by the *imago* of the human form, rather than an *Ein-fühlung* which seems clearly to be absent in early infancy, which, between the age of six months and two and a half, dominates all the dialectic of the behavior of the child in the presence of his counterparts. . . .

. . . This erotic relationship in which the human individual fixes upon himself an image which alienates him from himself, is the energy and the form from which there originates that passionate organization which he calls his *moi*.

In effect this form becomes crystallized in the conflictual tension internal to the subject which determines the awakening of his desire for the object of the desire of the other. Here the primordial coming togther is precipitated into an aggressive concurrence, and it is from this concurrence that there is born the triad of the other, the *moi,* and the object . . . (*Ibid.,* p. 379).

In his prewar, phenomenologically oriented writings, Lacan had emphasized the function of perception as information. This is related to the function of the *moi*: formation, information, deformation. It is the strength of the alienated *moi,* rather than its "disintegration," which would therefore account for the paranoid structures of identification with the aggressor, persecution mania, erotomania, doubling, jealousy, and so forth, all related to the subject's internal rivalry with himself. In his thesis of 1932, Lacan had sought to show that his patient's persecutors were identical with the images of her ego ideal. In studying what he called "paranoiac knowledge" he formulated the view that the paranoiac alienation of the ego through the *stade du miroir* was one of the preconditions of human knowledge. Thus the *moi* is essentially paranoid; it is "impregnated with the Imaginary." His "genetic theory of the ego," as the reader can see from the translator's notes and from the article of 1953, "Some Reflections on the Ego," depends upon treating the relationship of the subject to his own body in terms of his identification with an *imago.* The key point here is the notion of totality. The narcissistic component of the child (or man) who sees himself in the other, without realizing that what he contemplates as his self *is* the other, is quite different from that which is commonly thought to mean an autoerotic relationship between the subject and his own body (or parts of it). As others had said before Lacan, it is the notion of the *body image* which is involved rather than the notion of the body itself. The Romantic and existentialist heroes who face their mirrors know this.

The *stade du miroir* is called a turning point. Lacan sometimes speaks as if it occurred in the newborn baby's fascination with human faces, or in his relationship to the mother—note the "primary identification" of t.n. 68, where it is the mother in a Kleinian sense who is evoked—or with "stature, status, and statues"—in other words the child's fascination with the images of other human beings as harmonious totalities at a time when he himself is still unable to control his own functions or movements. At other times, he speaks of the mirror phase as occurring much later (six to twenty-one months). What seems fairly clear is that the *stade du miroir* never "occurs" at all—any more than the genesis of the ego does. If we consider the multivalency of the Schema L, it is evident that the *stade du miroir* is a purely structural or relational concept, conceived before postwar "structuralism" had been heard of. The Imaginary components of the mirror play of the child (as a perceptual relationship) absolutely require the *stade du miroir* to be read in three ways at once: backwards—as a symptom of or a substitute for a much more primordial identification; forwards—as a phase in development; and timelessly—as a relationship best formulated in algorithmic terms. The subject's "fixation" on (or in) the Imaginary is a matter of degree.

There is less emphasis on the justification of the *stade du miroir* in Lacan's writings of the sixties—the concept is simply integrated into the Lacanian algorithms. But the empirical facts of narcissism, identification, fascination, and, of course, the double (the *Doppelgänger* sometimes appears reversed, as in a mirror), as well as their vast progeny in literature and in the various explanations offered by the psychologists who write literature, make the topic especially important. This one concept may stand as one of Lacan's most important contributions to the interpretation of psychological data. What makes it more interesting is the fact that Lacan regards the *stade du miroir*—the vision of harmony by a being in discord—as at the origin of the phantasy or dream of the *corps morcelé*. The image of the "body in bits and pieces," or as put together like a mismatched jigsaw puzzle, is one of the most common phenomena in our normal dreams and phantasies, and also in certain forms of schizophrenia and of course in the LSD "trip," to say nothing of literature, from Romanticism to existentialism. For Lacan, then, the paranoid twist of the *moi* in the Imaginary is directly related to the peculiar twists we give to our own body image.

The category of the Imaginary can be fairly quickly defined—whether it can actually be separated logically from the Symbolic is quite another matter. From the point of view of intrasubjectivity, the concept of the

Imaginary order accounts for the narcissistic relation of subject and *moi* outlined in the foregoing. From the point of view of intersubjectivity, the Imaginary is the dual relationship of the Schema L—the capture of the *moi* by another, in an erotic or aggressive relationship. In relation to the environment, the Imaginary is the area of the biological maturation through perception. In relation to meaning, the Imaginary is that in which perceptual features like resemblance operate—that is to say, in areas where there is a sort of coalescence of the signifier and signified, as in traditional symbolism. For Lacan, the Imaginary relationship, of whatever kind, is also that of a lure, a trap. In this sense he is close to the normal usage of the word "imaginary" to describe something we believe to be something else.[7]

But, in spite of the fact that the Imaginary is present in all human relations, Lacan avers that intersubjectivity cannot be conceived within its limits, since intersubjectivity is ultimately dependent upon the intentionality of the discourse. The fact is that intersubjectivity *has* generally been conceived in entirely Imaginary terms throughout the Platonic and Cartesian tradition—and one might recall the well-known fact that "I know" (οἶδα) in Greek, from which "idea" is derived, is the present perfect of "I see" (εἴδω). Lacan's original attempt to restate in psychological and empirical terms the philosophical reversal which Heidegger had begun is thus of singular importance for anyone concerned with the discourse. But the question the reader must ask himself is whether Lacan's attempt to differentiate and restate the three modes of human relationship, subject-object, object-object, and subject-subject, is in the end successful. In other words, we must ask how he actually relates the Imaginary to the Symbolic, and the question would be unfair only if he had not claimed to have answered it. Obviously the relationship is there; obviously the distinction between the two is a valid methodological concept—but so much of Lacan's theoretical development of the notion, including the question of the partial object and the phantasy, is dependent upon one single piece of empirical data from Freud (the *Fort! Da!*) that one naturally asks what other psychological data there are to support the interpretation. Certainly if Lacan shared Freud's tentative and careful use of hypotheses instead of so readily employing the aphoristic, all-conclusive generalization, the lack of other empirical data would be less

---

[7] See the entry in: Laplanche and Pontalis, *Vocabulaire de la Psychanalyse* (Paris: PUF, 1967), p. 195.

disquieting, for even when Freud extends his own speculations far beyond the limits of the available data, he never lets the reader forget that what he is doing is based on hypothesis and speculation.

Lacan faces the problem squarely, but his explanations are less than complete. Taxed with explicating the unconscious phantasy in the terms of an unconscious "structured like a language," Lacan replies that "once it is defined as an image put into a function within the signifying structure, the notion of an unconscious phantasy presents no difficulties." [8] The reader will recall that this definition of the phantasy in the terms of a signifying function is dependent upon Lacan's interpretation of the rerepresentation at the Symbolic level of an original discovery of presence and absence at the Imaginary level (the *Fort! Da!*). And, presumably seeking to meet further objections about neurotic or hysterical symptoms (actions) which are not vocal parts of the discourse, he answers that Freud considered them *structurally* identical to facts of language (the hysterical symptom "joins in the conversation"—t.n. 52). He goes on:

> Leave to one side my remarks on the fact that overdetermination is strictly speaking only conceivable within the structure of language. In neurotic symptoms, what does this mean?
>
> It means that there is going to be an interference between the effects which correspond in the subject to any determinate demand and the effects of a position in relation to the other (here, his counterpart) which he sustains as subject.
>
> Which he sustains as subject means that Language permits him to consider himself as the engineer, or the *metteur en scène* of the entire Imaginary capture of which he could not be otherwise than the living marionette (p. 198).

Other immediate difficulties concerning the concept of the Imaginary and the *stade du miroir* are fairly clear. Compared with Lacan's remark about "the true subject" (t.n. 135) and the use of the verb "s'être" in translating Freud's "Wo es war soll Ich werden" (t.n. 110), the *stade du miroir* seems to imply a monadlike absolute subject (similar to Freud's last formulation of primary narcissism) which has to find itself again by "speaking from" the *je* rather than from the *moi*. According to Laplanche and Pontalis, however, Lacan has denied this difficulty by asserting that there is indeed an intersubjective relationship before the turning point of the mirror phase, whose importance he declares lies

---

[8] "La Direction de la cure" (1961), p. 199.

primarily in the *interiorization* of the image of the other as a totality. This formulation is close enough to Freud's view of the interiorization or introjection of the ideal ego, although Freud is also concerned with the partial identifications ("impersonations") involved in this relationship between subject and other.

The Cogito and the "True" Subject

Thus the Symbolic coexists with the Imaginary, since intersubjectivity is viewed by Lacan as primarily a symbolic relationship, and the Imaginary alone cannot explain intersubjectivity. Consequently, it is difficult to say precisely what it means to speak of the restoration of subjectivity to the *infans* through his appropriation of language except insofar as one interprets it somewhat tautologously to mean that this restoration "in the universal" allows the *je* to speak. If we leave aside the difficulties of the word "restoration," however, it can be said very simply that the child begins outside the Symbolic. He is confronted by it, and the significant question—ultimately the "Who (or what) am I?"—is articulated on the problem of entry into it. It has sometimes been suggested, for instance, that there is no neurosis within the highly complex symbolic structures of so-called primitive societies. Although there is empirical evidence against this position, which is primarily a theoretical one partly involving the impossibility of confronting a pristine or totally "authentic" native society, the possibility of seriously considering it devolves from the importance of the native's own symbolic position in societal interchanges. In other words, in the ideal case, he cannot pose the question of identity, because he has already been identified (as the mother's brother, for example). The question of identity may be for him a meaningless and therefore unaskable question similar to that involved in the native informant's puzzlement with the anthropologist who asks, "Well, what *would* happen if you married your sister?" In other words, the native's entry into the Symbolic order of his society is (ideally) more carefully defined than our own, and it may be the white man who teaches him to ask the question (cf. t.n. 80, 168, 188).

For Lacan, then, intersubjectivity becomes a wider or narrower concept, depending on the context, and it reflects the vacillating use of the idea in many other writers, notably since Husserl's struggles with bringing the concept into his own *cogito* philosophy in the *Méditations cartési-*

ennes, lectures delivered in Paris in 1929.[9] Husserl had tried unsuccessfully to solve the accusation that phenomenology entails solipsism, by recourse to the notion of empathy—which Lacan, following Heidegger, rejects as a primordial phenomenon—and by a further recourse to an "intermonadology." I doubt that Lacan has solved the technical problem of solipsism either, but his approach is considerably more subtle, and in any case it depends upon empirical, as opposed to apodictic, evidence. Possibly Lacan's insistence on the alienation by another through the *stade du miroir* can be more fully appreciated if we compare it with the following passage from Husserl's Fifth Meditation: "These two primordial spheres, mine which is for me as ego [*Ich*] the original sphere, and his which is for me an appresented sphere—are they not *separated* by an abyss I cannot actually cross, since crossing it would mean, after all, that I acquired an original (rather than an appresenting) experience of someone else?" (p. 121). Husserl's great difficulty was surely a lack of understanding of the sociological sphere, since some have found the truth of Saint Augustine's "interior man," which is evoked at the end of the *Meditations,* in an illusion stemming from our failure to recognize to what extent we are determined by social structures.

Many sociologists and anthropologists (notably Lévi-Strauss) regard individual psychology as more or less totally subordinated to social structures, certainly insofar as these structures are outside the psychopathological sphere. This assertion of the primacy of society, buttressed by a vast amount of anthropological evidence, is surely related to Lacan's introduction of "the Other" and "the other" (concepts to which I shall return) into his interpretation of the Freudian texts, which, we remember, tend to assert the primacy of psychology over sociology. Certainly many of Lacan's theoretical choices cannot be properly understood except as at least partly the products of a climate composed of the conflicting claims of phenomenologists, sociologists, existentialists, psychologists, and anthropologists. Thus he seems to steer between individualism on the one hand and sociology on the other, by asserting that the alienation of the *stade du miroir* is presocial yet dependent on the other, that it occurs at the level of family yet does not necessarily involve specific family relationships.

[9] Fifth Meditation. See the English rendering of the received text (which is not the same as the original French), translated by Dorion Cairns: *Cartesian Meditations* (The Hague: Nijhoff, 1964), p. 89ff.

For Lévi-Strauss the individual tends to disappear entirely within the social structure. But the question of the individual is fundamentally an ideological and socioeconomic one, and neither Lacan nor Lévi-Strauss ever goes beyond the values of the dominant ideology in this respect. From a philosophical perspective, one attempt to deal with the relationship of others and individuals was that of Heidegger, who begins, not with the *cogito,* but with *Mitsein.* Heidegger naturally poses difficulties as well: the concept that Dasein is "in each case mine" has been criticized as begging the question of the *cogito.* But insofar as psychoanalysis supposes what Philip Rieff has called Freud's "ideal of normalcy"—usually expressed (amusingly) in the Freudian terminology as the "genital character"—or, in Lacan's terms, a "true Word," a *parole pleine,* psychoanalysis is concerned with the problem of authenticity, just as Heidegger was, whereas for the sociologist the concept has less meaning. It must be remembered that Freud was extremely pessimistic about authenticity, unlike the more recent promoters of "social adaptation," who tend to identify it with the same sort of social conventions which Freud attacked so vigorously. Moreover, Lacan is a psychoanalyst who has never failed to point out Freud's ultimate conception of analysis as an infinite process. Death, says Lacan, has the last word. But, although it is true that in making his often implicit rapprochement between Freud and Heidegger, Lacan perhaps leaves too much unsaid, so much of his work is imbued with a Heideggerean viewpoint that it is informative to note the similarity between his view of the "true" subject and Heidegger's view.

"Who is speaking and to whom?" is one of Lacan's central questions, and if one compares it with the analysis of the "who" of Dasein in *Sein und Zeit* (1927),[10] it is perhaps not surprising to discover Heidegger's concern for the status of the "I" in the discourse—as well as negative echoes of the textbook Freud.

Husserl had said in the *Logische Untersuchungen* (1900), II, "Das Wort 'ich' rennt von Fall zu Fall eine andere Person, und es tut dies mittels immer neuer Bedeutung" ["The word 'I' as the case may be, designates a different person, and in this way constantly takes on a new signification."]. Heidegger takes up the same idea in terms very close to Peirce's concept of the "I" as one type of indexical symbol, substituting

---

[10] Trans. Macquarrie and Robinson, SCM Press, London, 1962. To avoid possible confusion, I have suppressed the capitalization of the noun "Other" in the quotations and replaced "entity" (*das Seiendes*) by "existent."

the concept of designation for that of signification: "The word 'I' is to be understood only in the sense of a non-committal *formal indicator,* indicating something which may perhaps reveal itself as its 'opposite' in some particular phenomenal context of Being. In that case, the 'not-I' is by no means tantamount to an existent which essentially lacks 'I-hood,' but is rather a definite kind of Being which the 'I' itself possesses, such as having lost itself [*Selbstverlorenheit*]" (pp. 151–52). Through his rejection of empathy (*Einfühlung*) in the sense that Husserl tried later to use it as an intersubjective bridge, Heidegger turns the concept inside out, as it were. " 'Empathy' does not first constitute Being-with; only on the basis of Being-with does 'empathy' become possible . . ." (p. 162). Being-toward-others is not a projection, in the psychological sense, of one's own Being-toward-oneself into something else, creating the other as a "duplicate of the Self" (that is, as a doubling from the point of view of a "given" self or *cogito*), because empathy, unlike *Mitsein,* is not a primordial existential phenomenon. In everyday inauthentic *Mitsein,* Dasein is *in subjection* to the "they": "[Dasein] itself *is* not; its Being has been taken away by the others . . . . These others, moreover, are not *definite* others. On the contrary any other can represent them . . . . The 'who' [of Dasein] is the neuter, *the 'they'* [*das Man*]" (p. 164). "Everyone is the other, and no one is himself" (p. 165).

Later on, he sums up the previous analysis before beginning the analysis of conscience (*Gewissen*), by saying in effect that the "I" is captured by the other: "For the most part *I myself* am not the 'who' of Dasein; the they-self is its who" (p. 312). In dealing with the "I," Heidegger is talking about one type of "shifter," [11] and he has already mentioned Humboldt's remarks (1829) on certain languages which represent the "I" by "here," the "thou" by "there," and the "he" by "yonder" (p. 155). He calls these locative adverbs "Dasein-designations." He goes on to distinguish the "authentic self" from the "they-self" in which Dasein has lost itself. He begins his analysis of this alienation through consideration of "the voice of conscience," which, he says, discloses through its being an appeal or call to Dasein (in a discourse). "Losing itself in a publicness and the idle-talk of the 'they,' it *fails to hear* [*überhort*] its own Self [*Selbst*] in listening to the they-self" (p.

[11] The passage from Husserl is quoted by Jakobson in his "Shifters, verbal categories, and the Russian verb," Russian Language Project, Harvard University Press, 1957.

315). The appeal of conscience is to "one's *own Self.*" Obviously the specific terminology used here by Heidegger is not the same as Lacan's, nor is his point of view that of psychology; moreover, Heidegger is talking about conscience as something which, for him, "discourses solely and constantly in the mode of keeping silent." Nevertheless, the parallel between Heidegger and Lacan seems explicit: "But we shall not obtain an ontologically adequate interpretation of the conscience until it can be made plain not only *who* is called by the call but also *who does the calling . . .*" (p. 319).

He goes on: " 'It' calls (*'Es' ruft*), against our expectations and even against our will. On the other hand the call does not come from someone else who is with me in the world. The call comes *from* me and yet *from beyond me*" (p. 320). The following paragraphs reject the concept of conscience as the "voice of God" ("an alien power by which Dasein is dominated") and continue Heidegger's implicit argument against the psychoanalytical notion of the superego. But when Heidegger seeks to fix the call of conscience as something both immanent to the subject and yet beyond him, the psychoanalyst is free to read *"Es ruft"* as *"Ça parle"* in the sense that Lacan employs the phrase. The reader will remember that in Lacanian and Freudian psychology the "true subject" is the barred subject ($), and that Lacan constantly plays on the homophony of "$" and "Es." Dasein calls itself, concludes Heidegger, but: "The caller is unfamiliar to the everyday they-self; it is something like an *alien* voice." This "es" calls Dasein back to its potentially-for-Being, back from its alienation in the "they."

Heidegger's conception of this conscience is of course the very opposite of the usual psychoanalytical view of conscience as determining the individual's adaptation to "reality," or his conformity to social and familial *mores.* It is no less the opposite of the "religious" conscience; its voice may be alien to everyday Dasein, but it is ours; it is not other-worldly. The subject is ex-centric to himself, and consciousness is not the center of his being (to consciousness, the voice of Heidegger's conscience is a *silent* discourse).

But these similarities are much more apparent in the Lacan of the fifties than they are later. If the reader has noticed Lacan's seemingly "existential" concern in the *Discours* for the fate of the individual in the neo-Freudian theories of social adaptation, as well as his apparently approving references to Leenhardt's Westernized "man in his authenticity" (t.n. 80, 168)—the Christianized native who has evolved from the status of a locus in relationships to that of a "person"—he will find the later Lacan moving further and further from any correlation of "subject" with *"cogito."* In the sense that "Go do kamo" is a Melanesian *cogito,* it is precisely the opposite of Lacan's logical view of the subject as the "empty subject"—a subject defined only as a locus of relationships, but in more than the two dimensions employed by Leenhardt (t.n. 188). We do not know what a subject *is,* any more than we know what an electron is, but we do know to a certain extent how it behaves in certain relationships and how it is related to the functions which intersect in it.

Many problems of interpreting Lacan are difficult to resolve because he does not approach the developments of his own theory in an unequivocal fashion. I cannot recall many published passages in which he says, for instance, that at such and such a time he thought one thing whereas now he thinks another. His views are always presented *en bloc* as if they had never evolved, with the result that one tends to assume that any formula or aphorism which is repeated always means more or less the same thing, whereas closer examination shows that this can not be so. Given these difficulties, the reader should therefore approach with some caution my opinion that, provided the very different orientation between Heidegger and Lacan is kept in mind, Lacan's early view of the unconscious as "the discourse of the Other," his notion of the neurotic as "appealing to the Other," and the ideological concept of the alienated *moi,* are in part a *psychological* development of a point of view which, while not exclusively Heideggerean, is particularly emphasized and developed in the Heidegger of *Sein und Zeit.* Later on, however, similar expressions will occur in contexts where the divergence between the philosophical epistemology of Hegel and Heidegger and the "linguistic" epistemology of Lacan is much more advanced.

Lacan's critique of the philosophical *cogito* in the late fifties is expressed in the following terms, where "subject of the signifier" and "subject of the signified" presumably represent the conscious and the unconscious subject. He begins with the formulation *" 'cogito ergo sum,' ubi cogito, ibi sum,"* and continues:

Certainly this formulation limits me to being there in my being only insofar as I think that I am in my thought . . . .
The real question is this: Is the place which I occupy as subject of the

signifier concentric or ex-centric in relation to the place I occupy as subject of the signified?

It is not a question of knowing whether I am speaking about myself in conformity with what I am, but rather that of knowing whether, when I speak of it, I am the same as that of which I speak . . . .[12]

The unconscious is an area of thought, as Freud asserted; consequently, says Lacan, the philosophical *cogito* is at the base of the mirage which makes modern man so sure of being himself in his incertitudes about himself. Thus the *cogito ergo sum* must be replaced by the following formula (p. 70): "Je ne suis pas, là où je suis le jouet de ma pensée; je pense à ce que je suis, là où je ne pense pas penser." ["I am not, there where I am the plaything of my thought; I think about what I am, there where I do not think that I am thinking (that is, at the level of the unconscious).] In essence, then, for Lacan, the conscious *cogito* is supplemented by an unconscious subject who may be the subject saying "I think" or "I am," but never both at once, since the question of the subject's being is posed at the level of the unconscious.

Shifters

Although the topic is not specifically mentioned in the *Discours,* Heidegger's reference to "Dasein-designations," or to what linguists now call "shifters," is an indication of the usefulness of this methodological concept in the interpretation of the discourse. Jakobson has taken up the problem of the status of what C. S. Peirce called "indexical symbols," more or less equivalent to Russell's "ego-centric particulars," with the intent of defining the notion more precisely for linguistics. These terms have often been applied to what are generally called indices, like "here," "there," "now," and so on, but especially to personal pronouns. But in defining his use of Jespersen's term "shifter," Jakobson includes within it what Postgate called the "subjective elements." He discards most of the definitions offered of these terms, denying to personal pronouns the primordial status accorded them by Humboldt. He notes that pronouns are the latest acquisitions of the child and one of the first losses

---

[12] "L'Instance de la lettre" (1957), pp. 69–70. Note that whatever Lacan says about the *theory* of the *cogito*, psychoanalysis deals only with the *subject* of the *cogito*, not with the id. Thus he reformulates the *cogito* for the Abbé de Choisy, a celebrated seventeenth-century transvestite, as: *"Je pense quand je suis* celui qui s'habille en femme."

in aphasia. For Jakobson, shifters are differentiated from other parts of the linguistic code only by their obligatory reference to the *message,* and thus to the sender.[13] Consequently a "but," a "probably," a conditional mood, or anything of a similarly "subjective" nature must be defined as a shifter. One example Lacan has employed, for instance, involves the so-called pleonastic or optional "ne" used in certain French subjunctive clauses.

Of course the shifter is only a methodological tool, since it does not necessarily increase our understanding. But Freud would almost certainly have wished to employ the notion in his lengthy discussion of the representation of a common phantasy in neurosis by the words: "a child is being beaten." [14] As the analysis progresses, this "neutral" message is re-presented in different ways. In each successive feedback or communication (*Verkehrung*) the new representation introduces the shifter without which the message cannot be interpreted, because without the shifter it refers only to the code. "My father is beating the child," says the subject. "My father is beating the child *whom I hate.*" Eventually the wording (Freud's expression) runs: "I am being beaten by my father," and so on. By designating the sender, the shifters thus move on to designate the receiver of the message. The fact that this transformed message oscillates between the conscious and the unconscious subject of the discourse, the fact that it depends upon the dialectic of identification which Lacan emphasizes so constantly, and the fact that Freud sees so much in this one phrase, will serve to suggest that Lacan's definition of the unconscious as "the discourse of the Other" (*de Alio in oratione*) is in essence a valid interpretation of Freud's experience, if not precisely in the words Freud would have chosen. Yet in a sense Freud had in fact chosen these terms, since for him the discourse of the schizophrenic is the discourse of the unconscious.

In any event, the question of who is speaking in the analytical discourse is no different in essence from the problems of locating the speaking subject in any one of the various voices of a literary or philosophical text at any particular moment—the author, the author's second self, the narrator, the questioner, the respondent, the omniscient or the restricted consciousness, the "I," the hero, and so forth—although in the

[13] The foregoing is taken from "Shifters, verbal categories, and the Russian verb," *loc. cit.* These passages date from 1950.
[14] See: " 'A Child Is Being Beaten' " (1919), *Standard Edition,* XVII, 179.

case of the literary text the question may be of a more formal than existential importance, and at the same time it may be more difficult. In both cases, however, linguistic analysis employing methodological concepts like that of the shifter is particularly useful. On the other hand, as Roland Barthes has long pointed out, we must be prepared also to recognize that the over-all exigencies and constraints of speech (*parole*) are different from those of writing, a distinction which Freud never made except by implication, as in his analysis of dreams, jokes, and slips of the tongue. To take a simplistic example, if the schizophrenic says "I'm the black sŭn," the psychiatrist may well catch the significant ambiguity of "sŭn," but how would the literary author spell it? And if he were to spell it "son," what would his decision mean in the context of any particular sentence or paragraph, or in the context of his work as a whole?

II

Need, Demand, and Desire

Before the preceding remarks on the possible ancestry of Lacan's "true" subject, I had quoted a passage from "La Direction de la cure" (1961) (p. 198) concerning the relationship of subject and analyst, in which the word "demand" occurs. The distinction between need, demand, and desire is an important aspect of Lacan's theory (t.n. 68, 143), and the distinction is related to the Imaginary order.

The *parole vide* is an Imaginary discourse, a discourse impregnated with Imaginary elements which have to be resolved if the subject and analyst are to progress to the ideal point of the *parole pleine*. For Lacan, the main features of this Imaginary discourse are the demands (intransitive in fact) which the subject makes of the analyst. Desire, for him, on the other hand, is "an effect in the subject of that condition which is imposed upon him by the existence of the discourse to cause his need to pass through the defiles of the signifier." This is in effect an important and radical restatement in a structural terminology of the essentially genetic view of the subordination of the pleasure principle to the reality principle, since reality for the subject is literally *re-presented* by the signifier (cf. Freud's article on "Negation"). Lacan's view of desire, apart from its Hegelian ancestry (which I shall deal with in a moment), involves an attempt to correlate several Freudian concepts: the libido, *Trieb,* Eros, the pleasure principle, and wish fulfillment (*Wun-*

scherfüllung). Lacan's earlier works stress the libido, as my previous quotations from the "Agressivité en psychanalyse" (1948) indicate, whereas the later ones, "La Direction de la cure" (1961), for example, which I am attempting to follow here, stress wish fulfillment. Obviously these concepts are interrelated; the difficulty is to say in what way. The situation is further complicated by Lacan's assertions that the phallus is a signifier—the signifier of signifiers in fact—but the passage from the discourse to the phallus is never clearly explained.

The difficulty derives from the way that Imaginary elements may enter the Symbolic as signs, signifiers, and symbols, and, conversely, from the way that symbolic elements may be reduced to Imaginary functions. Lacan's views on the relationship between the Symbolic, the Imaginary, and the Real, and their relationship to the phallus and to what is called the object relation in psychoanalysis are developed at length in the seminars on "La Relation d'objet et les structures freudiennes" (beginning in 1956), but since these seminars depend on a lengthy structural analysis of a number of case histories, it is not possible to go into the details here. Lacan's main point is that traditional psychoanalysis has so concerned itself with the "reduced" dialectic of the subject and his relation to objects conceived of by analysts as either imaginary (hallucinated) or real, that the most essential part of the object relation has been ignored: the notion of the lack of object. Analysts have forgotten that "between the mother and the child, Freud introduced a third term, an Imaginary element, whose signifying role is a major one: the phallus" (Seminar of November–December, 1956, p. 427). This relationship of three terms, mother, child, and phallus, is changed through the function of the father, which "inserts the lack of object into a new dialectic" and provides for what psychoanalysis calls the "normalization" of the Oedipus complex. But the father involved is not the real father, or an *imago* of any real father—he is what Lacan calls the "Symbolic father." Thus "little Hans" (1909), through whose phobia Freud first revealed in detail the extraordinary effects of castration fear in the child, was deprived of either a real or Imaginary father by the fact that his own father—by whom the analysis and cure were actually conducted— had abdicated his responsibilities in the Oedipal triangle in favor of the mother. The Symbolic father in this case, asserts Lacan, was "the Professor"—Freud himself.

Lacan is concerned with elucidating the Symbolic, Imaginary, and

Real relationships between three subcategories of "the lack of object"—castration (Imaginary object); frustration (removal of the real object: for example, the breast); and privation (the real absence of the organ in the woman)—and the further relationships between the people involved. Thus castration (which is neither real, nor really potential) is part of the child's relationship to the father, that of the "symbolic debt." Frustration is part of the child's relationship to the mother, that of an "Imaginary injury" (*dam imaginaire*), connected with the later symbolization of the relationship of presence and absence through the *Fort! Da!*. Privation, however, is real—nothing is lacking (nothing can be lacking in the Real, which is a plenum)—and the subject's relationship is not so much to a person as to "reality" itself. Since privation concerns "what ought to be there," the object involved is symbolic. These distinctions are related to Lacan's view of *Verwerfung* (rejection), *Verneinung* (denial), *Verdrängung* (repression), and *Verleugnung* (disavowal) in Freud's metapsychology, topics which are dealt with in greater detail in Section IV.

Since the phallus is not real, but Imaginary—though not necessarily hallucinated—Lacan relates it to (unconscious) desire and to (conscious) demand. The fetishist, for instance, is in fact demanding that there be something where there is nothing. His demand is a disavowal of reality (Freud). But the fetish (the shoe, the bound foot) is not simply a symbol for the phallus, since the phallus is already an Imaginary symbol. The fetish is a metonymic displacement—and displacement of any kind is always onto "something insignificant" (that is, onto something highly meaningful)—and it is this displacement, not the symbolic substitution of the phallus for the organ itself, which maintains the lack of being (the lack of object) in the subject's relation to objects, by directing the subject's conscious demand onto something he does not want. Why speak of the phallus and not of the penis? Lacan asks.

. . . Because the phallus is not a question of a form, or of an image, or of a phantasy, but rather of a signifier, the signifier of desire. In Greek antiquity the phallus is not represented by an organ but as an insignia; it is the ultimate significative object, which appears when all the veils are lifted. Everything related to it is an object of amputations and interdictions . . . . The phallus represents the intrusion of vital thrusting or growth as such, as what cannot enter the domain of the signifier without being *barred* from it, that is to say, covered over by castration . . . . It is at the level of the Other, in the place where castration manifests itself in the Other, it is in the mother—for both girls and boys—that what is called the castration complex is instituted. It is the desire of the Other which is marked by the bar (Seminar of April–June, 1958, p. 252).

The phallus is a *manque à être*—a lack which is brought into being.

Thus, insofar as the signification of a signifier is always another signifier (the metonymic reference of signifier to signifier which relates signifier to signified), the fetish would be a signifier of an original signifier, the phallus. After about 1956, then, Lacan's use of the term "signifier" may be more than usually ambiguous. One notes even in the *Discours* his reference to the Sanskrit noun *lakshana,* which means both signifier and phallus (t.n. 177). As with the unresolved question of the relation between signifier and symptom, however, the phallus is sometimes described, not as a signifier, but as something with a "signifying function."

To return to "La Direction de la cure," which summarizes in laconic fashion the seminars to which I have referred, it is important to realize to what extent Lacan's view of need, desire, and demand depends upon the notion of symbolic exchange in anthropology (t.n. 98), which is dealt with in detail in Section IV. This view seems to account in part for his assertion that the phallus is a signifier (or has a signifying function), since in psychoanalytical theory the phallus does indeed fulfil the task of an "object" whose exchange fixes the subjects in their respective roles as givers and receivers. The phallus is moreover part of the Symbolic order into which the child is born; it is not something he creates, but something he encounters. If the child is identified with the phallus by the mother, he is thus being required to conform to the desire of the Other. The symbolic value of castration—in which the agent is the Symbolic father who incorporates the *law:* the interdiction of incest—is in fact that of breaking this incestuous circuit, thus opening up object choices outside it. The symbolic exchange within the family is thus ideally free to escape the original dialectic and enter into a displacement of it at another level of signification. Through the child's accession to language, which for Lacan governs the Symbolic order, and through his advent to the intersubjectivity of rivalry (ideally with the parent of the opposite sex), the boy, by repressing castration, and the girl, by rejecting it (*Verwerfung*), emerge from the Oedipus complex into the subjectivity of normality (again ideally). Language provides the means of splitting off from each other the original confusion of need and demand (in the baby) and thus for the genesis of desire, which is never articulated as such.

The transformation of need into demand is repeated at the level of the relationship between analyst and patient, where it is never a question of need:

> Whether it intends to frustrate or to gratify, any reply to demand in analysis brings the transference back to suggestion.
> . . . The fact is that the transference is also a suggestion, but one which can only operate on the basis of the demand for love, which is not a demand resulting from any need. That this demand is constituted as such only insofar as the subject is the subject of the signifier, is what permits it to be abused by reducing it to the needs from which these signifiers have been borrowed —which is what psychoanalysts, as we know, never fail to do (pp. 196–97).

Since demand is articulated and addressed to another in a situation where the other has nothing to give, it is distinguished from need (for an object which will satisfy a need) by the fact that the object involved is nonessential; thus any demand is essentially a demand for love. As Laplanche and Pontalis repeat and summarize the formulations of Lacan's seminars under the entry *"Désir (Wunsch,* sometimes *Begierde* or *Lust)"*: "Desire is born from the split between need and demand. It is irreducible to need, because it is not in principle a relation to a real object which is independent of the subject, but a relation to the phantasy. It is irreducible to demand, insofar as it seeks to impose itself without taking language or the unconscious of the other into account, and requires to be recognized absolutely by him." Demand is thus *for* something, whether that something is desired or not, whereas desire, as an absolute, is fundamentally the Hegelian desire for recognition, in that the subject seeks recognition as a (human) subject by requiring the other to recognize his (human) desire; in this sense one desires what another desires. And in the sense that desire is unconscious, one desires what the Other (here the unconscious subject) desires.

In the process of analysis, says Lacan, the power of the analyst is "the power to do good. No power has any other end, which is why power has no end." In analysis, it must therefore be noted

(1) that the Word is all-powerful there, that it has the special powers of the cure

(2) that, by the fundamental rule, the analyst is a long way from directing

the subject towards the full Word, or towards a coherent discourse, but that the analyst leaves the subject free to try his hand at it

(3) that this liberty is what the subject tolerates least easily

(4) that demand is properly that which is put into parentheses in analysis, since the analyst is excluded from satisfying any of the subject's demands

(5) that since no obstacle is put in the way of the subject's avowal of his desire, it is towards this avowal that he is directed or even shepherded

(6) that his resistance to this avowal, in the last analysis, can only be the result of the incompatibility of desire with the Word.[15]

It is in the sense that desire ultimately seeks the annihilation of the other as an independent subject (or of oneself) that Lacan seeks to show both the impossibility of any fundamental satisfaction of desire (as opposed to the curative value of its recognition) and the role of demand in the discourse, where some sort of reciprocity is actually possible. At the same time the Hegelian view of desire, which is what pervades Lacan's earlier works, is supplemented by the more primordial notion of the lack of object which provides for the genesis of desire itself. If the newborn child can indeed be regarded as in a monadlike (lack of) relationship to "reality," then the desire for unity with the other, of which N. O. Brown speaks, expresses a *derivative* of the most fundamental of "relationships," the "megalomania" of primary narcissism. But primary narcissism is *not* in fact a relationship, since we assume that no objects "ek-sist" for the subject at this point, as Freud points out in his article on "Negation." The absolute character of the subject's desire matches his original status as an "absolute subject." But the absolute subject is an inexpressible, asubjective entity, since the absolute subject is a contradiction in terms, whether it be the primordial monad or the goal of the Hegelian *Phenomenology*. And it is not the fact that the child at the stage of primary narcissism "feels" all-powerful (another contradiction) which is significant for him, but rather his discovery of the absolute power of the whim of the Other whom he is totally unable to control. Since the early Lacan viewed both the paranoid character of the *moi* and its master-slave relationship to others as characteristics of modern civilization developed since the end of the sixteenth century (correlative to the discovery of the Cartesian subject whose primacy Lacan rejects), the implication seems to be that the Imaginary death struggle between egos is how things are, rather than how they

---

[15] "La Direction de la cure" (1961), p. 202.

have to be, whereas the subject's profoundest desire to be "One" again (to control the Other to whom he becomes subjected) is totally and absolutely irreducible. It is this desire for what is really annihilation (non-difference) that makes human beings human. And if we employ the insights of the mathematical metaphor, as Lacan does in the later works, we realize that this primordial "One" cannot be one at all, since one requires two. What it can be is *zero,* in the precise sense that, logically speaking, for mathematics the function of zero is to be the concept under which no object falls (all objects being defined as identical with themselves), because in order to "save the truth," zero is assigned to the concept "not identical with itself" (Frege). Zero makes a lack (but not a "nothing") visible, and thus it provides for the linear movement of integers in the same way as *absence* constitutes the subject of the *Fort! Da!,* who has previously known only the asubjectivity of total presence. In other words, the lack of object is what enables the child to progress to the subjectivity of "I," or, in the mathematical metaphor, from the not-nothing-not-something of zero to the status of "One," who can therefore know two. The subject *is* the binary opposition of presence and absence, and the discovery of One—the discovery of difference—is to be condemned to an eternal desire for the nonrelationship of zero, where identity is meaningless.

Whatever the value of this particular analogy—and it seems that if Freud had not reported the *Fort! Da!,* it would have been necessary to invent it, since it plays the role of the necessary "myth of origins" in Lacan's theory—the foremost consideration is the denial to the Cartesian subject of any but a derivative and essentially misconstrued function. When Lacan defines the signifier as "what represents the subject for another signifier," which is his most recent formulation, he is reducing the status of the subject from entity to locus, that is to say, to the linguistic function of the subject in the discourse—which is simply to be an intersection of relationships in the same way as the subject of the *Fort! Da!* is the intersection of presence and absence (t.n. 183).

To return to more familiar ground, Lacan's attempt to reformulate the psychoanalytical view of desire is by far the most interesting development of a tradition whose most influential exponent was Hegel. Freud, on the other hand, was not part of that tradition. In his writings he makes no methodological distinction between need and desire except in passages in the *Interpretation of Dreams* where he views the wish as something growing out of a need which once had known satisfaction (*Befriedi-gung*). Desire (*Wunsch*) is thus indissolubly linked to "mnemonic traces," and, since these memory traces have to be interpreted in terms of words or images, there is a considerable latitude in interpretation here. (The difficulty of relating words and images is commonly avoided by reference to "signs," a word whose ambiguity I shall consider later on.) Thus the wish, according to Freud, is an attempt to establish a present identity of perception (*Wahrnehmungsidentität*) or identity of thought (*Denkidentität*) between a present situation of nonsatisfaction and a previous situation of satisfaction. There are two ways to interpret *this* ambiguity in terms of the discourse (or in terms of writing, in the sense that dreams are a form of writing—t.n. 66): one may either speak of these signs as being "structured like a language," as Lacan tends to put it, or one may deny meaning to thought insofar as it is not an internal flow of words, with the corollary that any perception (image) is meaningless until intentionalized by words—and Lacan does this as well. The danger of the first is that it may only be an analogy, however informative the resultant *reflected* structure (or in another terminology, "homology") may be. The second view has a highly respectable ancestry, but both depend upon a metaphysical rather than upon an empirical choice. Certainly, for Freud, any reading of his works in the terms of a desire mediated by the other (as in the Oedipal triangle, for instance) is implicit rather than explicit, since the relationship of rivalry or, at another level, the desire for absolute recognition, is never examined outside an essentially dual situation. Furthermore, one can easily appreciate Lacan's difficulties in assimilating somatic symptoms, for instance, into a theory of the discourse which claims to be more than an all-encompassing semiology. Thus Lacan vacillates between asserting structural similarity and actual identity, as do the anthropologists from whose interpretations of social relationships the present notion of structure in the human sciences is derived (Mauss, Lévi-Strauss).

Kojève and Hegel

Sartre's notion of desire as a lack (t.n. 107), as well as his concept of desire as an attempt to appropriate the liberty of another, is basically Hegelian, and it bears obvious similarities to Lacan's view. This seems to be the result of what is probably their common source, the lectures of Alexandre Kojève on the *Phenomenology* at the Ecole des Hautes

Etudes between 1933 and 1939, later edited by Raymond Queneau and published as the *Introduction à la lecture de Hegel*.[16] The notion of temporality and the self in Sartre's *L'Etre et le Néant* (1943)—the Hegelian "Wesen ist was gewesen ist—can be found spelled out in Kojève's especially influential first chapter (for example, pp. 12–13), which was published in *Mesures* in 1939. This chapter is Kojève's translation of and commentary on the master-slave dialectic in the *Phenomenology,* the dialectic of the desire for recognition. In the same way, Lacan's early use of the Hegelian notion of desire repeats Kojèvian formulas (t.n. 68). There are in fact few contemporary readings of Hegel which do not owe a considerable debt to Kojève's commentary, and he himself owes an equal debt to Heidegger.

"Man is Consciousness of self," begins Kojève, ". . . Man becomes conscious of himself at the moment when—for the 'first' time—he says: '*Moi.*' Understanding man by comprehending his 'origin' is therefore to understand the origin of the *Moi* revealed by the Word." ". . . It is the (conscious) Desire of a being which constitutes that being as a *Moi* and reveals him as such by bringing him to say: '*Je*'" (p. 11). The human *Moi,* continues Kojève, following the *Phenomenology* closely, is "the desire of a Desire"—Lacan calls it "the metonymy of desire"—desire being "the revelation of a void, the presence of an absence of a reality." And the being of this *Moi* will be a project of becoming; its universal form will be time: "It will be (in the future) what it has become by the negation (in the present) of what it was (in the past), this negation being effected in view of what it will become" (pp. 12–13). The humanity of desire is expressed by the desire for recognition (as a subject) upon which is articulated the struggle between the master and the slave. Kojève's first chapter ends: "Thus it is that when all is said and done, all servile labor realizes not the will of the Master, but that—unconscious at first—of the Slave, who finally succeeds where the Master necessarily fails. It is therefore actually the Consciousness which was originally dependent, serving, and servile which realizes and reveals in the end the ideal of the autonomous Consciousness-of-self, and which is thus its 'truth'" (p. 34).

Kojève's commentary depends explicitly upon his theory of language —that is to say, upon his theory of truth (t.n. 130). Although it is some-

---

[16] Paris: Gallimard, 1947.

times difficult to tell whether it is Kojève, Heidegger, or Hegel who is speaking, Lacan's works seem often to allude directly to Kojève. Lacan's epistemology is thus a further development in the tradition of what used to be called "idealism" before the concern for the analysis of language and its function in our century revealed the misconceptions which are so easily engendered by such a label. Kojève, for one, was particularly insistent upon developing the notion of "discursive truth" in Hegel, as opposed to the "static truth" of the Cartesian and Kantian tradition. This approach naturally leads to a re-evaluation of Hegel's views about language, and his remark, repeated throughout the *Phenomenology* in various ways, that "die Sprache [ist] das Dasein des Geistes" reveals wide possibilities of interpretation in relation to history, to the collective and individual memory, and to the myth of the Spirit itself. Certainly we are more receptive now to what Hegel was doing when he criticized the idealisms and realisms of his day by distinguishing the perception of the *hic et nunc* from its representation in language:

[These philosophers] speak of the being-there of *exterior* objects, which can be even more exactly determined as effectively real [*wirkliche*], absolutely *unique, entirely personal* and *individual* things, each of which has absolutely no equal; this being-there, according to them, has absolute certitude and truth. They intend [*meinen*] *this* piece of paper on which I am writing *this,* or rather I have already written it; but what they intend they do not express. If they wanted to express this piece of paper in a way which would be actually real . . . , it would be impossible, because the sensible *hic* which is intended is *inaccessible* to language, which belongs to consciousness, to the universal in itself . . . . Therefore, what we call the inexpressible is nothing other than the non-true, the non-rational, that which is simply intended.[17]

All that I can express by language, says Hegel, is a universal; even if I say "this thing here" I am still expressing it by an abstraction, and I cannot attain the "thing-itself" in speaking of it. Speech "has the divine nature of immediately inverting the thing I intend [*Meinung*] in order to transform it into something else," because of my movement in time and space (p. 89; I, p. 92).

Through the "miracle" of the understanding (*Verstand*), with its power of abstraction, it is the negation of the thing itself which provides it with a universal essence in the concept. And since the named thing

---

[17] *Phänomenologie,* ed. J. Hoffmeister (Hamburg: Felix Meiner, 1948), p. 88; *Phénoménologie,* trans. J. Hyppolite (Paris: Aubier, 1938–41), I, 91.

is still a universal, so, too, is the *Ich*. But the "I" is in a category different from other words. When the subject seeks to express his own singularity by saying "I," he is only asserting what any man can assert. A modern linguist would say that the obligatory reference of this "shifter" to the message rather than to the code alone makes it less concrete and more easily alienable than other words. The modern philosopher would insist that the concept of "subject" outside of language, in perception, for instance, is only an analogy from language, and that the *cogito* and the *percipio* are primarily discursive phenomena. Since language, for Hegel, is the *Dasein* of the universal in itself, then "Language is in fact the *Dasein* of the pure Self as Self," and ". . . language alone contains the *Ich* in its purity; alone it enunciates the *Ich* . . . . *Ich* is *this Ich,* but it is also the universal *Ich*. Its manifestation is immediately the alienation and the disappearance of *this Ich* and is therefore its permanence in its universality" (p. 362; II, p. 69). It is only in language that it is possible to conceive of the identity of the particular and the universal, and, as for the *cogito,* it is not only temporal, but it must come from outside; it cannot come from a purely internal certitude. The attainment of what Hegel calls the consciousness-of-self can only come from the confrontation of the two consciousnesses in the struggle for recognition (an Imaginary conflict) and reconciliation, from Hegel's optimistic view of the eventual dialectical surpassing (*Aufhebung*) of this stage in a reciprocal recognition. For Hegel, language is the active mediator in this confrontation.

Kojève has brought most of Hegel's theory of language into his own systematic view of the *Phenomenology,* attempting to integrate the Concept (the signifier in the wide sense) with time, the discourse, the consciousness-of-self, and consciousness-of-death, and equating the wisdom of the Hegelian Sage with the authentic Dasein of Being-towards-death (t.n. 125, 186):

In Chapter VIII of the PhG, Hegel says that all *conceptual*-comprehension (*Begreifen*) is the equivalent of a murder . . . .
As long as the Meaning (or the Essence, the Concept, the Logos, the Idea, etc.) is incarnate in an entity existing empirically, this Meaning or this Essence, as well as the entity, *are alive* . . . . But when the Meaning (the Essence) "dog" passes into the *word* "dog," that is to say, when it becomes an *abstract* Concept which is *different* from the sensible reality which it reveals by its Meaning, the Meaning (the Essence) *dies* . . . .
. . . If the dog were eternal, if it existed outside Time or without Time,

the Concept "dog" would never be *detached* from the dog itself [it would be a "natural sign," univocal]. The empirical existence (*Dasein*) of the Concept "dog" would be the living dog, and not the *word* "dog" (thought or pronounced). There would therefore be no *Discourse* (Logos) in the World . . . and therefore no Man in the World (pp. 373–74).

Kojève's argument at this point seems a little confused, but his intent is clear. The detachment of the meaning from the reality is possible only because spatial reality is temporal, because the real of the present is annihilated by its passage into the past. But it is nevertheless maintained by the memory of man, itself dependent upon *words,* both within him (personal memory) and outside him (concrete discourses, books, inscriptions). "Without Man, Being would be mute: it would be there (*Dasein*), but it would not be *true* (*das Wahre*)" (p. 464). Error, and therefore truth, are only possible where there is language:

For the meaning incarnate in the word and the discourse is no longer subjected to the necessity which regulates essences bound to their respective natural supports, determined in a univocal manner by their *hic et nunc* . . . . It is this "separated liberty" and the "absolute power" from which it comes which condition the possibility of *error,* which the pre-Hegelian philosophies were never able to take into account. For this "liberty" *permits the meanings incarnate in words to combine in ways other than those of the corresponding essences,* bound to their natural supports (p. 546) (my italics).

It was in seeking to explain this fact, says Kojève, that Hegel discovered the ontological category of Negativity: "the energy of thought," the divisive and abstractive power of the understanding. "The miracle of the existence of the discourse . . . is nothing other than the miracle of the existence of Man in the world" (*ibid*). Needless to say the exigency of communication between men posed by the intersubjectivity of the discourse supposes an "existential" man without God, for if there were a God, then Cartesian truth, franked *in silence* by the Deity, would prevail, whereas for Hegel truth is temporal and discursive; it is a matter of communication, and therefore of the otherness of intersubjective discourse.[18]

---

[18] This conclusion follows rather naturally from all non-Platonic discursive views of truth, that is, from the Hegelian Lukàcs as well as from Kojève. See also the expression of an identical view in J. Hyppolite, "Phénoménologie de Hegel et psychanalyse," *La Psychanalyse,* III (1957), pp. 17–32. Cf. Lacan: "The full Word, in fact, is defined by its identity to that of which it speaks." "Réponse au commentaire de J. Hyppolite" (1956), p. 42.

Freud: the Rational and the Real

It is therefore precisely in the Hegelian sense that for Freud the rational is real and the Real is rational. He has often been criticized for his emphasis on "verbalization" (for example, by Philip Rieff) and for his ambiguities concerning thought and perception (by Ernest Jones)— the latter because of his use of the ubiquitous German term *Vorstellung,* whose primary meaning is simply "placed before" (presentation) but which appears as "idea," "presentation," "representation," "image," and even "thought" in English translations. Criticism directed at Freud's emphasis upon language and linguistic structures in psychic life is readily understandable in those outside the Hegelian and Heideggerian tradition, which is often rejected rather too hastily as "metaphysics," especially by people who are perhaps unwilling to seek to comprehend the metaphysical choices they have themselves made, including the metaphysical choice to avoid "metaphysics." Thus Freud's lack of concern over distinguishing phantasy from so-called reality has been a source of irritation to some, principally, it would seem, because of a misunderstanding of the role of language in perception (hallucinated or otherwise), but more especially a misunderstanding of the role of *meaning* or recognition in cognition. The subject is constituted by the signifier, and it is the signifier which constitutes reality. It seems to be the essence of great works to reflect in their ambiguities the very center of the problem they are seeking to solve. For Freud it is the metaproblem of representation itself which is reflected both in the term *Vorstellung* and in the very considerable number of metaphorical (reflected) representations of psychic structures which he introduces into the various stages of his work.

In order to avoid misunderstanding, therefore, and before coming to some remarks about Heidegger's view of the rational and the real, it is worth digressing slightly with a view to establishing Freud's own position in respect of the "intellectual scaffolding" (as he called it) which he constructed around psychic *relationships,* a scaffolding which has so often been taken in two persistent misreadings of his text: that he was describing anything other than psychic reality, or a psychical system which is not in itself psychic, by these metaphors, and that he was describing "substances" rather than the interrelation of parts of a structure whose real nature is beyond definition or grasp. Like his Romantic forebears, Freud was an "idealist," but more specifically (explicitly, I should say), a Kantian insofar as the relationship of the *Vorstellung* to the real was concerned. Once he entered this path—and however strong the influence of J. S. Mill on the young Freud, his experience bore him out—it makes very little difference in the end whether he believes in an inaccessible noumenal realm or in no outside reality at all, since by asserting *any* kind of discontinuity between language, perception, and reality, one ends with a theory of reflection implying a *total* discontinuity. For Freud, it seems clear that in the world of language, this discontinuity was a historical evolution from a mythical earlier time of "symbolic and linguistic identity" (t.n. 80).

Apart from the fact that even the concept of *Trieb* (drive—always a psychic entity for Freud) is itself an attempt to order the real through a reflected conceptualization, Freud was not consciously deluded about the status of the representations and metaphors he used. Particularly since Whorf's indications of the drastic differences between the conceptual organization of reality in Western languages and that in languages not of the Indo-European stock, since Lévi-Strauss's controversial restatement of Frazer's view of the cosmological function of the myth in "primitive" societies, and since the many pronouncements from the 1920's on by scientists and mathematicians on the existential status of the algebra they use to structure reality or to structure structures, we are surely more than ever ready to understand the import for his own theoretical pronouncements of Freud's remark in his letter to Einstein, "Why War," in 1933: "It may perhaps seem to you as though our theories are a kind of mythology and, in the present case [the theory of the death instinct], not even an agreeable one. But does not every science come in the end to a kind of mythology like this? Cannot the same be said of your own Physics?" [19] And even in the present era of what is called "structuralism" in France—the emphasis on relationships rather than on things—it is perhaps not so surprising after all to find Freud expressing himself in very much contemporary terms: "The processes with which [psychoanalysis] is concerned are in themselves just as unknowable as those dealt with by other sciences, by chemistry or physics, for example; but it is possible to establish the laws which they obey and to follow their mutual relations and interdependences unbroken over long stretches— in short, to arrive at what is described as an 'understanding' of the field

[19] *Standard Edition*, XXII, 211.

of the natural phenomena in question." [20] And later in the same work: "Reality [*das Reale*] will always remain 'unknowable.' The yield brought to light by scientific work from our primary sense perceptions will consist in an insight into connections and dependent relations which are present in the external world, which can somehow be reliably reproduced or reflected in the internal world of our thought . . . . We [the analysts] infer a number of processes which are in themselves 'unknowable' and interpolate them in those that are conscious to us" (pp. 196–97).

In spite of the possible ambiguity in this last passage, where it might be objected that Freud is dealing with two kinds of "unknowables"— outside reality on the one hand and unconscious reality on the other— the contradiction can, I think, be resolved at least at the level of intent. Twenty years earlier he had stated quite adamantly the discontinuity between psychic and other realities (biological reality in this particular instance), but he had nevertheless indicated his own carelessness about maintaining the distinction in his writing. In this respect the charge of carelessness against Freud's use of terms is obviously valid. In part it reflects his tendency to exploit the German language to the fullest extent by employing ordinary words in special senses rather than by coining neologisms. (He never really forgave James Strachey, for example, for coining the word "cathexis" to translate *Besetzung,* which normally means "occupation," and which the French translate by "investissement.") He expresses the distinction as follows:

> We have said that there are conscious and unconscious ideas [*Vorstellungen*]; but are there also unconscious instinctual impulses [*Triebregungen*], emotions, and feelings, or is it in this instance meaningless to form combinations of this kind?
>
> I am in fact of the opinion that the antithesis of conscious and unconscious is not applicable to instincts. An instinct can never become an object of consciousness—only the idea that represents the instinct can. Even in the unconscious, moreover, an instinct cannot be represented otherwise than by an idea. If the instinct did not attach itself to an idea or manifest itself as an affective state, we could know nothing about it. When we nevertheless speak of an unconscious instinctual impulse or of a repressed instinctual impulse, the looseness of phraseology is a harmless one [*sic*]. We can only mean an instinctual impulse the ideational representative [*Vorstellungsrepräsentanz*] of which is unconscious, for nothing else comes into consideration.[21]

[20] *An Outline of Psycho-Analysis* (1940 [1938]), *Standard Edition,* XXIII, 158.
[21] "The Unconscious" (1915), *Standard Edition,* XIV, 177.

In reference to "unconscious affective impulses," he goes on to say: "Yet its affect was never unconscious; all that had happened was that its *idea* had undergone repression" (p. 178). Or, in Lacan's terminology: "c'est le signifiant qui est refoulé" (t.n. 66).

It is the interpretation of this and similar passages, besides analyses of concrete examples from Freud, which allows Lacan to declare that the "unconscious is structured like a language," and it is this reading of Freud which brings us to see how often Freud is in fact observing, commenting, representing, and interpreting at one level of reality: discursive reality. The relationship between conscious and unconscious in Freud is not necessarily that of the psychic and the biological, or of the verbal and the real, or of letter and meaning, but essentially a relationship of *interpolation* (or decondensation) at the level of the signifier. I shall return to a specific example of this interpolation later. But whatever final status we assign to Freud's attempt to represent the structure of the mind, or to Lacan's interpretation of that attempt, we should probably keep in mind that it was not simply an old man's irony which prompted Freud, at the very end of his life, to compare the constructions of the analyst to the delusions of his patient. What is true inside the analytical situation is surely equally true outside it. Both constructions and delusions, like myths, are "attempts at explanation and cure," [22] and all intellectual explanations would seem to be a cure for something, be it the human condition.

Thought and Speech: Heidegger, Sapir, Merleau-Ponty

For Lacan, and I suggest also for Freud, psychic reality is primarily the intersubjective world of language. With Heidegger, Lacan views the subject as subordinated to language and thus cuts across the distinction often made between interpersonal and intrapersonal relations by representing the second as a subset of the first in the chains of signifiers which link them. This view is hardly to be found explicitly in Freud, since it depends upon a contemporary notion communication of which Freud was unaware. It can, I believe, be applied to the Freudian texts in the sense of a continuation of the experience which informs them, as I shall try to show later.

Heidegger has been the most influential exponent in our century of a

---

[22] "Constructions in Analysis" (1938), *Standard Edition,* XXIII, 268.

philosophical theory of the discourse which matches the more technically oriented views of a number of linguists, especially Sapir, who preceded him. The *ratio* of the Aristotelian ζῷον λόγον ἔχον is for Heidegger a description of "that living thing whose Being is essentially determined by the potentiality for discourse [*Rede*]." [23] He continues: "The real signification of 'discourse,' which is obvious enough, gets constantly covered up by the later history of the word λόγος .... Λόγος gets 'translated' (and this means that it is always getting interpreted) as 'reason,' 'judgment,' 'concept,' 'definition,' 'ground,' or 'relationship' [*Vernunft, Urteil, Begriff, Definition, Grund, Verhältnis*]" (p. 55). Heidegger goes on to justify these various translations in the terms of his interpretation of Aristotle's view of the function of the discourse as letting something be seen. "The λόγος lets something be seen (φαίνεσθαι)—namely, what the discourse is about; and it does so either *for* the one who is doing the talking (the *medium*) or for persons who are talking with one another . . ." (p. 56). "When fully concrete, discoursing . . . has the character of speaking [*Sprechens*]—vocal proclamation in words" (*ibid.*). And further: "*Discourse is existentially primordial with state-of-mind and understanding.* The intelligibility of something has always been articulated, even before there is any appropriative interpretation of it" (p. 203). *Gerede* ("idle talk")—which is not intended as disparaging in Heidegger as the *parole vide* is disparaging in Lacan—is explicated as a "discoursing which has lost its primary relationship-of-Being towards the existent talked about, or else has never achieved such a relationship." The word has become the thing itself. As a result, *Gerede* "does not communicate in such a way as to let this existent be appropriated in a primordial manner, but communicates rather by following the route of *gossiping* and *passing the word along* [des *Weiter-* und *Nachredens*]" (p. 212). "The doctrine of signification is rooted in the ontology of Dasein" (p. 209). Although these disjointed quotations tend to obscure the subtlety and length of Heidegger's argument, there is a significant and less technical expression of Heidegger's views quoted by Jean Reboul in his "Jacques Lacan et les fondements de la psychanalyse" (1962), which, for lack of the original, is translated here from the French: "Man behaves as if he were the creator and master of Language, whereas on the contrary, it is Language which is and remains his sovereign .... For in the proper sense of these

---

[23] *Being and Time,* trans. Macquarrie and Robinson (SCM Press, London: 1962), p. 47.

terms, it is Language which speaks. Man speaks insofar as he replies to Language by listening to what it says to him. Language makes us a sign and it is Language which, first and last, conducts us in this way towards the being of a thing" (p. 1060).[24]

Sapir had already expressed in 1921 a view of the relationship between imagery and thought which is correlative to Heidegger's philosophical development of a similar concept in his distinction between αἴσθησις and λόγος. Although Sapir did make a qualitative distinction between thought and ordinary speech (thought being a "refined interpretation" of the content of speech), which bears a technical similarity to Heidegger's differentiation between *Rede* and *Gerede,* he decided it was an illusion to consider that one can think without language:

> The illusion seems to be due to a number of factors. The simplest of these is the failure to distinguish between imagery and thought. As a matter of fact, no sooner do we try to put an image into conscious relation with another than we find ourselves slipping into a silent flow of words. Thought may be a natural domain apart from the artificial one of speech, but speech would seem to be the only road we know that leads to it. A still more fruitful source of the illusive feeling that language may be dispensed with in thought is the common failure to realize that language is not identical with its auditory symbolism . . . . One may go so far as to suspect that the symbolic expression of thought may in some cases run along outside the fringe of the conscious mind, so that the feeling of a free, non-linguistic stream of thought is for minds of a certain type a relatively, but only a relatively, justified one . . . . The modern psychology has shown us how powerfully symbolism is at work in the unconscious mind. It is therefore easier to understand than it would have been twenty years ago that the most rarefied thought may be but the conscious counterpart of an unconscious linguistic symbolism.[25]

These reflections lead him to the problem of the genetic primacy of thought versus speech. On this point, his views are essentially those maintained by many contemporary philosophers and anthropologists:

> We may assume that language rose pre-rationally—just how and on what precise level of mental activity we do not know—but we must not imagine that a highly developed system of speech symbols worked itself out before the genesis of distinct concepts and of thinking . . . . We must rather imagine that thought-processes set in, as a kind of psychic overflow, almost at the

---

[24] The passage is from *Dichterisch wohnt der Mensch,* trans. André Preau, *Les Cahiers du Sud,* No. 344 (1957).
[25] *Language* (New York: Harvest Books, n.d.), pp. 15–16.

beginning of linguistic expression; further, that the concept, once defined, necessarily reacted on the life of its linguistic symbol, encouraging further linguistic growth . . . . The word, as we know, is not only a key, it may also be a fetter (p. 17).

Merleau-Ponty, writing during World War II at the same time as Sartre, reflects the growing philosophical and anthropological interest in the discourse in this century:

We live in a world where the spoken word is *instituted* . . . . The linguistic and intersubjective world does not surprise us, we no longer distinguish it from the world itself, and it is in the interior of a world already spoken and speaking that we reflect [on it] . . . .
Thought has nothing "interior" about it; it does not exist outside of the world and outside of words. What deceives us about it, what makes us believe in a thought which supposedly exists for itself before being expressed, are the thoughts which have already been constituted and expressed, which we can recall silently to ourselves, and by means of which we create the illusion of an interior life. But in fact this supposed silence echoes with spoken words; this interior life is an interior language.[26]

A similar view of the relation between thought and language emphasized by Heidegger and Merleau-Ponty, as distinct from the accepted views of Husserl and Descartes, was expressed by Plato in the *Sophist* and the *Theaetetus*. Although the context of truth conceived by Plato made no distinction between the truth of language and the truth (adequacy) of perception—since Plato believed that the judgment (δόξα) and perception (αἴσθησις) involved in the "appearing" (φαίνεσθαι) of external objects (in the process by which I decide what the object is) to be of the same *nature* as statement (λόγος)—the Stranger says in the *Sophist*: ". . . Thinking [διάνοια] and discourse [λόγος] are the same thing, except that what we call thinking is, precisely, the inward dialogue carried on by the mind with itself without spoken sound" (263c, Cornford translation). Since Plato also said that all discourse depends on the "weaving together" (συμπλοκή) of forms—their context—it has been possible for some commentators, as Cornford points out in his *Plato's Theory of Knowledge* (New York: Bobbs-Merrill, 1957 [1934]), to suggest that for Plato thinking means predicative, discursive judgment and that the notion of the isolated meaning of *words,* as directly connected with their essences —what most people consider to be Plato's theory of meaning—is not an

[26] *Phénoménologie de la perception* (Paris: Gallimard, 1945), p. 214.

accurate interpretation of the text. This attempt to discover modern theories of language in Plato is rejected by Cornford (p. 259)—but perhaps only because of his own epistemology. However this may be, the whole question of meaning, reference, and the relationship between thought, language, and perception will occupy a central part of the following discussion of the linguistic terminology of Ferdinand de Saussure, whose theories have been developed and applied outside his own discipline: in anthropology, psychology, and psychoanalysis.

III

Ferdinand de Saussure

The technical differentiation between "speech" and "language" owes its impetus in the methodology (the language) of modern linguistics to Ferdinand de Saussure, the originator of the specific methodological concepts of synchrony and diachrony, and of the sign, signifier, and signified, if not in the precise sense in which they are now employed (*Cours de linguistique générale,* 1915).

For Saussure, *la langue* was *le langage* minus *la parole*. The distinction he employed is consequently: *langue/parole*—in other words: the social and collective institution of language as a system of signs possessing certain values and beyond the conscious control of the individual, opposed to the individual act of combination and actualization (in a discourse) of speech, which, for Saussure, would be an essentially conscious use of unconsciously determined structures. Obviously the two can be separated only formally and not existentially, since language and speech are in constant dialectical interaction. This is particularly true if we remain at the level of the historical evolution of a language, for it is through speech that it evolves. The distinction solves no problems, but it was an essential move in the transformation of philology into linguistics, and it has been the inspiration of the increasingly more subtle attempts by many linguists to clarify the relation between what is now usually called the (social) code and the (individual) message.

Synchrony and Diachrony

Synchrony and diachrony (t.n. 85) refer in Saussure's terminology to the "timeless" or synchronic cut one can make in a language at any stage of its evolution in order to examine the interrelationships of that particular language system at a moment in time. "Diachrony" refers to the evolution through time in a language of individual words, individual phonemes, or individual morphological elements, and so forth (semantic, pronunciation, and syntactic changes), or to the evolution of the totality of one synchronic system to another one (Vulgar Latin to French, for example). Saussure's prime intent was to separate philology into "synchronic linguistics" and "diachronic linguistics," but the terms have since been revived and employed in their own right, particularly in structural anthropology. Needless to say the relationship between one synchronic system and the next (its diachronic change) is impossible to specify except on the basis of "this" becoming "that," and entailing a further change "here," and so forth. Theoretically speaking, a change in any single element of any system will have repercussions throughout the whole system, whether from the diachronic or the synchronic point of view, or from both.

It was the extension by Lévi-Strauss of the concepts of synchrony and diachrony to the relationship between static ("cold") societies and dynamic ("hot") ones that indicated the value of these terms, as well as the difficulties involved in explicating the relationship between the two categories. Theoretically speaking, it is possible to say that a "primitive" society remains essentially synchronic; it has no history, only events. An evolving society on the other hand may be conceived as in the grasp of History itself—without, of course, necessarily deifying history in the Hegelian or Marxian sense, since what we mean by History may be the myths of history. Obviously one of the key differences between the two types of society lies in the introduction of writing, and therefore of an objective kind of memory, into a society. The memory of a primitive society lies in its myths—which speak the narrator rather than being spoken by him, as Lévi-Strauss has put it (t.n. 103)—and the function of the oral myth differs from the function of writing in the sense that both the oral myth and the supposedly synchronic society could evolve over a long period of time, but nobody would know about it. ("Evolution" is here distinguished from the change, usually that of degradation, brought on by outside factors, or events: ecological change, wars, the coming of the white man, and so forth.) Theoretically speaking, the "structuralist" approach will concentrate upon discovering and comparing the structure of synchronic systems—within history, for instance—without concerning itself with how or why any diachronic evolution has taken place. The historian, on the other hand, would tend to concentrate on the elements accounting for diachronic change at a specific level of society: economics, politics, or the class struggle, for example. Thus Lévi-Strauss, viewed as the man who might be able to prove to us that, *structurally speaking,* our society is identical with the society of the eighteenth century and distinguished from it only by events, has been opposed to the later Sartre, viewed as the man who must concentrate on the diachronic historical change which *has* taken place in order to discover what grounds there may be for hope that really fundamental changes can be brought about through History.

In addition to this general and simplified summary of the notions of synchrony and diachrony, it should be indicated in what sense these ideas, and their relationship to the notion of structure itself, are a transformation of the theses of the *Cours de linguistique générale*. Saussure did not in fact write this text; it was put together from lecture notes and scattered manuscripts by his students. Thus there is a certain systematization involved which was not necessarily that of Saussure himself, as Lévi-Strauss sought to indicate in 1960:

> For the editors of the *Cours de linguistique générale* there exists an absolute opposition between two categories of facts: on the one hand, the category of grammar, the synchronic, the conscious; on the other, the category of phonetics, the diachronic, and the unconscious. Only the conscious system is coherent; the unconscious infra-system is dynamic and in disequilibrium. At one and the same time, it is made up of past legacies and future tendencies, which have not yet come to realization.
>
> The fact is that Saussure had not yet discovered the presence of differential elements behind the phoneme. At another level, his position indirectly prefigures that of Radcliffe-Brown, who was convinced that structure is of the order of empirical observation, whereas structure is in fact beyond it. This unawareness of hidden realities leads both of them to opposite conclusions. Saussure seems to deny the existence of a structure wherever it is not immediately given; Radcliffe-Brown affirms its existence, but, since he sees structure where it does not exist in fact, he deprives the notion of structure of its force and import.

Today, Lévi-Strauss continues, we can see in both anthropology and linguistics that the synchronic may be as unconscious as the diachronic, which makes them both less separate from each other than they seem to have been for Saussure's editors. "On the other hand, the *Cours de linguistique générale* posits relations of equivalence between phonetics, the diachronic, and what is individual, forming the domain of *parole*; and between the grammatical, the synchronic, and what is collective, in the domain of *langue*. But we have learned from Marx that the diachronic could exist in the collective, and from Freud, that the grammatical could come to fruition in the heart of what is individual" (pp. 23–24).[27]

Synchrony and diachrony not only have a specific application in some of Lacan's formulations about the unconscious, but they are of course of especial relevance to psychoanalysis in the most general sense. It is after all the psychoanalyst who is always telling us that for the neurotic, structurally speaking, nothing has changed since his infancy, or that this or that person has regressed to this or that stage, both of which are manifestly untrue from the point of view of diachrony. A great deal has changed in the neurotic's life since infancy (but we have to decide nevertheless whether events or history—relative maturity—have operated), and it seems absurd to speak of regression or of fixation as if it were self-explanatory when we can see quite clearly that this miser today is not the constipated child of yesterday. Lévi-Strauss, for similar reasons, makes a distinction between linear, unidirectional time (diachronic time) and omnidirectional, reversible time (synchronic time). These are the times of *parole* and *langue,* respectively. The myth shares these two categories of time and adds a third by combining them: the eternity of past, present, and future in mythical time.

One difficulty in employing these terms outside systems like language, or even the relatively simple social systems of primitive societies, is that one is not even sure whether one is resorting to analogy or not. The neurotic, like the primitive society, may well depend to some extent upon a myth (personal or societal) which is speaking him repeatedly at the unconscious level of his symptoms (the unconscious is timeless, says Freud). On the other hand, his memory (the "magic writing pad") contains written on it all the pristine traces which would enable him to compare the unilinear relationship of present and past, and thus to resolve their conflict. Freud's central concept of *Nachträglichkeit,* which Lacan was one of the first to emphasize, requires this conception in fact, since deferred action, whether conscious (in the sense that I suddenly understand a book I read a year ago) or unconscious (in the more usual

---

[27] "Discours inaugural" at the Collège de France (1960), reprinted in *Aut Aut* (Milan), No. 88 (July, 1965), pp. 8–41.

psychopathological sense of suddenly discovering what a memory means to me, and repressing it), is one of the most commonplace facts of life. The "writing" of the dream—in its widest sense of a symptom—could be called an instance of the myth which is speaking us, since we do not know what it is trying to say. In this wide sense, the dream contains a message *to* someone (from the Other—I shall return to this point); it is an attempted explanation of the subject's reality. But it is also uttered by someone other than the subject who perceives and intentionalizes it, and the relationship between the manifest and latent content could be described as that between two versions of a myth which has evolved or been supplanted without a society's realizing it. Until recently, at any rate, Lévi-Strauss would say that this evolution is not important. All versions of the myth are part of the myth and structurally identical with it. This is in fact what the analyst would also say. If "primitive" myths are the public cosmological and conscious memory of a society which simply repeats its unconscious synchronic structure through time, then any important dream or symptom can be regarded as a similarly symbolic conscious private memory of the original system of relationships which the subject also repeats synchronically and unconsciously.

There is a great deal more to be said about these conjectures, which are open to criticism on the grounds of assimilating society to the individual, or vice versa, although it does seem that modern sociology offers a solution here. The central feature which separates this use of synchrony and diachrony from pseudo-organic views of society or pseudo-historical views of the individual is simply its reference to the societal memory, to the collective history of the society: Language itself. Meaningful memories (or myths) for society, as Lacan points out in his remarks on history in the *Discours,* are essentially indistinguishable from meaningful memories for the individual: to have meaning, they must be intentionalized in the *present,* through speech in the individual, through the historical consciousness in the collective. And this is in fact what happens within analysis itself through *rememoration* (inevitably *nachträglich*), where regression must be understood in the same way as we attempt to relate synchrony to diachrony in history. Needless to say, it is not only the neurotic who repeats, and the problem of relating synchrony to diachrony is also faced by the literary critic, especially in relation to the novel, where he must (ideally) relate any one novel, as a relatively independent structure, to the diachronic evolution of the rest of the novelist's work, as well as (again ideally) consider the relationship of any individual novel both to all the others produced or being read at its particular synchronic moment in history and to all the others produced in the novelist's lifetime. Moreover, if he takes a specific or extranovelistic approach, the same situation will repeat itself in the society, economy, psychology, or history of ideas to which he refers the novel or novels he seeks to explicate.

Synchrony and diachrony are related to Lacan's use of two basic concepts, metaphor and metonymy, in his attempt to deal with the structure of conscious and unconscious relationships. These concepts are partly dependent upon Saussure's notion of the signifier and signified, to which I shall now turn.

Sign, Signifier, Signified, Symbol, and Symptom

Saussure's linguistic "sign" is represented as the unity: $\frac{\text{Signified}}{\text{Signifier}}$, which is equivalent in his terminology to: $\frac{\text{Concept}}{\text{Acoustic Image}}$. This representation is accompanied in the notes published by his students by another one which equates the "concept" with a visual image (the picture of a tree) and the "acoustic image" with a word (the word "tree"). However, he adds, "in normal usage" the term "sign" "generally designates only the acoustic image—for example, a word (*arbor,* and so on). One forgets that if *arbor* is called a sign, this is only insofar as it includes the concept 'tree,' in such a way that the idea of the sensory part implies that of the whole." [28]

The distinction between the *significans* (τὸ σημαῖνον) and the *significatum* (τὸ σημαινόμενον) goes back to the Stoics, who were careful also to take into account the third element involved (the denotation; the thing intended: τὸ τυγχανον), which I call the "object" (in another terminology, the referent). The complications and contradictions of Stoic theory are many and varied, but insofar as the three elements mentioned are basic Stoic distinctions, they also correspond respectively to the "sound," the "sense" (τὸ λεκτόν) and the "external object." The *lekton* is variously defined and used; fundamentally it means "that which foreigners do not understand when they hear a Greek word." In Chapter II of his *Stoic*

[28] *Cours de linguistique générale* (Paris: Payot, 1963 [1915]), p. 99.

Logic (Berkeley: University of California Press, 1953) Benson Mates relates these distinctions as closely as he can to Frege's *"Zeichen," "Sinn,"* and *"Bedeutung"* ("sign," "sense" or "meaning," and "signification"), respectively, and to Carnap's distinction between "designator," "intension," and "extension." As I indicated in the Introduction, "sense" (*sens*) tends to indicate subjective intention and "signification" (*signification*) objective definition, but Frege uses *Sinn* to denote objective meaning (the *lekton* for the Stoics) and distinguishes it from the (subjective) presentation or idea (*Vorstellung:* φαντασία for the Stoics), which is the fourth term involved. Thus *Bedeutung* for Frege is the denotation of the external object, *Sinn* somehow falling "between" the subjective presentation or idea and the object. The point is that outside the question of meaning itself, in employing the categories of "signifier" and "signified" in their wider acceptation, there are at least four possible terms involved: "word," "concept," "image," and "external reality."

Saussure himself, although he expressly defined the signified as the concept (psychic reality) and not the object (external reality), nevertheless tended to confuse the two in his writing, as Emile Benveniste has pointed out.[29] Not only is this the most common kind of error we all make, but even if the object is distinguished from the signified in the rather limited area of language concerned with the application of substantives to reality, one has not advanced beyond the elementary level of designation or nomination, and nothing has been said about the further question, which seems to be quite separate from the question of the relationship of the signifier to reality: that of signification or meaning. And needless to say, nothing has been said about the other, purely functional parts of speech, about the relationship of verbs and "events," about shifters (which designate the subject but do not signify him), or about substantives referring to what are traditionally called "abstract (general) ideas." Moreover it seems clear that the only substantives which properly correspond to the Stoic view of denotation are those substantives devoid of meaning: proper names. The denotation theory is not of course confined to substantives, since, as in Stoic logic, one may apply it at the level of propositions. But it is confined to propositions about reality involving curious academic questions about "existence" (What is the object of

---

[29] "Nature du signe linguistique" (1939), in: *Problèmes de linguistique générale* (Paris: Gallimard, 1966), pp. 49–55. The "acoustic image," of course, as a set of frequencies, *is* real (material)—but it is not "reality."

"Dion" in the proposition "Dion is dead"? Does the golden mountain exist?), which are symptomatic of what seems to be a total impasse in the theory once one moves away from the most elementary kind of statements. The epistemological problem is on the one hand that "valid" statements are uniformly dull, and on the other that "Cartesian" or "static" truth cannot handle the sort of realities twentieth-century man is interested in. To paraphrase Lacan, it is not a question of the reality of the subject, but of his Truth.

We might reiterate at this point Hegel's definitions of truth as a process (*Bewegung*—cf. t.n. 130), as a totality, and as "effectively real" only as a system (one might say, immanent within an ongoing structure), all contained in the celebrated image: "The true [*das Wahre*] is the Bacchantic frenzy in which no member [*Glied*] is not drunken; and because each as soon as it differentiates itself, immediately dissolves [itself]—the frenzy is as if transparent and simple repose" (*Phänomenologie*, p. 39; *Phénoménologie*, I, 40).

As will become progressively clear, neither Lacan nor Saussure is primarily concerned with the relationship of the word to autonomous external reality, whereas when Lévi-Strauss employs the terms "signifier" and "signified" he is concerned on the one hand with the relation of thought (signifier) to the cosmos (signified) and on the other with that between the phenomenological "thing itself" he studies (for example, a social reality as a system of signifiers) and the underlying structure (a system of signifieds). The terms are generally employed in such loose and undefined ways that, outside linguistics itself, only the context will indicate a particular dichotomy. In linguistics on the other hand, one can usually rely upon the linguist's attempt clearly to differentiate and define his use of the terms in the context of his own work. What is often simply glossed over is that the most common acceptance of signifier and signified in linguistics refers, as it did ultimately for the *Cours de linguistique générale,* to the *sound* (the signifier) as opposed to the *sense* (the signified).

Even if we assimilate word and concept as essentially indistinguishable (Saussure does not regard thought and speech as ultimately separable), and if we disregard for the moment the fact that meaning is not simply denotation, we do not confront simply a new set of three terms—"word-concept," "image," and "reality"—but in fact four, since the linguist is obviously methodologically concerned with sounds (ultimately the non-semantic level of the distinctive features) and their relationship to word concepts, which he methodologically assumes to mean precisely what they say. Thus when the *Cours de linguistique générale* speaks of signifier and signified, it is not really a question of metasemantics, as Saussure's choice of examples clearly shows. *Arbor* means *arbre,* and *arbre* means "tree." When Saussure (or his students) speaks of the arbitrariness of the linguistic sign, he means primarily that the relationship between the sound and the word concept is discontinuous. Language could call chairs tables without affecting its semantics. Moreover, the sliding (*glissement*) of the signifier over the signified is for Saussure primarily a diachronic, evolutionary process. *Rem* (thing) becomes *rien* (nothing) over a period of time, but at any particular moment of time, words within any linguistic system mean what they say. And when he speaks of this sliding relationship in a wider context (pp. 156–57), comparing it to the wind ruffling the waters of the sea, the two pertinent terms are not "signifier" (or "sign") and "reality," but "thought" and "sound." It is Saussure's diacritical theory of meaning, to which I shall return, which is his only excursion, and an important one, into metasemantics.

Much of the problem behind this discussion is simply terminological, resulting in part from conflicting definitions of symbols as opposed to signs. Aristotle, for example, defined the spoken word as the "token" (σύμβολον) *or* the "sign" (σημεῖον) of "mental affections," which are the likenesses of things (πράγματα). The written word is similarly a token of the spoken word. For some linguists, however, a symbol is not the same as a sign—I shall clarify this distinction in a moment. But even the categories of "sound," "word," "concept," "image," and "external reality" (or "object") are deficient in themselves without some sort of definition and amplification. Since the category of "sound" is primarily material and non-semantic (the secondary articulation of phonemes), it can be ignored at this point. By "word" we really mean "syntagm" or "proposition"; the vague use of "word" is only the result of bad habits hanging on from the commonsense view that a single word is some sort of entity with a meaning. What a "concept" is outside its existence as a syntagm or proposition is difficult to say; it is surely inseparable from its expression. Certainly the fairly common translation of the technical use of *Vorstellung* in Freud as "concept" is misleading, since *Begriff* exists (and is etymologically more justifiable) to supplement and describe the indeterminate gap between "thought" and "speech," between "idea" and "proposition."

"Image" is surely too restricted a term for the fourth category, since what we require is something less restricted to visual connotations. This is why the German *Vorstellung* is so peculiarly apt to designate the private experience of "things," the private experience of the world, denoted by the less suitable φαντασία of the Stoics ("imagination" for Aristotle; "appearing" for Plato), which tends to imply something being revealed visually (as does "idea") rather than the composite notion of "presentation" actually involved. The concept of truth as dependent upon visual reference, as in the Platonic notion of intuition or noesis expressed by the verb κατιδεῖν, seems to be a restrictive metaphor; a presentation of an object may be *adequate* to that object, but it cannot be true or false. Thus Michel Foucault in *Les Mots et les Choses* (Paris: Gallimard, 1966) has made much of the deliberate transition, at the end of the Renaissance, away from notions of truth as adequacy or resemblance (to the great book of nature) and toward notions of truth as the *logos* of language, dependent upon the privileged verb "to be"—which in many of its uses corresponds or refers to nothing in nature at all. In the words of modern psychology, one could say that the language of the great book is purely analog language: a rich language of relationships (unlike the *digital* mode of discourse), a language with vast descriptive powers but no negation, no truth, no falsity. (Language may of course be both digital and analog; it may be purely expressive, or simply musical.) The "presentation," therefore, taken in this instance as covering experience outside the discourse as such (perception, phantasies, emotions, and so forth) —but necessarily mediated by it—is the category of the *referent* of the signified. In this sense, as Julius Laffal has pointed out in *Pathological and Normal Language* (New York: Atherton Press, 1965), it will in most contexts be equivalent to the Freudian *Sachvorstellung* or "thing presentation" (sometimes translated "concept of the thing" or "concrete idea"). The term avoids any necessary implication that the referent is *real*. The referent may of course be almost entirely subjective or almost entirely objective depending on whether what is presented is personal, like a phantasy, or collective, like a normal visual perception—for the visual perception can usually be defined ostensively whereas the phantasy never can. Naturally, the referent may also be a word, a proposition, an event, an experience, a system of signifiers, and so forth. It is obviously not the meaning. Abstract general nouns (or their related propositions), for instance, have no separate referent in this sense, only a signified (or concept), which coalesces with the referent in their signification. Unlike the possibility there is of ostensively defining certain visual thing presentations (but only with the help of words and in an already constituted language context), the chain of words in an abstract general proposition can only be defined by substitution. This is a substitution of signifiers, or verbal definition, to which all ostensive definitions can also be reduced. For Freud, this is clearly the category of the *Wortvorstellung* or "word presentation."

Let me now relate this terminology of signifier, signified, and presentation specifically to the more well-known terminology of Ogden and Richards' *The Meaning of Meaning* (New York: Harvest Books, 1966 [1923]). The authors of this celebrated work, from which many Anglo-Saxon attempts at resolving the epistemological or psychological problems of meaning take their departure, summarily dismiss Saussure from the very beginning. They had perhaps not read the *Cours de linguistique générale* very carefully, for, quite apart from their misreading of Saussure's view of the difference between the linguistic sign and the symbol, they failed to see the significance of Saussure's "diacritical" theory of meaning. The significance of this theory of meaning (the signification of a signifier is its differentiation from all other signifiers) lies in how it differs from the presuppositions behind the traditional use of commutative definitions—replacing "obscure symbols" by more suitable ones, as Ogden and Richards put it. Saussure is talking at a different and more profound level; he is talking about the *conditions* of meaning, as meaning operates immanently and unconsciously within the discourse, whereas Ogden and Richards are primarily concerned with the type of metasemantics implied in the title of the book—which is why Lacan smites what he calls their "logical positivism" hip and thigh in "L'Instance de la lettre" (1957). Their interest is not primarily in how what we say makes sense but rather in making sense of what we say. And if Ogden and Richards have elaborated a theory going far beyond the hints—usually related primarily to the philological question of why "mouton" has both a wider and a narrower referent than "sheep"—thrown out by the *Cours de linguistique générale,* these hints are highly significant. They could perhaps have given pause even to Ogden and Richards. Besides the common misinterpretation of the sound and sense distinction already mentioned, it is only because of the unfortunate diagram (including the picture of the tree) attached to Saussure's original algorithm that one might become misled as to Saussure's view of meaning. All that this formulation tells us is that Saussure—or Saussure as interpreted by his students—was not primarily concerned to distinguish the presentation or referent from the signified in the way that the psychologist or philosopher would be. The diagram is in fact modified later in the *Cours de linguistique générale* and the picture replaced by a word within quotation marks. Elsewhere Saussure specifically denies that his view involves relating a word to a real thing (p. 100). But what in this case can be meant by the notion of the arbitrariness of the sign (or signifier)? As Benveniste has pointed out in the article already cited on the nature of the linguistic sign, the sound and sense distinction is not arbitrary *in fact;* it is *necessary.* "Sister" and the signified sister are not actually divisible for the speaker of English; the word comes to him already defined by a collective context. This point is supported by the fact that Saussure, as a philologist first and a structural linguist second, can be seen shifting his terminology in response to the surreptitious third term not covered by the dichotomy of signifier and signified; this third term is either the presentation (referent) or the "real object" (since Saussure is not concerned with that particular distinction). When one examines the contradictory statements of the *Cours de linguistique générale* more closely, it is clear that Saussure's concern for philological problems of semantics—the relationship between "soeur" and "sister," for instance—is in conflict with his structural approach, which implicitly disregards philological semantics.

Consequently, when he talks about the dichotomy of the sign in a structural context, meaning the distinction between sound and sense, he is concerned with the conditions of the communicational circuit between sender and receiver: how *this* sound generates *this* sense in the "speech circuit" which he was the first to formulate expressly (p. 12). It is immaterial in this context to know what the signified represents; what is important, of course, is Saussure's emphasis upon language as the *form* of *communication* rather than as the substance of expression. Although the distinction between acoustic image and concept seems to share the mentalist view of Ogden and Richards—that speech is the expression of thought content—the indivisibility of the sign as emphasized by Saussure suggests that this would be a misinterpretation. At the same time the notion of the arbitrary relationship of sound and sense becomes largely irrelevant. In a communicational context, the relationship is *necessary*, otherwise there would be no *langue* to which the *parole* could be related. The sound/sense distinction is only arbitrary to a *transcendental observer*.

But Saussure as a philologist *is* a transcendental observer of languages other than his own, and this is where his confusion arises. The relationship between "boeuf" and "Ochs" *is* arbitrary, as he says (p. 102), but since that between cognates and derivatives in various languages is not, as he does not say, it is clear that the arbitrariness lies between the signifier and "reality"—that is, between the signifier and either "real objects" or whatever is represented as reality by the social consensus of mutually shared presentations or referents. Thus, although Saussure speaks of the arbitrariness of the *signifier,* he really means what he says when he uses the expression "the arbitrariness of the *sign*" as a synonym, for the linguistic sign *is* arbitrarily related to referents, which were probably conceived of by Saussure as "real objects."

Now obviously Saussure (or his students) were ill-advised to place so much apparent emphasis upon the notion of the word as an element of meaning. But this is hardly unexpected, since he is usually thinking in the terms of philological semantics, where words in one language do mean something in another, because in both languages a whole communicational system lies behind our ability to discover that "soeur" means "sister." Saussure would obviously have been better advised to speak explicitly of the signifier as a proposition or syntagm; nevertheless, his structural formulation allows this substitution without changing the model he is using.

But what is much more important, what Ogden and Richards could have learned from Saussure, is the wide implication of his "second" theory of meaning, derived from the notion of the arbitrariness between sign and referent. This is the "diacritical" view already mentioned, which is rigorously concerned with the conditions of meaning in the way that his discussion of "boeuf" and "Ochs" is not. This view depends upon the notion of differentiality in linguistics, which is entirely original with Saussure and which has seen its fullest development in phonology. At the semantic level, he expresses it as follows: "Since there is no vocal image whatsoever which would correspond more than any other one to *what it is charged with saying,* it is evident, even a priori, that *a fragment of language* can never be founded, in the last analysis, except on its *non-*

coincidence with the rest. *Arbitrary* and *differential* are two correlative qualities" (p. 163, emphasis added). This point was taken up in 1951 by Merleau-Ponty:

Coming back to the spoken or living language, we discover that its expressive value is not the sum of the expressive values belonging to each element of the "verbal chain." On the contrary, these elements become a system in the synchronic order in the sense that each one of them signifies only its difference in relation to the others—signs, as Saussure says, being essentially "diacritical" —and since this is true of all of them, in any language there are only differences of signification. If eventually the language means or says something, it is not because each sign carries a signification belonging to it, but because they all allude to a signification forever in suspense, when they are considered one by one, and toward which I pass them by without them ever containing it [30] [cf. t.n. 8].

The diacritical theory of meaning is a structural notion which deprives us of the transcendental dictionary Wittgenstein spoke of in the *Philosophical Investigations*. It implies a circularity of meaning, a system of signification arbitrarily related to "reality" and in fact only related to itself. "Wood," for instance, can only be finally defined by itself, because it is not any other signifier in the system. It is this implied circularity and autonomy of language that leads Lacan into postulating a sort of fault in the system, a hole, a fundamental lack into which, one might say, meaning is *poured*. It is this primordial *manque* which allows substitutions, the movement of language essential to signification, to take place. Saussure's view is in fact more radical, although it is unlikely that he concerned himself with its widest implications. It is the same radical statement of the modern notion of structure that can be found in Jacques Derrida's *L'Ecriture et la différence* (Paris: Editions du Seuil, 1967), where in an article on the sign, structure, and what he calls "freeplay" (*jeu*) (pp. 409–28), Derrida brings out the *unthinkable* novelty of Lévi-Strauss's concept of structure. For Lévi-Strauss a structure is totally autonomous, a system of interchangeability permitted by a sort of internal freeplay, but lacking the "center" or fixed point (the transcendental referent) implied in all the traditional notions of structure. Thus Lévi-Strauss's structural analysis of myths is, as Lévi-Strauss says himself, itself a myth, and the "myth of reference" which he employs is only

[30] "Sur la phénoménologie du langage," in: *Signes* (Paris: Gallimard, 1960), p. 110.

privileged by the method, not by "reality." It is a sort of Newtonian universe without any God to wind it up, or better, a whole system of utterances without a speaking subject. This is precisely the same sort of paradox for which Saussure has been reproached by linguists: a system without a center is unthinkable, and the diacritical system of meaning has no center. Parenthetically, whereas Derrida's notion of freeplay (which is a center related only to the system) is clearly conceived as something immanent to the structure (like the freeplay in a gear train), Lacan's notion of a primordial "lack" is precisely the "lack of a fixed point" (the impossibility for desire to recover the lost object) toward which desire and consequently the metonymic movement of discourse is aimed. It is a lack providing for the absent center (the object) and is thus simply a reversal of the fixed point. Lacan's view does not seem to dispense with the transcendental referent presupposed in psychoanalysis: for him this referent is the lost object at the origins. Presence (*Vollheit*) becomes absence (*signifiant*); and no substitute (representation) in the system is ever adequate to its object (presentation).

To return to the less metaphysical problem of terminology, Ogden and Richards also missed the point that Saussure's conception of the necessary commutability of signifiers and the non-commutability of (traditional) symbols rested mainly on definitions, not on some sort of misunderstanding of language, as they suggest. Although Saussure sometimes uses the expression "linguistic symbol," his remarks about the "natural" or "rational" link between the (traditional) symbol and the thing symbolized imply simply that symbols depend on or at one time depended on their Imaginary resemblance to "things." Thus, algebraic "symbols" are signifiers in Saussure's terminology. Neither things nor thing presentations are commutable, because reality and perception are continuous, whereas language can only be communicated in reality (by the continuous frequencies of sound waves) because it is segmented into commutable "bits." As long as they are not intentionalized as signifiers, symbols therefore remain non-commutable. In other words, whereas the symbol in this sense is mediated by perception so that the contiguity or continuity between adjacent symbols (the house, a balcony) may reflect a contiguity or continuity between what is symbolized by them (a woman), the contiguity of signifiers bears no relation to the contiguity of their referents. This is in part what Kojève was saying, albeit in a more traditional context, when he spoke of Hegel's "solution" of the problem of error in pre-Hegelian philosophy (in the passage previously quoted): "this liberty permits the meanings incarnate in words to combine in ways other than those of the corresponding essences, bound to their natural supports" (p. 546). Although this is a view far less radical than Saussure's diacritical theory of meaning and Lacan's assertion of the primacy of the Symbolic order, it is nevertheless more radical than the simple notion of convention in language—man giving names to thoughts and things—because the convention theory, like the theory of denomination in the child, presupposes language, and, presumably, thought without language, whereas for Kojève man and language are synonymous.

What is true of symbols seems to be true of gestures also, and of similar acts of communication (voluntary or otherwise). Since a gesture is "natural," has no subject function (apparently employs no substitutable shifters), and cannot be defined by a meta-gesture in the way that a statement may be defined by a metastatement, it cannot be accurately retransmitted in its own terms, or it may not be retransmissible at all. No other subject can substitute his gesture for mine because commutability —the primary requirement for the intersubjectivity of language—requires what André Martinet and other linguists have termed a "double articulation," that is, a non-semantic level of material signals (noises, marks, movements) forming a non-semantic code (an alphabet, phonemes) with commutative rules concerning the formation of words. At another level of articulation these words are combinable into syntagms or propositions where meaning arises. Thus the meaning of a gesture is quite different from the meaning of a proposition, because beyond the most elementary levels of glandular reactions to threats and so forth (signals), the gesture has to be raised to another level of articulation before becoming meaningful. I must interpret a look which says "He is sad," whereas no such interpretation is necessary if he says "I am sad." Gestures have no alphabet or dictionary and consequently very little syntax. This is once again a mode of the distinction between digital and analog communication, a notion modeled on the difference between digital and analog scales. There is a direct rational or quantificative relationship between an analog scale and what it represents (for example, the rise of the column of mercury in a thermometer), a relationship which imposes limits on the system. Similarly, an analog computer, which operates on a logarithmic scale and thus has no zero, employs a continuous linear scale to represent continuous linearities, such as the sequence of real numbers (which is an uncountable, continuous infinity). The digital computer, on the other hand, like language itself, employs discrete "bits" whose relationship to what they represent is constitutively arbitrary or conventional, and not limited in the same way. It may be used to represent the sequence of discrete units represented by the integers, for instance, or by the rational numbers, both sequences being discontinuous and countable—and separated by what in language would be called zero-phonemes. There are no discrete "bits" in a gesture language, unless it has become conventionalized as a system of signals (as in the deaf and dumb alphabet), and no zero-phonemes. Given a communicational situation in which gestures of any kind are being employed and recognized, it is clearly impossible for the situation of non-gesture ever to occur. (Note that in this context a traffic light is not a sign or a symbol, but precisely what we say it is, a traffic *signal*.) A digital computer, however, can theoretically be programmed (like language) to represent the behavior of any other system, including thought and language themselves.

François Bresson has pointed out this distinction in an article, "La Signification," appearing in *Problèmes de Psycho-linguistique* (Paris: Presses Universitaires de France, 1963, pp. 9–45). He cites various authorities to show that at certain stages of the evolution of a linguistic system, it may have depended to a large extent on analog "signs" like gestures—and, one might add, on similarly analogic groups of onomatopeic phonemes (which, *ipso facto,* are not *words*). But since these signs are *necessarily* linked to what they stand for (at least originally), that is, because they are symbolic in Saussure's sense of a natural link implying *continuity* between what signifies and what is signified, rather than the *arbitrariness* necessitated in the double articulation, "the symbolic character of [these] signs is more an obstacle than a help to communication." "Languages," Bresson adds, "are *simultaneously* doubly articulated and devoid of symbolic value" (pp. 14–15). This would seem to indicate that the metaphor as usually conceived (dependent on resemblance) is not something developed out of an originally digital language, but rather that language itself, as Vico, Condillac, Rousseau, and others believed, is originally metaphorical. Bresson goes on to point out, as Wittgenstein had already done from a purely logical standpoint, that studies of children seem to show that the primal "attitude of denomination" which is often postulated in discussions of the origins of language, and particularly in theories about language learning in the child (by Bertrand Russell, for instance), is clearly not a "spontaneous verbal attitude: it belongs in fact to metalanguage" (p. 21). It supposes, in other words, a comprehension of language which is clearly beyond the child, for whòm language is identical to "reality." This view of denomination lies behind all of Lacan's attacks on the supposedly causal relationship between "reality" and language, with its usual implication that language is subordinate to "reality." The theory of denomination clearly presupposes an anterior knowledge of language as a context, a system of relationships, without which naming would be impossible.

In modern psychology, particularly that derived from the behavioral school in the United States, the considerations generated by the notions of reference in the philosophical problem of meaning have lost ground in favor of a purely pragmatic approach. The meaning of a word has been simply defined as what the subject or subjects associate with it in the traditional word-association tests. The commonest association for "black," significantly enough, is "white," so that although this emphasis upon the meaning of *words* may seem somewhat archaic, it does in fact presuppose that the word is involved in an unstated syntagm, as well as implicitly insisting that the word be defined *differentially* within a linguistic system. The referent of black is obviously not the same as the referent of white, and yet black can only be defined verbally—it being understood that in such a test neither "black" nor "white" are or can be isolated from their subjective and objective contexts—by a differential reference to all other colors, and notably to its polar opposite "white." Similarly, but less clearly, with the most common response, "chair," to the stimulus "table," for the actual referent in both instances is not a specific presentation (or "real object"), but rather a whole subsystem of signifiers —what Ogden and Richards would call a (linguistic) "sign-situation"— in which one item is defined by its distinction from the others.

To return now to the question of the sign versus the symbol, it is clear that in Saussure's system a gesture is a symbol, not a signifier (or sign), provided that it affords or once afforded interpretation by a mimetic link. The distinction made by Ogden and Richards, on the other hand, is that the special group of signs which men use to communicate with one another, that is, "words, arrangements of words, images, gestures, and such representations as drawings or mimetic sounds" (p. 23), are to be called symbols. They add in a note that psychoanalytical symbols "are, of course, signs only; they are not used for purposes of communication" —an error to which I shall return. For Saussure, then, we can infer that a conventionalized gesture, like "sign language," becomes a signal equivalent to, but not the same as, the phonemic level of articulation in language. At any level beyond the animal level of communication—as in the case of dolphins who communicate by sounds, and who can be trained by the stimulus-response technique to communicate within the games they have been taught to play—the gesture is mediated by the linguistic context which provides the possibility of interpretation. A word or syntagm, however, is a "linguistic sign." What Ogden and Richards might have noted, therefore, is that Saussure's linguistic sign makes up the largest subset of what they chose to call symbols, thus confusing the discursive with the non-discursive. But insofar as "symbol" signifies something communicable in their terminology, it would seem that all the symbols to which they refer are in fact intentionalized as signifiers, since "symbolization" is elsewhere defined as "directly naming" (p. 117)—as ostensive definition. What they call a "sign" is in consequence what I term a "traditional symbol," as distinct from the signifiers of the Symbolic order. This does not imply that traditional symbols may not become signifiers or vice versa. To modify radically a definition from Ogden and Richards, one might say (with Lacan) that a symbol or signifier in this sense refers to "what it is actually used to refer to" by the subject in the sender-receiver relationship and in the system or subsystem in which it occurs, complete with its overdeterminations. This seems to be the only way in which we might approach the poetry of schizophrenia, for instance, as in the following statements by a young girl—who had undoubtedly never read Nerval or seen Durer's *Melancholia*—quoted by R. D. Laing in *The Divided Self* (Harmondsworth: Penguin Books, 1965):

> I'm thousands.
> I'm an in divide you all.
> I'm a no un. [. . .]
> She was born under a black sun.
> She's the occidental sun. [. . .]
> I'm the prairie.
> She's the ruined city. [. . .]
> She's the ghost of the weed garden.
> The pitcher is broken, the well is dry (pp. 204–5).

"Noun," "nun," "no one," "not one," "nothing," "black son," "accidental son," "sunset"—a whole permutative series of signifiers and referents, some of which ("nun," for example) are also symbols.

Let me now introduce the well-known triangle from *The Meaning of Meaning* (p. 11) in order to bring together the various terminologies more precisely, without, of course, implying an acceptance of the theory of "real meaning," causality, and necessary reference to "things" behind it:

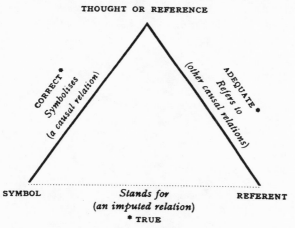

THOUGHT OR REFERENCE

CORRECT *
Symbolises
(a causal relation)

ADEQUATE *
Refers to
(other causal relations)

SYMBOL   *Stands for*   REFERENT
          (an imputed relation)
          * TRUE

From The Meaning of Meaning *by Charles K. Ogden and I. A. Richards. Reproduced by permission of Harcourt, Brace & World, Inc.*

The triangle represents the opposition between adequacy and truth, avoids the problem of the "real object," and shows the relationship between "symbol" and "referent" as mediated by something that is neither ("thought or reference"). If we employ Saussure's terminology, we would simply substitute "sign" for the left-hand relationship between "symbol" and "thought," in order to emphasize their indivisibility, and then write "signifier" for "symbol" and "signified" for "thought." "Referent," as I have said, would be equivalent to what I have called the "presentation." Thus the relationship between signifier and presentation, or symbol and referent, is mediated by the system of signifieds, that is, by the system of *signification*. Since signification rather obviously has no ultimate meaning outside language, we can simply say that in any context the apex of the triangle represents the particular given system of language. Similarly, and for the same reason that any set or subset of signifiers (a proposition) cannot not refer to the whole of which it is part, the referent represents the system of presentations or, in more general terms, the world of experience outside language ("the complex of associations made up of the greatest variety of visual, acoustic, tactile, kinaesthetic and other presentations" of which Freud speaks in the passage from his work on aphasia quoted below). In the same way, the left-hand side of the triangle covers Freud's "word presentation," and the referent is equivalent to his "thing presentation."

This interpretation of Ogden and Richard's triangle is derived in part from the following modification of it by Bresson in the article on signification previously cited (p. 12):

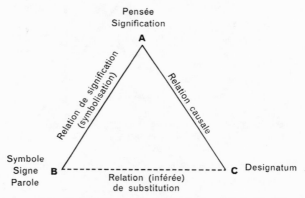

Reproduced from "La Signification" by François Bresson, in Problèmes de Psycholinguistique, *by permission of the Presses Universitaires de France.*

The terminology of Frege's theory of sense and reference (or signification), which is not however applicable to the concept (*Begriff*) or to relations, but only to the "proper name"—defined as "a sign [*Zeichen*] which stands for or signifies [*bedeutet*] an object [*Gegenstand*]"—would be related to this diagram in the following way. Apex B represents the sign (the proper name, the designation) which "expresses" the "sense" (apex A) and stands for the "object" or the "reference" (apex C). More accurately, apex C should be labeled *Vorstellung/Bedeutung/Gegenstand,* since Frege regards the referent as real, the *Bedeutung* as objective reference or signification, and both as in opposition to the personal and subjective *Vorstellung.* The relationship between object and presentation can be regarded as mediated by the sense. Thus in his "Ueber Sinn und Bedeutung," published in 1892, he states: "The reference or signification of a proper name is the object itself which we designate by its means; the presentation we have in that case is wholly subjective; in between lies the sense, which is indeed no longer subjective like the idea, but is yet not the object itself." To complete these terminological comparisons: in the Stoic armory, the respective labels would be as follows: B, the *semainon* (other possible synonyms are the *sema,* or the *sumbolon* and *semeion* used by Aristotle); A, the *semainomenon* (*significatum*), or *lekton;* C, the *phantasia, tunchanon,* and *pragma.* To these last remarks, we add Wittgenstein's warning in the *Philosophical Investigations* that *Bedeutung* is being used illicitly "if it is used to designate [*bezeichnet*] the thing that 'corresponds' ['*entspricht'*] to the word. That is to confound the *Bedeutung* of a name with the *bearer* of a name" (#40).

The "(imputed) relationship of *substitution*" in Bresson's diagram is precisely what we have seen in Lacan as the "metaphoric" relationship between a symptom and the presentation it replaces, neither of which "means" the other, as in the traditional sense of the meaning of a symbol or symptom, but one of which "stands in" for the other as a result of repression, or rather, as a result of the return of the repressed. When Lacan rewrites the Saussurian diagram, with the signifier over the signified, and uses the resulting algorithm $\left(\dfrac{S}{s}\right)$ to represent "la topique de l'inconscient," that is, the topology of the various levels of presentations as defined by Freud (t.n. 64), as we shall see in detail in the discussion of metaphor and metonymy below, he seems to be using "signified" to stand for the *referent* (apex C), which may, of course, be itself a signifier, rather than for the signification (apex A). But since the return of the repressed referent to consciousness is always eventually mediated by an intentionalization within the system of language or signification, since, in other words, there is no *direct* relationship between apex B and apex C, the return of the repressed means that "the unconscious speaks"—because of the intentionalization of the referent in a manner unacceptable to the conscious subject.

Lacan seems to oscillate between viewing the signified in some instances as representing preconscious or unconscious "psychic reality" and in other instances as simply the meaning of the signifier (cf. t.n. 85). It is clearly never "reality" in the sense that the "actual" referent for Ogden and Richards is a means of verifying a reference. Some readers have interpreted the algorithm $\frac{S}{s}$ as representing the metaphorical relationship between consciousness and the unconscious, and there are some statements in "L'Instance de la lettre" which seem to authorize such a reading. But the actual relationship as viewed by Lacan is more complicated, and it is difficult to see how the relation of signifier to signified thus expressed takes us beyond the notion of the manifest as the letter and the latent as the sense, which is precisely the viewpoint combatted by Lacan. Leclaire and Laplanche do in fact modify the representation radically in their lengthy article "L'Inconscient" (1961), without giving up the notion of a metaphorical relationship between two "levels" of discourse, but since Lacan does not accept their modification in certain respects, the question remains an open one. However this may be, when Lacan speaks of the primacy of the signifier in the genesis of the signified (as does Lévi-Strauss), all that he says about the signifier and signified seems to coalesce in the central idea that language in itself generates both meaning and reality (t.n. 91). In other words, the primacy of the Symbolic order is that it makes the ordering of reality possible (as Cassirer had said)—as in the crucial example of the *Fort! Da!*—at the same time as it *provides* and *constitutes* the "real" referents which are erroneously supposed to "cause" language. For Lacan, the interaction between discourse and perception is such that language, and not perception, is or becomes primary. This is a viewpoint supported by the Gestalt and other psychologists who assert that we perceive relationships, not objects, in reality, and that it is language or thought which supports our belief in the perception and knowledge of concrete objects.

In parallel fashion, it becomes impossible to make a valid and operational distinction in practice between the informative and the evocative (or expressive) aspects of language. The notion of language as information seeks to separate speech from motivation. The notion of evocative or expressive language complements this error by conferring a privilege on a theoretically bi-univocal and unambiguous correspondence between syntagm and referent and thus plays down the informative aspect of evocative language. But, as *communication,* the primary function of language is clearly to establish *relationships,* which is precisely what the theory of information and the privilege conferred on logical or digital language seeks to ignore. Freud's theory of overdetermination and Gregory Bateson's emphasis on the integral and indivisible "report-command" aspect of any statement (*Communication: The Social Matrix of Psychiatry* [New York: W. W. Norton, 1951], pp. 179–82) surely tell us that all punctuation of the communicational circuit set up by any statement is inevitably arbitrary. This is in effect what Lacan is repeating in a different form when he dwells on the mediated relationship of transference and countertransference between analyst and patient. It is in fact by means of an overload of information that the patient (or the analyst) may seek to *jam* the evocative circuit between them—or in other words, seek to *resist* the revelation or recognition of crucial relationships. Moreover, as Bateson suggests, it is unlikely that any one subject is capable of recognizing both the "report" and the "command" aspect of his or another's statement simultaneously, and his resistance may well depend upon which aspect he has chosen to recognize in any particular situation.

Of course, if we believe that there is something abnormal about the structure of the relationship between analyst and patient, much of what Lacan says can be successfully resisted. If we do not, it is of interest to see how Ogden and Richards, for example, use their "information" or "reports" in the highly aggressive and commanding manner characteristic of a certain period of British philosophizing, whereas the later Wittgenstein uses a largely evocative "command" approach to communicate a great deal of information (reports). In this sense, the general notion that truth depends on words having specific, particular, and causally related referents, without regard to the principle of overdetermination (which implies a series of statements on statements, communication on communication, information on information—in a word, a whole series of metalanguages) or to what a signifier is intended or interpreted to mean, irrespective of its particular syntactical form (Ogden and Richards, pp. 88, 103–4), seems to be in essence an aspect of the natural human resistance to the unthinkable consequences of the loss of the transcendental referent. It is a view apparently motivated by a search for identity in life which, as Hume implied, is only possible in language. It may correspond to what Sartre—from his own experience—so aptly called "la nostalgie de la pierre," in itself a derivative of a kind of psychosis (as exemplified in Sartre's analysis of the role of this nostalgia in the psychology of the bigot, as in his *Anti-Semite and Jew* and in the prewar short story "L'Enfance d'un chef") or a kind of neurosis (as in certain religious activities). It seems to be related to a fear that the pursuit of meaning in life—call meaning "goal directed activity," if needs be—will leave us only with Hamlet's "words, words, words." The consequence is that constructs like the notion of an ideal language are developed as defenses against this fear. Human communication is constitutively asymmetrical, and the pursuit of truth in these terms corresponds to the desire for symmetry implied by Freud's principle of inertia or constancy (homeostasis), expressing the impossible quest for the lost object—in a word, death. Truth, as both Hegel and Freud implied, is relative to the system or subsystem within which the seeker is inscribed: at any level beyond that of "I had breakfast this morning" (which is in fact a relationship of adequacy), truth is always a statement about another statement in the arbitrary punctuation of a relationship. Absolute Knowledge in Hegel corresponds to death in Freud—but this last remark may be inadequate to the subtlety of the role of death in the *Phenomenology*.

These considerations seem to lie behind Lacan's substitution of "truth" for "reality" in the *Discours*—since philosophy and commonsense have always tended to confuse the two—and it is in this sort of context that we should read Lacan on the meaning of meaning in "L'Instance de la lettre" (1957):

. . . We shall fail to stick to the question [of the nature of language] so long as we have not freed ourselves of the illusion that the signifier corresponds or answers to the function of representing the signified, or better, that the signifier has to answer for its existence in the name of any signification whatever.

For even if reduced to this last formulation, the heresy is the same. It is the heresy which leads logical positivism in quest of the meaning of meaning, as its aim or object [*objectif*] is named in the language its followers snuffle and snuggle in (p. 52).

On the other hand, when the psychologist studying the relationship of perception to the discourse evokes something similar to the Saussurian concept of the arbitrary sign (as Hegel does)—related to the notion of intentionality in phenomenology—he assimilates the sound, the image of the word, and the thing presentation to what is sensory and relates these "sensations" to conceptualization. He is not fundamentally concerned with meaning in the sense of the theoretical relationship between word and sense, because he generally assumes that the meaning is given (a picture of a table is not a picture of a house) or that the meaning is only that conferred by the subject (Rorschach tests). Considerations of arbitrariness are generated by the experiment itself, not necessarily by fundamental questions about language. But the philosopher tackles the same four elements in a different way, since "arbitrary" for him is an idealist, realist, or nominalist position, depending upon whether the arbitrariness of the sign is conceived as between presentation and reality (idealism), word and presentation, and thus between word and reality (nominalism) or between word and concept (realism). Thus Descartes, who formulated the modern notion of the "idea" from which philosophy has had to liberate itself through language, wants to be a realist: ". . . Since we attach our conceptions to certain words in order to express them orally and since we remember the words rather than the things, we can hardly conceive anything as distinctly as if we separate entirely what we conceive from the words which have been chosen to express it" (*Principes*, I, 74).

The philosopher who conceives of the world as his idea will be called in the textbooks a subjective idealist (for example, Kant). If the world for him is *our* idea, he is called an objective idealist (for example, Hegel). If he says that language bears no necessary relation to reality at all, he will be called a nominalist. But a label has not yet been devised for the philosopher who seeks to relate the linguist's view of language as an autonomous system to the system of perception and to the system of reality, each being viewed as somehow "mapping" the other through a process of abstraction or metaphor or metacommunication. Certainly, as my earlier remarks imply, the trend seems to be toward a view of phenomenological intentionality as conferring a subjective meaning on perception (or consciousness in general) out of the objective stock of language, so that if I always see church steeples, it is because everybody does, whereas if I see (mean, intend) the phallus, it will be related to subjective determinants derived from my personal relationship to my familial and societal environment as well as from my personal gifts of imagination.

Psychoanalytical Symbolism

The psychoanalyst is in yet another position, because he is concerned with symbols in the traditional textbook sense of Freud's last theory of symbolism. Symbols in this sense are not discursive phenomena; no doubt this explains why the psychoanalyst has not been primarily concerned with the problems of a theory of language, since he has supposed a natural connection between word and thing (spider) and a further natural connection between the symbol and the thing symbolized (mother). This view of symbolism, notably in the dream, accounts further for the traditional psychoanalytical interest in the symbolism of individual substantives rather than in the enchainment of words in a discourse.

Apart from the inevitably one-way interpretation of the symbol in traditional psychoanalysis (but not in Freud)—one does not often hear of the phallus standing as a symbol for a church steeple (and surely, sometimes at least, as Freud was wont to remark, a cigar is just a cigar?) —it has long been obvious that sexual, incorporative, and other "depth-psychology" symbols are so prevalent in life, in dreams, and in books that their recognition or discovery, outside the therapeutic realm, adds very little in the end to our understanding—and certainly does not provide us with the privileged level of "real meaning" as has so often been supposed. In literature, for instance, the analyst has tended to concern himself not so much with "nonliterature," as literary prudes are accustomed to wail—since everything about an author or his text has its relevance—but rather with one level and one means of interpretation to the exclusion of all others. But the real failing of many psychoanalytical or psychological approaches to literature and philosophy has lain not simply in the superiority of the symbol hunter, who knows what the author does not know because he has cracked his unconscious code and who confers a privilege on his knowledge because of that fact, but more significantly in his essentially nonsocial and nondialectical view of the symbol. It is not enough to talk about the universal symbols of the human race, all referring, as Jones had said, to a very limited number of human relationships, if one then returns to a kind of automatic and essentially solipsistic interpretation based upon allegory or analogy, which tends to negate the particular social, historical, and personal conjunctures in which the producer of the symbol is involved.

It is against the notion of a fixed symbolic code (*die Symbolik:* t.n. 86) that Lacan directs his attack in the *Discours*. Analogical interpretation is in fact only a step past the oriental dream books Freud was writing against in the early part of the *Traumdeutung*. Much of Lacan's orientation comes from his knowledge of the use of symbolism in anthropology, which differs in important ways from the usually accepted notion in psychoanalysis, although not from the general psychological sense of symbolic behavior. For example, in the extraordinary complex systems of primitive exchange examined by Mauss in the celebrated *Essai sur le don* (1923) (see the passages referred to in t.n. 80), the gifts exchanged can be called symbols. But they do not stand for what they "represent" in some fixed relationship to an unconscious "meaning." They are the symbols of the act of exchange itself, which is what ties the society together. Thus they cease to be symbols in any important sense; it is the *act* of exchange, with its attendant mana or *hau* (t.n. 98), which symbolizes the unconscious requirement of exchange through displaced reciprocity (I give you this, he gives me that) as a means of establishing and maintaining relationships between the members of that society. They are only symbols insofar as the idea of symbol includes the notion of the *tessera* (t.n. 32) as that which forms a link. In Lévi-Strauss's terminology, these objects of exchange are often referred to as "signs," which are exchanged like words in a discourse. The object (or woman) exchanged is part of a symbolic discourse responding to a requirement of communication. It is thus part of a symbolic function, but it symbolizes nothing in itself. Even the appellation "sign" turns out to be a dubious one in certain instances, since if we employ C. S. Peirce's definition of the sign as "something which replaces something for someone," Lévi-Strauss will ask how we can call an object with a specific function of its own, like a stone axe, a sign, since we cannot answer the question of what it replaces, or for whom.

Lévi-Strauss's own evolving terminology contributes to the confusion, since, outside the sociological sphere as a whole, he has equated the signifier with the symbol, in the traditional sense. Speaking of the shaman who cures his patients by driving out devils, in a process similar to the generally discarded notion of psychoanalytic abreaction, he says: ". . . The relation between monster and illness is interior to this one mind, conscious or unconscious: it is a relationship of the symbol to the thing symbolized, or, to use the vocabulary of linguistics, a relation of signifier to signified." The symbol is a "significative equivalent of the signified, from another order of reality than that of the signified."[31] Saussure's usage, however, was to distinguish the symbol from the signifier (or the sign), since the symbol, unlike the linguistic sign, is not entirely arbitrary. Unlike the arbitrary sign, there is a "rudimentary natural link"

[31] "L'Efficacité symbolique" (1949), in: *Anthropologie Structurale* (Paris: Plon, 1958), pp. 218, 221. Freud's early interest in catharsis as the key to the cure (later rejected) has been revived in the therapy of the psychodrama.

Lacan expresses himself similarly to Lévi-Strauss: "The symptomatic signifier [that is, horses in the "myths" of "little Hans"] covers the most multiple of signifieds" (Seminar of March–April, 1957, p. 854).

or a "rational relationship" between the symbol and the thing symbolized (pp. 101, 106), as I have already emphasized.

Lacan obviously does not deny the existence of *la symbolique,* the more or less fixed symbolic code developed by Freud, Jones, and others out of Stekel's intuitions, but he certainly seeks to weaken the overriding importance it had subsequently been accorded in traditional psychoanalysis. There is in Freud both a wide and a restricted sense ascribed to symbolism: the first and earliest is the notion of a symbolic action as something displaced, or figurative, or having a latent meaning; the second is that of the fixed code to which the analyst may resort when the dreamer is unable to supply his own interpretation of an image. Consequently Freud added to the *Traumdeutung* a series of "typical dreams," as in a dreambook. But at the beginning of the chapter on symbols in dreams (mostly added between 1909 and 1925), he acknowledged his debt to Stekel as to a man who had possibly damaged psychoanalysis as much as he had benefited it. Since Freud had very early insisted that the dreamer interpret his own dream text by means of his associations—the method Freud employed in interpreting most of his own dreams—he was perhaps aware of the danger of a purely automatic system of interpretation replacing the dialectical interpretation upon which his method had been founded. But the two methods of interpretation, one associative and personal, the other tied to the collective experience of humanity, exist side by side in his text. The difference between them is that emphasized by Saussure, the apparently "natural" reference of symbols as opposed to the arbitrary reference of signifiers. A symbol is not distinguished by its differentiation from other symbols as is the signifier, nor can it generally be replaced by other symbols, and it certainly cannot be defined by them. Symbolism in this sense is a sort of natural language or, more accurately, a semiology, rather than a language. Insofar as traditional symbolism depends upon visual resemblances, Lacan would relegate it to the Imaginary. But insofar as both the associative and the coded method of interpretation manifest a structural (semiotic) similarity (in the sense that one does speak of a "language of symbols"), there will be instances where the second will be subsumed under "le symbolique," a concept derived from the anthropological concept of the symbolic function, which is treated in Section IV.

The central aspect of the Symbolic order is communication, and with the introduction of the concept of *le symbolique,* the word symbol sheds its traditional sense in psychoanalysis to become a stronger term. In his article on "Le Symbolique" (1960), Rosolato distinguishes between sign, signal, and symbol on the basis of the multivalency or overdetermination (t.n. 70, 81, 86) which is possible only in, or in reference to, the intersubjectivity of language. Although his somewhat Lacanian style makes difficult reading, one or two points seem clear. The multivalency of the symbol ("a transmuted sign") "entails, *conjointly,* for a *signifier,* the correspondence of several *signifieds,* and, vice-versa, for one of these signifieds, *any one whatever,* several *signifiers*" (p. 225). This is in effect how Freud described the relationship between the manifest and latent details of the dream in the early part of the *Traumdeutung.* The linguistic sign, on the other hand, in its daily use in language is more or less fixed and consequently easily decodable. Rosolato goes on to say that "the Symbolic appears as a category when the sign acquires the supplementary dimension of the symbol; the Symbolic also assures the accession to a *state* (a stage) of comprehension, a state open to thought which thinks itself, to the *relation* which comes out, the subject being inserted into it or having taken it into account" (p. 227). These multivalent relationships between signifiers and signifieds are, *simultaneously,* several to one, one to several, or one to one. The symbol, notably in the dream, may institute a *function,* relating an element *x* of a set E to an element *y* of another set, F. "In opposing the sign to the symbol, it is possible to attribute to the former the *Imaginary which becomes solidified,* breaking with the Symbolic. . . . Reintroducing the Symbolic consists in opposing the *degradation* into signs or images" (p. 230). This last assertion is presumably to be related to the psychological tendency which makes us believe that words stand for things, whereas the fundamentally symbolic nature of language (in the sense of *le symbolique*), its constitutive ambiguity and dependence on its own internal relationships rather than on any necessary reference to "reality," clearly denies any legitimacy to this belief. Rosolato sums up:

Le symbolique remains in a close relationship with the Imaginary [author's capitalization] through the sliding towards the sign. Here a scansion is obligatorily set up. The sign is indispensable to the symbol; the symbol is vital for the sign. Every symbol is of language, just as every *Parole vraie* is symbolic. . . . This inclination of the signifier towards the sign, this sedimentation, like its inverse, the return to the symbol, implies the *unconscious,* an appeal to signification which must have been discovered—traced in the sign—and which will be discovered—but already giving way—since it has already been *conscious*. For, as it has been said, 'the symbol exists only in the nascent state' . . . (p. 231).

From this scansion, and from that which is produced between the Imaginary and the Symbolic [author's capitalization], from the osmosis between signs and symbols, issues the Real: *in truth, they are together* (p. 232).

In this context, then, the symbol is distinguished both from the traditional reifications of the "second theory of symbolism"—which ignores the role of the symbol in communication—as well as from the linguistic sign as such, insofar as the sign is considered to be a word "with" a meaning outside of its context. It is, of course, the context of *convention* itself which provides linguistic signs with the "inherent" meanings which common-sense ascribes to them, and which leads us erroneously to overcompensate for the total and irresolvable ambiguity of any communicational circuit with others or with the Other by means of theories of information, belief in "getting the facts straight," nostalgia for the "real" meaning, the "real" Freud (or the real Lacan), and so forth. This is a powerful epistemological scepticism—and potentially corrosive for those who lack the courage to accept the consequences of the "vanity of their gifts" (t.n. 31). It is not a new attack on error or on the outworn and faintly ridiculous notion of absolute truth, but a far more radical attack on all our little truths. If it entails what we have always known—that all reasonably intelligent interpretations are equal—it forces us to face up to the decision why some interpretations are more equal than others.

This distinction of the first from the second method of reading the symbol follows logically from Freud's own premise of overdetermination, as well as from the examples he employs.

As an example of the use of the first method where the second might have been used, that is, an example of a reading *à la lettre,* one might mention Alexander the Great's "satyr" dream on the night before his capture of Tyre. Presumably there is some obvious, fixed symbolic interpretation of this image in terms of the sexual propensities of that lusty conqueror, but in fact the image of the satyr (a regression to perception from the dream thoughts), once it was reintegrated into Alexander's discourse, revealed itself to be a simple statement in the discourse of the Other: σὰ Τύρος: "Tyre is thine." Obviously, if Alexander had described the image as a "funny-looking goat," this particular wish-fulfillment (however overdetermined) would have remained incomprehensible without Alexander's further associations. Freud comments at this point that "it is impossible as a rule to translate a dream into a foreign language." [32]

Thus when Lacan uses "signifier," even in a clearly linguistic sense, it is not always a precise equivalent for the Saussurian term. In the general sense it is more nearly an equivalent for "word plus concept" or for "sign," since at the level of *Rede,* word and concept cannot in fact be separated (whereas definitions can be improved), nor is it now usual to attempt to differentiate them, as Descartes had done. Certainly the purely linguistic distinction of sound and sense seems to have had only a secondary interest originally for Lacan; his mathematical propensities have since led him to emphasize the notion of the signifier as made up of the combination and substitution of the phonemic chain, the substratum of the discourse. He seems to have settled on signifier for a number of reasons: one, its clear implication that something is signifying something for someone (the intentionality of the discourse)—whether that something is an individual, a society, or language itself; two, its differentiation from "signal," too easily assimilated under the term "sign"; three, its implication that no direct or necessary relationship to a real object or to reality is involved (t.n. 144); four, its autonomous nature (split off from "sense") as reducible to combinatory distinctive features. Thus the reader is always faced with deciding how Lacan is using the term in any particular context.

In the sense that the most important level of meaning of "satyr" for Alexander was a proposition in a discourse, Lacan uses "signifier" in a contextual theory of meaning, and would obviously subscribe to Wittgenstein's slogan: "The meaning is the use." Thus he also uses "signifier" to avoid the implication that any given word "contains" or "has" a meaning of its own, outside its diacritic reference to other signifiers. In this sense, even Saussure's distinctions give rise to ambiguities, for if the meaning of a signifier is its differentiation from other signifiers, it can nevertheless be defined by them. Thus the loose use of signified to mean "signification" is just another way of saying the signified is a signifier after all.

Saussure likens the relationship of signifier (sound) and signified (sense) to the two sides of a single piece of paper. This image brings to mind the analogy of the Moebius strip sometimes employed by Lacan

[32] See: *Standard Edition,* IV, 99, note 1.

to describe the subject, where the apparent division of conscious and repressed turns out to be the unity of the writing on one continuous side. Analogies are of course the weakest and most dangerous form of argument, however valuable they may be as illustration. It is in this restricted latter sense that one might liken the relationship between signifier (word-concept) and reality, which is the essentially irresolvable problem here, to that between a map and the countryside it represents. One might then recall the assertion of topologists that if a map is crumpled up and thrown down on another identical map, at least one point will be exactly where it would be if the two had been simply superimposed. For Lacan, the symptom is a twisted signifier, but it is still related somehow to the original map, just as the nodal point of the dream in analysis is a transferential point aimed at the "significant other" the analyst represents.

But symptoms may be simply somatic, or they may be actions. Lacan never really resolves this ambiguity, an ambiguity which might be resolved if he assimilated the discourse to a generalized semiology (t.n. 70). To do so, however, is perhaps only another way of begging the question. Nevertheless there is a distinction to be made on the basis of his view of the signifier and the sign. The reader should not be misled by Lacan's directing his attack in the *Discours* against the tendency of psychoanalysis towards an interpretation of behavior, into thinking that for him the discourse may not depend on a gesture, an act, a sigh, a moment of silence. Psychoanalysis is the "talking cure," but symptoms join in the conversation, too. A gesture may have all the value of a verbal signifier, or more value; Lacan does not deny this, but his point is that the gesture already includes the necessity of a second level of interpretation. It may be a signifier in the discourse of the subject, just as the ending of the session is a punctuation, but before being a signifier, it is a sign (something which replaces something for someone) to which a discursive meaning must be ascribed.

On the other hand, the hysterical symptom or obsessive action may actually be directly derived from the discourse. A symptomatic sign, in other words, may be the subject's interpretation of a signifier, just as a word may be used in place of a symptomatic action—as in the case of the Rat Man's prayer: *"Samen."* Many examples could be quoted. One favored by Lacan is that of the fetishist (at the beginning of Freud's article on fetishism [1927], *Standard Edition,* XXI, 152) for whom erotic satisfaction depended on a "shine on the nose" which he actually projected on to his partner's nose. The expression in German is "Glanz auf der Nase," but as Freud discovered, the word "Glanz" was not connected directly with its German meaning "shine," which is how the subject interpreted it, but rather with its English homonym "glance." The subject had in fact spent his early childhood in England but had since forgotten the language: his disavowal (of castration) was an Imaginary displacement on the body itself exactly parallel to the displacement from the English to the German word. What his action meant was "a glance at the nose," dependent upon the Imaginary resemblance of the two words.

Freud and Language

Freud's own explicit theory of the relationship of word and thing presents an interesting parallel with Saussure's diagram, if not with Saussure's considered theory. His "linguistic" representation of the unconscious depends upon a distinction between the primary (*Ucs.*) level, where only thing presentations are found, and the secondary (*Cs. Pcs.*) level where both thing presentations and word presentations operate (t.n. 66). In the following extract from Freud's 1891 book on aphasia, the thing presentation would correspond to "idea" in traditional philosophical terminology.[33]

In this article Freud speaks of our learning to speak in the traditional terms of the association of a "sound image" with the "sense" of a word, and continues:

A word . . . acquires its *meaning* by being linked to a thing-presentation at all events if we restrict ourselves to a consideration of substantives. The thing-presentation itself is once again a complex of associations made up of the greatest variety of visual, acoustic, tactile, kinaesthetic and other presentations. Philosophy tells us that a thing-presentation consists in nothing more than this—that the appearance of there being a 'thing' to whose various 'attributes' these sense-impressions bear witness is merely due to the fact that, in enumerating the sense-impressions which we have received from an object, we also assume the possibility of there being a large number of

[33] An extract from this book is included in *Standard Edition*, XIV, following the 1915 article "The Unconscious." There is a slight difference in terminology, the "object-presentation" of 1891 being the equivalent of the later "thing-presentation." To avoid confusion, I have substituted accordingly. The word translated "image" is *Bild.*

further impressions in the same chain of associations (J. S. Mill). The thing-presentation is thus seen to be one which is not closed and almost one which cannot be closed, while the word-presentation is seen to be something closed, even though capable of extension (pp. 213–14).

He goes on to distinguish between "first-order aphasia" (verbal aphasia), where only the associations between the separate elements of the word presentation are disturbed (speaking, writing, reading), and "second-order aphasia" (asymbolic aphasia), in which the association between the word presentation and the thing presentation is disturbed. He explains that he uses "symbolic" to describe the relationship between word and thing presentation rather than that between object and thing presentation.

In the process he produces a diagram which, if we simplify it by leaving out the elements external to the reflected relationship involved, can be represented as:

$$\frac{\text{Visual object association (thing presentation)}}{\text{Sound image (word presentation)}}$$

which is more or less equivalent to the loose interpretation of the Saussurian notion of the concept or image (of the object) over the acoustic image (the word). "Among the object-associations," Freud explains, "it is the visual ones which stand for the object, in the same way as the sound-image stands for the word." And in the 1915 article on the unconscious, he uses the term "object-presentation" to stand for the unity of the thing presentation and word presentation, or for what Saussure would call the "sign." Thus he supposes a similar discontinuity between the word, the image, and the thing.

Metaphor and Metonymy

Freud's practice, however, never depended upon this traditionally simplified view of signification, as the *Interpretation of Dreams,* the *Psychopathology of Everyday Life,* and the work on *Witz,* in particular, bear witness. And Lacan, using his own inverted version of the Saussurian algorithm $\left(\frac{S}{s}\right)$, is quick to point out that what he views as the Saussurian signifier and signified are not of the same order of reality (in the same way as word and image, or word and thing, or sound and sense are not) and that the signified is not the thing itself. But the signified is not simply the meaning of the signifier, although he has implied that it is (t.n. 85), since the meaning is another signifier, and the only correspondence between them, on Lacan's—and Lévi-Strauss's—view, is that of the totality of the signifier to the totality of the signified (t.n. 70).

In "L'Instance de la lettre" (1957), Lacan makes his distinctions between signifier and signified and their relation to the Symbolic order somewhat more clear, revealing a certain evolution in his thinking since the *Discours de Rome*. Taking up Lévi-Strauss's notion of the signifier as preceding and determining the signified (see Section IV), he describes the formula $\frac{S}{s}$ (signifier over signified) as representing two distinct and separate orders separated by "a barrier resisting signification." Using this algorithm, he says, will allow an exact study of the "liaisons proper to the signifier" and an examination of the function of these relations in the genesis of the signified. Referring to Augustine's *De magistro* (the chapter entitled "De significatione locutionis"), he reiterates the view that "no signification can be sustained except in its reference to another signification" (p. 51). (Cf. the seminar of November, 1957, p. 295: "Only the relationship of one signifier to another signifier engenders the relationship of signifier to signified.") Consequently, he brushes aside the philosopher's and anthropologist's concern to relate signifier and reality on the basis of denotation by condemning as an illusion the notion "that the signifier corresponds to the function of representing the signified, or better, that the signifier has to answer for its existence in the name of any [particular] signification whatever" (p. 52). But the function of the algorithm is not in his view simply to represent two separate but parallel orders, since without some sort of relationship between them language would simply be a total mystery.

Thus he replaces the Saussurian diagram of the tree by an amusing perversion of it (not necessarily more correct, he says), with the intention of indicating the empirical falsity of the theory of nomination or pointing, since in language the object is constituted at the level of the concept, which is not the same as "any particular nominative." It might be added that the theory of the genesis of learning of language as a reflex originally conditioned by pointing (a signal) cannot account for the obvious fact that for "table" to mean table, the child must already be constituted in a world of language. He must in fact already know all there is to know about language outside its specific vocabulary, grammar, and syntax. Lacan's diagram represents something that might be seen in a railway station (p. 53):

HOMMES DAMES

Thus, he concludes, if the algorithm $\frac{S}{s}$ is an appropriate one, the crossing of the bar itself between signifier and signified cannot in any case entail any signification—"For the algorithm, insofar as it is itself only a pure function of the signifier, can reveal by this transference only a signifying structure [*une structure de signifiant*]," and the structure of the signifier is that of being articulated (p. 55). The signifier is subject to the double condition of being reducible to "ultimate differential elements" and of "combining them according to the laws of a closed order." This second property of the signifier in his view requires the notion of a topological substratum (the phonological level), which he usually calls the "signifying chain" and which he describes as analogous to the rings of a necklace which is itself sealed as a ring into another necklace made of rings (p. 55).

What this analogy seems destined to imply is the circularity of the signification of any particular signifier, itself caught in the circularity of the signification of the system of language itself, which is commonly regarded by linguists and philosophers as an autonomous and closed order, opposed to the open order of "reality." Lacan seems to be balancing on the razor's edge between what are traditionally called "idealism" and "nominalism" (but language itself is not *post res*). Fundamentally, however, Lacan's point is that if any particular signifier refers directly to a particular signified "reality," it can only do so through the mediation of the rest of the signifying system making up language. His assertion of the primacy of the signifier corresponds to the empirical fact of "the dominance of the letter in the dramatic transformation that the dialogue may bring about in the subject" in analysis. The (symbolic) dominance of certain signifiers in the discourse is analogous for Lacan to the buttons pinning down quilted upholstery at certain points. These signifiers are what he calls the *"points de capiton"* (p. 56)—which will be mentioned again in reference to his theory of psychosis.

He goes on to evoke the Saussurian concept of the *glissement* or sliding of one system over the other (t.n. 67), which accounts in Saussure's terms for the transference of meanings during the evolution of a language. (Here Lacan slides more or less imperceptibly from the notion of signifier and signified as "word concept" and "signification" to the Saussurian distinction [p. 156] of "thought" and "sound," with language serving as an intermediary between them. Language, for Saussure, "organizes" the amorphous mass of thought by selecting from an equally amorphous mass of sounds, language being in this respect comparable to the piece of paper already mentioned, thought on one side and sound on the other.) This transposition which describes the signifying function in language is *metonymy* for Lacan, the point being that there is no connection between word and thing in the way metonymy operates. We speak of "thirty sail" meaning thirty ships, but the usual definition of this figure as the "part for the whole" is totally misleading when we reflect that each ship undoubtedly has more than one sail. Thus for Lacan the connection between the part and the whole, between ship and sail, is totally included in the signifier itself: the relationship is one of "word to word" (*mot à mot*), or of signifier to signifier, not of word to any reality. The other versant of the signifying function is *metaphor,* or "one word in place of another one" (*un mot pour un autre*) (pp. 59–60). The image in the dream, in particular, once it is assumed by the subject as a signifier, metaphorical or metonymical, will as often as not have nothing whatsoever to do with its "objective" signification, any more than the words of the politician or the propagandist mean what they say. One of the prime functions of speech, like Orwell's Newspeak, is not to reveal thoughts, but to conceal them, especially from ourselves.

Since he is concerned with the discourse of the unconscious, and with its relationship to the poetic metaphor and the joke, Lacan goes on to employ the algorithm $\left(\dfrac{S}{s}\right)$ in a different sense from that he had begun with, the "S" and "s" now representing the *Cs.* and the *Ucs.* discourse, respectively. As he had said in the seminar of November–December, 1956: "There is nothing in the *signified*—the lived flux, wants, pulsions— which does not present itself marked by the imprint of the *signifier,* with all the slidings of meaning which result from it and which constitute symbolism," which is another way of saying that "the *Es* designates what in the subject is capable of becoming *Je,* not a brute reality" (p. 427). In order to account for the repression, condensation, and displacement of signifiers (for Freud the *Vorstellungen*), as well as for the diacritical theory of meaning, he seeks to replace the original algorithm by formulations which can be represented as $\dfrac{S'}{S}$ (metaphor) and $\dfrac{S.\,\ldots\,S'}{s}$ (metonymy). The actual representations he uses are more complicated. In what follows, "(—)" represents the retention of the bar resisting signification, "(+)" represents the crossing of this bar, and "≡" designates equivalence or congruence. Both formulations are derived from rewriting the original algorithm as: $f(S)\,\dfrac{1}{s}$:

(1) Metonymic structure:

$$f(S\ldots S')S \equiv S(-)s$$

(2) Metaphorical structure:

$$f\!\left(\frac{S'}{S}\right)\!S \equiv S(+)s$$

The difference between the metonymic structure and the metaphoric structure corresponds to the task of displacement and substitution in psychoanalytic theory. Thus, metonymy is a displacement from signifier to signifier, but since the original term, which is latent, remains unexplained, it corresponds to the censorship's seeking to escape the significant term by calling up another one contiguous to it (for example, "the "*Wespe:* S. P." of the Wolf Man). The meaning or significance of the original term (unconscious or otherwise) is still to be discovered; hence the retention of the bar. Moreover metonymy, by the displacement of the "real" object of the subject's desire onto something apparently insignificant, represents the *manque d'être* (lack of being) which is constituent of desire itself. ". . . It is the connection of signifier to signifier which permits the elision through which the signifier installs lack of being in the object relation, by employing the value of reference-back of the signification in order to invest it with the desire which is aimed at the lack which [desire] supports" (p. 68). In this way need becomes (unconscious) desire by "passing through the defiles of the signifier" and becomes manifest as (conscious) but displaced demand.

The metaphorical structure, on the other hand, is more profound. As a substitution, the S′ accounts for "the passage of the signifier into the signified"—that is, it accounts for the repression of a particular signifier, S. The patent or manifest term represents the (distorted) "return of the repressed" (the symptom), equivalent in every way to the mechanism involved in the poetic metaphor, where it is what is not said which gives the metaphor its evocative power. This crossing of the bar is constitutive of the emergence of "signification." The crossing differs from that previously mentioned in the railway station example in that no "reality" is involved.

In their article on the unconscious (1961) Leclaire and Laplanche seek to relate Lacan's formulations to the Freudian "linguistic view" of the relationship between consciousness and the unconscious (t.n. 66 and Section I). They are led to modify Lacan's formulas—the details need not concern us here—and in doing so, they reveal that if Lacan is seeking to develop Freud's notions at this point, the "s" must either be regarded as another signifier—as in the case of normal repression or disavowal—or it must be regarded as an image or as the unconscious intentionalization of an image (*Sachvorstellung:* thing presentation)—as in what Freud describes as the topographical regression "through the unconscious" to perception in the dream. Naturally both Freud's view and Lacan's formulation are necessarily oversimplified; nor do I think Leclaire and Laplanche resolve the difficulties involved. But repression still remains such a mysterious process that these difficulties should not deter us if, as it seems, the new formulation, or a variant of it, can add to our understanding in both the pathological and the normal spheres. It is this particular distinction between the signifier and the signified which Lacan employs when he goes on to speak of the question of locating the subject as subject of the signifier or as subject of the signified (in his remarks on the *cogito* cited towards the end of Section I), and the ultimate distinction he made in 1956 was between two "areas" of thought, or between the conscious and the unconscious discourse, which are related metaphorically.

Fortunately there is an excellent example in one of Freud's earliest psychological works which can be employed as a practical illustration of what is expressed so ambiguously in Lacan's theoretical writings. It is such a significant case of repression that if it were ever completely dealt with in theoretical terms, the problem of formalizing the structure of repression would surely be solved. In parentheses, let it be noted that although Lacan has referred to this incident in Freud's life many times, he has never sought in print to do more than hint at how it might be dealt with.

I am referring to Freud's forgetting of the name "Signorelli" (in 1898) and to the paralogisms which replaced it when he sought to recall the name. The details are too lengthy to go into here, but the repression of "Signorelli" can be formalized in the terms of its meta-phorical relation to the symptom "Botticelli," which replaced it. Thus one writes the relationship as: $\frac{\text{"Botticelli"}}{\text{"Signorelli"}}$. If Freud's own structural analysis of this act of forgetting at the beginning of the *Psychopathology of Everyday Life* is rewritten in Lacanian terms, and the two signifiers treated as condensations in a chain of signifiers, their decondensation reveals that the substitution of the one for the other is an exemplary instance of the irruption of the "discourse of the Other" into Freud's conscious discourse (the return of the repressed, distorted by the censor-ship). The explanation of the significance of "Signorelli" (the name of an Italian painter and thus meaningless in itself, like all proper names, before it was forgotten) can be worked out in purely linguistic terms, almost entirely from Freud's own associations (his discourse) and with-out any necessary recourse to symbols, analogies, or instinctual processes. At the same time, as it happens, all the central theoretical concerns of psychoanalysis, as well as the central theme of death and sexuality, and the master-slave dialectic of father and son are revealed. But before dealing further with this example, let us consider the linguistic ante-cedents of Lacan's theory of metaphor and metonymy in greater detail.

Lacan's use of these terms (t.n. 67) and their correlation with the Freudian condensation (for Lacan, the symptom) and displacement (for Lacan, desire), respectively, is a specialized development of Jakob-son's theory of the relation of similarity and the relation of contiguity.[34] Any linguistic sign, says Jakobson, involves two methods of arrange-ment: combination and contexture, and selection and substitution (or concatenation and concurrence in Saussurian terms). Thus there are always two possible interpretants (Peirce's term) of the sign, one re-ferring to the code and the other to the context of the message. The

---

[34] What follows is taken from R. Jakobson, "Two Aspects of Language and Two Types of Aphasic Disturbances," in: *Fundamentals of Language* (The Hague: Mouton, 1956), pp. 55–82.

interpretant referring to the code is linked to it by similarity (metaphor), and the interpretant referring to the message is linked to it by
contiguity (metonymy). For example, the word "hammer" is linked by
metaphor to the code where hammer stands for a "tool for driving nails"
and linked by metonymy to the rest of the message ("Bring me the
hammer," "This is a hammer," "Hammer," "Hammer?").

Selection (the relation of similarity) and combination (the relation of
contiguity)—the metaphoric and the metonymic ways—are considered
by Jakobson to be the two most fundamental linguistic operations,
whether at the level of phonemes (like the *Fort! Da!*) or at the level of
semantemes or words. In psychopathology he discovers that aphasia can
be divided into variants of two broad types: contiguity disorder (where
contextual, connective, and auxiliary words are the first to disappear)
and similarity disorder (where the same contextual words are those
most likely to survive). In the first, the patient may employ a telegraphic
style, or he may be able to understand and say "Thanksgiving," for instance, but be totally unable to handle "thanks" or "giving." In the
second, he might be unwilling or unable to name objects pointed to,
but will perhaps offer some associated remark about them instead of
the name. In the final chapter of his remarks on aphasia, Jakobson deals
with "the metaphoric and metonymic poles" in the wider context of
normal speech and literature:

In normal verbal behavior both processes are continually operative, but
careful observation will reveal that under the influence of a cultural pattern,
personality and verbal style, preference is given to one of the two processes
over the other . . . .
In manipulating these two kinds of connection (similarity and contiguity)
in both their aspects (positional and semantic)—selecting, combining and
ranking them—an individual exhibits his personal style, his verbal predilec-
tions and preferences (pp. 76–77).

In literature, he continues, poetry is of course predominantly metaphorical, but the "realistic" trend in modern literature (for instance the rise
of the "realistic" novel) is predominantly metonymic. Jakobson goes
on to consider the application of this polarity in Freud: "A competition
between both devices . . . is manifest in any symbolic process, either
intrapersonal or social. Thus in an inquiry into the structure of dreams,
the decisive question is whether the symbols and the temporal sequences
used are based on contiguity (Freud's metonymic "displacement" and

synecdochic "condensation") or on similarity (Freud's "identification and symbolism")" (p. 81). It will be seen that Lacan's use of this polarity between metaphor and metonymy—the two processes cannot, of course, be actually separated from each other—is slightly different from Jakobson's. Freud's usage in this respect is ambiguous (t.n. 53), but Lacan's equation of these terms with condensation and displacement is not incompatible with that of Freud, since the importance of metaphor and metonymy in the discourse is correlative to the importance Freud assigns to condensation and displacement in the formation of jokes, slips of the tongue or pen, dreams, and symptoms in general (t.n. 67): ". . . One . . . of these logical relations is very highly favoured by the mechanism of dream-formation; namely, the relation of similarity, consonance or approximation—the relation of 'just as.' . . . The representation of the relation of similarity is assisted by the tendency of the dream-work towards condensation." [35]

Although Lacan's formulations could be regarded as prefigured in the way Freud employed the concepts of "concatenations of pathogenic trains of thought" and of symbolic replacement (mnemonic symbols or symptoms) in explicating hysterical symptoms in the *Studies on Hysteria* (1893–95),[36] Lacan goes much further toward systematizing Freud when he assimilates the dream mechanism of displacement ("metonymy") to desire and that of condensation ("metaphor") to the symptom or substitute. For Freud, any means of "indirect representation" is a symptom, that is to say, a substitute for something else (cf. the term *Verschiebungsersatz:* "formation of a substitute by displacement"). At this point in the development of his views, Lacan is in fact attempting to deal with specific linguistic concepts employed by Saussure and other linguists, the "vertical" *paradigmatic* mode of language and the "linear" (horizontal) *syntagmatic* mode, which is another way of stating the opposition of synchrony ("the axis of simultaneities") to diachrony ("the axis of successivities"). But Saussure, as I have pointed out, applied the distinction between synchrony and diachrony to the *science* of language (*langue*), rather than to language itself, and certainly not to speech (*parole*). This is the effect of Saussure's view of the chain of signifiers as strictly linear, temporal, and one-dimensional, which is obviously true

---

[35] *The Interpretation of Dreams* (1900), *Standard Edition*, IV, 319–20.
[36] *Standard Edition*, II, 92; 152; 288; and elsewhere.

for the formal study of utterances, since one cannot say two words at once. It is to his concept of value as opposed to signification that one might turn for the germ of Lacan's symbolization of a repressed signifier as $\dfrac{\text{Signifier B}}{\text{Signifier A}}$. A word, says Saussure (p. 160), has two qualities: exchange value (it can be exchanged for an idea or another word) and signification (its reference and opposition to other words). Thus "sheep" and *"mouton"* have the same signification, but not the same value, since the value of *"mouton"* in French can only be exchanged against "sheepmutton" in English.

However these details may be, Lacan's formulation can be related to these previously unsynthesized views in the following way, although he has never specifically done so in print:

←——METONYMY (desire, "displacement," contiguity, the syntagmatic)——→

| *Cs. Pcs.* | "Botticelli" | ↑ | METAPHOR (symptom, "condensation," |
| *Ucs.* | "Signorelli" | ↓ | similarity, the paradigmatic) |

The example does not have to come from psychopathology, of course, but it is on the Signorelli incident that this particular formulation heavily depends. One can decondense either of the terms, by using Freud's own associations, to include Freud's own desire for his mother (Eros) and his desire for the death of his rivals: his father, Fliess, and others, as well as his desire for his own death (Thanatos). The fact that this paralogism was first announced in a letter (t.n. 69) to Fliess (the master), and the fact that it occurred at the time that Freud (the slave) discovered the Oedipus complex, are not without significance in this heavily overdetermined symptom. The key term, the "switch word," is of course *Signor,* meaning *Herr.* The last words toward which the metonymic displacement within these signifiers intend are in fact "death and sexuality," and part of the result of this particular discovery of Freud's, so fraught with meaning for him, was to give him the absolute mastery he desired. What also makes this example interesting, although I would think it an error to push it too far, is that in fact nothing but a new formulation, an exchange of structures, has been substituted for Freud's own attempt to deal with it structurally.

Freud did in fact employ a schematic representation of a joke in the work on *Witz,* an example which Lacan has not failed to use and which is similar enough to the representation of the Signorelli incident to make it worth introducing. One of Heine's characters meets Baron Rothschild, who, he says, "treated me quite famillionairely [*familionär*]." This example is designated by Freud as a "condensation accompanied by the formation of a substitute" (*Verdichtung mit Ersatzbildung*), making a "composite word," and he decondenses the pun as follows:[37]

(1)
$$\begin{array}{c} \text{FAMILI} \quad \text{ÄR} \\ \underline{\textit{MILIONÄR}} \\ \textbf{FAMILIONÄR} \end{array}$$

(2)   'R. treated me quite *familiär*,
              that is, so far as a *Millionär* can.'

(3)   'R. treated me quite *famili* on *är*.'
              (*mili*)   (*är*)

One is immediately reminded of similar associations (as opposed to symbols)—in the poetry of Nerval, for instance.

The structural relationship between what is conscious and unconscious in both these examples can clearly be regarded as a relationship of *interpolation* which establishes the continuity of the conscious discourse. In the case of Heine's joke, the analogous interpolation from the "unconscious level" is discovered by reading the joke backwards; in the case of Signorelli, infinitely more profound, there is a gap in the discourse (the absence of the signifier "Signorelli") which Freud cannot adequately fill and whose existence torments him until somebody re-establishes the continuity of that discourse by telling him the name he cannot for the life of him remember. The principle of intentionality to which I have constantly referred is also involved, since as long as the name remained repressed, Freud had an "ultra-clear" but ineffable image in his mind of Signorelli's own self-portrait in the fresco at Orvieto: *The Four Last Things: Death, Judgment, Hell, Heaven,* which played a central part in the repression. Thus he was quite correct in naming this image "Botticelli," since the name was only a distorted substitute for "Signorelli." And when the original name was restored to him, the image of the painter's sober face "faded away," along with Freud's anxiety. Thus the image of "Signorelli" was itself a screen memory, a

[37] *Standard Edition*, VIII, 16–20.

visual displacement of the abhorred themes of the fresco onto something apparently unimportant, an Italian painter whose name Freud knew as well as his own.

IV

The Symbolic Order: Lévi-Strauss and Marcel Mauss

Lacan's notion of the Symbolic order is primarily derived from anthropology, notably from Lévi-Strauss, as I have already indicated. Since this concept is so ambiguous in Lacan, it is to Lévi-Strauss that one naturally turns for clarification about the notion as a whole. It involves several features: a view of the unconscious different from the usual Freudian acceptation, the concept of structure as used in structural anthropology, the relationship between linguistic and social structures as systems of communication (t.n. 98), and the unconsciously determined phonological laws of distinctive features or phonemic opposition (Troubetskoy, Jakobson) (t.n. 119, 183, 184). Consideration of these points will also serve to clarify Lacan's direct allusions to Lévi-Strauss in the *Discours*.

It seems best to refer first of all to the early Lévi-Strauss's general concept of the unconscious as something imposing form on a content which is outside it. This view was expressed in an article seeking to explain the relationship between psychoanalysis and shamanism (no malice intended), which Lacan had read in 1949.[38] The "symbolic efficacity" of the title of the article refers to the shaman's proven ability, by reference to collective myths, actually to effect cures by taking the patient's sickness onto himself in a symbolic fashion and driving the evil out, or by his "psychological manipulation" of a sick organ. Lévi-Strauss employs his knowledge of Freud to clarify certain aspects of shamanism— and hopes that shamanism may one day help to clarify Freud. The principal difference between shamanism and psychoanalysis, he declares, even if neurosis should eventually turn out to be derived from a "physiological substratum," lies in "the origin of the myth which is found again in the one instance as an individual treasure, and received, in the other, from the collective tradition" (p. 223). He disputes the importance accorded in French psychoanalysis (Marie Bonaparte) to the reality of the

---

[38] What follows is taken from the last pages of "L'Efficacité symbolique" (1949) in: *Anthropologie Structurale* (Paris: Plon, 1958), pp. 205–26.

traumatic memory: "What should really be considered is whether the therapeutic value of the cure depends upon the reality of rememorated situations, or whether the traumatizing power of these situations is not the result of the fact that at the moment when they present themselves, the subject experiences them immediately in the form of a lived myth" (p. 223). "Traumatizing power" means not something intrinsic to these situations, but rather the propensity of certain events "coming forth in an appropriate psychological, historical, and social situation, to induce an affective crystallization which comes about within the mold of a pre-existing structure." "In relationship to the [actual] event or to the anecdote, these structures—or more exactly, these laws of structure—are really non-temporal" (p. 224).[39]

The same structures are to be found in pathological cases, in normal people, and in primitive cultures. Under the "catalyzing action of the initial myth," the psychic life and the experiences of the subject become organized "as a function of an exclusive or predominant structure."

The whole set of these structures, in my view, would form what we call the unconscious . . . . The unconscious ceases to be the ineffable refuge of individual particularities, the depository of a unique history, which makes of each one of us an irreplaceable being. The unconscious can be reduced to a term by which we designate a function: the symbolic function, a specifically human function, no doubt, but which is exercised in all men according to the same laws; which is in fact reduced to the ensemble of these laws (p. 224).

On this view, he remarks, we must make a distinction between the unconscious and the subconscious (*subconscient*), a distinction which is not to be found in the psychology of the 1940's:

The subconscious, a reservoir of memories and images collected in the course of each life,[40] becomes a simple aspect of memory. At the same time as it affirms its lasting nature, it implies its own limitations, since "subconscious" refers to the fact that memories, although retained, are not always available. On the other hand, the unconscious is always empty; or, more precisely, it is as much a stranger to images as is the stomach to the food which

[39] These remarks would now require interpretation in the sense of the existentialist project and the Freudian concept of deferred action, mentioned briefly in Section V. For Freud the value of the reality of the traumatic memory is that of a myth; it makes no difference whether it is real or phantasy.

[40] Lévi-Strauss notes: "This definition which has been so heavily criticized takes on meaning again by the radical distinction between subconscious and unconscious."

passes through it. As an organ of a specific function, the unconscious limits itself to the imposition of structural laws . . . on unarticulated elements which come from elsewhere: pulsions, emotions, representations, memories. One could therefore say that the subconscious is the individual lexicon where each of us accumulates the vocabulary of his personal history, but that this vocabulary only acquires signification, for ourselves and for others, in so far as the unconscious organizes it according to the laws of the unconscious, and thus makes of it a discourse. . . . The vocabulary is less important than the structure (pp. 224–25).

Whether the myth is recreated by the subject or borrowed from a tradition, he continues, it draws only the *material* of the images it employs from individual or collective sources (between which there are constant interpenetrations and exchanges), "but the structure remains the same, and it is through it that the symbolic function operates." Moreover the laws of the symbolic function, however diverse the material with which they deal, are "few in number," in the same way that the whole galaxy of words in all languages can be reduced to a very few phonological laws (p. 225). One notes that the distinction he makes between subconscious and unconscious is similar to Freud's distinction between the preconscious (ordinary memory, the area of language) and the unconscious, and that his notion of the unconscious could be compared to those passages in which Freud includes in the unconscious not only "after repression" but also the "primal repression," which was never conscious in the usual sense.

In the final part of *Les Structures élémentaires de la parenté*,[41] Lévi-Strauss examines the general problem of synchrony and diachrony in primitive societies. He has developed at length the thesis of the incest prohibition as inexplicably at the frontier between (biological) nature and (human) culture. His reaffirmation of Tylor's notion of the incest prohibition as a positive law is stated as the obligation undertaken by one family to give one member to another family. It follows from this view that it should be possible to formulate the marriage rules of primitive societies as systems of exchange in what is in fact an unconsciously determined system of communication. This is precisely what Lévi-Strauss sets out to prove.

This radical interpretation of Mauss's intuitions about the gift is further radicalized by the apparently scientific correlation between the

[41] Paris: PUF, 1949, pp. 592–617.

structures of kinship, and therefore the structures of society, and the distinctive features of the phonemic structures underlying language. With Mauss, Lévi-Strauss points out that it is not what is given, but the act of exchange which holds any society together, including our own. In a similar sense, we all know only too well how in normal conversation, it is the exchange of words and not their content which is important, since most of what we say consists of redundancies rather than of information. And this act of linguistic intercourse can no more be separated from the world of discourse into which we are born than an individual marriage—the exchange of a woman for one previously given or one to be given—can be separated from the "universe of rules" englobing the single act of giving. The marriage, setting up its participants as a new locus of other relationships, is "the archetype of exchange" (p. 599), and, for Lévi-Strauss, the attendant rules of kinship are not simply something necessary for society, but, like language, they *are* society.

This view leads him to reject the "theory of origins" (myth or fact) so damaging to Freud's *Totem and Taboo* (1912–13), since, as Rousseau had also supposed, it supposes a mythical society preceding the necessary conditions of society. Yet in doing so he arrives at a modern comprehension of what Freud was trying to do, in terms (only faintly visible here) of the later "symbolic order." This ahistorical view promised to account for the Lamarckian difficulties one encounters in Freud as well as for those of the genetic approach, and those of relating the individual to society: "Ontogenesis does not repeat phylogenesis, or vice-versa. The two hypotheses result in the same contradictions. One can only speak of explication from the moment that the past of the species is played out again, at every instant, in the indefinitely multiplied drama of each individual's thoughts, doubtless because it is itself only the retrospective projection of a passage which has come about because it continually comes about" (p. 609). Thus Freud's "myth of origins" paradoxically explains the present, not the past, and accounts not for the prohibition of incest, but rather for the fact that incest is unconsciously desired. Freud's myth perhaps "translates, in a symbolic form, a dream which is both enduring and ancient." But the power of this dream has nothing to do with any historical event. Thus the symbolic satisfactions through which, according to Freud, we commemorate our regret for the lost opportunities of incest, are, in the eyes of Lévi-Strauss, "the permanent expression of a desire for disorder, or rather, for counter-order" (pp. 609–10).

These considerations lead Lévi-Strauss to emphasize in a Kantian sense Freud's remarks elsewhere upon permanent structures in the human mind,[42] which are in apparent contradiction with the historical or evolutionist view of *Totem and Taboo*. These "hesitations" on the part of Freud, he says, reveal that psychoanalysis, which is a "social science," is "still floating between the tradition of a historical sociology, which seeks, as Rivers did, the *raison d'être* of a present situation in a far-off past, and a more modern and more solidly scientific attitude, which expects knowledge of the future and the past from the present" (p. 611).

But there is one science, Lévi-Strauss goes on to say, in which diachronic and synchronic explanation come together, "because the first permits the reconstitution of the genesis of systems as well as bringing them to a synthesis, while the second brings out their internal logic and grasps the evolution which directs them towards a goal" (p. 611). This science is phonology, as developed out of the work of Troubetskoy and Jakobson in the 1930's. He pushes the analogy, if it is an analogy, as others had done, to the point of declaring that linguists and sociologists not only employ the same methods, but in fact study the same object. He quotes a remark of W. I. Thomas,[43] to the effect that exogamy and language have the same fundamental function: "communication with others and the integration of the group." Whether the assimilation of the "same object" to the "same function" actually holds good is not discussed further at this point by Lévi-Strauss.

Naturally rejecting the simplistic notion of language as an inert intermediary between men, he goes on to quote Cassirer (p. 613): "Language does not enter into a world of objective and complete perceptions, thence simply to add 'names' to individual objects, clearly distinct in relation to each other, 'names' which are purely exterior and arbitrary signs. On the contrary, language is itself a mediator in the formation of objects; it is in one sense the denominator par excellence." [44] With the remark that "the conception of speech [*parole*] as

---

[42] For example, the universality of anxiety analyzed in "Inhibitions, Symptoms and Anxiety" (1926), *Standard Edition*, XX.

[43] *Primitive Behavior* (New York: McGraw-Hill, 1937), p. 182f.

[44] E. Cassirer, in the French translation: *Le Langage et la construction des objets* in: *Psychologie du language* (Paris: Alcan, 1933), p. 23. See also Cassirer, *An*

verbe, as power and action, certainly represents a universal tendency of human thought" (cf. t.n. 80), Lévi-Strauss develops almost all the full implications of his thesis: that "the relations between sexes can be conceived as one modality of a vast 'function of communication,' including language" (p. 613), and draws on further anthropological evidence. Certain societies have strict rules against a number of actions which can apparently be subsumed under "abuses of language": "What does this mean except that women themselves are treated [in these societies] like *signs,* which are *abused* when they are not employed in the way reserved for signs, which is to be communicated?" (p. 615).

The passage from phonology to the discourse and back to anthropology is a slippery one, but Lévi-Strauss sets out forthrightly to complete it: "When we pass from the discourse to the marriage-tie, that is to say, to the other domain of communication, the situation becomes reversed. The emergence of symbolic thought must have required women to be things [reciprocally] exchanged like spoken words" (p. 616). This reciprocity, for Lévi-Strauss, is what explains how the incompatibility in the dual role of the woman of one's own family (whom one desires and who yet must be delivered up to the desire of another man) is resolved, since giving her up to another forges the reciprocal bond which is its purpose.

But women could never become a sign, and only a sign, since, in a world of men, she is nevertheless a person, and since, in so far as she is defined as a sign, one is obliged to recognize her as a producer of signs. In the matrimonial dialogue of men, a woman is never purely that of which one speaks, since . . . each woman maintains a particular value, which depends upon her maintaining her part in a dual relationship,[45] both before and after her marriage. In opposition to the word, which has totally become a sign, woman has remained both a sign and a value at the same time. Thus is explained, no doubt, how the relations between the sexes have been able to preserve that affective richness, that fervor and that mystery, which probably filled the whole universe of human communications originally (p. 616) (t.n. 80).

Essay on Man (New Haven: Yale University Press, 1944), p. 31f; and M. Leenhardt, "Ethnologie de la parole," *Cahiers Internationaux de Sociologie,* Vol. 1 (Paris, 1946); R. Firth, *Primitive Polynesian Economics* (London: Routledge & Sons, 1939), p. 317.

45 This duality is to be viewed in the light of his previous remark, referring to the theory of games, that "mathematical studies confirm that in any combination involving several partners, the dual game must be treated as a particular case of a triangular game" [*jeu à trois*] (p. 574).

Part of the thesis of the "Introduction à l'oeuvre de Marcel Mauss" [46] is to establish the subordination of individual psychology to sociology in their respective roles as explanations of human relationships in society. It seems clear that the movement towards a social psychology from the thirties onward, both by the "neo-Freudians" and by independents like Harry Stack Sullivan (a friend of Sapir's)—who introduced the terms "interpersonal relations" and "significant others" into psychiatry, as well as the concept of the psychiatrist as the "participant observer"—reflected a defeat of the sociological aspirations of traditional psychoanalysis.

Lévi-Strauss notes that in 1924 Marcel Mauss had defined social life in an address to French psychologists as "a world of symbolic relationships," and goes on to declare that a "psychological formulation [of these relationships] is only a translation, at the level of the individual psyche, of a structure which is properly sociological" (pp. xv–xvi). "It is in the nature of society that it is expressed symbolically in its customs and its institutions; on the other hand, normal individual behavior *is never symbolic by itself:* individual actions are elements out of which a symbolic system, which can only be collective, is constructed. It is only abnormal behavior which, because it is de-socialized and more or less abandoned to itself, realizes at the individual level, the illusion of an autonomous symbolism" (pp. xvi–xvii).

After further discussion of these remarks, which set his views clearly apart from individual psychology, he provides the central notion from which the idea of the symbolic function is derived: "Every culture can be considered as an ensemble or set of symbolic systems, amongst which the most important are: language, marriage-rules, economic relationships, art, science, and religion" (p. xix). All these systems seek to express certain aspects of social and physical reality, he says, as well as the relationship between these two realities. But these symbolic systems are "fundamentally incommensurable" and "irreducible" the one to the other. The result is that "no society is ever integrally and completely symbolic; or, more precisely, that no society ever manages to offer all its members, and in the same degree, the means to fully employ themselves in the edification of a symbolic structure which, for the normal person, is only realizable on the level of social life. Properly speaking,

[46] In: Marcel Mauss, *Sociologie et Anthropologie* (Paris: PUF, 1966 [1950]), pp. ix–lii.

it is the one we say has a healthy mind who alienates himself, since he consents to existing in a world which is definable only by the relation of self [*moi*] and other" (p. xx).[47]

Passing from these considerations, which he feels are conclusions we must draw from Mauss's work, to the notion of the "total social fact" in the *Essai sur le don* (1923), Lévi-Strauss deals first with one of the problems most personal to his own experience: the relationship of the observer to the observed in ethnology, and within our own social groupings. The ethnologist is involved in an attempt to identify with what is an alien object to him: "This difficulty would be insoluble, since subjectivities are, by hypothesis, incomparable and incommunicable, if the opposition between self [*moi*] and other could not be overcome at a certain level, which is also that where the objective and the subjective meet, I mean the unconscious" (p. xxx). He seeks to deal with this unconscious, in the terms which Mauss had already employed, as connected with the notion of mana, at the level of a sort of "fourth dimension" of the mind, where "the concept of 'unconscious category' and that of 'category of collective thought' would come together as one." "Thus the unconscious would be the mediator between self [*moi*] and other." Analyzing the unconscious would "put us in coincidence with forms of activity which are at one and the same time *ours* and *other*." This knowledge would of course be objective, in the sense that knowledge, for Lévi-Strauss, is always of an object, but it would lead to subjectification, since this is an operation of the same type as that which makes it possible in psychoanalysis "to reconquer for ourself our most alienated *moi*." Consequently the difficulty of the ethnologist in identifying with the alien other will perhaps be solved at the unconscious level of human conduct, just as it is apparently solved in psychoanalysis where the problem is the same: "that of a communication sought, at one time between a subjective *moi* and an objectifying *moi,* at another, between an objective *moi* and a subjectivity which is *other*" (p. xxi). In this way Lévi-Strauss seeks to develop a theory of intersubjectivity which will provide him with an objective scientific base for his relationship to the object he studies: other men. His concern will be all the more understandable if we recall the date at which he wrote. In the France of the

[47] Author's note: "This is at any rate the conclusion which it seems to me we must draw from the profound study by Dr. Jacques Lacan: 'L'Agressivité en psychanalyse,' *Revue Française de Psychanalyse,* No. 3 (July–September, 1948)."

late forties and early fifties, the existentialist and phenomenological theories of the intentionality of consciousness, along with their rejection of the unconscious, had seemed to show that our apprehension of the other was always as an object.

As for these unconscious structures which we share, the whole point, as Lévi-Strauss saw it, was to distinguish between purely phenomenological data ("the things themselves" of which we are individually conscious), which cannot be treated by science, and an infrastructure which is more simple than that data and to which that data owes all its reality, especially as this distinction had been employed in phonology by Troubetzkoy and Jakobson. Structural linguistics was founded on the notion of relationship and combination, the theory of binary phonemic oppositions having been solidly established by 1938. Mauss had already conceived of "function" in society as an algebraic idea, one social phenomenon being viewed as a function of others, their interrelationship being constant. Thus the later establishment of an identical series of ideas in the study of language could not but reinforce the probable success of applying the science of one domain[48] to another domain determined to become a science: "Like language, the social *is* an autonomous reality (the same, in fact); symbols are more real than what they symbolize, the signifier precedes and determines the signified" (p. xxxii)—but, for Lévi-Strauss, what is most crucial is to pass beyond the suggestion (which can be found in Mauss) that the relationship between signifier and signified, as Saussure is assumed to have put it, is an *arbitrary* one (p. xlv, note).

There are two problems here, however, and it is not entirely clear from the context whether Lévi-Strauss is making a clear distinction between them. What one might call a relationship between "appearance" (things) and "reality" (relationships) is being looked at in two different but complementary ways. Does "infrastructure" mean something "beneath" the phenomena (signifier over signified) or does it simply imply something existing in an unconscious mode *within* a "superstructure" (that is, the structure of the relationships of signifiers as functions

---

[48] The value of the use of notions from linguistics outside their own sphere is rather well brought out by Nicolas Ruwet (who is not a structural linguist) in an article on Lévi-Strauss: "Linguistique et sciences de l'homme," *Esprit* (November, 1963), pp. 564–78, where the whole question is reviewed and a number of misinterpretations, both of linguistic theory and of Lévi-Strauss, are cleared up.

of other signifiers, rather than the phenomena *qua* individual elements)? Since a structure is by definition unconscious and since Lévi-Strauss clearly defines the "reality" of "more real" in terms of scientifically discoverable "objective" relationships, it seems that he views the problem primarily from the second or "horizontal" or "immanent" viewpoint. Thus the reference to Saussure may be misleading—because one immediately thinks of the Saussurian diagram representing the sign as a "vertical" relationship and tends to forget Saussure's rather more subtle metaphor of the signifier and the signified as being related like the two sides of a piece of paper. Lévi-Strauss evidently wants to avoid falling into the unscientific mode of viewing social reality as equivalent to the ideology of the human beings involved in it and at the same time to define the structure of social relationships as immanent to the "language" of social reality, just as phonemes are immanent to a word, without, however, being the same as the word. One could simplify the whole problem—into which we have been led here by a particular concern for a particular category, the signifier—by asking simply whether the structure is arbitrary in relationship to what it structures (thus avoiding the awkward spatial metaphor). It seems, however, that the question could be even better stated in the terms of Carnap's theory of object language and metalanguage, calling a structure a particular kind of metastatement. From a purely epistemological point of view, one might add parenthetically that however Lévi-Strauss's use of the categories of signifier and signified is related to Saussure's or Lacan's employment of the same terms—there is clearly a confusing alternation of convergence and divergence in this respect—the statement that "the signifier precedes and determines the signified" is an assertion of the primacy of language over reality which is shared by Lacan.

The assimilation of the methods of phonology to anthropology is certainly not a self-evident step, and Lévi-Strauss's formulations have naturally raised a certain amount of criticism on purely theoretical grounds. It is not my intention to enter into this controversy in any detail, but it does seem clear that we must distinguish between models and analogies. Phonological oppositions are not employed by Lévi-Strauss as analogies to buttress an argument at another level; rather he is employing the notion of the relationship between the infrastructure of binary phonemic oppositions and the superstructure of morphemes as a model of the relation of "reality" (the underlying or immanent structure) to "appearance" (phenomenological data). This methodological model is not employed because of some a priori theoretical or axiomatic necessity, but rather because it seems to *work,* and Lévi-Strauss has always left a hypothetical door open for a more adequate model should new information or new understanding require it. He is in fact entirely faithful to his own concept of *bricolage*—working with what is at hand, building an interpretation out of the available conceptual "odds and ends" which are used as instruments in a process of invention, without concern for their origin or homogeneity. Thus it seems that any one model he employs is indeed a model, whereas the totality of these models can be called a series of analogies. The problem, however, is to decide to what the analogies refer. As Jacques Derrida has pointed out in "La Structure, le signe et le jeu dans le discours des sciences humaines" (*L'Ecriture et la différence* [Paris: Editions du Seuil, 1967], pp. 409–28), Lévi-Strauss seeks in effect to break with a philosophical and epistemological tradition which has always in the past related the notion of structure to some privileged point of reference, some *epistemē:*

It would be easy enough to show that the concept of structure and even the word "structure" itself are as old as the *epistemē*—that is to say, as old as western science and western philosophy. . . . Nevertheless, up until the "event" which I wish to define [that is, the change in the use of the concept of structure], the structure—or rather the structurality of the structure— . . . has always been neutralized or reduced, and this by a process of giving it a center or referring it to a point of presence, a fixed origin. The function of this center was not only to orient, balance, and organize the structure—one cannot in fact conceive of an unorganized structure—but above all to make sure that the organizing principle of the structure would limit what we might call the *freeplay* [*le jeu*] of the structure. . . .
 . . . The center also closes off the freeplay it opens up and makes possible. *Qua* center, it is the point at which the substitution of contents, elements, or terms is no longer possible (pp. 409–10).

Lévi-Strauss's use of *bricolage,* however, especially in relation to the structure of a series of myths such as those analyzed in *Le Cru et le Cuit* (1964) results in a sort of decentered and self-criticizing discourse on myths which is itself a myth:

It is here that we rediscover the mythopoetical power of *bricolage*. In fact, what appears most fascinating in this critical search for a new status of the discourse is the stated abandonment of all reference to a *center,* to a *subject,* to a privileged *reference,* to an origin or to an absolute *archia* (p. 419).

. . . In opposition to the *epistemic* discourse, the structural discourse on myths, the *mytho-logical* discourse must itself be *mytho-morphic* (p. 420).

In a sense, Lévi-Strauss is simply denying the possibility for a being which is within a system to step outside it, and all the problems of the "impartial observer," such as that implicit in the Marxist view of ideology or that explicit in the nineteenth-century view of physics are involved. In another terminology, one could say that the lack of a center is equivalent to a lack of an ultimate, completely transcendental metalanguage which could comment on the relationships within language and between human beings. It will be clear to the reader that Lacan is very much a *bricoleur* in the sense that Lévi-Strauss uses the term, a judgment reinforced by Lacan's reply to a question in a recent conference. He had been employing the model of the Moebius strip to speak of the subject's relationship to himself, as well as using the theory of integers to discuss the theoretical ramifications of how the child discovers the Other (how he progresses from "one" to "two"). Taxed by a historian of science on the subject of his "analogies," Lacan simply replied: "Analogy to what?"

Lévi-Strauss's methodology, like Lacan's, involves a number of special assumptions (which Derrida compares to Rousseau's "brushing aside the facts" in his analysis of society, or to Husserl's "parentheses"). It is already clear that Lacan presupposes an undeterminable "break" between humanity and the animal world (without, of course, denying the possibility of continuity or the actuality of the animal functions of man). For Lacan, the split between nature and culture is defined by the difference between animal need and animal communication, on the one hand, and human desire and human language on the other. This methodological break is employed by him as an *instrument* of analysis, just as a similar break is employed by Lévi-Strauss, without any necessary acceptance of its transcendental *truth-value*. If we return to the essay on Marcel Mauss, we can see how this sort of presupposition is part of Lévi-Strauss's own developing theory, notably in his answer to the problem of the development of language:

. . . Language could only have been born in one fell swoop. Things were not able to set about signifying progressively . . . . At the moment when the entire Universe suddenly became *significative,* it was not for all that better *known,* even if it is true that the appearance of language must have precipitated the rhythm of the development of knowledge. There is therefore a fundamental opposition in the history of the human mind between symbolism, whose nature is to be discontinuous, and knowledge, marked by continuity . . . .

The result of this difference is

that the two categories of signifier and signified were constituted simultaneously and jointly, like two complementary units; but that knowledge, that is to say, the intellectual process which permits us to identify in relationship to each other certain aspects of the signifier and certain aspects of the signified —one might even say: that which permits us to choose from the set of the signifier and the set of the signified those parts which present the most satisfactory relationships of mutual agreement between them—only began very slowly . . . .

Thus Lévi-Strauss can say: "The Universe signified long before we began to know what it was signifying . . . ." Moreover, "the Universe signified, from the very beginning, the totality of what humanity could expect to know about it" (pp. xlvii–xlviii). The work of equation of the signifier in relation to the signified, he continues, given on the one hand by symbolism and pursued on the other by knowledge, is not fundamentally different in any kind of society, except insofar as the birth of modern science has introduced a difference of degree. Outside the specialized area of science, in his view, the human condition rests on a fundamental antinomy resulting from the fact that "from his earliest origins man has at his disposition an integrality of signifier whose allocation to a signified—which is given as such, but not in fact known —is a source of great perplexity to him."

Thus in his attempts to comprehend the universe, man has at his disposition "a surplus of signification." This he divides among things "according to the laws of symbolic thought," in order that "on the whole, the available signifier and the signified it aims at may remain in the relationship of complementarity which is the very condition of the use of symbolic thought" (p. xlix). From these considerations, Lévi-Strauss posits the notion of mana as the zero-symbol in the system of symbols which go to make up any cosmology, as "a sign marking the necessity of a symbolic content supplementary to that with which the signified is already loaded, but which can take on any value required, provided only that this value still remains part of the available reserve [of "floating signifier"]" (p. xlviii) (t.n. 98).

The Symbolic Order: Lacan and Freud

The transition from these notions of a symbolic function, reflected in the individual by the symbolic relationships of the group, to Lacan's notion of the Symbolic order seems fairly clear. Lacan's use of the term tends to rely heavily upon the ambiguity of the use of the term "symbolic" in psychoanalysis and in anthropology. But insofar as Lacan seeks to relate the Symbolic order primarily to Language and the family rather than to intragroup communication and society in general, or to a semiology, he employs it to buttress his concept of the unconscious as the "discourse of the Other." Nevertheless, the twin aphorism of the unconscious as "structured like a language" betrays an ambiguity he has not seen fit to resolve. The ambiguity derives in part from Freud, for whom the concept of the unconscious shifts between something seemingly biological—an infrastructure, at any rate (the so-called instincts)—and the more obviously psychic representation of this level (*Triebrepräsentanz*), between memory in the very wide sense (including "inherited" memories) and simply the repressed, which may also include the "deepest" level (the primal repression). It is sometimes equated with all that is not in consciousness (*Pcs. Ucs.*), sometimes only with that not immediately available to (*Pcs.*) memory. Lacan's view of the unconscious is essentially a combination of the dynamic view (metaphor) and the economic view (metonymy). He supposes an unconscious discourse interfering with the conscious discourse, and responsible for the distortions and gaps in that discourse. In one sense, there is an unconscious subject (barred from consciousness) seeking to address itself to another unconscious subject (the Other). In another sense, this unconscious discourse is that of the Other in the subject who has been alienated from himself through his relationship to the mirror image of the other. But whether one can actually say that the unconscious is a discourse, or that it is structured like a language, depends upon the level at which one views the unconscious. What is involved is the fundamental contradiction implied by the notion of censorship, or whatever it is in the subject which makes his symptoms twisted signifiers or twisted signs. The dream, for instance, is not the unconscious, but rather the distortion (*Entstellung*) of the unconscious dream thoughts as they regress to the level of perception. The subject's verbalization of the dream is his intentionalization of these images, and, outside the level of "natural" symbolism, it is always the dream text—which only accounts for that part of the dream which is actually remembered—which is interpreted, not the dream itself. Within analysis, this seems invariably to be that part of the dream which is addressed to the significant other whom the analyst, through transference, represents. Thus Freud can interpret a patient's one-word dream: "Kanal" and find that it is derisively directed at himself through his work on jokes, by means of a play on words. The "channel" refers to the "Pas de Calais," as he discovers from the dreamer; the ridicule depends upon the pun: "Du sublime au ridicule il n'y a qu'un pas." [49] The only part of the dream which was originally remembered was the "nodal point" aimed at the analyst.

But it is surely not the unconscious which imposes laws like those of condensation, displacement, and symbolism upon the conscious discourse or the subject's symptomatic acts. It is rather whatever it is that seeks to deny the recognition of unconscious wishes while still obeying the compelling need of the subject to communicate them "to him that hath ears to hear," as Lacan puts it—or in other words, to the significant other to whom those wishes were originally directed in a nondistorted form. Whatever its content may be, no wish is really intransitive, nor can it remain intrasubjective. One can certainly say that the unconscious speaks *through* the conscious discourse, but whether one can then employ this factual description as a metaphor about the unconscious itself is not easy to decide. Aphorisms have the merit of revealing truth in a striking way, but they must by their very nature be both ambiguous about their truth and a simplification of it. This leads one to remark that Lacan's tendency to depend on the aphorism may well lead the reader to regard Lacan, even more imperiously than he may already regard Freud, as literary or cultural phenomenon, outside whatever importance his theories may have in their own right. Thus Lacan's style is perhaps symptomatic not just of the man, but also of his time—and *préciosité* is a recurrent phenomenon in French literature, especially during periods of intellectual reorganization.

With this in mind, we can perhaps better understand why Lacan has chosen to express ambiguous ideas and unresolved difficulties in an ambiguous and perhaps ultimately impenetrable style. It is not possible, for instance, to define the Other in any definite way, since for Lacan it

[49] *Standard Edition*, V, p. 517, note 2. Lacan refers to this example in his introduction to the commentary on the Freudian *Verneinung* (1956).

has a functional value, representing both the "significant other" to whom the neurotic's demands are addressed (the appeal to the Other), as well as the internalization of this Other (we desire what the Other desires) and the unconscious subject itself or himself (the unconscious is the discourse of—or from—the Other). In another context, it will simply mean the category of "Otherness," a translation Lacan has himself employed. Sometimes "the Other" refers to the parents: to the mother as the "real Other" (in the dual relationship of mother and child), to the father as the "Symbolic Other," yet it is never a *person*. Very often the term seems to refer simply to the unconscious itself, although the unconscious is most often described as "the locus of the Other." In this sense the concept of "Otherness" is valid and important, because the identity and difference of "the other" in the Imaginary relationship is a false kind of "otherness" in the human world: a relationship to objects, not to subjects. In this sense the unconscious is the Other for the subject, since it is the unconscious subject who tells the truth, and the test of truth in human relations is not the reality or perception it represents, but intersubjectivity. The unconscious, in its necessary dialectical relationship to the unconscious of others, is the test of the truth of the message. As the locus of the code, the unconscious is not "within" the subject; it is the third position through which the sender is provided with a receiver. As I interpret it, in the sense that all messages, articulated or not, involve us in a dialogue mediated by the locus of the code (the unconscious), the desire to communicate rather than the content of the communication is surely what enables Lacan to reformulate the notion of "the unconscious is the discourse of the Other" by defining the idea as "Your concern is with the Other in the discourse," for it is by the Other that you are unconsciously controlled (t.n. 59, 79). This is true in the purely formal sense that our choice of messages is limited by the code; it is also true in the existential sense that the conscious subject has only a limited control over the content of his messages, and less over their reception. In any event, not even an apparent monologue can take place without the mediation of "Otherness."

What is surely essential to keep in mind about Lacan's use of the terms "unconscious" and "Other" is their relationship to the concept of *transsubjectivity* that he emphasizes in the *Discours,* which entails a correlative: the position of both unconscious and Other as third terms in any dual situation. Like Lévi-Strauss, Lacan seeks to rebut the notion of the unconscious as an individual, intrapsychic entity, and to restore it as a function to the collectivity which in fact creates and sustains it. Beyond the Kantian universality and apparently innate nature of the (mythical) "fixations" established at the level of the primal repression, and whatever the individual factors involved, it is clear that at least the after repression of the unconscious is constituted in and by the subject's relationship to what is other. Its advent as such seems therefore to be indistinguishable from the advent of phonemic organization (and desire) in the child. R. D. Laing has recently spoken of repression as inconceivable outside an interpersonal relationship, which is surely what Lacan is saying in the *Discours* when he defines the unconscious in the early part of Chapter I as "that part of the concrete discourse insofar as it is *transindividual,* which is not at the disposition of the subject to re-establish the continuity of his concrete discourse." Discourse requires both a sender and a receiver, as well as a message mediated by a code in a reciprocal interpretation or "reading": it *is* transsubjective. The concrete discourse suffers from *lacunae,* distortions, negations, and disavowals generated by its *relationship* to the unconscious, however difficult it is in fact to formalize the evidence we have of that relationship. In a more specific sense, it can hardly be doubted that Lacan was thinking of the Signorelli incident when he coined this definition. It will be recalled by the reader familiar with the incident that the *lacuna* in Freud's discourse at this point came about in a *conversation* concerning death and sexuality. Freud tells us that he was concerned with consciously wishing to *suppress* certain information on the subject of sex because of the social niceties required in a conversation with a stranger. The suppression then became converted into a profound repression of something with no manifest relationship to death or sexuality at all. In other words, Freud's first extended analysis of repression was explicitly an example of transsubjective repression. Because of Freud's concern for that aspect of the discourse of the Other represented by conscious social constraints, his avoidance of a specific topic turned into something far more significant, as a result of its association with the profoundest of unconscious prohibitions derived from the Other. From the moment that the repression operated—however difficult it is to conceive of this extraordinary mechanism—"Signorelli" *became* the discourse of the Other; in its simplest form, it was a message saying on the one hand: "You want to kill your father and sleep with your mother" (report aspect); and on the other: "Do not kill your father and sleep with your mother" (command aspect), neither of which can possibly be understood in the terms of atomistic individualism or the biological need of an individual. To employ a Lacanian expression, one could say that it was from the Other behind the other (Freud's companion) that the repression came, for the driving force of a repression is as unconscious as what is repressed.

Lacan is more precise about the Other when he calls it the "locus of the signifier" or "of the Word," since he is obviously talking about the collective unconscious without which interhuman communication through language could not take place. Thus in "La Chose freudienne" (1955) he defines the Other as "the locus where there is constituted the *je* which speaks as well as he who hears it [speak]" (p. 248). Lacan's point is surely that even outside the formal necessity of a collective unconscious as constituted through the objectively determined code of language itself, the unconscious, as the repository of personal and social myths, as the locus of socially approved hostilities, illusions, and identifications, could not be otherwise than collective. And even if for Freud these collective characteristics, outside the unconscious aspects of the introjected superego, seem ultimately to depend upon a theory of inherited racial memories like that of the "myth of origins" in *Totem and Taboo* (and we do inherit myths, for it is the structure of society and the individual which generates them, and not vice versa), Freud's answer to Jung's particular heresy is itself unanswerable: "the unconscious is collective anyway." Consequently the unconscious Symbolic relationship between "Es" and "Es" would seem to be governed by the Other as the locus of the symbolic function itself, which is by definition collective, whereas the Imaginary (but not necessarily entirely conscious) relationship of self and other remains a dual one insofar as it is not mediated by the Other (cf. Lacan's remarks on telepathy at the end of Chapter I of the *Discours*). One is led to suspect that the substitution of the words "the unconscious" for "the Other" in many of Lacan's formulations will produce an adequate translation, provided it is remembered that the unconscious in question may be the unconscious of the other or the "collective" unconscious (see the passages of the text referred to in t.n. 50, 51). In this second sense, however, when the unconscious is viewed by Lacan as the "locus of the signifier," he may in fact be referring to the "topological substratum" of the "signifying chain"—or in other words, to the combinations and substitutions of the distinctive features at the phonological level, which is another level of the collective unconscious. (Cf. his remarks on stochastics, kinship, and numbers in the *Discours*.)

On the other hand, the notion of "the Other" makes clearer sense in some contexts if Lacan is deliberately not distinguishing between repression and disavowal (see Section V) when he speaks of the *Spaltung* of the subject (Freud's *Ichspaltung*: "splitting of the ego"). He refers to the notion of *Spaltung* as "le sujet en *fading*": either the barred subject in the process of fading "in the *coupure* of demand" ($\$ \Diamond D$) or the barred subject in the process of fading "before the object of desire" ($\$ \Diamond a$), respectively the pulsion and the phantasy. The $\Diamond$ refers to the relationships: "envelopment-development-conjunction-disjunction," in other words, to the relationships expressed by the "Z" of the Schema L ("La Direction de la cure" [1961], p. 196, n.1; see also the Seminar of November, 1958–January, 1959), and the $\$$ seems simply to refer to the Other subject in the subject's division from himself. (The *a* now denotes an object of identification rather than simply the image of another person in his totality—see t.n. 183.) Freud, of course, makes two structural divisions: the first and earliest between id and ego in neurosis (governed by repression) and the later one between two or more "egos" in psychosis (governed by disavowal). The immediate difficulty is that if this reading of Lacan's text is correct, and quite apart from the obvious change in terminology since the *stade du miroir*, Lacan is no longer talking about the same Freudian unconscious as he is elsewhere, the unconscious we might legitimately conceive of as the "primary system" somehow between the id and ego (t.n. 66). The fact is that there is more than one "unconscious" in Freud's structural view of the subject, a position forced upon him by the primacy of empirical data in his work. It is unfortunate, therefore, that Lacan's reformulations so often leave the reader to decide which particular psychoanalytical referent or referents will clarify any particular Lacanian statement. The lacunae of the unpublished seminars inevitably put the reader in the position of reading Lacan as the discourse of the Other. Certainly the transformation of *l'autre* into *l'autre* (*petit a*) (after the introduction of *L'Autre* in the late fifties), thence into the shorthand, *le petit a,* and finally, notably in the "Schema R" in Section VI, into *l'objet petit a* (which is the subject of his more recent seminars) is correlative to more and more explicit statements derived from the Kleinian observations of children. But in 1953 Lacan was less concerned with his theory than with his impact: hence the abstractions of the

Discours, which become more explicitly part of established psychoanalytical positions in the later works.

Distinguishing the Other—as a category of Otherness, or as related to the "significant others"—from the other (or present counterpart) is methodologically useful. The analyst may be viewed as the (neutral) other who is constituted as the Other by the subject (who is not talking to *him*) on the basis of the original or primordial constitution of the subject by Otherness. This is why self-analysis absolutely requires another to whom the subject's discourse is apparently addressed—just as Fliess served this function in Freud's self-analysis. The subject begins by addressing a *discours imaginaire* to the analyst: it is addressed to the projection of an internalized *imago* who isn't there. This view, dependent upon an implicit, if selective, interpretation of Freud, is an important correction to the atomistic individualism Freud inherited from the nineteenth century and which he in fact exploded without, it seems, fully realizing what he had done. In this context, Lacan naturally turns to the work on jokes and reads it seriously, because the joke is not only structurally equivalent to a derivative of the unconscious, employing mechanisms similar to those involved in any kind of symptom, including the dream, but it also necessarily involves someone to whom it must be told (the *"third* person"–t.n. 78), without which it may be comic, but cannot be a joke. Lacan's introduction of the notion of the Other is of value here, since Freud expressly says that what distinguishes mechanisms like condensation, displacement, and indirect representation in the dream from the same mechanisms in jokes is that jokes are of a social nature, whereas dreams are not. Freud describes the dream as "having nothing to communicate to anybody else; it arises within the subject as a compromise between the mental forces struggling in him, it remains unintelligible to the subject himself, and is for that reason totally uninteresting to other people." A dream is a wish, whereas a joke is "developed play." But their function is not in fact so dissimilar: "Dreams serve predominantly for the avoidance of unpleasure [*Unlust*], jokes for the attainment of pleasure; but all our mental activities converge in these two aims." [50] Today one would say that the dream wish is certainly addressed to someone; it is part of an interhuman discourse, which, although expressed intrasubjectively, will also be expressed intersubjectively.

[50] *Jokes and the Unconscious* (1905), *Standard Edition,* VIII, 179–80.

The very fact of the dream presupposes the existence of others; its message can be used for or against others; one of the "mental forces" within the subject *is* another. Obviously someone is trying to tell someone something; the dream wish is addressed ambiguously to the (significant) other and distorted in such a way as to hide the truth expressed. It is not a monologue, and it is the task of the analyst in the end to reveal to whom the dream is speaking.

To sum up: in view of the multiple ways in which Lacan employs "the Other," we might supplement the suggested translation of *l'Autre* as "the unconscious" or "Otherness" by the expression "Thirdness." Thus in a recent broadcast over French radio, Lacan defined the Other as follows: "The Other with a big 'O' is the scene of the Word insofar as the scene of the Word is always in third position between two subjects. This is only in order to introduce the dimension of Truth, which is made perceptible, as it were, under the inverted sign of the lie."

Lacan's view of the dream as communication is not entirely an addition to Freud, however, for when Freud introduced the concept of the "splitting of the ego" in his later works, he laid emphasis upon the message of the dream, which, in psychosis, may actually provide a straightforward and undistorted interpretation of the subject's delusions for him. In this instance the dream is a message from the level at which "reality" is recognized to the coexisting level at which it is disavowed, the two attitudes existing in simultaneous contradiction. Moreover, even in acute cases of hallucinatory psychosis, the subject will speak of a "normal" person in the corner of his mind, watching the psychosis pass by like a spectator.[51]

This view of the dream returns us to Lacan's use of the Symbolic. If no man's actions are symbolic in themselves, as Lévi-Strauss asserts, then their symbolic nature is dependent upon the Other (upon the unconscious and the other). Even if the subject is "talking to himself," the category of the Other plays its part. But in the analytical relationship itself there is always another waiting to assume the function of the Other; thus the subject's dreams become an external dialogue, whether the analyst replies or not. The dialogue is symbolic in that it is one unconscious seeking out another unconscious—demanding countertransference in fact—since the Other is the guarantor of Truth.

[51] See Chapter VIII of the posthumous *Outline of Psychoanalysis* (1940), *Standard Edition,* XXIV, notably pp. 201–4.

The Symbolic has wider connotations also. In another sense it is exactly equivalent to Lévi-Strauss's notion of the "world of rules" and the "symbolic relationships" into which we are born and to which we learn to conform, however much our dreams may express our wish for a disorder or a counterorder. The "familial constellation" into which we arrive as strangers to humanity is already part of it. The Symbolic is the unconscious order for Lacan, just as it is for Lévi-Strauss, however divergent their intentions. Thus it designates a symbolic structure based on a linguistic model composed of chains of signifiers (some of which, however—the somatic symptoms, for instance—are in fact signs). And in the same way that Lévi-Strauss's concept of the "symbolic function" in human society depends upon the *law* which founds society (the law of incest), so Lacan's notion of the Symbolic order depends upon the law of the father. This is his notion of the Symbolic father, or what he calls the Name-of-the-Father—that is, a signifier in a linguistic model—which is related to his theory of psychosis (t.n. 96).

The Name-of-the-Father: Lacan and Psychosis

The Symbolic father is not a real or an Imaginary father (*imago*), but corresponds to the mythical Symbolic father of *Totem and Taboo*. The requirements of Freud's theory, says Lacan, led him "to link the apparition of the signifier of the Father, as author of the Law, to death, or rather to the murder of the Father, thus demonstrating that if this murder is the fruitful moment of the debt through which the subject binds himself for life to the Law, the Symbolic Father, insofar as he signifies that Law, is actually the dead Father." [52] This primal of all primal scenes is related in Freud to the "primal repression," for which Lacan substitutes the terms "constituting metaphor" or "paternal metaphor." It is through the failure of this paternal metaphor, according to Lacan, that the psychotic is induced to foreclude (*verwerfen*) the Name-of-the-Father. Since the Name-of-the-Father has never been successfully repressed, it is rejected, and with it, asserts Lacan, the whole Symbolic order. If the subject employs figures of speech and metaphors in his delusions, it is because the signifier and the signified have coalesced for

[52] "Traitement possible de la psychose" (1958), pp. 24–25. This article, which is a summary of Lacan's interpretation of the case of Schreber analyzed by Freud and of Schreber's own book, *Memoirs of my nervous illness* (1903), develops the notion of the Symbolic and the Law in detail.

him to the point that he cannot tell symbol from the thing symbolized, or word from thing presentation. In some respects his discourse may resemble what linguists call autonomous messages, that is to say, messages about words rather than messages employing words. But eventually he will lose all his metalinguistic capacities, or so it will seem from outside.

In the seminar of March–April, 1957, Lacan clarifies somewhat the notion of the symbolic function of the father. "Through the Oedipus complex," says Lacan, "the child takes on the phallus as a signifier, which supposes a confrontation with the function of the father." Whereas the girl's passage through this stage is relatively simple, the boy's is not. The Oedipus complex must permit him to identify himself with his own sex and must provide for him to accede to the position of a father, through what Lacan calls the "symbolic debt." He has the organ; the function must come from the Other (the Other beyond the other represented by his father, says Lacan) : the Symbolic father.

. . . The boy enters the Oedipus complex by a half-fraternal rivalry with his father. He manifests an aggressivity comparable to that revealed in the specular relation (either *moi* or other). But the father appears in this game as the one who has the master trump and who knows it; in a word, he appears as the Symbolic father. The Symbolic father is to be distinguished from the Imaginary father (often . . . surprisingly distant from the real father) to whom is related the whole dialectic of aggressivity and identification. In all strictness the Symbolic father is to be conceived as "transcendent," as an irreducible given of the signifier. The Symbolic father—he who is ultimately capable of saying "I am who I am"—can only be imperfectly incarnate in the real father. He is nowhere. . . . The real father takes over from the Symbolic father. This is why the real father has a decisive function in castration, which is always deeply marked by his intervention or thrown off balance by his absence . . . .

Castration may derive support from *privation,* that is to say, from the apprehension in the Real of the absence of the penis in women—but even this supposes a symbolization of the object, since the Real is full, and "lacks" nothing. Insofar as one finds castration in the genesis of neurosis, it is never real but symbolic, and it is aimed at an Imaginary object (pp. 851–52).

The notion of the primal repression (*Urverdrängung*) is difficult enough in Freud; it remains to be seen whether Lacan's view of the primal metaphor helps to clarify it. Freud was led to suppose the existence of a primal repression in his metapsychology by the empirical fact that repression works in two ways: on the one hand the repressed idea is

pushed out of consciousness; on the other, it is attracted into the unconscious by the ideational representatives already there. This double
movement seems in fact to have operated in the Signorelli incident,
where Freud's conscious desire to suppress his thoughts on death and
sexuality seems to have been converted into a repression lasting several
days because of the attraction exerted by unconscious representatives of
Eros and Thanatos.

The primal repression stands for Freud at the level of the constitution
of the unconscious (for Lacan, the creation of the barrier) at some time
during the child's advent to humanity. It has all the characteristics of a
mythical supposition, like that through which Lévi-Strauss supposes language to have been constituted in one fell swoop, or that in which he
posits the incest prohibition as the determining factor in the progress
from nature to society. It is unlikely that any of these notions will ever
be verifiable. But as a methodological supposition in Freud's metapsychology, the primal repression is that which denies to consciousness
or to the preconscious certain primordial instinctual representatives in
certain forms, and which seems to account for certain types of universal
repression (of the death instinct, perhaps). But since he also views the
psychotic as speaking his unconscious discourse directly ("treating words
like things," that is, like the thing presentations of the unconscious), the
notion of a miscarrying of the primal repression—whose duty it is to
establish an (undefined) "fixation," according to Freud—in psychosis
is not entirely foreign to the text of Freud. Lacanian analysts have thus
sought to describe this fixation in terms of an anchoring or fixing of the
"non-verbal" unconscious chain of the discourse which would allow the
symbolization essential to the conscious chain to take place.[53]

Outside these seemingly irresolvable theoretical difficulties, the fact
that the theory of psychosis in psychoanalysis is closely related to the
function of the father in the Oedipal triangle puts Lacan's theory of the
paternal metaphor well within the Freudian tradition. And his insistence on its linguistic aspects is also derived from the Freud who said
of Schreber's case: ". . . It is a remarkable fact that the familiar principal
forms of paranoia can all be represented as contradictions of the single
proposition: '*I* (a man) *love him* (a man),' and indeed that they exhaust

[53] See: Leclaire and Laplanche, "L'Inconscient," *Les Temps Modernes,* No. 183
(July, 1961), pp. 81–129, notably p. 115.

all the possible ways in which such contradictions could be formulated." [54] (This remains true whether one regards homosexuality as a cause or as a symptom in psychosis.)

In seeking to view the Symbolic as providing a means of anchoring our personal appropriation of language to the linguistic code controlled by the Other (t.n. 183), Lacan is pleased enough, since Lévi-Strauss, to call this theory a myth. The notion of anchoring is logical enough. Certainly, if the meaning of a word is always another word, a determined perusal of our linguistic dictionary will eventually return us to our starting point. Perhaps language is in fact totally tautologous in the sense that it can only in the end talk about itself, but in any event, Lacan has suggested that there must be some privileged "anchoring points" (the *points de capiton*), points like the buttons on a mattress or the intersections in quilting, where there is a "pinning down" (*capiton-nage*) of meaning, not to an object, but rather by "reference back" to a symbolic function. The tautologous, "unanchored" *glissement* of the signifier over the signified is in fact an aspect of certain types of schizophrenic language, where the correspondence of the subject's language to the "reality" accepted in normal discourse has somehow become unhinged, so that one may discover the schizophrenic at the mercy of binary semantic oppositions structurally similar to the child's first semantic or phonemic acts, but in which the opposition is valued over the content. The similarity is not an actual one—that is, there is no question of real regression—but, as Jakobson has noted in his influential article on aphasia (1956), in certain kinds of aphasia the patient loses first what the child learns last—usually shifters relating him to his entourage—and retains to the end what the child learns first.

In their article on the unconscious Leclaire and Laplanche have this to say about the constitution of the Symbolic order:

It is here that J. Lacan introduces his theory of the *'points de capiton'* through which, at certain privileged points, the signifying chain, in his view, comes to fix itself to the signified. It would be incorrect to see in this theory a surreptitious return to a nominalist theory, where the function of controlling the circulation of language might be considered as having devolved on to a link with some 'real' object, or on to what certain modern experimenters call 'conditioning.'

[54] *Standard Edition,* XII, 62–65.

In dealing with their use of the "primal metaphor," Leclaire and Laplanche go on to quote from one of Lacan's unpublished seminars (1958), noting that the possibility of meaning in language is absolutely dependent upon the nonunivocity of words, for otherwise no substitutions (definitions, metaphors, synonyms) could take place:

"Between the two chains . . . those of the signifiers in relationship to all the ambulatory signifieds which are in constant circulation because they are always in a process of transposition [*glissement*], the 'pinning down' I speak of, or the *point de capiton,* is mythical, for no one has ever been able to pin a signification on a signifier; but on the other hand what *can* be done is to pin one signifier to another signifier and see what happens. But in this case something new is invariably produced . . . in other words, the surging forth of a new signification . . ." (p. 112).

In Lacan's "Subversion du sujet et dialectique du désir" (1966), the *point de capiton* is defined in purely linguistic terms as that by which the signifier brings the indefinite *glissement* of signification to a stop. The diachronic function of the *point de capiton* in the sentence, according to Lacan, is that function which describes the process of signification in speech. The signification of a sentence remains "open" until its final term (including punctuation). Each term is anticipated by those which precede it in the construction of the sentence, and, inversely, the *meaning* of the sentence is *retroactively* revealed by a sort of reading backwards from the end.

This progressive-regressive movement is symbolized in a diagram (*Ecrits,* p. 805):

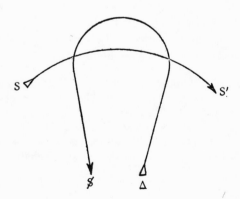

in which the vector $S \rightarrow S'$ represents the "support of the chain of signifiers" (the passage of the subject) and $\Delta \rightarrow \$$, the reading backwards which Lacan expresses by saying that the subject receives his own message from the Other in an inverted form (t.n. 147). This "general formula of transsubjective communication" is clarified elsewhere by another diagram in which the *loci* where the vector $S \rightarrow S'$ crosses $\Delta \rightarrow \$$ are defined respectively as the locus of the message and the locus of the code. In other words, for the complete message of the conscious subject to be understood (by the emitter or by the receiver) at any level at all, there must be an unconscious reading in reverse at the *end* of the message, a reference to the locus of the code *after* the complete message has been received (the message consisting if necessary of a series of significant "bits"). This reading backwards is the interpretation of the message (cf. *Ecrits,* p. 56), and the general notion of the *point de capiton* outside any particular sentence or discourse is that fixed relationship to a symbolic function which is the prerequisite for any messages at all to pass between subjects. It is this "fixation" which is rejected in advanced psychosis, where all attempts to communicate apparently cease but speech may not.

Lacan's interpretation of psychosis and its relation to the Symbolic order stems in part from widely accepted conclusions about the language of psychosis, as expressed, for example, in the following passage from Kurt Goldstein, where the latter is comparing schizophrenic language and the language of patients with brain damage. The patient's capacity for abstract attitudes and abstract thought is impaired:

. . . The process of disintegration in the direction of concrete behavior does not prevent the arousal of ideas and thoughts; what it actually affects and modifies is the way of manipulating and operating them. Thoughts do arise, but they can only become effective in a concrete way: just as the patient cannot deal with outer-world objects in a conceptual frame of reference, so he deals with ideas simply as things which belong to an object or situation. Concepts, meaning, categories—other than situation means-end relations— are not within his scope.

And later:

Concrete behavior means that in our behavior and activity we are governed, to an abnormal degree, by the outer-world stimuli which present themselves to us, and by the images, ideas, and thoughts which act upon us at the moment . . . . The demarcation between the outer world and [the schizophrenic's] ego is more or less suspended or modified in comparison with the normal . . . . He does not consider the object as part of an ordered outer world separated from himself, as the normal person does.[55]

It will at once be seen how Goldstein's view matches Freud's meta-psychological remarks on the language of schizophrenia in 1914 and 1915. Although Freud generally regards condensation and displacement as distinguishing marks of the primary (unconscious) physical process and considers language to be part of the (conscious and preconscious) secondary process, his distinction between word presentations and thing presentations (t.n. 66) enabled him to account for both the similarities and the differences between dream language and schizophrenic language. In the dream the dream thoughts regress "through the unconscious" to images (thing presentations) and are modified by condensation and displacement in the process. In schizophrenia on the other hand, *"words are subject to the same process as that which makes the dream-images out of latent dream thoughts—to what we have called the primary psychical process. They undergo condensation and by means of displace-ment transfer their cathexes to one another in their entirety. The process may go so far that a single word, if it is especially suitable on account of its numerous connections, takes over the representation of a whole train of thought."* [56] "The dream-work too," he adds, "occasionally treats words like things, and so creates very similar 'schizophrenic' utterances or neologisms." But there is an important difference between the two "languages": "In [schizophrenia], what becomes the subject of modifica-tions by the primary process are the words themselves in which the pre-conscious thought was expressed; in dreams, what are subject to this modification are not the words, but the thing-presentations to which the words have been taken back. In dreams there is free communication between (*Pcs.*) word-cathexes and (*Ucs.*) thing-cathexes, while it is characteristic of schizophrenia that this communication is cut off." [57] Thus at the end of the article on the unconscious he states simply that an attempted characterization of the schizophrenic's mode of thought would be to say "that he treats concrete things as though they were ab-stract" (p. 204).

---

[55] "Methodological Approach to the Study of Schizophrenic Thought Disorder" (1939), in: *Language and Thought in Schizophrenia,* ed. J. S. Kasanin (New York: Norton, 1964), pp. 20–21, 23.

[56] "The Unconscious" (1915), *Standard Edition,* XIV, 199.

[57] "The Metapsychology of Dreams" (1915), *Standard Edition,* XIV, 229.

In speaking of the "paternal metaphor," Lacan is dealing with the wider theoretical justification of his view of the role of *Verwerfung* in psychosis.

The notion of *Verwerfung* springs from Freud's use of the term in the Wolf Man's "rejection (repudiation) of castration in the sense of repression" (t.n. 104)—and as Lacan notes in the *Discours,* the Wolf Man did eventually become psychotic. From the terminological point of view, the notion of *Verwerfung* is to be related to the more strictly discursive term *Verleugnung* (disavowal), which is that upon which Freud relies in his discussion of the psychoses after about 1923. The idea is sometimes expressed as "a withdrawal of cathexis [*Besetzung*] from reality," related to the so-called loss of reality in psychosis. *Verleugnung* is central to his remarks on fetishism (1927)—which, as a perversion, is closer to psychosis than neurosis—where he makes the distinction between "repression" (*Verdrängung*) and "disavowal" (of castration).[58] That his views depend upon an interpretation or value judgment—the castration complex —as well as upon observation, does not of course necessarily invalidate their more general application, especially since the concept of repudiation is intimately connected with the function of judgment itself in his metapsychological article of 1925 on the *Verneinung*. Lacan, as I have noted, relates the whole question to the phallus, the partial object, castration, and frustration.

Insofar as the *Verleugnung* is both a "disavowal of reality" connected with the "splitting of the *Ich*" in the later articles on neurosis and psychosis, as well as a disavowal of castration, the use of the term does seem to be comparable to the use of the term *Verwerfung* in the much earlier analysis of the Wolf Man (1914). Moreover, although Freud does speak of repression in connection with the psychoses, this usage seems to be the result of an incompletely formalized distinction, since his considered view is that repression is the operative factor only in neurosis. And indeed Freud does note in the very first paragraph of the article "Repression" (1915)[59] that "repression is a preliminary stage of condemnation."

The German terms involved are variously translated in the *Standard*

[58] "Fetishism" (1927), *Standard Edition,* XII, 152.

In the article "Anatomical Sex-distinction" (1925), *Standard Edition,* XIX, Freud describes disavowal as "a process which in the mental life of children seems neither uncommon nor very dangerous but which in an adult would mean the beginning of a psychosis" (p. 253).

[59] *Standard Edition,* XIV, 148.

Edition. Provided we keep in mind the normal fluctuation that is constitutive of Freud's terminology and hypotheses, it seems that "rejection," "repudiation," "condemnation," "negative judgment," "condemning judgment"—the various renderings of *Verwerfung, Verurteilung,* and *Urteilsverwerfung*—are synonymous in the text of Freud. In both the case of little Hans (1909), and the case of the Wolf Man (1918 [1914]), "repression" is distinguished from "condemnation" or "condemning judgment." [60] And in the 1925 article on "Negation," of which Lacan's commentary (1956) is the first to deal systematically with the concept of *Verwerfung* (t.n. 23), Freud states that: "A negative judgment [*Verurteilung*] is the intellectual equivalent of or substitute [*Ersatz*] for repression; its 'no' is a hallmark, a certificate of origin as it were, something like 'Made in Germany.' " Through the mediation of the "symbol of negation" (*Verneinungssymbol*), thought frees itself from the consequences of repression and enriches itself with a content which is essential for its accomplishment.[61] This conception, notes the editor, goes back at least to the work on jokes (1905), where Freud points out that there is no way of telling whether any element in a dream which has a possible contrary is actually positive or negative. No process resembling "judging" seems to occur in the unconscious, he goes on: "In the place of rejection by a judgment, what we find in the unconscious is 'repression.' Repression may, without doubt, be correctly described as the intermediate stage between a defensive reflex and a condemning judgment." [62]

In Freud's metapsychology, the *Verneinung* to which the negative judgment is related is described as the "derivative of expulsion" from the "primary *Ich,*" a concept described elsewhere in the article on negation by the verb *werfen* (eject). Affirmation (*Bejahung*) is correlative to introjection. This idea is central to Lacan's view of "repudiation," and, as Laplanche and Pontalis note in their article *"Forclusion,"* Freud had said of psychosis in 1894 that it involved a much more energetic and successful "means of defense" against "incompatible ideas" than "repression" or "transposition of affect" in neurosis and hysteria: "Here, the ego rejects [*verwirft*] the incompatible [*unverträglich*] idea together with

[60] See, for example: *Standard Edition,* X, 145; and XVII, 79–80 ("eine Verdrängung ist etwas anderes als eine Verwerfung").
[61] *Standard Edition,* XIX, 124.
[62] *Standard Edition,* VIII, 175.

its affect and behaves as if the idea had never occurred to the ego at all." [63] This is clearly the germ of the much later technical use of the term *Verleugnung* to describe the psychotic's "incomplete attempts at detachment from reality." "The disavowal is always supplemented by an acknowledgment; two contrary and independent attitudes always arise and result in the situation of there being a splitting of the ego [*Ichspaltung*]." [64] This split differs from that in neurosis, where it is repression which occasions a split between "ego" and "id," since the contrary attitudes in psychosis are entirely at the level of the concrete discourse. Laplanche and Pontalis note the other terms used by Freud in similar ways: *ablehnen*[65] and *aufheben*.[66]

Lacan develops the concept of *Verwerfung* out of the case of the Wolf Man and the metaspsychology of the *Verneinung,* which he describes as "mythical." Laplanche and Pontalis point out that Lacan's view corresponds to Freud's constant attempts to define a defense mechanism proper to psychosis. In the case of Schreber, for instance, the concept of projection, which is for Freud on the one hand the counterpart of introjection, and on the other, a defense typical of paranoia, is first viewed as a rejection toward the exterior and distinguished (as a symptom) from the "return of the repressed" in neurosis. But Freud goes on to correct himself: "It was incorrect to say that the perception which was suppressed [*unterdrückt*] internally is projected outwards; the truth is rather . . . that what was abolished [*das Aufgehobene*] internally returns from without" (*loc. cit.*). This conception is the key to Lacan's commentary on the *Verwerfung* (1956). In demonstrating how the Wolf Man interpreted the "primal scene" (parental intercourse, real or phantasied, *a tergo*) *nachträglich,* that is to say, how it became meaningful for him, Freud shows how the "literal" interpretation by the subject—at an age before he could conceive of castration—co-existed in the adult with the deferred interpretation of what he had seen, in the light of castration.

[63] "The Neuro-Psychoses of Defence" (1894), *Standard Edition,* III, 58.
[64] *An Outline of Psycho-analysis* (1940 [1938]), *Standard Edition,* XXIII, 204. See also the unfinished paper on the splitting of the ego in the same volume (pp. 275–78) where Freud comments: "The whole process seems so strange to us because we take for granted the synthetic nature of the processes of the ego" (p. 276).
[65] "Turning away," "keeping at a distance," for example, in: "Repression" (1914), *Standard Edition,* XIV, 147; and in: "The Unconscious" in the same volume, p. 203.
[66] "Suppress and conserve," usually translated "abolish" or "lift." See the case of Schreber, *Standard Edition,* XII, 71; and the article on negation already cited.

"He rejected [*verwarf*] castration and held to his theory of intercourse by the anus . . . . He would have nothing to do with [castration], in the sense of repression. This really involved no judgment upon the question of its existence, but it was the same as if it did not exist." [67] Thus two contrary ideas existed side by side at the level of the discourse, the disavowal and the acknowledgment. Lacan formulates his view on the basis of the "primary process" in the child, as described in the article on negation, involving two operations: "the *Einbeziehung ins Ich,* the introduction into the subject, and the *Ausstossung aus dem Ich,* the expulsion outside the subject," [68] which, as I have already pointed out, are related by Freud to *Bejahung* and to *Verneinung,* respectively. Since the rejection of castration by the Wolf Man was in Freud's words "as if it did not exist," and since part of Freud's argument in the article on negation is to describe the function of judgment (*Urteil*) as (1) affirming (*zusprechen*) or disaffirming (*absprechen*) attributes to things, and (2) asserting or disputing the existence of a presentation in reality (*Realität*), Lacan seeks to view affirmation or introjection as a "primordial symbolization" of reality, and negation or expulsion as "constituting the Real [for the subject] as the domain which exists outside symbolization" (p. 48). *Verwerfung,* as a form of negation, consists therefore in *not* symbolizing what should have been symbolized—castration, in the case of the Wolf Man. The *Verwerfung* consequently amounts to a "symbolic abolition" (p. 46): "The *Verwerfung* therefore cut short any manifestation of the Symbolic order [for the Wolf Man]. That is to say, it cut short the *Bejahung* which Freud posits as the primary process in which attributive judgment is rooted, and which is nothing other than the primordial condition for something out of the Real to offer itself to the revelation of being, or, to employ a Heideggerean term, for it to be 'let be' " (p. 47). But what was not "let be" in that aborted *Bejahung?* Since the subject, in Freud's words, wanted to know nothing about castration "in the sense of repression," Lacan proposes that it was this very meaning itself which was lost in the incomplete symbolization. With castration not repressed, there was nowhere for the "return of the repressed" (the symptom) to return to (as it returns to the subject's

[67] *Standard Edition,* XVII, 84.
[68] "Réponse au commentaire de J. Hyppolite sur la *Verneinung* de Freud" (1956), p. 48.

"history" in normal neurosis). And if Freud means what he says about affirmation and negation, then what was wrongly rejected (expulsed), that is to say, what never "came to the light of the Symbolic," *must logically appear in the Real* (the domain outside symbolization). In Freud's words: "what was abolished internally returns from without."

And this is precisely what happened. ". . . The castration which was 'cut out' [forecluded] of the limits even of the possible by the subject," Lacan continues, "and furthermore, by this very fact, withdrawn from the possibilities of the Word, will appear erratically in the Real—that is to say, in relationships of resistance with no transference—or, as I would put it . . . it will appear as a punctuation without a text" (p. 48). What happened was that unlike the neurotic symptom which is always an interpretation of what is repressed (for example, "Botticelli") and which provides a form of defense or gratification in itself, the equivalent incident in the Wolf Man's case was a hallucination. In one version he thought he had cut his finger off; in another, he cut into a tree and blood oozed from the wound. In both incidents the subject was horrified to the point of *speechlessness*. This, says Lacan, is an "interversion" of the Signorelli incident: "In the latter, the subject lost the disposition of a signifier; in the present case, he halts before the strangeness of the signified" (p. 50). Both correspond to gaps in the Symbolic order, where "the voids are as significant [*signifiants*] as the plenums." The hallucination itself in this instance is not simply Imaginary, because it is a symbol which has been originally cut out of the Symbolic itself.

". . . Reading Freud today, it certainly seems that it is the gaping of a void which constitutes the first step of his whole dialectical movement [that is, the Signorelli incident of 1898]. This seems certainly to explain the insistence of the schizophrenic in reiterating this step. In vain, since for him all the Symbolic is real" (p. 52). Thus—to quote Laplanche and Pontalis—foreclusion as a psychotic mechanism is to be considered as "a primordial rejection of a fundamental 'signifier' (for example: the phallus in so far as it is a signifier of the castration complex) from the symbolic universe of the subject." It differs from repression in that (1) "the forecluded signifiers are not integrated into the unconscious of the subject," and that (2), "they do not come back 'from the interior,'" as in the return of the repressed, but return "in the heart of the real, singularly in the hallucinatory phenomenon."

Lacan's view of the loss of reality (*Realitätsverlust*)[69] in psychosis is therefore that of a loss of symbolic reality. In the widest sense, this seems to be a double-pronged idea. On the one hand the psychotic's difficulties in relating to people around him would correspond to a loss of the "symbolic function" of which Lévi-Strauss speaks. Thus the psychotic's world, in the extreme case, is totally nonsymbolic; he has withdrawn not from reality, but from human reality (t.n. 102). On the other hand, the very common instances in aphasia (of which Goldstein speaks), where the subject has lost the "divine power of abstraction [*Verstand*]," in Hegel's terms, is clearly related to his inability to employ what Lévi-Strauss calls *la pensée symbolique*. The aphasiac who cannot classify different colored and different shaped pieces of card or cloth has lost the taxonomic power of human thought, which appears to be universal in all societies and especially developed in the *pensée sauvage* of the so-called primitive cultures. What he has lost, it seems, is the power of *mapping* external reality which we exert by placing that reality on a symbolic "background." This is in effect the loss of the ability to intentionalize reality; the psychotic is simply too close to it. Thus, in speaking of amentia (an acute type of hallucinatory confusion), Freud points out that "not only is the acceptance of new perceptions refused [by the ego], but the internal world, too, which, as a copy of the external world, has up till now represented it, loses its significance [*Bedeutung*] (its cathexis)." [70] And later:

> But, whereas the new, imaginary external world of a psychosis attempts to put itself in the place of external reality, that of a neurosis, on the contrary, is apt, like the play of children, to attach itself to a piece of reality—a different piece from the one against which it has to defend itself—and to lend that piece a special importance and a secret meaning which we (not always quite appropriately) call a *symbolic* one. Thus we see that both in neurosis and psychosis there comes into consideration the question not only of a *loss of reality* but also of a *substitute for reality*.[71]

In Lacan's terminology, the substituted reality in neurosis or psychosis could be called metonymic (a displacement from one instance of reality

---

[69] For Freud, this concept goes back to the Draft K in the correspondence to Fliess (1896). See: *The Origins of Psychoanalysis* (1954), p. 146. The "alteration" or "malformation" of the *Ich* at this date is not without relevance to the much later idea of the splitting of the ego.

[70] "Neurosis and Psychosis" (1924), *Standard Edition*, XIX, 150–51.

[71] "Loss of Reality in Neurosis and Psychosis" (1924), *Standard Edition*, XIX, 187.

to another) or metaphorical (a symbolic substitute), except that the "loss of reality" in psychosis would amount to a loss of the ability to distinguish the system of signifiers from the system of signifieds, and thus the coalescence of what for the neurotic is still symbolically separated. Lacan's view is thus also an interpretation of Freud's distinction between normal language (sustained by repression)—where both word presentations and thing presentations are found—and schizophrenic language (dependent on rejection)—where, as in the unconscious, only thing presentations are found, according to Freud. The loss of the abstractive power of thought in psychosis would correspond to the loss of the ability to handle word presentations in their normal symbolic way, since they have coalesced with the conscious and unconscious thing presentations. At the same time, what Freud describes as communication between (*Pcs.*) word cathexes and (*Ucs.*) thing cathexes has been cut off —what we call "meaning" has become "detached" from what we call "reality" (the reality of the *Vorstellungen*) by the fact that the psychotic can no longer distinguish one from the other.

And here at least one aspect of the multivalency of the structural view vindicates itself as an especially successful shorthand. If Lacan means "things" by "the signified," the psychotic is handling signifiers like signifieds (words like things); if Lacan means "images," the psychotic is handling words like unintentionalized images. On the other hand, if Lacan means "the unconscious discourse," there has been a crossing of the bar between consciousness and the unconscious in the psychotic: he speaks Freud's schizophrenic language. Yet again, if the psychotic is at the mercy of any kind of binary opposition, and he often is, then the semantic values of his discourse have "regressed" to phonemic values; Lacan can speak of the "unconscious chain of signifiers" (the signified is ultimately a signifier) and mean a series of opposing distinctive features governed by the compulsion to repeat (the *Fort! Da!*) and its relation to the phantasy.

To sum up rather simply: repression is thwarted by the coalescence between consciousness and the unconscious in the psychotic (who *says* he wants to murder his father and sleep with his mother); the subject has to protect himself and attempt his own cure by a different process: rejection (condemnation) or disavowal (he does *not* want to kill his father; his father wants to kill him . . . .). And in the light of these views, however systematically simplified they may be for the purposes of this exposition, one especially interesting idea is revealed: that for Freud "the withdrawal of cathexis," and perhaps the whole notion of cathexis itself, has ultimately to be interpreted in terms of meaning (intentionality). Reality doesn't lose its significance for the psychotic, it loses its signification.

V

The Belle Âme: *Freud, Lacan, and Hegel*

Lacan makes constant reference in his earlier works to the dialectic of the *belle âme* (*die schöne Seele*) in the *Phenomenology,* which is a repetition at another level of the confrontation of the master and the slave. The *Phenomenology* is in fact a repeated dialectic of the confrontation of self and other. This confrontation is external in the dialectic of the master and the slave, or in that of the noble consciousness and the base consciousness, or in that of the sinning and the judging consciousness, or in that of the active consciousness and the *belle âme.* It becomes internal, for instance, through the internalization of these conflicts within the unhappy consciousness. Although the otherness involved is sometimes itself or "the world" in a modern phenomenological and existential sense, and although the various stages of the journey of consciousness are tied to historical and literary models, the level of abstraction and the quality of intuitive psychological insight is such as to allow a more or less coherent reading in terms of "interpersonal relations" mediated by the discourse. The traditional reading of the *Phenomenology* has always had either to accept or to gloss over the implied necessity or causality of the movement from one moment of the over-all dialectic to another—which reminds us that Hegel is primarily describing what *has* happened (in history) and not what must happen (for us). But there is another Hegel waiting to be read today: the man who accomplished an extraordinary *tour de force* in a conceptual coalescence of the diachronic and the synchronic, the man who showed precisely what Goethe meant to say by "man remains the same but humanity progresses [changes]." It is for this reason that the man who *also* reads Hegel the way he would read Proust will always come to a wider comprehension of the *Phenomenology* than the man who reads him *only* as he would read Kant.

Moreover, the role of necessary alienation (*Entäusserung*) through otherness in the dialectical formation of the human "personality"—explicitly or implicitly dependent upon a repeated desire for recognition—is clear enough, and not necessarily to be confused with the use of a stronger word (*Entfremdung*) in the Marxian or modern sense. Jean Hyppolite has summarized the notion of formation lying behind Hegel's systematic elaboration of alienation in the following terms:

> . . . The two terms formation [*culture: Bildung*] and alienation [*Entäusserung*] have a very similar meaning [for Hegel]. It is by the alienation of his natural being that a determinate individual cultivates and forms himself for essentiality. One might put it more precisely by saying that for Hegel self-formation is only conceivable through the mediation of alienation or estrangement [*Entfremdung*]. Self-formation is not to develop harmoniously as if by organic growth, but rather to become opposed to oneself and to rediscover oneself through a splitting [*déchirement*] and a separation.[72]

The dialectic of the *Phenomenology* is a dialectic of cognition, miscognition, and recognition, based on the notion that through consciousness of the other one attains consciousness of self on the condition of being recognized by the other. But this recognition is further to recognize that one's self is the other or that the other is oneself. Hegel seeks an intersubjective recognition, that is to say, a reconciliation of the opposition of self and other. The repeated reversal of opposites is like what the French would call *un jeu de miroirs;* the role of identification is constitutive in these reversals. The similarity of the dialectic to the actual progress of an analysis was first noted by Lacan in the "Intervention sur le transfert" in 1951, where he analyzes Freud's countertransference onto Dora in Hegelian terms (t.n. 159). There is an unconscious in the *Phenomenology* which would bear analysis in the light of Freud; equally interesting, perhaps, would be the application of the discursive mechanism of *Verneinung* (t.n. 11) both to Hegel's conception of negativity and to the repeated denials or repressions of the truth expressed by the various stages of the consciousness on its journey toward absolute subjectivity.

Freud does in fact extend the notion of *Verneinung* to a conception constitutive of judgment itself, and in the discussion of the relationship of the *Verneinung* to repression, he is very naturally led to employ the Hegelian terms of dialectical negation (*Aufhebung*) as well: "The content of a repressed presentation or thought can thus make its way through to consciousness on the condition that it lets itself be negated. The *Ver-*

[72] *Genèse et structure de la Phénoménologie de l'Esprit* (Paris: Aubier, 1946), II, 372.

neinung is a way to take cognizance [*Kenntnis*] of what is repressed; indeed it is already a 'lifting and conserving' [*Aufhebung*] of the repression, but not for all that an acceptance [*Annahme*] of what is repressed." [73] In another terminology, one would say that repression in history is constitutive of our essential social myths—such as the myth of the American Revolution, for instance. In Freud's article, moreover, the whole concept of negation (which is a fact of the discourse) is related to death, exactly as the time of the discourse in Hegel is so related:

> Affirmation—as an equivalent of unification [with external reality]—belongs to the Eros; negation—the derivative of expulsion [from the "primary ego"]—belongs to the instinct of destruction [the death instinct].[74] The pleasure in universal denegation, the negativism of many psychotics is very probably to be understood as a symptomatic-mark or sign [*Anzeichen*] of the defusion of the instincts [*Triebentmischung*] through the withdrawal [*Abzug*] of the libidinal components (*ibid.*).[75]

These similarities between Hegel and Freud require a much closer examination than it is possible to enter into here. But it is not surprising to find Norman O. Brown calling for an interpretation of Freud in the light of Kojève's commentary on Hegel's concept of time and for an interpretation of Hegel in the light of the Freudian doctrine of repression and the unconscious. He goes on to point out that "It is not the consciousness of death that is transformed into aggression, but the unconscious death instinct; the unconscious death instinct is that negativity or nothingness which is extroverted into the action of negating nature and other men." [76]

To return to the Hegelian dialectic: Kojève notes its circularity. In fact, however, it is more like a spiral whose two ends are synchronically (or structurally) identical but which are separated diachronically in time by History—that is to say, by the Sage's coming to be conscious of his own absolute mortality. Detached from the unacceptable philosophy of nature which underlies Hegel's dialectic, and with no necessary acceptance of the final transcendance and reconciliation, the *Phenomenology* remains one of the truly profound psychological works of the nineteenth century.

[73] "Negation" (1925), *Standard Edition*, XIX, 239. Translation slightly modified.
[74] "Die Bejahung—als Ersatz der Vereinigung—gehört dem Eros an, die Verneinung—Nachfolge des Ausstossung—dem Destruktionstrieb." See the commentary by Lacan and Hyppolite (1956).
[75] See Section IV, on the "withdrawal of cathexis."
[76] *Life against Death*, p. 102.

Indeed, its very repetitions of similar structures beg to be considered in the light of the psychoanalytical compulsion to repeat.

It is worth noting at this point that René Girard's pioneering work on identification, rivalry, and mediated desire in the novel, from Cervantes to Proust,[77] was once thought by some to have been influenced by Lacan, at a time when Lacan was generally unknown in the United States. But it was the Hegelian, Freudian, and existentialist sources which were similar in the two writers, whereas the approach and conclusions remain fundamentally different. Girard is concerned among other things with what he calls the "Romantic solipsist," exemplified with especial éclat by the Roquentin of Sartre's *La Nausée* (1936), whose influence it is unnecessary to go into. It is a similar desire for autonomy *against* the other which is to be found in the *pour soi* of *L'Etre et le Néant* (1943). The existential hero of that period has also been interpreted as an example of Hegel's unhappy consciousness (the internalization of the master-slave dialectic), but, given the diachronic repetition which is so characteristic of the *Phenomenology,* one may find the Romantic solipsist even more precisely defined in the dialectic of the *belle âme*—and for the very good reason that Hegel is dealing with a whole tradition of the Romantic "literature of the self," beginning with Rousseau's great novel, the *Confessions,* and including Goethe's *Werther,* his "Confessions of a noble soul" in *Wilhelm Meister,* and the Karl Moor of Schiller's *Brigands* (whose prototype is to be found in Diderot's *contes*). These characters are inevitably linked to the master and the slave, to the noble and the base consciousness, in Diderot's *Neveu de Rameau* and *Jacques le Fataliste.*

Karl Moor, the "ethical bandit," the Romantic Robin Hood, is for Hegel the epitome of the sentimental subjectivism to be found in Rousseau and in Goethe's Werther. His identification with the individual versus society and the alliance of his personal well-being with the well-being of humanity makes him the figure most characteristic of what Hegel calls the law of the heart (*das Gesetz des Herzens*). His essence is to be *pour soi,* negating the *en soi* of social necessity.

The heartfelt identification with the universal well-being of humanity by the individual governed by the law of the heart passes into madness

---

[77] *Mensonge romantique et vérité romanesque* (Paris: Grasset, 1961). Translated by Yvonne Freccero as: *Deceit, Desire, and the Novel* (Baltimore: Johns Hopkins Press, 1966).

(*Verrücktheit*) when he discovers the opposition and indifference to his good intentions of those he wishes to save from themselves. His madness is the delusion of his self-conceit (*der Wahnsinn des Eigendünkels*); he projects his inner perversity (*Verkehrtheit*) onto the other and seeks to express (*aussprechen*) it as other (pp. 266ff.; I, pp. 302ff.). He condemns individuality in the other, but not in himself.

The structure of the individual subjected to the law of the heart is repeated in a slightly different way at the later "moment" of the *belle âme*. Hegel condemns the *belle âme*—which he had not done in the theological writings of his Romantic youth—and Lacan equates the *belle âme* with the subject in analysis, giving a widely accepted interpretation of the Alceste of Molière's *Le Misanthrope* in the process (t.n. 111). This is to condemn the subject of the *parole vide* or, in Girard's view, the subject who has not discovered himself through the *expérience romanesque* in the others he condemns. The early Lukàcs, for another, a man who is personally seeking to escape the fate of the Hegelian *belle âme,* attempts to view the contradictions of the novel of "abstract idealism" (*Don Quixote*) and those of the novel of "romantic disillusion" (*L'Education sentimentale*) as coming to a sort of synthesis in the *Bildungsroman* (*Wilhelm Meister*).[78] Whatever the success or persuasiveness of this or other attempts at dealing with the alienation of the individual from himself and from society inside or outside literature, the similarity between psychoanalysis, the novel, and the *Phenomenology* is unavoidable, if only because of their mutual influences and intersecting structures.

The transformation of the consciousness into the *belle âme* begins with the dialectical moment when this consciousness, certain of himself, discovers himself in his discourse, creates an *en soi* of his Self, and thence discovers his autonomy to be an abstraction:

Language is the consciousness of self which is *for others,* which is immediately *present as such* and which, as this *consciousness of this self,* is *universal* consciousness of self. It is the Self which separates itself from itself and becomes objectified [through speaking of itself] as pure *Ich bin Ich* and which, in this objectivity, fuses immediately with the others and is their consciousness of self . . . . However, language comes forth as the mediating

[78] *Die Theorie des Romans* (Berlin: Luchterhand, 1966 [1920]). For similar reasons of the common influence, Lucien Goldmann has been able to draw parallels between the early Lukàcs and Girard's independent interpretation.

element of the independent and recognized consciousnesses of self . . . (pp. 458, 459; II, pp. 184, 186).

Faced with the poverty of its object (its Self), the consciousness is divided between its subjectivity and its own existential poverty: "The absolute certitude of self changes therefore immediately for it as consciousness into a dying echo, in the objectivity of its being-for-itself; but the world thus created is its *discourse* [*Rede*] which it has heard similarly non-mediately and whose echo keeps on coming back to it . . ." (p. 462; II, p. 189). The consciousness lives in the anguish of sullying its purity by action or contact: "The hollow object it creates for itself thus fills it with the consciousness of the void. Its occupation is a nostalgic aspiration which simply loses itself . . . —it becomes an unhappy *belle âme* . . ." (*ibid.*).

The *belle âme* is a consciousness which judges others but which refuses action. In his vanity, the *belle âme* values his ineffective discourse above the facts of the world and expects it to be taken as the highest reality (p. 469; II, p. 195). He is recognized (like the master) by the active consciousness which he judges, but he is recognized as an equal. The active consciousness, "drawn by the vision of itself in the other" (p. 471; II, p. 198), "confesses itself openly to the other" and waits for the other (the *belle âme*), apparently on the same level as the active consciousness, "also to repeat its discourse, and to express in this discourse his equality with it. The active consciousness waits for the being-there [of language] which effects recognition" (*ibid.*).

But the reply of a similar confession does not follow the confession of the evil: "This is what I am." The judging consciousness [the *belle âme*] . . . refuses this community . . . it rejects continuity with the other. Thus the scene is reversed. The confessing consciousness sees itself repelled and sees the other's wrong, the other who refuses to bring his interior life out into the being-there of the [intersubjective] discourse, opposes the beauty of his own soul to the [other's confession of] evil, opposes to the confession the obstinate attitude of the character always equal to itself and the muteness of one who retires into himself and refuses to lower himself to the level of the other . . . .

This *belle âme* cannot attain to equality with the [other] consciousness . . . he cannot attain being-there . . . (pp. 469, 470; II, pp. 196, 197).

Thus the *belle âme* refuses the world and attains, not being, but non-being, "an empty nothingness." ". . . The *belle âme* therefore, as consciousness of [the] contradiction in his unreconciled immediateness, is unhinged to the point of madness and wastes away in a nostalgic consumption" (*ibid.*).

The "False-Self System"

The *belle âme* is a schizoid personality: his fundamental question is the question of his being in an expressly existential sense. He not only asks: "What am I in my being?" but he fears the loss of the very void he discovers he is. His relationship to being-in-the-world and to being-with-others can very aptly be characterized as the "splitting of the ego" (the self)—into many possible "parts"—which is described by R. D. Laing as the opposition of an "inner-self system" to a "false-self system." Not that this inner-self is somehow absolutely true, unalienated, or authentic, or free of the necessity of the mask we all wear, but rather that it is less inauthentic. The *belle âme* fears the other because he wants so much to be the other, but being the other means losing himself. The whole paradox of identification is involved: seeking to be identical to the other, or seeking to possess the other's identity, is to lose one's own identity. The possibility that self-identity may simply be a more than usually all-persuasive myth need not detain us here. Hegel's point is that the "normal" relationship of being-with-others is both subjective and objective, whereas the *belle âme* seeks to preserve an unsullied subjectivity because of his fear of what modern psychologists would call the necessary and normal depersonalization (as opposed to Marxian reification) which is part of our interpersonal relations.

Thus Laing's existential approach to schizoid personalities on the basis of his own clinical experience provides an implicit analysis of the character of the *belle âme,* which Rousseau, for one, knew only too well. Schiller's *belle âme* had indeed been a "beautiful and noble soul," one in which moral duty was a matter of nature. For Goethe, however, in his middle years, the *belle âme* depended on the "noblest deceptions," on "the most subtle confusion of the subjective and the objective." [79] Hegel, thinking of Novalis, of the Romantic notion of pure subjectivity and immaculate beauty, of Fichte's *Ich bin Ich,* has developed the notion further: "The *belle âme* lacks the power of alienation, the power to make himself a thing and to support being" (*ibid.,* p. 462; II, p. 189).[80] For

---

[79] See: Hyppolite, *Phénoménologie,* II, p. 176, note 74; p. 189, note 95.
[80] "Es fehlt ihm die Kraft der Entaüsserung, die Kraft, sich zum Dinge zu machen und das Sein zu ertragen."

Hegel, the Spirit will eventually reconcile the split, revealed by the understanding, between the subjective and the objective, or between what Laing would call the "disembodied" and the "embodied" self, or between what the Romantic would call the official self and the unconscious or supernatural immediate unity of soul and nature. But the *belle âme,* in Freud's terms, has recognized the split by *disavowing* it in his discourse.

Thus the *belle âme* refuses necessary alienation and becomes more or less estranged from others and from the world as a result. He becomes alienated in the sense that *aliénation mentale, Geistesgestörtheit,* and derangement are employed in the vocabulary of psychiatry. Without mentioning the *belle âme,* Laing elucidates his view of this alienation and the schizoid "loss of reality" as follows:

> The false-self system to be described here exists as a complement of the 'inner' self [of the schizoid personality] which is occupied in maintaining its identity and freedom by being transcendent, unembodied, and thus never to be grasped, pinpointed, trapped, possessed. Its aim is to be a pure subject, without any objective existence. Thus, except in certain possible safe moments the individual seeks to regard the whole of his objective existence as the expression of a false self. Of course . . . if a man is not two-dimensional, having a two-dimensional identity established by a conjunction of identity-for-others, and identity-for-oneself, if he does not exist objectively as well as subjectively, but has only a subjective identity, an identity for himself, he cannot be *real.*[81]

The "false-self system" is, of course, more complex. Laing goes on to distinguish between three types of false self: the normal *persona,* the "false-front" of the hysteric (both part of Sartrean *mauvaise foi*), and the truly schizoid false self. Unlike the others, this last is experienced as alien to the subject; moreover, it does not serve as a vehicle for gratification of the desires of the "inner" self, as a similar construct may do in neurosis (p. 96).

The *belle âme* desires the absolute recognition of his subjectivity; he refuses reciprocity with the active consciousness. But for Hegel the coalescence of the subjective and the objective, of the universal and the particular, await the *belle âme* in the world of the absolute spirit. Unlike Freud, Hegel believes that "the wounds of the spirit are cured without leaving scars" (p. 470; II, p. 197), and the dialectic moves on to a new reversal: the renunciation of the pure self, and the acceptance of the

---

[81] *The Divided Self* (Harmondsworth: Pelican Books, 1965 [1960]), pp. 94–95.

objective self (for others), in the recognition on the part of the *belle âme* of his own inner baseness and hypocrisy, which leads to his pardon in "the reciprocal recognition of the absolute spirit" (p. 471; II, p. 198). (See t.n. 110.)

Hegel had skirted the problem of reciprocal recognition at the level of the master and the slave, but now of course he is approaching the goal of the *Phenomenology*. Kojève, in his remarkable commentary on the role of death in the *Phenomenology,* has this to say about that goal (cf. t.n. 125):

> It is only in knowing himself to be irremediably mortal that the Sage can attain the plenitude of satisfaction [*Befriedigung*].
>
> . . . This last consequence of Hegelianism is psychologically less paradoxical than it may seem at first sight. Certainly, the idea of death does not augment the *well-being* of man. . . . But it is the only thing which can *satisfy his pride,* that is to say, which can provide precisely the 'satisfaction' that Hegel has in mind. For Hegelian 'satisfaction' is nothing other than the full satisfaction of the anthropogenous and human desire for Recognition (*Anerkennen*), the satisfaction of man's desire to see all other men attribute an absolute value to his *free* and *historical individuality* or to his *personality.* It is only in being and feeling himself to be mortal or finite, that is to say, feeling himself as existing in a universe without a beyond or without God, that Man can affirm and obtain the recognition of his liberty, his individuality 'unique in the world' (p. 551).

A great deal more should be said about the individual and his absolute desire than is possible here. The problem is not an ontological or even a primarily metaphysical one. In a schizoid society, it can only be fundamentally ideological. The existentialist outlook, for instance (but not, I think, Laing's modification of it), which owes so much to the rightwing Hegel, seems for all its "realism" to fall into the toils of the noble self-deceptions of the *belle âme*. Kojève is certainly not free from them, nor is the Heidegger who influenced him so much. And in spite of the obvious existential elements in Lacan's own work, his rejection of much of Sartre's viewpoint is surely the result of his experience of the noble souls on both sides of the analytical couch. Yet, considering to what extent the existential views of responsibility and commitment permanently changed our views of psychoanalysis, philosophy, and literature by emphasizing both consciously and unconsciously the problem of the *belle âme* and his relationship to oppressive social institutions, it is somewhat ironic to see how French "structuralism"—which has now replaced both phenomenology and existentialism as intellectually fashionable—is in fact a regenerated disavowal of that problem. (Until very recently, of course, influential figures in psychoanalysis and literary criticism on both sides of the Atlantic had been doing the same thing for decades.) If Lacan shows Sartre's phenomenological premises to have been largely misguided, the Sartrean problematic of freedom and responsibility, individual and community, is still there. The structural approach has brought new understanding to *les sciences de l'homme,* and especially to psychoanalysis, but its own premises preclude a certain concern for the ideological problem of finding acceptable forms for the sublimation of individual desires in a repressive civilization. Certainly the goal which both the concept of sublimation and the expectations of the analytical cure imply—the goal of reconciliation (*Versöhnung*)—cannot be defined in psychology alone or in sociology alone, or entirely inside or outside a social and political morality still structured on our sadomasochistic desire to dominate the others we have chosen for our personal or societal scapegoats.

VI

The "Schema R"

This would be an incomplete summarization of what seem to me the more important of Lacan's views and antecedents, if I were to leave out the Schema R that expands and completes the earlier Schema L (t.n. 49) and the concept of the *stade du miroir*. It is introduced as an element of Lacan's commentary on Schreber's book and Freud's reading of it; thus it seeks to take into account the question of the "paternal metaphor" in psychosis. Later in the commentary ("D'une question preliminaire à tout traitement possible de la psychose" [1959]) it is employed in a twisted form to represent Schreber's delusions and the respective relationships between the Symbolic, the Imaginary, and the Real as Lacan sees them in Schreber's text.

The diagram on page 294 is a more detailed representation of the simplified "Z" in t.n. 49.

Like all of Lacan's formulations and diagrams, and deliberately so, the Schema R is designed to be read in various ways. The key, as well as what follows, are the results of my reading of Lacan and of other readings of the schema, notably those of André Green and J.-A. Miller in *Les Cahiers pour l'Analyse,* Nos. 1–2 and No. 3 (1966)—neither of which, unfortunately, is entirely conclusive.

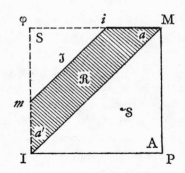

SCHÉMA R :

KEY

S   the subject

I   the Imaginary (at upper left)

R   the Real (shaded area)

S   the Symbolic (at lower right)

a   the figure of the Imaginary other of the *stade du miroir*

a′   the identification of the (child's) ego through the identification with the ideal of the ego (the paternal *imago*)

ϕ the phallus (Imaginary object)

I   the ideal of the ego

P   the position of the Name-of-the-Father in the locus of the Other

M   the signifier of the primordial object (*das Ding*—cf. Freud on negation)—the mother, who is the *real Other*.

i   the two Imaginary end-points of all later narcissistic relationships,

m   the ego (*m*) and the specular image (*i*).

*i*M   the axis of desires (object choice)

*m*I   the axis of identifications (narcissism)

SA   the *metaphorical* relationship between the subject and the Other or between the phallus (ϕ) and the Name-of-the-Father (P)—cf. Schema L.

The broken line delimits the Imaginary.

Beginning from the position of the (child) subject—identified as in classical analytical theory with the phallus—one notes the two lines of interest which link him to the ideal of the ego (I) and the signifier (M) of the real Other, the mother. The first represents the nonsexual relationship of identification with an ideal (being the other), described in

Section I; the second, the libidinal relationship of desire for the mother as an object (having the other). At the same time the primordial triangle of father-child-mother represented as I-S(ϕ)-M is given at a secondary level (m-S-i) representing all the later identifications, narcissistic relationships, and Imaginary captures in which the subject may be involved. The solid line joining i and M represents the *real* relationship between the child and the primordial object (the mother or a part of her body) at a time when the child cannot distinguish himself from "reality." This is of course in keeping both with Freud's remarks, previously referred to, in the article on the *Verneinung* as well as with Lacan's view of the Real as outside symbolization, since for the mother to symbolize "reality" she must become a signifier in the Symbolic for the subject, introjection and expulsion being neither Real nor Imaginary. On the other hand, the relationship between ego (m) and the ideal of the ego (I) is shown as a broken line; it is always Imaginary. Thus the distance between m and I and that between i and M represent the distinction the subject has achieved between the primordial relationships of being and having (I and M) and later ones; this delimits the Real for the subject. In psychosis this delimitation becomes warped or twisted. The Real and the Imaginary are represented more closely related to each other than is each to the Symbolic, Lacan's intention presumably being to assert the primacy of the Symbolic over both, since they derive their structure from it (the signifier precedes and determines the signified).

The *objectal* movement of the subject's desire toward the mother is complemented by the mother's desire. Her desire (the desire of the Other) that he *be* the phallus (the signifier of the desire of the Other) so that she may have it is met by the child's desire to conform to her desire (to be what his mother wants him to be)—in the Lacanian view the neurotic or psychotic subject has to learn that this is what he wants to be and precisely what he cannot be. The *identificatory* movement towards the ideal is a pure alienation along the lines of the *stade du miroir*, but again the subject meets a contrary law: his desire to be the father (in the father's place) complements the rivalry which his relationship to the mother also sets up. Naturally the respective lines of interest represent any number of intermediate positions, whether from the static or the historical point of view.

The Name-of-the-Father in this formulation means rather precisely what it says. P represents the Word of the father as employed by the mother—in other words, it represents the authority of the father upon which she calls in her dealings with the child. Thus is the Symbolic father the figure of the Law to which the real or Imaginary father may or may not conform. The anaclitic and primary relationship of the child to the mother is mediated by the "object *a*" (apparently complemented in the relationship to the *imago* of the father by its image in *a'*). Originally the child is involved in an identification with another springing from his identification with objects at a stage where he does not distinguish between object love and identification love; it is at this point, in Lacan's view, that the progressive splitting of demand from need and the resulting birth of desire occur. It is at this point—structurally speaking—that the mother introduces into the child's view of "reality" the fact of the lack of object upon which desire depends. This lack of object is an absence; the Imaginary other (*a*) is now only a substitute for it, since a lack cannot be "specularized" (cf. t.n. 183). Weaning, for instance, sometimes described in psychoanalysis as a primordial form of castration—inaccurately it seems, since the "castration" of the "castration complex" is not and cannot be real—is an especially significant discovery of absence for the child. With the constitution of the lack of object, need gives rise to demand and desire.

In 1966 Lacan added a note to the Schreber article explaining that the Schema R is to be read in three dimensions (*Ecrits*, pp. 553–54), the shaded area representing the projection into two dimensions of a Moebius strip. In a supplement to the second edition of the *Ecrits*, published separately in *Les Cahiers de l'Analyse* Nos. 1–2, J.-A. Miller adds the remark:

The surface *R* is to be taken as the flattening out of the figure obtained by joining *i* to I and *m* to M, that is, by the twisting which characterizes . . . the Moebius strip. The presentation of the schema in two dimensions is thus to be related to the cut which enables the strip to be laid out flat. It will be realized that the line IM cannot refer to the relationship of the subject to the object of desire: the subject is only the cutting of the strip, and what falls out of it is called 'the object *a*.' This verifies and completes the formula of Jean-Claude Milner on [Lacan's] '$\$ \Diamond a$' [the diamond standing for a relationship like that of the Z-shaped diagram in t.n. 49]: 'the terms are heterogenous, whereas there is homogeneity attached to the places' (*Cahiers pour l'Analyse*, No. 3, p. 96). That in fact is the power of the symbol (pp. 175–76).

Miller's remarks on the Schema R *in toto* are as follows:

This construction requires a double reading:
1) It can be read as a representation of the subject's static states. Thus one distinguishes the following: (*a*) the triangle *I* resting on the dual relationship of the *Moi* to the Other (narcissism, projection, captation), with the phallus (φ), the Imaginary object, "with which the subject identifies himself . . . along with his living-being [*avec son être du vivant*]" (*Ecrits,* p. 552), that is to say, how the subject represents himself to himself; (*b*) the field *S*, with the three functions: the Ideal of the Ego I, where the subject takes his bearings in the register of the Symbolic . . . , the signifier of the object M, and the Name-of-the-Father P in the locus of the Other A. One could regard the line IM as doubling the relationship of the subject to the object of desire by the mediation of the signifying chain, a relationship which Lacan later writes as $ ◇ *a* (but the line immediately reveals its inadequacies); (*c*) the field *R* framed and maintained by the Imaginary relation and the Symbolic relationship.
2) But it is also the history of the subject which is noted here. On the segment *i*M are placed the figures of the Imaginary other, which culminate in the figure (or face) of the mother, the real Other, the primary exteriority of the subject, which in Freud is called *das Ding* (cf. *Ecrits,* p. 656). On the segment *m*I succeed the Imaginary identifications the *Moi* of the child until he receives his status in the Real from the symbolic identification. Thus one finds a specified synchrony of the triangle *S*: the child at I is linked to the mother at M, as desire of her desire; in third position one finds the Father borne along by the vehicle of the mother's Word (p. 75).

To this summary should be added the transformation of the schema to represent Schreber's delusion, but the details upon which it is based are too complicated to be included here. It can simply be said that the foreclusion of the Name-of-the-Father at A (lower right) engenders problems related to the phallus to which it is linked metaphorically at S (upper left) : Schreber's desire to become a woman, his fear of being "unmanned," his desire to be the bride of God, and so forth. The interested reader should refer to the *Ecrits,* to Freud, and to Schreber's fascinating book if he wishes to make his own judgment about the adequacy of the demonstration. The further developments of Lacan's diagrammatic representations can be found in some detail in the published seminars and in the recent article: "Subversion du sujet et dialectique du désir" (1966).

Given his probable distance from the *Ecrits,* the reader may find the foregoing rather less than illuminating. However, he can certainly see the dangers inherent in Lacan's analogies: in the absence of concrete studies or case histories, they may lend themselves to ever more refined abstraction while the empirical evidence upon which they are based remains uncritically accepted. Nevertheless, the exigencies of hypothesis are such that the building of a theory often depends upon the privileged value conferred upon particular and perhaps seemingly insignificant evidence. Certain metaphysical decisions, recognized or unrecognized, are always at the basis of hypotheses; their task is to serve the creative function of myths. Thus the *Fort! Da!* has for Lacan the value of a myth. At the same time, since the structural approach is originally dependent upon analogies (which may not be analogies) and upon a theory of reflection (which may not be a theory of reflection), it will naturally bring together any fields or disciplines which seem to reveal similar *structures*—in the first place linguistics and anthropology, with Lévi-Strauss, and now mathematical logic and psychoanalysis, with Lacan. It is this very search for similar structures which is the strong point of the structural approach for its supporters and the weak point for its detractors.

Conclusion

It was with some misgiving that I finally decided to include the preceding section on the Schema R. In the first place, as the reader will no doubt have gathered, I am not entirely convinced of the precise relevance of the mathematical analogies employed by Lacan, mainly because of the inconclusive way in which they are presented. Secondly, the reader will surely have noted as well as I that the algebraic symbols employed are not simply multivalent—which would be perfectly acceptable, given the requirements of the representation—but that they seem to be employed without explanation in contrasting ways, at times within the same context. It is perfectly possible that I have misunderstood Lacan; on basic questions it is difficult not to. However, it was important to include the schema for the sake of supplementing the consideration of identification and narcissism with which this essay began.

This essay is necessarily incomplete, since on the one hand it is restricted by my own interests and understanding and since, on the other, Lacan is still writing and teaching; at least a decade of seminars remains unpublished. Moreover, as the reader who tackles the original text will discover, there is really no substitute for reading Lacan himself —provided the reader is interested enough to put the necessary time and

energy into it. What seems to me especially significant about that text is
not so much the "system" as the remarkable number of genuine and
original insights encompassing, renewing, and bringing into relation a
large number of the facets of contemporary thought, from phenomenology
through existentialism to "structuralism." On the other hand, there is
not the personal commitment and engaging honesty of the early Sartre
or the laborious logical progress of the Heidegger of *Sein und Zeit,* nor
is there the sweeping vision of Hegel or the ambiguous caution of
Freud. Readers with a distaste for Heidegger's fragmentation of the
German language or for Sartre's less than rigid logic, his repetitious
style, or his emotional *engagement* are likely to turn purple when confronted by Lacan. Ideologically speaking, Lacan's theories rest upon a
bourgeois psychology which is only one of the many faces of the
middle-class psychologies he attacks. At the moment it remains a
psychology for intellectuals, not for people. All there is, in fact, is a
revolution in psychoanalytical thought whose repercussions in other areas
cannot as yet be properly estimated—and a curious phenomenon called
Jacques Lacan.

In my attempt to introduce the English-speaking reader to Lacan and
to the intellectual context in which he formulated his views, there have
been many aspects that lack of space has prevented me from considering
in detail. I should have liked to deal at some length with the early
Sartre, for instance, whose somewhat misdirected critique of Politzer's
Freud did not prevent him from developing a brilliant analysis of
mauvaise foi (a synthesis of role-playing, the false self, *Verneinung,* and
Verleugnung). Moreover, Sartre's theory of the existential project, derived from Heidegger, demands analysis in the light of the concept of
deferred action in Freud, since for Freud the intentionalization (cathexis)
of a past memory projects the subject into a future different from that
which was possible while the comprehension or signification remained
deferred. As Marcuse has said in different terms, without the concept of
repression, man's past must be viewed as static (*en soi*); with repression,
the past becomes a dynamic projection of future possibilities (*pour soi*).
Perhaps it is even true that the old comparison between psychotics and
"primitive" man (or children), vigorously and convincingly combatted
by Lévi-Strauss, is partially connected with the thwarting of repression in
psychosis, resulting in a sort of synchronic fixation of structures in the
psychotic's life.

The reader will have noted to what extent Lacan was writing against the existential Sartre in the 1950's. In effect, Lacan was seeking to answer the questions which existentialism had posed. Sartre's concern for our recognition of our *mauvaise foi,* and his attempt to deal with it in terms of consciousness alone, is surely one of the questions implicit in Lacan's promotion in 1954 of the Freudian concept of the discursive *Verneinung.* Certainly Sartre's "existential psychoanalysis" was essentially but unwittingly derivative. However, it depended ultimately on the almost total intellectual rejection of Freud—partly for ideological reasons of responsibility resulting from the existentialist discovery of "total evil" during the Nazi occupation and partly because of the sheer incompetence of the French analytical movement—by the French against whom Sartre was writing. Nevertheless, Sartre paid the Freud he knew the compliment of seeking seriously to refute him, and in the process he regenerated the questions which Freud left his Einstein to solve. Freud has certainly not yet met his Einstein, but it is interesting to note the existence of a specific question in Sartre—apart from the question of his early distinction between the *je* (the later *pour soi*) and the *moi* (the later *en soi* of the "Wesen ist was gewesen ist") on the basis of a Husserlian intentionality of consciousness (consciousness is always consciousness of . . . .) and a prereflexive *cogito*—that is to say, the presence in his work of the question of the relationship of repression to the symptom, in almost precisely the terms which Lacan employs to give his own answer to it: "If the complex really is unconscious, that is, if the sign is separated from the signified by a barring [*barrage*], how would it be possible for the subject to *recognize* it?" [82]

In another sense, Lacan's work is also the beginnings of an answer as to why the problem of language is hardly treated at all by Sartre in his early work. Except for a page or so in *L'Etre et le Néant,* where he simply notes that language is intersubjective and a manifestation of the master-slave dialectic, before moving on to assimilate the Heideggerean notion of "I am what I say" to his own notion of human behavior: "I am what I do" (*ibid.,* p. 440), the early Sartre seems to subordinate language entirely to questions of consciousness. Moreover, Lacan's refusal of the primal *cogito* is surely related to the fact that Sartre and Merleau-Ponty between them so radicalized the notion as to destroy its psychological premises.

[82] *L'Etre et le Néant* (Paris: Gallimard, 1943), p. 661.

In a sense the omission of any detailed remarks on the positive and negative influence of Sartre on Lacan is just as well at the present time, since the journalistic furor in Paris which followed publication of Lacan's *Ecrits* in 1966 resulted in the creation of a tendentious opposition between Sartre and Lacan. This in itself was a derivative of the debate over "structuralism," history, and dialectical and analytical reason between the Sartre of the *Critique de la raison dialectique* (1960) and the Lévi-Strauss of *La Pensée Sauvage* (1962) (which is dedicated to Merleau-Ponty), and their respective cohorts.

It seems wiser to wait until the shouting has died down if we wish to put this debate into any sort of perspective. Nevertheless, it is worthwhile remarking that Lévi-Strauss has recently withdrawn from his previous invasion of other domains in the human sciences, and certain of Lacan's minor revisions to the *Discours* in 1966 consisted of toning down over-enthusiastic judgments about structural anthropology in 1953 and 1956.

Let me indicate briefly an example of the present direction of non-psychoanalytical studies of Freud in France and their detachment from the phonological notion of binary opposition which is so evident in Lacan.

In a recent article on the numerous metaphors employed by Freud to represent the mind, Jacques Derrida, manifestly influenced both positively and negatively by Lacan, seeks to interpret them in relation to the partial solution of the problem of memory offered by the metaphor of the "magic writing pad" (t.n. 108): the endlessly erasable children's plaything in which the original script is always retained in its pristine newness by the underlying wax, while new "perceptions" are constantly inscribed upon it. Dreams and memory for Freud, as we know, are a succession of comparisons with pictograms, hieroglyphs (*Bilderschriften*), the palimpsest, the double inscription (*Niederschrift*), *Wortvorstellungen,* the rebus, sentences and paragraphs blacked out by the censorship in Russian newspapers, and so forth. While dealing with many of the more strictly mechanistic and spatial metaphors employed by Freud (archeology, the telescope, the microscope, the camera, the various "systems" in the mind, the different *topoi,* and so forth), Derrida seeks to emphasize the metaphor of *writing* in Freud, noting the implication of a postscript, or supplement, in the concept of *Nachträglichkeit.* Of course there are considerable difficulties here, since writing is the most highly developed form of the discourse while memory seems to be the unarticulated and undifferentiated *absence* which we intentionalize. For the observer, memory is what is absent from the here and now and thus what has to be inferred; for the subject, it is the nature of memory's passage from absence to a particular kind of presence—the way in which the subject *reads* it—which governs his future possibilities.

Whatever the relationship between the neurological metaphors and the psychological metaphors with which neurology and psychology seek to formalize the structure and behavior of the mind, it is clear that there are repeating neurological circuits in the brain which can be considered structurally similar to the memory circuits of cybernetics. And as Derrida points out, this structural similarity is prefigured in the concept of the *facilitation* (*Bahnung: frayage*) of the "traces of reality" (*die Spuren der Realität*) in the neurological model built up by Freud in the *Project* of 1895. (When one discovers—*nachträglich*—in that extraordinary document the notion of feedback, as well as so many other conceptions essential to modern psychology and to the later Freud, one begins fully to understand the nature of *reading,* and especially the nature of reading Freud.) Derrida sees the metaphorical dimension of the *trace* as that which unites Freud's earliest discussion of memory to the metaphor of writing in the last model he employed, the "magic writing pad." *L'écriture* is, however, a rather special notion for Derrida, an aspect of his work which I shall not introduce here.

The import of Derrida's tentative analysis is indicated well enough by his own preliminary questions: "What is a text? And what must the psychic be for it to be represented by a text?" [83] For Derrida, insofar as the temporality of a text is historical and not linear (as unrecorded speech is essentially, but not constitutively, linear), that is to say, insofar as a text can be read backwards, comprehended at a glance, written up and down, or from right to left, or permanently modified after it has been written (like a dream),[84] it calls for a method of interpretation allied to the interpretation of the discourse rather than to the interpreta-

[83] "Freud et la scène de l'écriture," *Tel Quel,* No. 26 (Summer, 1966), p. 12. The text is part of a lecture given at Dr. André Green's seminar at the *Institut de Psychanalyse.* Derrida's position is partly indicated by his opening words: "If the Freudian break-through is historically original, it does not derive its originality from a pacific coexistence or a theoretical complicity with [a certain type of] linguistics, at least in its congenital phonologism" (p. 11).
[84] Thus Corneille does more than repeat the old dream-books when he says: "C'est en contraire sens qu'un songe s'interprète." *Horace,* I, iii (l. 223).

tion of speech—in other words, an interpretation bound by the laws of writing rather than by the laws of linguistics. If the distinction sometimes seems rather too nice, it is surely motivated by the necessity of escaping the dilemmas of formalistic binary oppositions as well as by the fact that literature, history, and philosophy are discursive and not linguistic forms.

In the domain of anthropologically oriented psychoanalysis, Marie-Cécile and Edmond Ortigues have made a significant contribution to the metapsychology of the Oedipus complex in a recent book *Oedipe Africain* (1966). Their work is the result of psychoanalytical therapy among the Africans of Senegal in a situation where the combined influence of colonialism, urban living, and a loosely structured native society have created family relationships so diverse that a mother may not remember how many children she has had and a father may not see his son for years at a time. "Father" and "mother" for the native child may have no biological significance, and "brother" or "uncle" includes people we would hardly consider relatives at all, situations common enough outside Western society.

The significance of the Ortigues' work lies in their use of Lévi-Straussian and Lacanian theses to confront the problem of employing the Western "civilized" notion of the Oedipus complex in this sort of society. Their point is that once the complex is viewed as Lacan views it —in other words, as a structure of intersecting relationships where the *loci* are "empty places"—it is indeed possible to speak of an Oedipal structure in Senegalese society. What is of especial interest is their theoretical justification, derived from Lacan, for the necessity of the "fourth term" in the Oedipus complex, the term which mediates (and thus grounds) the dual relationships between its three self-evident positions (father, mother, child). Just as Lévi-Strauss had pointed out that the transformation of the biological family into a societal unit in "primitive" societies is absolutely dependent upon the fourth term—the maternal uncle who *gives* his sister to the father (his brother-in-law) and thus provides for the exchange of women outside the family—the Ortigues note that the transformation from "nature" to "culture" in psychological terms similarly depends upon a fourth term, the image of the phallus, which founds, structures, and mediates the relationships of the biological family and converts it into a *human* family:

The fourth term which originally founds the relationship between the child, the mother, and the father is symbolically situated at the intersection of the body image and the words [*paroles*] which name and recognize. This is what psychoanalysis designates as the specific function of the phallus. What is mythically designated in this way is only designated by its place— between the image and the name, between the lost object and the promised object, at the frontier of the unnameable. This place is empty . . . but [it] is marked by its function . . . (p. 72).

Since the phallus "signifies the lack of object," it reveals the "irreducible necessity" of an intermediary between persons in any relationship.

Moreover, the "empty" fourth terms in both cases—the maternal uncle or the phallus—are interconnected: in the "sister." The incest prohibition is both positive ("give your sister") and negative ("do not desire your mother, your sister"); in the first case it regulates marriage ties (*alliance*); in the second it regulates kinship (*parenté*).

Therefore, when the incest prohibition names the 'sister,' it is not in order to designate a term which is already totally constituted as an 'object' but rather in order to signify the smallest difference at which it becomes forbidden 'legitimately' to transform 'virgin' into 'wife,' 'nature' into 'culture,' 'savage heart' into 'mistress of the house'. . . . And does the maternal uncle not similarly represent the *minimum* difference without which it would be impossible for a family to constitute 'marriage ties'? Here, as in linguistics the value of each term is always a difference (pp. 81–82).

Just as the maternal uncle mediates the marriage tie between his brother-in-law (to whom he is related by that tie) and his brother-in-law's wife (for whom he is a blood relative) in the same generation—that is to say, horizontally—the phallus mediates the "horizontal" relationship between man and wife in the same generation. And just as the maternal uncle is the mediator between parent and child in succeeding generations related by the marriage tie, so the phallus mediates that "vertical" relationship between generations related by blood. The "horizontal" debtor-creditor relationship is real, whereas the "vertical" relationship is what Lacan calls the "symbolic debt"—the exchange between father and son, where the child who *is* the phallus for his mother comes through the Oedipus complex to *have* the phallus for another woman.

Although the Ortigues' use of these Lacanian formulations still leaves many fundamental questions unanswered, their refutation of the concept of the Oedipal structure as a simple series of "attitudes" between real persons, and their replacement of this notion by that of more or

less unchanging relationships between *loci* leads to a persuasive development of the Freudian and Lacanian view of the "dead father," something
especially important in societies like the Senegalese, in which the
relationship of the present generation to its ancestors is consciously and
carefully formulated.

If one wished to archeologize the Oedipus complex, it could be said that
in the tribal society it is the collectivity which assumes the responsibility for
the death of the father [and not the son]. In the first place, traditional
Senegalese society states that the place of each person in the community is
marked by reference to an ancestor, the father of the lineage. The society
states that death has made the father of the lineage equivalent to the pure
authority of a name, equivalent to the law of speech [*parole*] which fixes
each in his place: the ancestor is the guarantor of custom and of the communal
law. The reference to the names of ancestors is the geometric locus of all the
occupiable places in the society; it defines the right of entry into each
lineage. The sire of Ego has not had to take the place of the former legislator,
since this place must remain empty. . . .
Senegalese society neutralizes as it were the diachronic series of generations
by establishing the law of the fathers. In fact the phantasies of the death of
young Oedipus are turned towards his collaterals: brothers or relations by
marriage. Instead of being displayed vertically or diachronically as a conflict
between successive generations, aggressivity tends to unfold in horizontal lines
within the limits of the same generation. . . . The solution [to the problems
of the Oedipus complex] consists in one's being integrated into an age
group which is supposed to be the immutable repetition of all the others
preceding it. For Ego a drama is repeated which has always taken place before, which has been lived by the preceding generation . . . and which long
before was already as if it were there as a destiny which is inherited at the
same time as the spirits of his ancestors.

Thus the Ortigues conclude that although there is indeed an "Oedipe
africain," the "anteriorization" and "mythologization" of the Oedipus
complex by this society renders the complex inaccessible as a clinical
entity. One might conclude that it is there, but that the society itself has
already employed it as an a priori myth in the same way that the clinical
entity is employed a posteriori in an essentially mythical way by the psychoanalyst in order to help the subject answer the question of who or
what he is. Correctly employed, the myth of the Oedipus complex in its
widest sense will tell the subject why his anxiety or his guilt is ultimately
dependent upon an ontological question which has to be reformulated
not in the terms of *who* he is, but rather in the terms of *where* he is.
To employ Heideggerean language, the "who" of Dasein is the un-

answerable question, whereas the "where" of Dasein is revealed in almost every word he speaks: the "who" of Dasein is the shifter "I," which is a locus and not a person.

Several additional points should be made. First, Lacan's pronouncements are obviously much more detailed than it has been possible to indicate here; further, I have ignored many of his mathematical formalizations, either because I cannot test their validity or because they are not presented very clearly; thirdly, I have said very little about the more recent aspects of his work. It should be emphasized also that my references to Hegel, Heidegger, Lévi-Strauss, and other thinkers are made with the double intent of what I would call text and context. There are textual similarities, direct references, and formulations derived or modified from many sources in Lacan; at the same time there is a context of contemporary thought centered around language and linguistics, with repercussions on anthropology, psychoanalysis, literary criticism, and philosophy. If Michel Foucault places ethnology and psychoanalysis in the van of contemporary thought, pervading all the other human sciences with their methods and their axioms, it is because of what Lacan and Lévi-Strauss have accomplished.

But Lacan is not a Heideggerean or a Hegelian or a structural linguist —he is a Freudian psychoanalyst. However much he may borrow from other disciplines and other thinkers, there is always an essential distinction to be made: that philosophy, or literature, or psychology are not "forms" of psychoanalysis, since there is only one form of psychoanalysis —and it rests squarely and firmly upon the base Freud built for it. To whatever extent Freud's specific formulations may be changed or modified, there is nothing in Lacan which is not ultimately viewed from the privileged status accorded to Freudian theory in the Lacanian corpus. For example, although the similarities between Hegel's *Phenomenology,* the *Bildungsroman,* and psychoanalysis are fertile and interesting, the Hegelian subject is not and cannot be the equivalent of the Freudian subject. The reader will have noted in the *Discours* that while Lacan *uses* the Hegelian notion of labor as what frees the slave from the master-slave dialectic, he does not *accept* it as a valid premise for the analytical dialectic. The obsessional neurotic, for instance, knows better than anybody else how to use his "labor" (his "working through") to maintain himself in the position of slavery he has chosen. Similarly Lacan refers to the concept of the "cunning of reason" in Hegel's philosophy of history (t.n. 131), but he notes the difference between the "mirror-game" of the *Phenomenology* and the working through of an analysis:

The promotion of consciousness as essential to the subject in the historical sequel of the Cartesian *cogito* is for me the deceptive accentuation of the transparence of the *Je* in action at the expense of the opacity of the signifier which determines the *Je*. Through Hegel's own rigorous demonstration, the *glissement* by which the *Bewusstsein* serves to cover over the confusion of the *Selbst* eventually reveals the reason for his error in the *Phenomenology of the Spirit*.

The very movement which offsets the phenomenon of the spirit towards the Imaginary relationship to the other . . . reveals its effect: that is to say, the aggressivity which becomes the beam [*fléau*] of the balance on which will become centered the decomposition of the equilibrium of counterpart to counterpart in the Master-Slave relationship, a relationship which is pregnant with all the tricks [*ruses*] through which reason sets its impersonal realm in motion. [. . .]

The struggle which sets [this inaugural servitude] going is wisely called a struggle of pure prestige, and the stake, life itself, corresponds nicely to the danger of the premature birth generic [to our species], which Hegel knew nothing of, and which I have put at the origin of the dynamics of the specular capture ("Subversion du sujet," *Ecrits*, pp. 809–10).

Lacan goes on to point out that since the whole dialectic of the master-slave relationship depends upon the slave's refusal of gratification (*jouissance*) (because of his fear of death) and his consequent acceptance of slavery, what is forgotten is that "the [final] pact is in every case preliminary to the violence" of the so-called struggle to the death, and that it is this tacit agreement which perpetuates the dialectic. Thus the slave can never escape his alienation, and the notion of the "cunning of reason," which supposedly informs the labor through which the slave will attain mastery, is an error.

Lacan is speaking at both the psychological and the political level, for he is attempting to show the impossibility of the final reconciliation of the *Phenomenology,* whether it is viewed at the individual or at the societal level. Given the Freudian notion of the discovery of difference and the "lost object," reconciliation (return to "One") is psychologically impossible either for the individual in relation to himself or in relation to the group to which he is linked both by identificatory ties and by the interaggressivity of the master-slave relationship itself. The subject-object relationship of the Imaginary order precludes anything but a phantasmatic "return to unity"; the goal of the *Phenomenology* is illusory.

This goal is absolute Knowledge (*Wissen*), and it is precisely in their relationship to Knowledge that the Freudian and the Hegelian subject differ. For Hegel, one can say that Truth is immanent in the progress of the dialectic towards Knowledge; for Freud, however, Truth is the unanswerable question of the "Who (or what) am I?" This desire to know, in the Freudian view, is fundamentally sexual:

. . . In Hegel it is desire (*Begierde*) which carries the charge of that minimum of liaison to 'antique' knowledge [*connaissance*] which the subject must retain in order for Truth to be immanent to the realization of Knowledge. Hegel's 'cunning of reason' [cf. t.n. 131] means that from the beginning and to the very end, the subject knows what he wants.

It is here that Freud reopens the splice between Truth and Knowledge to the mobility out of which revolutions come—and in this respect: that at this point desire is knit with the desire of the Other, but that in this knot lies the desire to know ("Subversion du sujet," *Ecrits,* p. 802).

In other words, for the Freudian subject, the distinction between Truth and Knowledge results from the question of recognizing the result of the lifting of the veil of Maia (t.n. 107).

In respect of Lévi-Strauss, nothing has been said about the later development of his views, notably his realization that a kinship system is not on an unconscious level equivalent to that of the phoneme, since many natives are able to analyze it in its own terms, and his later statements that the distinction of nature from culture should be considered only a methodological distinction. Moreover, he has also attempted to distinguish his structuralism from the formalism it more obviously resembled in his early works: ". . . In opposition to formalism, structuralism refuses to oppose the concrete to the abstract and to confer on the second a privileged value. *Form* is defined by opposition to a matter which is alien to it. But structure has no distinct content: it is the content itself, apprehended in a logical organization which is conceived as a property of the real." [85] Lévi-Strauss's strong tendencies to confer a privilege of purity on the natural sciences thus set him in a certain opposition to Lacan, although their mathematical propensities are somewhat similar.

What seems now a particularly fruitful future enterprise is to seek to read Lacan (in part) in the terms of Anglo-Saxon communicationally

[85] "La Structure et la forme," *Cahiers de l'institut de science économique appliquée,* No. 99 (March, 1960), pp. 3–36.

oriented psychotherapy and at the same time to see how many of Lacan's theses extend and amplify the theoretical work of people like R. D. Laing and Gregory Bateson in England and in the United States. The phenomenological and existential basis of many of these theorists, coupled with their interest in schizophrenia as a disease of communication, has led them to employ models derived from cybernetics and general systems theory to explain communicational contexts in the terms of *loci* and relationships. The notion of *feedback* (essentially what lies behind the notions of dialectic and transference), the "black box" concept of the subject (viewed as a locus of input and output), and Carnap's theory of object language and metalanguage provide an independent clarification of much of what Lacan is saying in his own terms. From their stated basis that all behavior is communication, the communications theorists may be readily interpreted in the light of the Lacanian categories of the signifier, and the Symbolic, the Imaginary, and the Real. Moreover, the notion of metalanguage and its logical consequence—that *the symptom is a statement in a metalanguage about an object language*—provides a solution to some of the problems of "reflection" which have cropped up in my own attempt to analyze the Lacanian standpoint. From this point of view, one can define the Other simply as the rest of the system in which the subject is involved, and the analysis will tend to concentrate on the relationship between a whole series of levels of communication (including the level of the phantasy) rather than upon any one level or any one element. What is of even greater nicety is that the notion of levels of communication (logical types) avoids the problems of reductionism, since it is clear that every level of statement has its own validity and cannot be reduced to any other level (in whatever way it may be related to it)—for the relationship, in Lacan's terms, is *metaphorical*. The further point might perhaps be made that insofar as Carnap's theory of metalanguage and Russell's theory of types presuppose, like all theories of logic, an *ideal speaker*—what for Chomsky would be the "fluent speaker" against whom the linguist measures grammar and syntax—it could be said that in the widest sense of Lacan's view of the Other as "the locus of the message," or "the locus of the Word," this ideal speaker is in fact Lacan's Other. In brief, it is clear that in spite of the differences in method and in point of departure, there is a significant convergence in context between these Anglo-Saxon writers and Lacan, especially in the use of models derived from outside psychology proper as well as in what is essentially a phenomenological approach—but an approach based on a phenomenology of language rather than on the phenomenology of consciousness as it was developed by the early Husserl and his followers.[86]

This book has been worked on and written like a mosaic of many layers, reflecting to a certain extent Lacan's own *modus operandi*. I can only express my hope that the pattern of the book does not prevent the reader from coming to terms with it. I must nevertheless ask his indulgence with the evolution of my own understanding as it is represented here—I don't know now whether the book could have been written in any other way. The reader will have noted now and then my reservations about Lacan's expression of his views and his approach to his public. Difficult as it may be, however—for I cannot think of a more irritating author—we must give Lacan his due. In spite of all the reservations one might make, there is no discounting the unique value and wide influence of Lacan's work in France. By the mere fact of going back to the German text and reading it seriously in a contemporary framework, he converted the limited, medical, and positivist approach of French analysts into something with repercussions in all the spheres of *les sciences de l'homme*. It seems banal to say it now, but Lacan introduced us to another Freud, and a whole new generation of analysts and psychiatrists bear his imprint. Apart from the obvious ramifications of the concept of the *stade du miroir* and the importance of his rebuttal of the notion of the "autonomous ego" (a Trojan horse, says Lacan), he has introduced us to the less than obvious fact that psychoanalysis is a theory of language. Not that Freud had not been read seriously and carefully before, but I doubt whether any other commentator has been as daring and as innovating as Lacan. Lacan's work has surely resulted in the final demise of the *cogito* that Husserl, Merleau-Ponty, and Sartre once struggled with, besides giving us the wherewithal to brush away the last vestiges of the atomistic, linear, and essentially solipsistic psychology inherited by the modern world, and to replace it by analyses of relationships, dialectical

[86] Unfortunately, I became fully aware of the wide development of communicationally-oriented therapy only after this book was already in the press; consequently, I have not been able to employ its insights to clarify and exemplify those portions of the preceding analysis where they would have been especially helpful both to myself and to the reader. I can only refer the reader to a recent book which provides an admirably lucid account of what a number of leading psychologists have derived from communications theory and related sources, notably since the late fifties: Paul Watzlawick, Janet Beavin, and Don Jackson, *The Pragmatics of Human Communication* (New York: W. W. Norton, 1967).

opposition, and communication. At the time of writing, Lacan's weekly seminar at the Ecole Normale is still strictly standing room only. My personal debt to Lacan remains very great—let me employ the words of Louis Althusser, the neo-Marxist philosopher, to acknowledge it:

It is to the intransigent, lucid, and for many years solitary, theoretical efforts of Jacques Lacan that we owe today the result which has drastically modified our *reading* of Freud. At a time when what Lacan has given us which is radically new is beginning to pass into the public domain, where anyone may make use of and draw advantage from it in his own way, I must insist on recognizing our debt to an exemplary lesson in reading, which in some of its effects, as will be seen, goes far beyond its original object.[87]

And when all is said and done, even if the curious mixture of penetration, poetry, and wilful obscurity in the *Ecrits* seems designed to force the reader into a perpetual struggle of his own with the text, perhaps there is a method even in that madness. Lacan has always told his readers that they must "y mettre du sien," and as Hanns Sachs once said: "An analysis terminates only when the patient realizes it could go on for ever."

[87] *Lire Le Capital* (Paris: F. Maspero, 1965), I, 15.

Bibliography

Section A contains the works of Lacan and the *compte-rendus* of his seminars by J.-B. Pontalis; Section B, those items in which he collaborated with others; Section C, items dealing with Lacan and items by authors employing or commenting on Lacanian themes. Section D includes a brief list of items of relevance to the *Discours de Rome* as well as works referred to by the translator. An attempt has been made to provide as complete a bibliography of Lacan as possible, including items not published in a regular format or otherwise unobtainable, and including items of primarily therapeutic or psychiatric interest. However, a number of items previous to 1930 have been left out, and it should be noted that the bulk of Lacan's seminars during sixteen years of commentary on Freud have never been published.

Items preceded by an asterisk will be found in: Jacques Lacan, *Ecrits* (Paris: Editions du Seuil, 1966). This collection includes a series of "introductions" bridging the gaps between the various texts (which are carefully arranged in nonchronological order); some of the texts reprinted in it are slightly modified from their original form or include explanatory notes added in 1966. Four of the articles had not been previously published.

SECTION A

LACAN, Jacques
   "Structure des psychoses paranoïaques," *Semaine des Hôpitaux* (July, 1931), pp. 437–45.
   De la psychose paranoïaque dans ses rapports avec la personnalité,

313

Paris: Le François, 1932. (Thèse pour le doctorat en médecine, Diplôme d'état.)

Review of: E. Minkowski, *Le Temps vécu: Etudes phénoménologiques et psychopathologiques,* in: *Recherches Philosophiques,* V (1935–36), 424–31.

Review of: Henri Ey, *Hallucinations et délire,* Paris, 1935, in: *L'Evolution Psychiatrique* (1935), No. 1, pp. 87–91.

* "Au delà du 'Principe de réalité,'" *L'Evolution Psychiatrique* (1936), No. 3, pp. 67–86.

"La Famille," *Encyclopédie Française* (ed. A. de Monzie), Vol. VIII, 1938. (The title of this volume is "La vie mentale de l'enfance à la vieillesse.")

Résumé by the author of his "De l'impulsion au complexe," *Revue Française de Psychanalyse,* XI (1939), 137–39. (Session of October 25, 1938.)

* "Le Temps logique et l'assertion de certitude anticipée: un nouveau sophisme," *Cahiers d'Art* (1945), pp. 32–42.

* "Propos sur la causalité psychique," *L'Evolution Psychiatrique* (1947), No. 1, pp. 123–65. Reprinted in: *Le Problème de la psychogenèse des névroses et des psychoses* (ed. Henri Ey). Paris: Desclée de Brouwer, 1950, pp. 23–54. (Paper delivered at Bonneval, September 28, 1946).

"La Psychiatrie anglaise et la guerre," *L'Evolution Psychiatrique* (1947), pp. 293–312.

* "L'Agressivité en psychanalyse," *Revue Française de Psychanalyse,* XII (1948), 367–88. (Delivered at the 11th Congrès des psychanalystes de langue française, Brussels, May, 1948.)

* "Le Stade du miroir comme formateur de la fonction du Je, telle qu'elle nous est révélée dans l'expérience psychanalytique," *Revue Française de Psychanalyse,* XIII (1949), 449–55. (Delivered at the 16th International Congress of Psychoanalysts, Zürich, July 17, 1949. The original paper on the *stade du miroir* was delivered at the Marienbad Congress, June 16, 1936, but never published in its original form.)

* "Intervention sur le transfert." *Revue Française de Psychanalyse,* XVI, Nos. 1–2 (1952), 154–63. (Intervention at the Congrès des psychanalystes de langue romane, 1951.)

"Some Reflections on the Ego," *International Journal of Psycho-Analysis,* XXXIV (1953), 11–17. (Address to the British Psychoanalytical Society, May 2, 1951.)

"Le Symbolique, l'Imaginaire et le Réel," Conférence à la Société française de psychanalyse, July, 1953. (Unpublished.)

"Le Mythe individuel du névrosé ou 'Poésie et vérité' dans la névrose." Centre de la documentation universitaire, Paris, 1953. (Mimeographed.)

* "Variantes de la Cure-type," in *Encyclopédie Médico-Chirurgicale* (ed. Henri Ey), *Psychiatrie,* Vol. III (1955).

* "Fonction et champ de la parole et du langage en psychanalyse (Rapport de Rome)," *La Psychanalyse,* I (1956), 81–166. (September 26–27, 1953. Here called the *Discours de Rome.*)

"Discours de Jacques Lacan (26 septembre, 1953)," *Actes du Congrès de Rome, La Psychanalyse,* I (1956), 202–55. (This is the address and discussion which followed delivery of printed copies of the Rapport. All quotations from this source are from Lacan's remarks.)

* "Introduction au commentaire de Jean Hyppolite sur la *Verneinung,*" *La Psychanalyse,* I (1956), 17–28. (Seminar of February 10, 1954.)

* "Réponse au commentaire de Jean Hyppolite sur la *Verneinung* de Freud," *La Psychanalyse,* I (1956), 41–58. (Seminar of February 10, 1954.)

* "Le Séminaire sur *La Lettre volée,*" *La Psychanalyse,* II (1956), 1–44. (Given April 26, 1955.)

* "La Chose freudienne ou Sens du retour à Freud en psychanalyse," *L'Evolution Psychiatrique* (1956), pp. 225–52. (Amplification of a lecture at the Neuro-psychiatric Clinic of Vienna, November 7, 1955.)

* "Situation de la psychanalyse et formation du psychanalyste en 1956," *Etudes Philosophiques* (1956), No. 4, pp. 567–84.

* "La Psychanalyse et son enseignement," *Bulletin de la Société Française de Philosophie,* II, No. 2 (1957), 65–101. (Session of February 23, 1957.)

* "L'Instance de la lettre dans l'inconscient ou La Raison depuis Freud," *La Psychanalyse,* III (1957), 47–81. (May 14–26, 1957.) [English translation by Jan Miel, *Yale French Studies,* No. 36–37 (October, 1966), pp. 112–47.]

* "D'une question préliminaire à tout traitement possible de la psychose," *La Psychanalyse,* IV (1958), 1–50. (December, 1957–January, 1958. This article summarizes the work of the first two terms of the seminar of 1955–56.)

* "Jeunesse de Gide ou la lettre et le désir," *Critique,* No. 131 (April, 1958), pp. 291–315.

* "A la mémoire d'Ernest Jones: Sur sa théorie du symbolisme," *La*

Psychanalyse, V (1959), 1–20. (January–March, 1959).

* "La Direction de la cure et les principes de son pouvoir," *La Psychanalyse,* VI (1961), 149–206. (Report delivered at the *Colloque international de psychanalyse,* Royaumont, July, 1958.)

* "Remarque sur le rapport de Daniel Lagache," *La Psychanalyse,* VI (1961), 111–47. (Easter, 1960.)

"Maurice Merleau-Ponty," *Les Temps Modernes,* Nos. 184–85 (1961), pp. 245–54.

* "Kant avec Sade," *Critique,* No. 191 (1963), pp. 291–313. (September, 1962.)

* Resumé by the author of his "Du *Trieb* de Freud et du désir du psychanalyste," *Archivio di Filosofia* (1964), Nos. 1–2, pp. 51–60. (Includes discussion following. University of Rome, January, 1964.)

* "Propos directifs pour un Congrès sur la sexualité féminine," *Ecrits* (1966), pp. 725–36. (Written in 1958. The Congress took place at Amsterdam in September, 1960. See *La Psychanalyse,* VIII.)

* "La Signification du phallus: Die Bedeutung des Phallus," *Ecrits* (1966), pp. 685–95. (Delivered in German at the Max Planck Institute at Munich, May 9, 1958.)

* "Subversion du sujet et dialectique du désir dans l'inconscient freudien," *Ecrits* (1966), pp. 793–827. (Communication to the Congress at Royaumont organized by Jean Wahl on "La Dialectique," September, 1960. Cf. the seminar of 1957.)

* "Position de l'inconscient," *Ecrits* (1966), pp. 829–50. (Written in March, 1964. Summarizes Lacan's interventions at the Bonneval Congress organized by Henri Ey in November, 1960, where the Leclaire–Laplanche paper on the unconscious was originally delivered.)

* "La Science et la vérité," *Cahiers pour l'Analyse,* No. 1 (January, 1966), pp. 1–31.

"Réponses à des étudiants en philosophie," *Cahiers pour l'Analyse,* No. 3 (May, 1966), pp. 5–13.

PONTALIS, J.-B.

Compte-rendus of Lacan's seminars 1956–59. These are published in the *Bulletin de Psychologie* as follows:

Seminar of November–December, 1956: "La Relation d'objet et les structures freudiennes," *BP,* X/7 (April, 1957), pp. 426–30.

Seminar of January, 1957: "La Relation d'objet et les structures freudiennes," *BP,* X/10 (April, 1957), pp. 602–5.

Seminar of January–February, 1957: "La Relation d'objet et les structures freudiennes," *BP*, X/12 (May, 1957), pp. 742–43.

Seminar of March–April, 1957: "La Relation d'objet et les structures freudiennes," *BP*, X/14 (June, 1957), pp. 851–54.

Seminar of May–July, 1957: "La Relation d'objet et les structures freudiennes," *BP*, XI/1 (September, 1957), pp. 31–34.

Seminar of November, 1957: "Les Formations de l'inconscient," *BP*, XI/4–5 (January, 1958), pp. 293–96.

Seminar of December, 1957–March, 1958: "Les Formations de l'inconscient," *BP*, XII/2–3 (November, 1958), pp. 182–92.

Seminar of April–June, 1958: "Les Formations de l'inconscient," *BP*, XII/4 (December, 1958), pp. 250–56.

Seminar of November, 1958–January, 1959: "Le Désir et son interprétation," *BP*, XIII/5 (January, 1960), pp. 263–72.

Seminar of January–February, 1959: "Le Désir et son interprétation," *BP*, XIII/6 (January, 1960), pp. 329–35.

SECTION B

LACAN, MEIGNANT, LEVY-VALENSI

"Roman policier. Du délire type hallucinatoire chronique au délire d'imagination" (April 30, 1928), *Revue Neurologique*, XLIX (1928), 738–39. (Presentation of patient.)

LACAN, J., CLAUDE, H., and MIGAULT, P.

"Folies simultanées," *Société Médico-Psychologique* (May 21, 1931), *Annales Médico-Psychologiques*, I (1931), 483–90.

LACAN, Jacques, MIGAULT, Pierre, and LEVY-VALENSI, J.

"Troubles du langage écrit chez un paranoïaque présentant des éléments du type paranoïde (Schizographie)" (November 12, 1931), *Annales Médico-Psychologiques*, I (1931), 407–8. (Résumé of report on patient.)

"Ecrits inspirés: Schizographie," *Annales Médico-Psychologiques*, L (December, 1931), 508–22. (The full report on the patient presented on November 12, 1931.)

LACAN, Jacques, and EY, Henri

"Parkinsonisme et syndrome démentiel" (November 12, 1931), *Annales Médico-Psychologiques,* II (1931), 418–28.

LACAN, J., and CENAC, M.

* "Introduction théorique aux fonctions de la psychanalyse en criminologie," *Revue Française de Psychanalyse,* XV (1951), 7–29. (Delivered at the 13th Conférence des psychanalystes de langue française, May 29, 1950.)

LACAN, J., LEVY, R., DANON-BOILEAU, H.

"Considérations psychosomatiques sur l'hypertension artérielle," *L'Evolution Psychiatrique* (1953), pp. 397–409.

LACAN, Jacques, and GRANOFF, Vladimir

"Fetishism; the Symbolic, the Imaginary, and the Real," in: *Perversions, Psychodynamics, and Therapy* (ed. M. Balint) New York: Gramercy Books, 1956. (Pp. 265–76).

SECTION C

AUDOUARD, X.

"Pourquoi Hegel?" *La Psychanalyse,* V (1959), 235–56.

BOUTONIER, Juliette

"A propos du 'Problème de la psychogenèse des névroses et des psychoses,'" *L'Evolution Psychiatrique* (1951), pp. 355–63.

DUROUX, Yves

"Psychologie et logique," *Cahiers pour l'Analyse,* Nos. 1–2, second edition (January–April, 1966), pp. 31–38.

GREEN, André

"La Psychanalyse devant l'opposition de l'histoire et de la structure," *Critique,* XIX (1963), 649–62.

"L'Objet (a) de J. Lacan, sa logique, et la théorie freudienne," *Cahiers pour l'Analyse,* No. 3 (May, 1966), pp. 15–37.

LAPLANCHE, Jean

Hölderlin et la question du père. Paris: PUF, 1961.

LAPLANCHE, Jean, and LECLAIRE, Serge

"L'Inconscient," *Les Temps Modernes,* No. 183 (July, 1961), pp. 81–129.

LECLAIRE, Serge

"A propos de la 'Cure-Type en Psychanalyse' de M. Bouvet," *L'Evolution Psychiatrique* (1956), pp. 515–40. (First of three articles: I, critical.)

"A la recherche des principes d'une psychothérapie des psychoses," *L'Evolution Psychiatrique* (1958), pp. 377–411. (II, theoretical.)

"L'Obsessionel et son désir," *L'Evolution Psychiatrique* (1959), pp. 324–409. (III, clinical.)

"Point de vue économique en psychanalyse," *L'Evolution Psychiatrique* (1965), pp. 189–213. [Partial translation by D. Palin: "The Economic Standpoint: Recent Views," *International Journal of Psycho-Analysis,* XLV (1964), 324–30.]

MIEL, Jan

"Jacques Lacan and the Structure of the Unconscious," *Yale French Studies,* No. 36–37 (October, 1966), pp. 104–11.

MILLER, J-A.

"La Suture," *Cahiers pour l'Analyse,* Nos. 1–2, second edition (January–April, 1966), pp. 39–51.

"Les Graphes de Jacques Lacan," *Cahiers pour l'Analyse,* Nos. 1–2, second edition (January–April, 1966), pp. 169–77. (Appears in the second edition of Lacan's *Ecrits*.)

ORTIGUES, Marie-Cécile and Edmond

Oedipe Africain. Paris: Plon, 1966. Esp. pp. 51–92.

PICHON, Edouard

"La Famille devant M. Lacan," *Revue Française de Psychanalyse,* XI (1939), 107–35. (Comments on the encyclopaedia article "La Famille.")

PONTALIS, J.-B.

"Freud aujourd'hui," *Les Temps Modernes,* Nos. 124, 125, 126 (May–July, 1956), pp. 1666–80; 1890–1902; 174–86.

REBOUL, Jean

"Jacques Lacan et les fondements de la psychanalyse," *Critique,* XVIII (1962), 1056–67.

ROSOLATO, Guy

"Sémantique et altérations du langage," *L'Evolution Psychiatrique* (1956), pp. 865–99.

"Le Symbolique," *La Psychanalyse,* V (1959), 225–33.

TORT, Michel

"De l'interprétation ou la machine herméneutique," *Les Temps Modernes* Nos. 237, 238 (February–March, 1966), pp. 1461–93, 1629–52.

WILDEN, Anthony

"Jacques Lacan: A Partial Bibliography," *Yale French Studies,* No. 36–37 (October, 1966), pp. 263–68.

"Freud, Signorelli, and Lacan: The Repression of the Signifier," *American Imago,* Vol. 23, No. 4 (Winter, 1966), 332–66.

"Par divers moyens on arrive à pareille fin: A Reading of Montaigne," *Modern Language Notes* (forthcoming, 1968).

"Death, Desire, and Repetition in Svevo's *Zeno,*" *Modern Language Notes* (forthcoming, 1968).

SECTION D

BARTHES, Roland
"Eléments de sémiologie" (1964), in: *Le degré zéro de l'écriture.* Paris: Gonthier, 1964.

BENVENISTE, Emile
Problèmes de linguistique générale. Paris: Gallimard, 1966.

DEWEY, John
"Peirce's Theory of Linguistic Signs, Thought, and Meaning," *Journal of Philosophy,* XLIII, No. 4 (1946), 85–95.

FLIESS, Robert (ed.)
The Psycho-Analytic Reader. London: Hogarth Press, 1950.

FREUD, Sigmund
Complete Psychological Works of Sigmund Freud (Standard Edition), ed. James Strachey. 24 vols. London: Hogarth Press, 1953——.

The Origins of Psychoanalysis (ed. Anna Freud, Marie Bonaparte, and Ernst Kris). New York: Basic Books, 1954.

"Sur quelques mécanismes névrotiques dans la jalousie, la paranoïa et l'homosexualité," trans. J. Lacan, *Revue Française de Psychanalyse* (1932), No. 3.

GREEN, André
"Les portes de l'inconscient (A propos des Journées de Bonnéval sur l'inconscient, November, 1960)," *L'Evolution Psychiatrique* (1962), pp. 569–613.

HEGEL, G. W. F.
Phänomenologie des Geistes, ed. J. Hoffmeister. Hamburg: Felix Meiner, 1948.

La Phénoménologie de l'Esprit, trans. Jean Hyppolite. Paris: Aubier, 1939–41.

HEIDEGGER, Martin
Being and Time (1927), trans. J. Macquarrie and E. Robinson. London: SCM Press, 1962.

"Logos," trans. J. Lacan, *La Psychanalyse,* I (1956), 59–79.

HYPPOLITE, Jean

Genèse et structure de la Phénoménologie de l'Esprit. Paris: Aubier, 1946.

* "Commentaire parlé sur la *Verneinung* de Freud," *La Psychanalyse,* I (1956), 29–39.

"Phénoménologie de Hegel et psychanalyse," *La Psychanalyse,* III (1957), 17–32.

JAKOBSON, Roman

"Two Aspects of Language and Two Types of Aphasic Disturbances," in: *Fundamentals of Language.* The Hague: Mouton, 1956. (Pp. 55–82.)

"Closing Statements: Linguistics and Poetics," in: T. A. Sebeok, ed., *Style in Language.* Cambridge: MIT Press, 1960.

JAKOBSON, Roman, and HALLE, Morris

"Phonology and Phonetics," in: *Fundamentals of Language.* The Hague: Mouton, 1956. (Pp. 3–51).

JONES, Ernest

Sigmund Freud: Life and Work. 3 vols. London: Hogarth Press, 1956–58.

KOJEVE, Alexandre

Introduction à la lecture de Hegel (Leçons professées de 1933 à 1939), ed. Raymond Queneau. Paris: Gallimard, 1947.

LAPLANCHE, Jean, and PONTALIS, J.-B.

Vocabulaire de la Psychanalyse. Paris: PUF, 1967.

LEENHARDT, Maurice

Do Kamo: La personne et le mythe dans le monde mélanésien. Paris: Gallimard, 1947.

LEVI-STRAUSS, Claude

Les Structures élémentaires de la parenté. Paris: PUF, 1949.

"L'Efficacité symbolique" (1949), in: *Anthropologie Structurale.* Paris: Plon, 1958. (Pp. 205–26.)

Introduction à l'oeuvre de Marcel Mauss in: Marcel Mauss, *Sociologie et Anthropologie.* Paris: PUF, 1950.

"Sur les rapports entre la mythologie et le rituel," *Bulletin de la Société Française de Philosophie,* 1, No. 2 (July–Sept. 1956), pp. 99–125. (Session of May 26, 1956, in which, among others, Lacan, Goldmann, Jean Wahl, and Merleau-Ponty took part).

PEIRCE, Charles Sanders
  "Logic as Semiotic: The Theory of Signs," available in: *Philosophical Writings of Peirce,* ed. J. Buchler. New York: Dover Books, 1955 (1940).
SAUSSURE, Ferdinand de
  Cours de linguistique générale. Paris: Payot, 1965 (1915).
WALLON, Henri
  Les Origines de la pensée chez l'enfant. Paris. PUF, 1945.

Index

N.B. Figures in italics refer to the translator's notes by *note number,* not to pages. For references to and quotations from the works of Freud and Lacan, see the entry under the author's name.

323